THE GROWNUP'S GUIDE

VISITING NEW YORK CITY WITH KIDS

Diane Chernoff-Rosen
with Lisa Levinson

GROWNUP'S GUIDE PUBLISHING LLC

TO THE READER:

The information in this book was accurate at the time of publication. However, due to the dynamic nature of small businesses and the Internet, business names, addresses, phone numbers and web addresses may change in the future.

The author and publisher apologize for any errors and, if notified, will adjust them for future editions of this book. If we have not included your favorite resource or you want to make us aware of additional information to be included in subsequent editions, you can contact the publisher at info@grownupsguide.com.

As of February 1, 2003, all calls within New York City will be made by dialing 1 plus the three-digit area code plus the seven-digit phone number. Unless otherwise indicated, all phone numbers listed in this book are in area code 212.

Published by Grownup's Guide Publishing LLC. Find us online at www.grownupsguide.com

Library of Congress Control Number 2002096827

ISBN 0-9663392-4-X

Book and cover design by Elizabeth Woll

Manufactured in the United States of America

10 9 8 7 6 5 4 3 2 1

 GROWNUP'S GUIDE PUBLISHING LLC

To Amanda, Oliver and Matthew
You continue to inspire me.
I love you.

TABLE OF CONTENTS

ACKNOWLEDGMENTS

A huge thank you to the many parents, friends, administrators, business owners and others who shared information and insights with us. A special thanks to Heidi Selig, whose tireless and energetic pursuit of local fact and lore was instrumental in helping us provide you with the best of New York City. Also, thanks to our copy editor, Karen Lane, who cheerfully and efficiently worked through many drafts and taught us the difference between 'that' and 'which.' Last, but never least, thanks to our families for their patience and support.

THE GROWNUP'S GUIDE®

VISITING NEW YORK CITY WITH KIDS

Chapter 1

WHEN IN NEW YORK . . .

Ａs shock and grief descended on New York in the aftermath of the events of September 11, 2001, it seemed hard to imagine that New York City would ever again become the destination of joy and wonder it was before that fateful day. Indeed, the terrorist attacks created a literal and figurative hole in our city and collective soul and broke the hearts of New Yorkers and others around the country and around the world. As time has passed, ever-resilient New Yorkers have forged ahead, refusing to surrender our city or ourselves to fear. From those dark days, New York has emerged, not unscathed, but surely empowered by the collective intention to remain one of the world's great cities.

Whether you visit daily or once in a lifetime, New York is a city of endless possibilities. As in all of the world's great cities, you can spend decades here and still not have sampled it all. The attraction of New York is found in its mountains of tall buildings, lights that seem to outshine the stars in the night sky, the unrivaled cultural

1

attractions, the pulsating energy of city life and the presence of enough people to populate a small country. While often considered primarily an adult experience, the Big Apple has a delicious piece carved out especially for children, and millions of families come here each year just to take a taste.

The joy of New York City is that there is something for every member of the family. The challenge for families planning an excursion here is to figure out how to access the tremendous resources of the city while finding a balance of activity and entertainment that will leave everyone happy and satisfied, or at least not exhausted, furious or dejected. While every parent knows that there is no guaranteed way to approach a sojourn that will put smiling faces on the whole family at the end of the day, we truly believe that it is indeed possible to maximize the chances of having a wonderful Big Apple experience and whet the urban and cultural appetites of your young explorers.

After writing *The Grownup's Guide to Living with Kids in Manhattan*, we wanted to give all families who visit New York City the opportunity to take full advantage of the incredible cultural, educational and recreational resources available here and have access to the inside information available to the locals. To that end, we created *The Grownup's Guide to Visiting New York City with Kids* with the goal of helping visitors with the practical side of planning a Big Apple adventure in child-sized portions.

So, whether you are planning a special vacation with your children, bringing them along on a business trip, passing through on your way to another destination or coming in for a day from the suburbs, our intention is to help you identify various considerations in planning your trip, prepare your children and yourself for your time here and lead you to and through the wonders of this great city. We have included hundreds of things to do, a variety of unique and special spots to share with your family and plenty of places to explore, stay and eat. Regardless of your familiarity with the city, the ages of the children or for how long you are staying, we want you to create good memories and be glad that you came.

The Grownup's Guide to Visiting New York City with Kids is designed as a ready reference. The book is divided into 10 chapters covering specific topics. Each chapter contains detailed relevant resources.

Chapters 5 (entertainment), 6 (children's activities and cultural attractions), 7 (shopping), 8 (restaurants) and 9 (hotels) are organized alphabetically for easy reference and are followed by indexes arranged by relevant categories. All telephone numbers listed are 212 area code unless otherwise indicated.

Please note that we do not rate or endorse stores, destinations, restaurants or other businesses, because we have found that no two people respond to the same experience in the same way. Even among our own husbands and children, we could not reach agreement on favorite restaurants, destinations, stores or activities. Therefore, rather than imposing our subjective evaluations on you, our goal is to provide you with the inspiration and resources to plan your own meaningful adventure.

Armed with resources, realistic expectations and the right attitude, the sky is the limit, and in New York that can be taken quite literally.

The Ten Principles of Visiting New York City with Kids

Organizing your urban adventure requires advance preparation. Planning, however, is not the only key to success. Even the most intricately planned day can end with someone in tears, whether it is you or your children. Suppose, for example, a special day is arranged to visit the city with the kids during the holiday season. You have purchased tickets for "The Nutcracker," and you plan to spend the day enjoying a long list of special spots: a trip to Rockefeller Center to see the giant Christmas tree, a walk up Fifth Avenue for a glimpse of the holiday windows, lunch and a walk through FAO Schwarz. Then it's off to Wollman Rink for a look at the skaters and a carriage ride through Central Park. A side trip to the Metropolitan Museum of Art is negotiated because of an unanticipated drop in temperature. As the afternoon wears on, everyone begins to wear out and the whining escalates.

At last, it is off to an early dinner, where relations are strained at best and then to Lincoln Center for "The Nutcracker." All is going well until the appearance of the multi-headed mouse king and his army of huge mice, at which time it becomes necessary for one of the adults in the party to sit out the first act with the now-terrorized preschooler. At intermission, two kinds of candy are requested and a denial brings tears and a tantrum. As the curtain rises for the second act, an immediate need for the bathroom develops followed by demands from the whole crew to be taken home immediately. By this time you are totally annoyed that you have shelled out a small fortune and taken off from work to make this day happen. It is clear that everyone is feeling the effects of the crowds and other obstacles that can sabotage a visit that is not organized with realistic expectations. Scenarios like this one would make any parent wary.

So how do well-meaning parents who want their children to have a memorable New York experience create one? There are no hard and fast rules, but the results of our own unscientific polling of native New Yorkers and visitors alike have helped us to identify some major themes in having a successful New York visit and avoiding the serious pitfalls that create the wrong kind of vacation or day-trip memories. The following Ten Principles of Visiting New York City with Kids consolidates years of collective experience and distills many hours of wonderful dialogue. These principles are by no means the only things to keep in mind as you put together your itinerary, but they will be a good starting point toward making your journey a little smoother.

▶ **1. Weather Counts.** Rain, sleet, snow (the precursor to horrible gray city slush), heat, humidity. New York has them all. But New York also has clear crisp autumn days, perfect white snowfalls, magnificent spring afternoons, sultry summer evenings and bright summer mornings. Wherever you hail from, as parents you know that **weather counts**. From struggling to get a snowsuit on a squirmy toddler to pacifying an overheated, dehydrated child, preparing for and adjusting to weather conditions can make a day go well or badly.

Unlike the non-urban dweller, New Yorkers do not spend much time in their own cars in the course of the day. Therefore, when getting around New York, you cannot count on stowing your extra gear in your car, warming up by turning on the seat warmers, cooling off with a blast of air conditioning or getting out of a downpour and back to home base with nary a drop of water ruining your favorite shoes.

New Yorkers travel from place to place by foot, cab, car, bus and subway, all of which require time out of doors both in terms of waiting time and making connections. Even if it is your intention to travel by taxi, that does not mean taxis will be readily available when and where you need them, particularly during peak rush hours or when inclement weather strikes. Exposure to the elements is absolutely part of the deal, and it is important to dress appropriately and comfortably.

Weather is also important when scheduling your activities. Good weather allows you to include outdoor experiences in your itinerary, since with more than 26,000 acres of city parks and playgrounds plus zoos, botanical gardens and outdoor café possibilities, New York has a great outdoor life. Bad weather does not mean you have to cancel all your plans, because that is the perfect time to explore museums, galleries, indoor sporting events, performances and the scores of available indoor family activities.

▶ **2. Be Flexible.** Many things happen spontaneously in New York. It is not always possible to anticipate traffic, sidewalk concerts, lines, and sudden cancellations, to name a few of the types of things that can impact the best laid plans. At the same time, there are those things that are planned by others but somehow not factored into *your* plans, such as parades, street fairs, charity walkathons, demonstrations, construction detours and running or cycling races.

While we are by all means strong advocates of planning, sometimes too much planning is not a good thing. A schedule too tightly packed doesn't allow for detours, and detours in a big city, especially when you are with curious children, are inevitable. Much of the wonder of this city is found in unexpected places. It is worth being prepared to abandon or modify your plans when something interesting appears, so you can let the moment redirect you. To pass such up such moments is to lose the very essence of the city. Hence, our second principle—**be flexible**.

This is not to suggest that when traveling with your family in tow you should walk out the door with no plans at all and wait for the city to happen to you. To the contrary, not having an idea of what you would like to do when you arrive can make doing anything substantially more difficult because there are simply too many choices and, if your families are anything like ours, too many opinions to create a consensus under pressure.

Flexibility is important not only when dealing with those things beyond your control that happen to you on your travels. It is also relevant when dealing with your own family as you see the sights. We have all had the experience of organizing something that we think will be fabulous but which turns out to be a big dud as far as the children are concerned. In these situations, we have observed that it is often not worth the effort to make the kids stick it out. If we can be flexible enough not to let our own disappointment get in the way and instead move on to something more appealing to the younger members of the party, everyone can have a better time.

▶ **3. Be Realistic.** There are certain truths about New York City: it is expensive, crowded and usually a very stimulating place for children. Even if your children are used to being in an urban environment and are incredibly adaptable, a quick reality check of your itinerary is always a good thing before you head out. Consider: things generally take longer than you would expect because there is a lot to see along the way; things will in all likelihood cost more than you are used to; crowds are exhausting and they are worse at certain times of year, on certain days and at particular times of day; and children get hungry, tired, bored and need to use the bathroom at totally inopportune times. To make the most of your time here, it is essential to **be realistic** about how much you and the kids are able to take on and avoid succumbing to the pressure to do it all.

New York City is full of great things to do, and there is certainly no shortage of activities or things to explore. If anything, the temptation is to try to do too much with your time here. As you make your lists of what you want to do during your visit, keep in mind the need to match the children with age-appropriate activities, the logistics of moving around town, the energy level of the kids as well as your own energy level, how much stimulation your children can handle before melting down and how often they need to rest and eat. The more realistic the plans, the better the experience for the whole family.

► **4. Location, Location, Location.** Manhattan may be only 24 square miles, but trying to hit the Statue of Liberty, Central Park, and the Bronx Zoo in one day is not a good plan. Unless you are a visiting dignitary traveling in a police-escorted motorcade, getting from one end of town to another will take time and cost money. Although transportation can be an activity of its own—and young children do love riding buses, subways and cabs—too much time in transit leaves less time for enjoying your destination. And so our fourth principle—**location, location, location**.

Keeping your day of adventure in a particular neighborhood or within a reasonable geographical area has many benefits. Being able to walk around the area is pleasant, allows for spontaneous and in-depth exploration, and saves the expense (and potential aggravation) of multiple taxi rides or the use of city buses and subways. Most of all, getting from one place to another in New York with children requires some effort, particularly if you are toting strollers, diapers, backpacks, shopping bags, snacks and whatever other travel gear you have along. Moving your brood and your stuff gets tiring, so the less distance you have to go, the better.

► **5. Size Matters.** Whether it is the size of your children, the size of your group or the size of your budget, **size matters** quite a bit when it comes to your time in New York. Your planning should take into account the different ages of your children, the logistics of moving your group around and the amount of money you are prepared to spend.

The ages of your children do in large part determine what kinds of activities will be appropriate. Small children are very curious and enjoy hands-on experiences. They also have short fuses and do not do well with more adult-oriented activities, such as long visits to art museums. Big kids on the other hand can enjoy doing more adult activities. They can also do more in a day. Consequently, for your own sake as well as that of the children, it is important to choose activities and destinations that make sense for the ages and tem-

peraments of your kids. If your children are of significantly different ages, a divide-and-conquer strategy might be well advised.

The size of your group is a major consideration when figuring
out logistics. Small groups (two adults and two kids) are easy to
accommodate. When the numbers get higher, however, the prob-
lems can begin. Traveling in a pack has many disadvantages,
including the difficulties in being seated together at restaurants or
at performances, fitting into taxis (which are not required to take
more than three adults), loading onto public transportation at rush
hour, keeping track of children in crowded situations and main-
taining the interest level of a large group of people of different ages.
Certainly you can make reservations to accommodate a crowd at
most restaurants, but it is harder to stay together at South Street
Seaport when you are traveling with four active children.

If you are traveling with a large contingent, for instance with
another family, consider breaking up for parts of the day or pre-
arranging meeting points and times so that you can find each other
if you get separated (accidentally or on purpose) along the way. If
that is not possible, try to schedule your activities for off-peak
times. You will have better luck being seated together in a restaurant, for example, if you arrive before or after typical mealtimes.

New York is "do-able" on any size budget. There are many ways
to take advantage of what the city has to offer without having to
spend a fortune, and conversely, there are many ways to spend a
fortune. Attending free events, using organization memberships
and subscriptions offering discounts, buying discounted theater
tickets and taking advantage of special travel service offers are just
some ways to keep costs down. As long as you come to terms with
the fact that you will probably spend more money here than anywhere else (except maybe Paris!), you will do just fine.

▶ **6. Your Comfort Level is Key.** If you survey your friends about
what to do in New York, you are bound to get long lists of "don't
miss" suggestions. When it comes down to planning your own trip,
however, we urge you not to feel compelled to do that which makes
you uncomfortable. To have a great experience here, you have to
relax and enjoy it, and therefore **your comfort level is key**.

If driving in the city makes you nervous, take the train or park in a garage that does not require you to negotiate your way through town. If you are unfamiliar with the city and are concerned about finding yourself somewhere you do not want to be, take a tour of the city and get the lay of the land. There are many ways you can prepare yourself to keep urban anxiety at bay so that you and your children can enjoy yourselves. On the other hand, we also urge you not to surrender totally to urban apprehension. While New York is not perfect, it is neither mayhem exemplified nor a battlefield. Multitudes visit, have a great time and live to tell the tale. So while it is not advisable to do anything reckless or without thought, it is worth pushing the envelope and expanding your comfort level just enough to let yourself experience the Big Apple.

If you are fortunate enough to live close to the city and can visit regularly, you will be surprised how quickly you will become acclimated to the beat of the city. However, if you are here for a once-in-a-lifetime visit, better to do the things with which you feel comfortable rather than to be a nervous wreck the whole time.

▶ **7. Heads Up.** The general safety basics go a long way in New York. This is a big city, and among all the normal everyday kinds of people here, New York has its share of urban dwellers with little anchoring in reality (although most of the people you might consider to be highly suspect may be, in relative terms, "normal"). New York also has its criminal element, and unfortunately, tourists are often their targets. Being aware and applying the same kind of caution you would in any unfamiliar situation is important. And so we urge you to keep your **heads up**.

Prepare your children for their city visit and review your safety rules and procedures with them in advance of your arrival. While New York has a reputation for being a dangerous place, in many ways it is no more or less dangerous than any other urban environment. It is therefore more crucial to give your children the tools to help them develop judgment and confidence combined with caution than it is to scare them about city hazards.

▶ **8. The Benefits of Regular Use.** If you are lucky enough to live within close proximity to New York City, you can transform it into an extension of your community. By selecting one or more of the larger cultural institutions (such as any of the major museums) and purchasing a family membership or subscribing to children's performance series, you will have a wealth of programming available to you, which can facilitate your use of the city. Subscribing to one of the local parents' papers or visiting their websites affords you the opportunity to find out what is going on for kids in and around the city and keeps you current on new shows, activities and other events worth attending. When you establish a routine that includes visiting the city, even on a quarterly basis, your level of comfort will increase, your familiarity will expand your areas of interest and the city will become another community resource.

▶ **9. A Lasting Impression.** After their visits, people leave the city with many different impressions. Kids, because they see things from a different perspective, not to mention a different elevation, have the most interesting impressions of all. They are fascinated by the dog walkers, rollerbladers, mounted park police, buses, subways, hotdog vendors, tall buildings, pigeons and manholes. The power to command a yellow car by simply raising a hand is nothing short of fantastic to a young child.

There is much in New York to catch the imagination of a child. Just being here and part of the action is an experience not to be quickly forgotten. Don't feel that you have to pull out all the stops when you visit. It simply doesn't take much for this amazing city to make **a lasting impression**.

▶ **10. When in New York, Do as the New Yorkers Do.** While most New Yorkers will admit they hate the noise, traffic and crowds, they by and large love their city and would think of living nowhere else. When you visit the Big Apple, look beyond the blemishes. The city is a special place for both kids and adults. Understandably it can be overwhelming, but with the right information, great resources and a little inspiration you and your children can play in the city like the natives.

Chapter 2

GETTING READY FOR NEW YORK CITY

P eople pour into the city to find fame and fortune, to ride on the subway and for just about every other reason imaginable. As a visitor, you can choose the slice of the Big Apple that you want to sample or devour it to the core. Since New York is a place where extraordinary things seem to happen spontaneously, it is easy to assume that it is not necessary to do much to prepare for your visit because the city will simply work its magic on you. The reality is that the magic is usually less the result of serendipity than the result of good planning.

Deciding what you want out of your time in New York is well worth the effort, whether you are planning a day trip or your annual family vacation. The purpose of your visit may be to expose your young explorer to some high-level culture, further develop an emerging interest, present the world in which you work, take advantage of all the amazing things there are to do or simply experience a different way of life for a moment. Identifying your objectives will help you organize your activities so that you can experience your own bit of New York City magic. In a city where dreams are made, the time you spend thinking through and organizing your New York City time will go a long way toward ensuring that your visit to New York is a dream come true.

🏙

When, How, What and Why?

In orchestrating your Big Apple visit, there are many factors that can affect your plans. Why are you visiting New York: a vacation, an add-on to a business trip, part of a family visit, a day in from the suburbs? How long will you be staying? How old are the children traveling with you? What time of year are you planning to visit? How do you intend to get to and move around the city? The answers to these questions can help you set your priorities as well as organize your time and effort.

▶ **Timing is everything.** What you can actually accomplish during your visit has everything to do with the length of your stay. Shorter visits work best when limited to smaller areas or a few discrete plans, allowing for a meaningful taste of the Big Apple without exhausting the troops. A day visit is most successful when you do only one or two things, while a weekend visit allows time to explore particular neighborhoods more fully. Longer visits enable you to tackle the entire Big Apple in bigger bites over more time.

While this may sound elementary, it is easy to arrive in New York and feel like that proverbial kid in the candy store who wants to sample it all and ends up leaving feeling sick. Being realistic about what can be done in any given time is very difficult when you're not a regular. Some tips:

◪ **Allow time to get from place to place.** New York City is a big place, and visitors often underestimate the time spent getting from place to place. Depending on the time of day, traffic can be simply impossible, making bus and taxi rides feel interminable. Whenever it is feasible, consider walking. Although walking may take time and requires comfortable shoes, endurance (yours as well as the kids') and the right equipment (a stroller or baby carrier) if you have little ones, it is a great alternative, the journey can be an adventure in itself and the price cannot be beat.

In organizing your day, it is a good idea to plan the activities for that day in a single area or at least in adjacent areas. If you plan geographically, you can usually incorporate more into your day without running out of gas. Pick an activity or destination and then investigate the shopping, restaurants and other points of interest within that area so that you do not spend all of your time and energy in transit.

▰ **Allow for time between activities.** Whether you are going to a musical or skating at Wollman Rink, allow some time for the members of your party to decompress between activities. If you are here for more than the day, a retreat to "home" base or a stop for a snack and a rest are excellent refueling techniques. If you are a day visitor, then a leisurely meal or a stop at a library or a bookstore with some space to spread out and relax with a book can make a world of difference.

If you are not used to urban hustle and bustle, remember that participating in city life and leisure involves a pace most people, particularly children, are unfamiliar with, and that pace can be exhausting. Exhausted people are generally not at their best, so avoid meltdowns by making sure you allow for downtime and plentiful snacks throughout the day.

▰ **Be prepared for lines or long waits.** Depending on the destination and time of year, you may be confronted with long lines or long waits to get into various attractions or to be served or to have your turn at something. For some attractions, it is possible to call ahead to find out if you should expect a long wait, but whatever the answer, it is always worth being prepared with age-appropriate distractions for your young explorer. It is very handy to have on hand things such as strings for cats cradle, paper and crayons or markers, books, hand-held electronic games, a portable CD or tape player as well as a mental inventory of spur-of-the-moment activities including old favorites such as "I Spy."

▶**Age matters, too.** When making plans, it is essential to consider the ages of the children who will be with you during your various activities. Children, and most adults, are creatures of habit and do best when following their usual routines. A trip to New York City, though certainly exciting, will stretch even children accustomed to a very flexible schedule. The odds of a successful visit with children significantly improves when you consider the ages and stages of the children involved. For families traveling with children of multiple ages and stages, the mix of activities should be carefully balanced so that there is something for everyone, in reasonable proportions scheduled throughout the visit.

▰ **Babies.** Babies are generally pretty easy to travel with. If you can organize your visit so that you are walking most of the time and the weather holds out for you, babies can be easily entertained in the seat of a stroller and will doze off when they need to nap. In fouler weather, baby carriers allow you to go, go, go. Admittedly, the bottles, diapers and other necessities are numerous and can make packing requirements overwhelming, but in general, the babies themselves are quite portable and adaptable.

As with most parenting issues, patience and flexibility are key survival skills. Conventional wisdom would suggest that the more you keep to your baby's regular sleeping and eating patterns, the better. However, many parents will confirm that even the youngest baby may realize that you are on vacation and be surprisingly cooperative, at least once they get past the time change!

▰ **Toddlers and pre-schoolers.** Toddlers are unpredictable travelers. While they are great fun to watch as they discover the world around them, they also are known to have spontaneous outbursts, experience the uncontrollable need to run and touch and on the whole have a very different agenda from their adult companions. This unpredictability makes planning for a visit challenging. While there is certainly plenty for this age group to explore in the Big Apple, keep in mind a toddler's level of curiosity, need for physical activity and limited attention span, and anticipate the potential safety hazards as you plan your activities. Toddlers do best with simple, less stimulating experiences, regular mealtimes and naps and not too much transition.

Pre-schoolers are somewhat more predictable than toddlers. Having had a bit more "world experience," these creative, curious and expressive children are more able to handle a busy day and less likely to melt down into a bona fide tantrum. However, pre-schoolers are not yet big kids and can move between coping and not coping with amazing speed. For this group, it is still best to keep the activities simple, the transitions minimal and the stroller handy.

◪ **School-aged children.** School-aged children are perfect city tourists. They are curious and intellectually ready to enjoy diverse cultural experiences. Their increasing attention span allows them to engage in activities in a more substantive manner and their enthusiasm generally makes the trip seem very worthwhile. It is important to keep in mind though that a school-aged child, however mature, is not a peer. While school-aged kids may be up to a great deal, they can burn out like a shooting star, suddenly and dramatically, so keep a close watch for overload. School-aged children also have definite ideas about what they would like to do, and so making sure to balance the itinerary with a sprinkling of their preferred destinations is a must.

◪ **Teens.** Teenagers can be the toughest audience to please. If you live within commutable distance to the city, your older teenagers will probably want to explore the city with friends, leaving parents behind. Younger teens generally love the opportunity to visit with their families, especially if it involves bringing a friend along and going to something special like a show, sporting event or great shopping. Depending on the interests of your teen, you can have wonderful experiences together.

The key to treating your teens to an "awesome" time is pursuing opportunities and activities that are in sync with their interests. For families traveling greater distances, you are in luck. The city is a destination most teens are curious enough about that getting the opportunity to check it out makes a trip with the family absolutely worth it.

▶ **'Tis the season...**The time of year is a major consideration in planning your trip. The most popular times for visiting the city, with or without children, are the Christmas holidays, Thanksgiving and Easter holidays and during the summer. That is not to say, however, that there is an official off-season in New York City. New York is always a popular destination, and there is an abundance of activity throughout the year to prove it.

While trying to plan your visit for a time when the city will not be overly crowded is pretty tough, it is not totally impossible. If you are able to visit outside of typical school breaks or holidays and can be in town on weekdays as well as over the weekend, you stand a good chance of not having to constantly navigate through crowds of tourists. Summer visits are also good bets, despite it being tourist season, because many city residents head out during the summer months, particularly on weekends. If you intend to be in New York during the summer, do keep in mind that the kinds of activities that appeal during the dog days of summer, such as a ferry ride to the Statue of Liberty, will appeal to a whole lot of other people, too.

If you want to be in New York for the Christmas or other holidays, then you have to be prepared to meet with crowds. This does not mean that you will not have a great time here. On the contrary, holidays are wonderful times to spend in New York, and in fact the hustle and bustle and special events that accompany the holiday season can be quite extraordinary. What is important, however, is to be prepared so that you will be less frustrated when you have to stand on line.

▶ **Dress for success.** The weather and what to wear are two additional important considerations. Without question the city can be fickle on both counts.

The mean daily temperature in Manhattan during the month of January is 32 degrees F (0 Celsius), and in July it is 76.5 degrees F (24.7 Celsius). The average annual rainfall is 47.25" and the average annual snowfall is 29.3". New York City can be hot, hot, hot during the summer with heat and humidity so intense it can actually melt the asphalt. The winters can be bitter cold with rivers of running slush. But on the whole, the city is a fairly comfortable place to be, given proper attire.

Be aware, however, that the weather can change frequently and without much notice. Keeping track of what the meteorologists have to say will at least prepare you for what might be. In this age of unpredictable climatic changes, it is not uncommon to have the kinds of weather patterns that bring snow in April and heat waves in January. Not unlike other locations in the world, if you don't like the weather, wait a bit, and it is sure to change.

Children seem to have a different heating and cooling system than do adults. It may hardly have reached 55 degrees and kids are stripping down to T-shirts and shorts while their seniors are still in parkas. While weather-appropriate attire can make your day pleasant, being too hot or too cold can be a distraction that is not easily overcome, particularly by children. Layers seem to work best.

Naturally, what you plan on doing here will impact your clothing choices. Unless you will be attending a wedding or other special event, formal attire is rarely required. Many of the nicer restaurants "recommend" jackets but few require ties. Young men should follow the lead of the adult males in their party, although boys can generally get away with a nice sweater or vest in lieu of a jacket. In general, the city

While weather-appropriate attire can make your day pleasant, being too hot or too cold can be a distraction that is not easily overcome, particularly by children. Layers seem to work best.

is much more informal than in decades past. You will see individuals attend Broadway shows in shorts and a T-shirt. Regrettably this informality takes away from the glamour that was once Broadway.

New Yorkers are, for the most part, a stylish bunch, known less for their classic style than for their sense of fashion adventure. Black still reigns supreme, and kids definitely have a good feel for fashion's edge. To blend with this crowd, leave the jogging suits home.

When selecting what should be jammed into the suitcase, make sure to pack comfortable shoes, and include a second pair (our children have been known to actually lose a shoe on an airplane). Despite much good advice you may have heard regarding how to travel light, much of it does not seem to work for many families. Children in particular have a hard time leaving their favorite items home, and parents usually need to be prepared with extra changes of clothes when faced with spills, outfit tantrums and items lost or forgotten in the course of the day's activities.

Some packing considerations: encourage (as best you can!) your children to travel light; bring stain-removing towelettes for quickly attacking stains; determine whether or not you will have access to laundry facilities during longer visits and pack accordingly; think in terms of comfort (sightseeing is not the time to break in new shoes) and layers. And finally the great comforter: you can always buy in the city anything you may have left home.

► **What's available?** Deciding what to do in New York City can be a complicated affair. Where do you start? What will be the most fun? What requires the least amount of effort? How can you enjoy the city without going bankrupt? What are the not-to-be-missed attractions, and which sights not only can be, but definitely should be, missed? Priorities and preferences are different for everyone, so the key to making your visit work is to do your research before you get into town.

The best way to access information is to go directly to the resources available to the natives. The local parents' publications are excellent sources for monthly descriptions of events and activities. You can either obtain copies of these publications or visit their websites. If you visit the city regularly, it may be worth the investment to subscribe to your favorite parent publication, as the subscription rates are quite reasonable. Other publications such as *The New York Times*, *New York Magazine* and *TimeOut* also cover activities for children. The foregoing publications are listed in the resource section following this chapter. We have also included a list of popular websites that focus on New York City, the most comprehensive of which are www.nyc.com and www.nycvisit.com (the website of New York City & Company, the official city tourism and marketing organization).

Chapters 4, 5 and 6 have extensive listings of attractions, destinations, activities and cultural events. The Appendix to this chapter has a calendar of annual city events and parades.

Another good source of ideas can be travel agents who have spent some time in the city and have a good feel for it. They can be helpful in selecting the things that will be meaningful for your family to do while visiting. Also, speaking with families you know who have gone or often go to the city with kids can be an important source of information. Remember to ask specifically why an activity was or was not great. You may find that an activity described through the eyes of the evaluator reveals clues as to the appropriateness for your family.

▶ **Get ready, get set, go.** Almost as important as deciding what to do during your stay is preparing the children for their visit. Build the trip up too much and the kids will feel let down. Conversely, without any preparation, the kids may find the city too overwhelming.

One way to paint a picture of the place you are going to visit is to read some stories or watch some movies that take place in that location. Mind you, Lyle the Crocodile doesn't really live on East 88th Street, but when you pass a townhouse in the city with your five-year-old, it might be fun to guess if that is the kind of house Lyle might have lived in, if he were real of course. Particularly for older children, a movie that follows a family through Ellis Island and their early days in the city as immigrants will make a visit to Ellis Island and the Lower East Side come to life a bit more. We have listed some books set in New York City and some videos that you might enjoy watching together as a family before heading to New York.

Keep in mind that building a context does not have to mean focusing exclusively on the city. You can also introduce books or films to your child that will be relevant in other ways. For example, if you will be attending the ballet, you can read books about ballet or watch videos of particular ballets. Or if you will be attending an exhibit of Van Gogh paintings, you might read a biography of the artist, show pictures of the paintings they will be seeing or even make some Van Gogh–like paintings of your own. With a little preparation, you may find the quality of your own experience greatly improved too.

General Information

www.allny.com

www.applevision

www.applevision.com

www.cityguideny.com

www.citysearch.com

www.dailycandy.com

www.digitalcity.com

www.go-newyorkcity.com

www.fieldtrip.com/ny/index

www.lasvegasroomfinders.com/newyork/kids.htm

www.metronewyork.com

www.nyc.com

www.nyc.gov
(official website of New York City)

www.nyc-arts.org

www.nyctourism.com

www.nycvisit.com

www.nytoday.com

www.souljourn.com
(African American travel guide)

www.stayinnewyorkcity.com

Publications

Big Apple Parent. Monthly. Free. Widely distributed throughout the city. Produces an annual Parents' Source Book. Subscriptions available. 889-6400. www.parentsknow.com

City Guide. Weekly, distributed free in hotels. www.cityguidemagazine.com

Family Entertainment Guide. Five issues per year (seasonal plus holiday). Free. Available at schools, libraries and family facilities. 787-3789. www.familybuzz.com

IN New York. Monthly, distributed free in hotels. www.in-newyorkmag.com

iNew York Quick Guide. Distributed free in hotels. www.cityspin.com

New York Family. Monthly. Free. Available at pediatricians' offices, schools, libraries and stores. Subscriptions available. Produces an annual Family Resource Guide. 914 381-7474. www.nyfamily.com

New York Magazine. Weekly magazine. www.metronewyork.com

New York Times. Daily newspaper. www.nytimes.com

New Yorker. Weekly magazine. www.newyorker.com

PARENTGUIDE. Monthly. Free. Available at pediatricians' offices, schools, libraries and stores. Subscriptions available. 213-8840. www.parentguidenews.com

Time Out New York. Weekly magazine. www.timeoutny.com

Village Voice. Weekly magazine. Free. www.villagevoice.com

Wall Street Journal. Daily newspaper (Monday through Friday). www.wsj.com (paid subscription required).

Where. Distributed free in hotels. www.wheremagazine.com

Some New York Stories

While this list represents some favorites, it is absolutely not intended to be comprehensive. We hope that you enjoy these titles and add others to your library.

Picture Books

Adams, Barbara Johnston. *New York City (Downtown America)* (Dillon Press, 1996). A photo tour of New York City, including a list of places to visit, a map and a historical time line.

Barracca, Debra, and Sal Barracca. *The Adventures of Taxi Dog* (Dial,1990). See New York from the front seat of a yellow cab through the eyes of Maxi the Taxi Dog.

Catrow, David, and Stephen P. Policoff. *Cesar's Amazing Journey* (Viking Children's Books, 1999). Cesar the tree frog explores New York City with the help of a hip spider, looking for a new home.

Cohen, Miriam. *Down in the Subway* (DK Publishing, 1998). A routine trip on the subway is made magic by the Island Lady.

Collier, Bryan. *Uptown* (Henry Holt, 2000). Discover Harlem through the eyes of a little boy.

Enderle, Judith Ross, and Stephanie Gordon Tessler. *Where Are You, Little Zack?* (Houghton Mifflin, 1997). Little Zack Quack is lost somewhere in New York City. With the help of his brothers, commuters, taxi drivers and some baseball fans, readers are guided through many city sites while trying to find Zack.

Gutman, Anne, and Georg Hallensleben. *Lisa in New York* (Knopf, 2000). Join Lisa, a puppy, as she sightsees in Manhattan. (Part of the Misadventures of Gaspard and Lisa series)

Jakobsen, Kathy. *My New York* (Little Brown, 1993). A young girl writes a letter to her friend in the Midwest describing her new home in New York, accompanied by detailed illustrations.

Karlins, Mark. *Music Over Manhattan* (Doubleday, 1998). A sweet story of a child finding his own special talent.

Kent, Deborah. *New York City (Cities of the World)* (Children's Press, 1997). Beautiful color photos plus brief descriptions highlighting the history, religion, landmarks, festivals and arts of the city. Includes a "fast facts" section.

Low, William. *Chinatown* (Henry Holt, 1997). Join a young Chinese American boy and his grandmother for a fictionalized walking tour of New York's Chinatown during the celebration of the Chinese New Year.

Marx, David F. *New York City (Rookie Read-About Geography)* (Children's Press, 1999). A non-fiction book all about New York for young readers.

Mayhew, James. *Katie's Picture Show* (Bantam Books, 1989). Join Katie as she steps inside paintings at the Metropolitan Museum of Art.

Munro, Roxie. *The Inside–Outside Book of New York City* (Seastar, 2001 [revised and updated]). A detail-rich tour of New York City Landmarks.

Thompson, Kay. *Eloise* (Simon & Schuster, 1969). The classic story of Eloise, the garrulous little girl who lives at New York's Plaza Hotel.

Torres, Daniel. *Tom* (Viking Children's Books, 1996). *Tom* is a story of an unusual tourist (a dinosaur) who loves the big city and is determined to land a job there.

Waber, Bernard. *Lyle, Lyle, Crocodile* (Houghton Mifflin, 1973). Join in the fun with Lyle the Crocodile who lives with the Primms in a townhouse on East 88th Street. There are several titles in the Lyle the Crocodile series.

Wasserstein, Wendy. *Pamela's First Musical* (Hyperion Books for Children, 1996). Join Pamela for her ninth birthday with Aunt Louise as they lunch at the Russian Tea Room and attend a matinee performance of a Tony Award–winning musical.

Chapter Books

Dreyer, Ellen. *Speechless in New York—Going to Series: Going to New York City* (Four Corners, 2000). Join the adventures of a group of aspiring young singers in New York City.

Giff, Patricia Reilly. *Next Stop, New York City! A Polk Street Special* (Bantam Books, 1997). Ms. Rooney's class is taking a trip to New York City and Emily has been named their "New York City expert."

Greenwald, Sheila. *Stucksville* (DK Publishing, 2000). Emerald, who lives in a small apartment with her actor parents, takes a new look at her home.

Konigburg, E. L. *From the Mixed-up Files of Mrs. Basil Frankweiler* (Yearling Books, 1977). Claudia and her brother run away to The Metropolitan Museum of Art where, upon the introduction of a new statue, they become involved in a mystery.

Lasky, Kathryn. *Dreams in the Golden Country: The Diary of Zipporah Feldman, A Jewish Immigrant Girl, New York City, 1903* (Scholastic Trade Books, 1998). Part of the Dear America Series, this is the story of a young Russian immigrant and her life in Manhattan's Lower East Side.

MacAulay, David. *Unbuilding* (Houghton Mifflin, 1980). This detailed, illustrated, fictional account of the unmaking of the Empire State Building provides a wonderful explanation of how such a building would be demolished.

Merrill, Jean, and Lyman Cumberly. *Pushcart War* (Yearling Books, 1987 [reissue edition]). A fictitious account of the "war" between pushcart vendors and trucks during the 1970s paints a colorful picture of the city landscape.

Neumann, Deitric. *Joe and the Skyscraper: The Empire State Building in New York City (Adventures in Architecture)* (Prestel, 1999). Experience the construction of the Empire State Building through the eyes of a sixteen-year-old boy who worked on it. Includes vintage photos.

O'Neil, Laura. *The Case of the Ballet Bandit (New Adventures of Mary-Kate & Ashley)* (Scholastic Paperbacks, 1998). Mary-Kate and Ashley take on the Big Apple and solve a mystery at the world-famous New York City Ballet.

Seidler, Tor. *A Rat's Tale* (HarperCollins Juvenile Books, 1999 [reprint edition]).Beneath the streets of New York, two young rats from different socioeconomic levels find adventure and true love.

Selden, George. *The Cricket in Times Square* (Farrar Straus & Giroux, 1970). The comic, sometimes tragic, side of life in the city is all part of the tale of Chester Cricket and his friends as they struggle to help their human friends save their Times Square newsstand.

Selden, George. *Harry Cat's Pet Puppy* (Yearling Books, 1975 [reissue edition]). Harry Cat and Tucker Mouse try to care for and find a home for a stray puppy that Harry brings home to their drainpipe in the Times Square subway station.

White, E. B. *Stuart Little* (Harper Trophy, 1999 [reprint]). This classic story follows the surprising arrival of the Little's second child, Stuart, who is a mouse.

Books for the Family
Greenberg, Stanley, and Thomas H. Garver. *Invisible New York* (Johns Hopkins University Press, 1998). Fifty-three black and white photos exploring the underpinnings and infrastructure of New York.

Johnson, Stephen T. *City by Numbers* (Viking Children's Books, 1999). Find the numbers in the lines, curves and shapes of city architecture in this "exercise in visual literacy."

Kannapell, Andrea (ed.). *The Curious New Yorker: 329 Fascinating Questions and Surprising Answers About New York City* (Times Books, 1999). A collection of 329 of the most intriguing questions and amusing answers from the popular "F.Y.I." column in the *New York Times* about the Big Apple's history, landscape, subways, architecture, laws and more.

Videos
AAA Travel Video Series – New York (1994).

Home Alone 2: Lost in New York (PG) (1992). This sequel to *Home Alone* has Macaulay Culkin's character boarding the wrong plane at Christmas time, only to find himself once again separated from his family.

Miracle on 34th Street (1947). The story of the misadventures of Kris Kringle as he plays Santa at Macy's Department Store in New York City. There is also a 1990s remake of this classic.

The Muppets Take Manhattan (PG) (1984). This Muppet adventure visits many NYC locations as the Muppets attempt to take their college show to Broadway.

New York (1999). This PBS five-tape history of the city of New York stars David Ogden Stiers.

New York: First City of the World (1997). From Museum City Videos, a tour of the Big Apple.

New York the Way It Was – The Old Neighborhood (1995). "The Old Neighborhood" is a view of New York City neighborhoods of the past and the struggles of the immigrant generation trying to better the lives of their children.

APPENDIX

Just the Facts

All travelers need some basic information about their destination in order to get the most out of their visit. To guide you through the essentials, here is a New York City primer.

Accessibility information

Big Apple Greeters, 669-2896, www.bigapplegreeters.org

Hospital Audiences, Inc., 575-7660, www.hospitalaudiences.org. Publishes *Access for All*, a guide to New York City cultural institutions for people with disabilities.

Lighthouse International, 821-9200, 800 829-0500, www.lighthouse.org

Mayor's Office for People with Disabilities, 788-2830,

www.nyc.gov/html/mopd/home.html

New York Society for the Deaf, 777-3900, www.nysd.org

Society for Accessible Travel & Hospitality, 447-7284, www.sath.org

Babysitters

While we do not necessarily recommend hiring a babysitter on your vacation, if you do decide to leave your child with a babysitter, make sure to check references and do not leave your child if you are at all uncomfortable with the sitter. Many hotels will have a list of babysitters. Expect to pay between $15 and $20 per hour with a several-hour minimum.

Avalon Nurse Registry and Child Service, 245-0250, www.avalonhealthcare.com

Babysitters Guild, 682-0227, www.babysittersguild.com

Barnard College Babysitting Service, 854-2035, www.barnard.edu

Fox Agency, 753-2686

Pinch Sitters, 260-6005

No representation is made as to the quality of the babysitters that may be sent by the foregoing agencies.

Banking

ATM (Automatic Teller Machine). ATMs are plentiful and accept a variety of bank, debit and credit cards. Beware—many institutions charge a fee of between $1 and $2 per transaction at their ATMs (plus potential additional fees for conversion of currencies). Safety tips: Do not use a machine in a poorly lit area or if there are suspicious people around the ATM; have your card handy before you approach the machine (avoid searching your purse or wallet at the machine); do not count your cash at the ATM—quickly and discreetly put it away; do not let anyone into a closed ATM area behind you; and do not let anyone see your PIN (personal identification number). To find the nearest ATM, you can purchase a copy of Money Map at local stores (see www.money-map.com for a list of stores stocking this handy publication).

Bank Hours.

Banks are typically open Monday through Friday from 9:00 a.m. to either 3:00 p.m. or 4:00 p.m. Some banks have extended or weekend hours.

Currency.

United States currency is very simple. There are six types of bills, all of them currently the same size and color: $1, $5, $10, $20, $50 and $100. Many smaller establishments (and virtually all taxis) will *not* accept $50 or $100 bills. There are six types of coins: 1 cent (penny), 5 cents (nickel), 10 cents (dime), 25 cents (quarter), 50 cents (rarely used) and $1.00 coins (silver-colored Susan B. Anthony coins and gold-colored Sacagawea coins, both of which are rarely used). One hundred cents equal one dollar.

Foreign Exchange.

Not all banks will accept or exchange foreign currency (although certain Chase or Citibank branches will). It is best to use credit cards or travelers checks for most purchases. Bureaux de change are not plentiful and are typically found only in tourist areas.

Chequepoint USA, 22 Central Park South between Fifth and Sixth Avenues, 750-2400, www.chequepoint.com.

Travelex, Broadway at Morris Street, 363-6206; Broadway at 48th Street, 265-6063; Madison Avenue at 53rd Street, 753-2595; Madison Avenue at 42nd Street, 883-0401, www.thomascooktravelex.com.

Travelers Checks.

The most widely accepted travelers checks are American Express, Thomas Cook and Visa. You will need photo identification to cash a travelers check.

American Express, 800 221-7282, www.americanexpress.com

Thomas Cook, 800 223-7373, www.us.thomascook.com

Visa, 800 227-6811, www.visa.com

Business hours

Most shops stay open all day, every weekday, usually starting some time between 10 a.m. and 11 a.m., and close for the day in late afternoon, usually some time between 5 p.m. and 6 p.m. Shops that open on Sunday tend to do so at noon. Many stores stay open until 7 p.m. on Thursdays and have extended shopping hours on sale days or during the Christmas holidays. Most offices open for business between 8 a.m. and 9:30 a.m. and close some time between 5 p.m. and 6 p.m.

Calendar of events

January

National Boat Show—Jacob K. Javits Convention Center, 216-2000, www.javitscenter.com

February

Black History Month—Celebrated with special programs around the city

Chinese New Year—Celebrations throughout Chinatown, including the dragon parade

New York International Children's Film Festival—349-0330, www.gkids.com

Westminster Kennel Club Dog Show—Madison Square Garden, 465-6741, www.thegarden.com, www.westminsterkennelclub.org

March

International Auto Show—Jacob K. Javits Convention Center, 216-2000, www.javitscenter.com, www.autoshow.com

International Cat Show—Madison Square Garden, 465-6741, www.thegarden.com

Ringling Brothers and Barnum and Bailey Circus—Madison Square Garden, 465-6741, www.ringling.com

St. Patrick's Day Parade—March 17, Fifth Avenue from 44th to 86th Streets

April

Central Park Easter Egg Hunt—Easter Sunday

Easter Parade—Easter Sunday, Fifth Avenue from 47th to 57th Streets

Macy's Flower Show—Rockefeller Center, the week before Easter

May

Bike New York Five Boro Bike Tour (a traffic nightmare)—932-2453

Cherry Blossom Festival—Brooklyn Botanical Garden, 718 623-7200, www.bbg.org

Fleet Week—End of May

Ninth Avenue International Food Festival—Ninth Avenue from 37th to 57th Streets

Throughout the Summer

Central Park Summer Stage—Free outdoor performances, 362-2777, www.summerstage.com

Metropolitan Opera Parks Concerts—Free outdoor concerts, 362-6000

Mostly Mozart Festival—Lincoln Center, 875-5030, www.lincolncenter.org

New York Philharmonic Concerts in the Parks, 875-5656, www.ny.philharmonic.org

New York Shakespeare Festival—Outdoor performances at the Delacorte Theater, 539-8750

June

Mermaid Parade—Coney Island, 718 372-5159, www.coneyisland.brooklyn.ny.us

National Puerto Rican Day Parade—First or Second Sunday in June

July

Macy's July 4th Fireworks

August

Brooklyn County Fair

Harlem Week, which includes the Black Film Festival and Taste of Harlem Food Festival

September

Festival of San Gennaro—Little Italy, Third week in September, www.littleitaly.com

U.S. Open Tennis Tournament—USTA National Tennis Center, Flushing Meadows-Corona Park, 718 760-6200

West Indian American Day Parade—Labor Day Weekend, Brooklyn

October

Big Apple Circus—Lincoln Center, 800 922-3772, www.bigapplecircus.org

Blessing of the Animals—Cathedral of St. John the Divine, First Sunday of the month, 316-7400

Columbus Day Parade—Fifth Avenue between 44th and 79th Streets

Greenwich Village Halloween Parade—www.halloween-nyc.com

November

Macy's Thanksgiving Day Parade—From Central Park West and 77th Street to Herald Square, www.macyparade.com

New York City Marathon—First Sunday in November, www.nycmarathon.org

Veteran's Day Parade

December

Christmas Spectacular—Radio City Music Hall, 247-4777, www.radiocity.com

Christmas-tree lighting at Rockefeller Center—www.rockefellercenter.com

Kwanzaa Holiday Expo—Jacob K. Javits Convention Center, 216-2000, www.javitscenter.com

Lighting of the Chanukah Menorah at Grand Army Plaza—First night of Chanukah

New Year's Eve Ball Drop in Times Square

New Year's Eve Fireworks in Central Park

The Nutcracker—New York City Ballet, Lincoln Center, 870-5570, www.nycballet.com

Credit cards

Credit cards are accepted at almost all shops and restaurants around the city. The most widely accepted are American Express, MasterCard (or Access, Chargex or Eurocard) and Visa (or Barclaycard). Some, but not all, establishments accept Diners Club, Discover/Novus and Carte Blanche.

Drinking age and purchasing alcoholic beverages

The legal drinking age in New York is 21. This age restriction applies to both the purchase and consumption of alcoholic beverages.

Electricity

The United States runs on 110V to 120V 60-cycle AC current. Most foreign appliances will need an adapter.

Emergency

In case of fire or to report an emergency requiring ambulance or police, dial 911.

Foreign entry requirements

Visitors to the United States may bring in one carton of 200 cigarettes or 50 (non-Cuban) cigars, one liter of liquor and $100 of gifts. No plants, fruit, meat or produce can be brought into the United States.

- ↪ Travelers coming to the United States for tourism or business for up to 90 days from one of the following 28 countries participating in the Visa Waiver Program do not need a visa to enter the country: Andorra, Australia, Austria, Belgium, Brunei, Denmark, Finland, France, Germany, Iceland, Ireland, Italy, Japan, Liechtenstein, Luxembourg, Monaco, the Netherlands, New Zealand, Norway, Portugal, San Marino, Singapore, Slovenia, Spain, Sweden, Switzerland, the United Kingdom and Uruguay.

- ↪ All travelers from other countries (except Canada, whose citizens only need proof of residence) must obtain a visa to enter the United States. Visas are obtained at the American Embassy or Consulate with jurisdiction over the traveler's place of permanent residence.

- ↪ Embassies to the United States are located in Washington, D.C., but many countries have either consulates or missions to the United Nations in New York City. Local consulate or mission phone numbers are listed in the phone directory (or directory assistance, 411 or 555-1212) and at www.embassy.org.

State Department Visa Information, 202 663-1225, travel.state.gov/visa_services.html

U.S. Immigration and Naturalization Service, 800 375-5283, www.ins.usdoj.gov

Handicap information (see Accessibility information)

Holidays

With the possible exception of New Year's Day and Christmas Day, most restaurants and shops are open on national holidays. Mass transit functions 24 hours a day, 365 days a year. On the following holidays, banks, most businesses (including the stock exchanges) and government offices will be closed.

New Years Day—January 1

Martin Luther King, Jr. Day—third Monday in January

President's Day—third Monday in February

Memorial Day—last Monday in May

Independence Day—July 4

Labor Day—first Monday in September

Columbus Day—second Monday in October

Election Day—first Tuesday following the first Monday in November (only Presidential elections are national holidays)

Veterans Day—November 11

Thanksgiving—fourth Thursday in November

Christmas Day—December 25

Insurance

The United States does not have a national health insurance system. Foreign travelers are encouraged to make arrangements for travelers health insurance, because individuals requiring medical services are personally responsible for payment for the services they receive.

Newspapers and other publications

Newspapers

New York Daily News—Daily newspaper. www.nydailynews.com

New York Post—Daily newspaper. www.nypost.com

New York Observer—Weekly newspaper. www.observer.com

New York Times—Daily newspaper. www.nytimes.com

Wall Street Journal—Daily newspaper (Monday through Friday). www.wsj.com (paid subscription required)

Magazines

New York Magazine—Weekly magazine. www.metronewyork.com

New Yorker—Weekly magazine. www.newyorker.com

Time Out New York—Weekly magazine. www.timeoutny.com

Village Voice—Weekly magazine. Free. www.villagevoice.com

Family publications

Big Apple Parent—Monthly. Free. Widely distributed throughout the city. Subscriptions available. 889-6400. www.parentsknow.com

Family Entertainment Guide—Five issues per year (seasonal plus holiday). Free. Available at schools, libraries and family facilities. 787-3789. www.familybuzz.com

New York Family—Monthly. Free. Available at pediatricians' offices, schools, libraries and stores. Subscriptions available. 914 381-7474. www.nyfamily.com

PARENTGUIDE—Monthly. Free. Available at pediatricians' offices, schools, libraries and stores. Subscriptions available. 213-8840. www.parentguidenews.com

Postal services

The main branch of the U.S. Post Office is at 421 Eighth Avenue at 33rd Street, 967-8585. Check the phone book or www.usps.com for other locations (there are more than 50). Stamps are available from the post office, mobile post office units and vending machines. The current postal rate for a standard letter is 37 cents and 23 cents for a postcard. Overnight (or other expedited) mail or package delivery is available from U.S. Post Office Express Mail, 967-8585, www.usps.org; FedEx, 800 463-3339, www.fedex.com; DHL Worldwide Express 800 225-5345, www.dhl.com; and United Parcel Service, 800 742-5877, www.ups.com.

Radio and television stations (Just a sampling)

Radio—Music

WBGO-FM 88.3 Jazz

WBLS-FM 107.5 Urban Contemporary

WCBS-FM 101.1 Oldies

WHTZ-FM 100.3 Top 40

WNYC-FM 93.9 Classical

WPLJ-FM 95.5 Top 40

WQCK-FM 101.9 Smooth Jazz

WQEW-AM 1560 Disney

WQXR-FM 96.3 Classical

WXRK-FM 92.3 Classic Rock

Radio—News/Talk

WABC-AM 770

WBBR-AM 1130

WCBS-AM 880

WINS-AM 1010

WOR-AM 710

Radio—Public

WBAI-FM 99.5

WFUV-FM 90.7

WNYC-AM 820

Radio—Sports

WFAN-AM 660

WJWR-AM 620

Television-Network Stations

FOX-WNYW 5

UPN 9

WABC 7

WB11 11

WCBS 2

WNBC 4

WXTV 41 and WNJU 47 (Spanish)

Television—Public

WLIW 21

WNET 13

WNYE 25

Television—Cable News

CNN, MSNBC, FOX NEWS (Station numbers will vary depending on the cable system)

Sales tax

There is an 8.25 percent sales tax on almost all retail purchases and restaurant meals. Exempt from sales tax are clothing and footwear under $110, prescription drugs and certain non-prepared foods purchased in grocery stores. The sales tax applies to hotel rooms, which are also subject to an additional 5 percent hotel tax and $2 hotel fee.

Smoking

New York has very strict smoking laws and regulations. Smoking is prohibited in taxis, subway stations and most public places, including building lobbies and restaurants that seat more than 35 people. An individual must be 18 to buy tobacco products.

Street Facts

Most of Manhattan is set up in a grid system. Streets run east-west and increase by number as you head north from Houston Street. Most even-numbered streets allow eastbound vehicular traffic; most odd-numbered streets allow westbound vehicular traffic. Below Houston Street (and in Greenwich Village), streets have names and are not in a regular grid pattern. Avenues run north-south. Fifth Avenue divides Manhattan into the east and west sides. Approximately 20 north–south blocks equal one mile.

Supplies and Equipment

Traveling with supplies and equipment for young children can add pounds to your luggage. Several services are available that can deliver to a Manhattan destination.

Baby Basics, 718 257-3000 (formula, specialty nutritionals, diapers and infant care essentials, hard to find medical products)

Baby Travel Solutions, 888 989-0302, www.babytravelsolutions.com (diapers, formula, baby food, etc.)

Travel Babies, 631 666-3484, www.travelbabies.com (cribs, strollers, high chairs, car seats, etc.)

Telephones

- ↪ Coin-operated telephones are located all around the city. Local calls are 50 cents (paid in coins other than pennies) or by prepaid phone cards (sold at newsstands, drug stores, candy stores). To activate a phone card, follow the instructions printed on the card.

- ↪ To report an emergency, dial 911 (free call from a pay phone).

- ↪ Phone numbers in the United States consist of a three-digit area code plus a seven-digit phone number. The local area codes are: Manhattan—212, 646, 917 or 347; Brooklyn, Queens, Bronx and Staten Island—718 or 347. Cell phone and pagers also use area codes 917 and 646. The area codes for toll-free calls (calls for which there is no charge) are 800, 888, 866 and 877. All calls within New York City are made by dialing 1 plus the three-digit area code plus the seven-digit phone number. Unless otherwise indicated, all numbers listed in this book are in area code 212.

↪ To make an international call, dial 011 plus the country code (found in the telephone directory or from the operator) plus the phone number. To make a call to Canada, dial 1 plus the three-digit area code plus the phone number.

↪ To dial the operator, dial 0.

↪ To make a credit card or collect (reverse the charges) call, dial 0 plus the three-digit area code and the seven-digit phone number. The operator will come on with instructions.

Useful telephone numbers:

Emergency 911

Better Business Bureau 533-6200

Directory assistance 411 or 555-1212

NYC Department of Consumer Affairs 487-4444

Time 976-1616 or 976-2828

Weather 976-1212 or 976-2828

Time zone

New York is in the Eastern Time zone. Late autumn to early spring, New York is on Eastern Standard Time (EST); the rest of the year it is on Eastern Daylight Time (EDT). In early April, clocks are moved one-hour ahead (later) for EDT; in late October, they are moved one-hour behind (earlier) to return to EST.

Tipping

The customary tip for waiters, taxi drivers, bartenders and beauty-salon service providers (hairstylists, manicurists) is 15 to 20 percent. The customary tip for coat checkers is $1 to $2 per coat; for bellhops is $1 to $2 per bag; for hotel maids is $1 to $2 per night (given at the end of your stay).

Toilets

New York does not have many public toilets, and those that exist are generally unsavory. Your best bets are facilities located in hotel lobbies, large department stores, museums, libraries, restaurants (facilities are generally for patrons only) and bus/train stations (not always clean or particularly safe). See Rovere, Vicki, *Where to Go, Second Edition* (Rovere, 2001) for a list of more than 800 facilities.

Travelers Assistance

City Hall Park Visitor Information Kiosk, Southern tip of City Hall Park on the Broadway side at Park Row (closed during winter).

NYC & Company (formerly the New York Convention & Visitors Bureau) is the city's official tourism marketing organization and provides information and assistance to visitors as well as travel professionals, media and businesses. General number, 484-1200, visitor information 484-1222, www.nycvisit.com

Official Visitor Information Center, 810 Seventh Avenue, between 52nd and 53rd Streets, 484-1222

Traveler's Aid Society 718 656-4870 (booths at JFK and LaGuardia Airports)

Visitor Information Counselors 484-1222

Chapter 5

NAVIGATING THE CITY

C ontrary to popular belief, New York City is an extremely accessible city. Served by three major airports, two train stations, an international harbor and a network of highways, it is easy to get to and get around once you are here. How you reach and navigate the city has less to do with the availability of any particular mode of transportation than with your comfort level with the various kinds of transportation, your personal preferences, your budget and the distances you are traveling. The key to getting to and around town is accumulating a little knowledge on the subject.

In this chapter we provide information on the area airports, trains, buses and ferries as well as helpful information on getting into the city by car. To ensure that you are properly prepared for navigating the city once you have arrived, we have also included tips for traveling by taxi, bus, subway or car. A list of resources to help you with your travel plans can be found at the end of this chapter.

While this chapter focuses on the logistics of getting from Point A to Point B, it is essential that you become familiar with the basic layout of the Big Apple. In Chapter 4 you will find maps that provide the basic geography of the city as well as descriptions of the different neighborhoods, their history, points of interest and other highlights. Note that any fares or prices for transportation quoted in this chapter are those in effect at the time of this writing and are always subject to change.

By Air

New York City wasn't always easily accessible by air. It was not until after 1930, when former World War I fighter pilot Mayor Fiorello LaGuardia pushed to develop an airport within the city, that airport development became a focus for city planners. Today, the area's three major airports—John F. Kennedy International Airport (JFK), LaGuardia Airport and Newark International Airport—bring tens of millions of passengers in and out of the city each year.

Newark International Airport is located in Newark, New Jersey, and, at 16 miles from Manhattan, is the furthest airport from the city. LaGuardia, located 8 miles away in Queens, is nearest to the heart of Manhattan. JFK is located 15 miles from Manhattan in the Jamaica Bay section of Queens. Incredibly, despite the difference in mileage between Manhattan and each of these three airports, travel time to each can be similar, due to the vagaries, challenges and surprises of city traffic. Whichever airport you use, always allow yourself plenty of time to get to and from the city.

While you may wonder which of the three local airports is the best one, and most New Yorkers have their personal favorites, in reality there is no "best" airport. All three airports are large and busy, sometimes lose luggage and often experience flight delays. Yet each airport has made many changes over the years to try to become more passenger friendly. To a great extent, which airport you fly into will have more to do with availability of flights by your preferred carrier, travel dates and time of arrival than with anything else.

If you do have a choice, it is worth noting that there are generally more bargains to be had flying in and out of Newark. Although it is perceived to be the least convenient to Manhattan because it is in New Jersey, Newark in fact can be the most convenient depending on the time of day you are traveling and where you are headed.

► **General airport information.** Make sure to leave yourself enough time for check-in when departing from any of the area airports. Recent times have necessitated more intensive check-in procedures at all airports, and so you cannot rely on immediate curbside check-in for your flight, particularly if you are on an international flight. In all likelihood, you will need to stand in one line or another before you can depart. When you check in, you will be required to show photo identification to the airline personnel for the adults in your party as well as answer a few questions about your luggage. International flights require identification for all passengers, including children.

If you are traveling with small children and their paraphernalia—strollers, car seats, diaper bags—give yourself time to maneuver through the airport. You may find yourself with a long walk to or from your gate.

It is also important to leave yourself plenty of time, because the reality of air travel today is that many flights are overbooked, and a last minute check-in can leave your family seatless. Finding a new flight for a family that has been bumped is a bummer, and, if you do not have pre-assigned seats, the likelihood of being seated together on a crowded flight when you show up ten minutes before departure is remote at best.

It is also important to leave yourself plenty of time, because the reality of air travel today is that many flights are overbooked, and a last minute check-in can leave your family seatless.

New York airports are extremely crowded and busy, especially at holiday time. We cannot emphasize enough the importance of keeping close watch on your children, making sure that they do not wander off and that they are never left unattended, even for a minute. Be especially careful about sending your child to the bathroom. We recommend that you not let them go without an adult.

Like the city they service, the three area airports never sleep, operating 24 hours a day. Should you become stranded at any of the area airports you will find that they all have similar amenities and equivalent food concessions.

▶ **Getting to and from the airport.** When determining how best to transport your family to and from the airport, consider the number of people and the amount of luggage you are hauling. Your choices include taxi, bus, van service, subway, private car service or limousine or, if you are very lucky, being met by a local friend or family member. Note that taxis are not required to take more than three adults and typically cannot accommodate huge amounts of luggage.

New York City taxis are yellow and have medallion shields on their hoods and medallion numbers on the roof (more about this later). New Jersey taxis that pick up at Newark airport come in many different colors. For your safety, always use uniformed airport taxi dispatchers to get a cab at the airport. You will find dispatchers stationed outside of the baggage-claim areas (just follow the queue to the source). Cab drivers are required to join the line for the dispatcher, which means you cannot hail a cab on your own or commandeer one from the back of the line.

There are ground-transportation service desks or courtesy phones at the baggage-claim areas at each of the airports to assist you in arranging transportation from the airport to the city by bus, shared van service or limousine service.

You can also arrange for a private car service or limousine to pick you up at the airport. Your hotel concierge can arrange this or you can call a service in advance to make arrangements (see the resource section at the end of this chapter for some local services). If your company has a New York City office, it may have a car service you can use. Car-service automobiles are usually dark-colored luxury sedans with a big trunk for lots of baggage. We caution you against taking rides from people who approach you and tell you that they can take you into the city for a price. It is recommended that you use only services that you have reserved in advance and that have sent a driver to meet you.

If you use a car service, it is important to make specific arrangements as to the pick-up point. While at some airlines you can be met directly outside of the baggage-claim area, at others you need to arrange a different pick-up point because drivers are not allowed to park at the baggage-claim area while waiting for you. It is enormously frustrating to circle the area looking for your car when you are trying to maintain your travel sanity with tired or excited children. Confirm the fare, tolls and tip and whether you can pay by credit card (versus cash only); procedures for what to do if your flight is delayed; and the contact number should there be a problem upon arrival.

If you prefer mass transit, you have options from each of the three airports. You can take public buses from each airport into Manhattan. You can also take a bus from JFK or LaGuardia to the subway. You can take the subway from Manhattan to JFK and LaGuardia, but in each case you will have to transfer to a bus which takes you the rest of the way. Be practical when deciding whether to use mass transit, because even though this may be the most economical way to travel as an adult, it may be totally impractical for a family or a small group with children requiring a lot of paraphernalia. And, of course, public transportation cannot provide you with door-to-door service.

Each airport is also served by private bus lines, which are listed in the resource section at the end of this chapter along with van lines providing minibus airport transportation.

If you absolutely cannot bear the thought of traffic or are feeling totally extravagant, you can also travel to and from the airport by chartered helicopter, one of the many ways you can burn through cash in a New York minute. Although this may sound like an appealing adventure for the kids, remember that you will still need to arrange transportation between the heliport and your accommodations.

Car rental in the city is really unnecessary as you will likely do most of your exploring on foot, by cab or by mass transit. For those who feel stranded without a car, the reality is that unless you have reasonably priced parking arrangements through a hotel, it's not worth the small fortune you will pay in parking for the limited benefit of getting around town by car. If you must rent a car, the car rental companies have locations in Manhattan and the other boroughs. It will be much easier on you and the kids simply to pick up a rental car for an out-of-town trip the day you need it.

See the resource section at the end of this chapter for detailed transportation information for each airport.

▶ **John F. Kennedy International Airport**. JFK handles more international passengers by far than any other airport. Formerly known as New York International Airport, in 1963 it was rededicated as John F. Kennedy International Airport. It is located 15 miles from midtown, but do not be deceived: it typically takes about 50 to 60 minutes to travel to midtown (and longer during rush hour). The airport has been undergoing extensive renovations, which, when completed, will render JFK truly state of the art in all respects.

In the meantime, JFK can be somewhat complicated and confusing to get around. In particular, it is often quite difficult to travel from terminal to terminal. Before you depart from or arrive at JFK, we recommend that you call your airline in advance to confirm from which terminal your flight will start or end, as the case may be. This information is quite useful when making pick-up and drop-off arrangements.

If you are traveling from the airport to Manhattan via taxi, note that currently the fare is a flat rate of $35 plus tolls and tip. The establishment of the flat rate for taxi service from the airport has prevented dishonest cabbies from taking advantage of arriving visitors. The flat rate does not, however, apply to trips from Manhattan to the airport. When leaving from the city to the airport, the rate is the amount on the meter plus tolls and tip (expect to pay between $30 and $45).

There is frequent bus service to and from JFK. Expect to pay around $13 per person and a bit more for door-to-door shared van service. See the resources at the end of this chapter for specifics.

▶ **LaGuardia Airport**. This little giant is small on size and big on volume. By virtue of its being the closest airport to Manhattan and the easiest to get to, LaGuardia is probably the city's most popular airport and the day traveler's best bet. If you are lucky and do not encounter any major traffic snarls, it is possible to get from Manhattan to LaGuardia in 25 minutes, although it typically it will take

35 to 45 minutes to get there in average traffic. LaGuardia is not permitted to service flights traveling in excess of 1,500 miles, so, depending on the origin or destination of your flight, flying into or out of LaGuardia may not be an option.

The airport has four terminals, including the historic Marine Terminal used by Delta Airlines for its shuttle service to Washington, D.C., and Boston. The Central Terminal is used by all airlines except Delta, US Airways and Northwest Airlines. Delta and Northwest share a separate terminal and US Airways has its own terminal. If you are flying Delta, be sure to confirm from which terminal your flight will originate or depart to avoid any confusion.

If you travel by taxi, expect to pay a fare of $20 to $30, plus tolls and tip. There is frequent bus service between LaGuardia and JFK. Expect to pay around $10 per person and a bit more for door-to-door shared van service. See the resources at the end of this chapter for specifics.

► **Newark International Airport.** While most New Yorkers would like to believe that the Big Apple consistently does everything bigger and better, Newark Airport may have the other New York airports beat. Opened in 1928, Newark Airport was New York's first commercial aviation location. It is located 16 miles from midtown and takes approximately 45 to 60 minutes to reach by car. It is the city's only hub airport (for Continental Airlines) and is the metropolitan area's busiest airport.

The airport has three terminals connected by roadways and an elevated monorail system. The monorail is an integral part of the successful transportation system that gives access not only to the terminals but to parking areas and car-rental facilities. The monorail system connects the airport to the NJ Transit commuter service and Amtrak's Northeast Corridor trains.

It costs a bit more to travel between Newark airport and Manhattan. In average traffic, taxi fares can range from $35 to $55, plus tolls and tip. Private car services are often the better way to go, as they offer a fixed rate. The least expensive per-person way to get into the city is the AirTrain to the Rail Link Station at Newark Airport, which links with NJ Transit, Amtrak and PATH service to Manhattan.

There is frequent bus service to and from Newark. Expect to pay around $11 per person and a bit more for door-to-door shared van service. See the resources at the end of this chapter for specifics.

By Train

Whether traveling from near or far, consider the train. Kids love the adventure of it, there are generally few hassles involved with train travel and the price may be just the ticket.

If you live in the metropolitan area, the train is a great way to travel into the city for a day trip or other excursion. There are four local commuter rail systems serving New York City: Metro-North, with more than 100 stations in New York and Connecticut; the Long Island Railroad (LIRR); New Jersey (NJ) Transit (consisting of the Hoboken and Newark Divisions and the Atlanatic City Rail Line); and PATH, the Port Authority Trans-Hudson Corporation.

Amtrak, which operates trains throughout the United States, provides the rail service into New York from points both inside and outside of the metropolitan area. Compared to the European rail system, Amtrak is not as reliable or as extensive a system, but for going from city to city, particularly along the East Coast, it is generally fast, reasonably priced and convenient. International visitors can purchase a USA Railpass, and Amtrak offers special packages and promotions for all travelers.

There are two major train stations in Manhattan. Grand Central Terminal (called Grand Central Station by many New Yorkers), perhaps the most famous station in the country, is located on 42nd Street and Park Avenue in Manhattan. Metro-North operates out of Grand Central. Pennsylvania Railroad Station, known as Penn Station, is located on Seventh and Eighth Avenues between 31st and 32nd Streets, directly underneath Madison Square Garden. Penn Station is home to Amtrak, the LIRR and NJ Transit trains.

▶ **General information.** On most train lines, children under the age of 12 travel at either a discount or for free. Depending on the train line, the price of a child's ticket may be contingent on the time of travel. It is wise to be aware of fare restrictions and policies so that you can plan to travel at the most advantageous time. Note that in general, purchasing a ticket on the train rather than at the station will add to the cost of an adult fare and, on certain train lines, perhaps to the cost of the child's ticket as well. We have included information about discounted children's fares, but note that policies are subject to change and it has been known for the railways to provide inconsistent information about their policies!!

Strollers are allowed on all trains and are not necessarily required to be folded. They cannot, however, interfere with the conductor's ability to move easily through a train car. Therefore, if you are not able to park your stroller out of the way, you will probably be asked to fold it. Make sure that while your child is in a stroller, he or she is properly secured during travel. It is recommended that when traveling with a child in a stroller, you do so during off-peak hours when space is more available.

Bathrooms are available on all trains with the exception of the PATH trains. Since the facilities are far from hygienic—and definitely not spacious—it is always a good idea to "try" before you get on the train.

There are two weekday commuter rail "rush hours" (the time when commuters are rushing to and from work), which impact travelers. Each commuter railway will define its own rush hour in terms of "peak" times, meaning the time when the rail service is most used by commuters. Generally speaking, it is safe to assume that the morning rush ranges from about 5:30 a.m. to 10 a.m. and the afternoon rush ranges from about 4:30 p.m. to 6 p.m.

Although there are more trains running at peak times than during "off-peak" times, during peak times, commuter trains will be crowded and it will be hard to get taxis at the train station (especially in bad weather). Unless you need to arrive or leave the city during rush hour, try to avoid rush hour when you travel with children. Refer to train schedules for on- and off-peak time periods.

If you use the commuter rails, take along a schedule for the train line you will be riding (also called a "branch schedule") so that if your plans change, you'll have the information you need to select an alternative departure time. Remember to check the dates for which the schedule is effective, as schedules tend to change a few times a year, typically around the change of seasons.

▶ **Amtrak.** While traveling by air is often perceived as being the fastest way to get from place to place, it can be far from the truth once you factor in getting to and from the airport and dealing with airport issues such as check-in and retrieving your luggage. For instance, if you are traveling to New York City from Baltimore, Washington, D.C., New Jersey, Pennsylvania, upstate New York, Boston or New England, consider taking Amtrak. Its express trains, such as the Metroliner and Acela (a high-speed train that runs between Boston and Washington, D.C.), deposit you in the heart of Manhattan at Penn Station and provide a reasonable alternative to flying or driving.

One adult can take up to two children between the ages of 2 and 15 for half of the adult fare. Children under two travel for free. Amtrak often runs specials that make it even less expensive to travel by rail. While the cost savings can be meaningful and traveling by train can be quite a family adventure (complete with sleeper cars on the longer runs), if you are traveling a long distance, be sure to consider whether the total time involved is worth the savings.

To explore all that Amtrak has to offer, including schedule and fare information, call 800 USA-RAIL (800 872-7245) or visit www.amtrak.com. Reservation Sales Agents or Customer Service Agents can help you with information about services for travelers with disabilities.

▶ **Metro-North.** The Harlem Line, the Hudson Line and the New Haven Line carry thousands of people each day from as far north as Dover Plains into Grand Central Terminal and back home again. Traveling with kids under the age of 12 is a relative bargain on any one of these lines. One adult can travel with up to four children between the ages of 5 and 11 for only 50 cents per child. Children under five are free. The catch is that you may not depart from the station before the conclusion of the morning rush hour. Rush hour is usually considered over after 10 a.m., although this may vary for certain stations. This fare restriction does not apply to evening peak hours or weekend schedules. If you must travel during the morning rush hour, children between the ages of 5 and 11 will be charged half the adult fare. Children 12 and over pay the adult fare.

Tickets can be purchased at the train station or from a conductor aboard the train. There is no surcharge for purchasing a ticket on a train into the city if the station ticket office is closed. There are surcharges for purchasing a ticket on the train when leaving from Grand Central Terminal or a station outside the city during station ticket-office hours. For schedule and fare information outside the city call 800 METRO-INFO (800 638-7646), or call 532-4900 from within New York or visit www.mnr.org.

If you are planning to purchase tickets to a Broadway show, be sure to check the Metro-North website, since, during special promotions, you can obtain free train tickets when you purchase tickets to certain shows. Also, from June through September, Metro-North typically offers a variety of one-day excursions outside of the city.

▶ **LIRR.** The Long Island Rail Road, often referred to as the "LI double R," maintains nine lines and over 130 stations serving Nassau and Suffolk Counties as well as Queens, Brooklyn and Manhattan. Trains originate from Penn Station in the heart of Manhattan and travel up to 120 miles from Manhattan to Montauk at the eastern tip of Long Island.

Children under five travel for free on the LIRR regardless of the time of day. During peak hours, children between the ages of 5 and 11 pay half the adult fare; off-peak, the fare is only 50 cents per child. Up to five children can travel with a paying adult and receive the discounted off-peak fare. There are surcharges for tickets purchased on trains when station ticket offices are open. For specific fare and schedule information call 718 217-LIRR (718 217-5477) in New York City, 516 822-LIRR (516 822-5477) in Nassau County and 631 231-LIRR (631 231-5477) in Suffolk County. Information can also be obtained on-line by visiting www.mta.nyc.ny.us.

The LIRR offers special promotional packages to various events and Broadway shows as well as seasonal tours. For families seeking an excursion outside of the city that does not require a car, this is one option worth checking out. Visit the website or call 718 558-7498 for further information.

▶ **NJ Transit.** NJ Transit has 614 trains servicing more than 380,000 passengers daily. It provides access via three commuter train divisions—the Hoboken and Newark Divisions and the Atlantic City Rail Line —to points in New Jersey, New York and Philadelphia. The lines and branches include the Atlantic City Line, the North Jersey Coast Line, the Northeast Corridor, the Pascack Line, the Main/Bergen Lines, the Boonton Line, the Raritan Valley Line and the Morris & Essex Lines (which include the Morristown Line and the Montclair and Gladstone Branches). Trains leave out of and arrive at one of three stations: Penn Station, Hoboken and Newark's Penn Station.

For specific fare and schedule information call 973 762-5100 outside of New Jersey and toll free in New Jersey at 800 772-2222. The official website of the NJ Transit can be found at www.njtransit.com. Check the website for information on special promotions and offers, including discounts to cultural events and free rides to shows. There is an "unofficial" site at www.nj.com/njtransit .

Up to three children under four years of age ride free with an adult passenger paying a full fare. Children from 5 to 11 years of age pay half the adult fare, provided that they are traveling with an adult passenger paying a full fare. The fare for children is the same off- or on-peak

You will pay a surcharge for tickets purchased on trains when station ticket offices are open or vending machines are available.

NJ Transit offers a Family Super Saver Fare, which allows two children between the ages of 5 and 11 to travel free with an adult passenger paying a full fare, provided that travel occurs between 7 p.m. on a Friday evening and 6 a.m. on a Monday morning. This Super Saver Fare is also available over federal and state holidays and is in effect between 7 p.m. of the evening prior to the holiday and 6 a.m. of the day after.

▶ **PATH.** The PATH system links New Jersey urban communities and suburban commuter railroads to Manhattan. Over 1,000 trains run daily, operating 24 hours a day, as frequently as every four to six minutes during rush hour.

The PATH fare is a flat rate of $1.50 for a ticket, regardless of the distance being traveled. Children under five ride for free. Trains leave from Newark, Jersey City and Hoboken and arrive in lower Manhattan, making stops along the route on Sixth Avenue. In Manhattan, you can catch a PATH train at various locations along Sixth Avenue between Christopher Street and 33rd Street. The World Trade Center and Exchange Place stations are expected to re-open in 2004. Schedules can be obtained at the stations, on-line at www.panynj.gov/path or by calling 800 234-PATH (800 234-7284).

The Newark station is New Jersey's Penn Station and should not be confused with New York's Penn Station located in the heart of Manhattan.

By Bus

If you are traveling into New York City from the metropolitan or so-called tri-state (New York, New Jersey and Connecticut) area, a number of local bus companies offer service. See the resources at the end of this chapter.

Bus service between the city boroughs is extensive and offered by seven different franchised private companies with over 91 routes. The bus lines and the areas they service have been listed in the resource section of this chapter.

Many bus companies bring visitors to the city from any number of locations across the country. Undoubtedly these travelers will pass through the Port Authority Bus Terminal, one of the largest terminals in the country, located on Eighth Avenue between 40th and 42nd Streets. The Port Authority has received a major face-lift in recent years and is packed with stores and places to grab a bite. In the resource section we have listed bus companies offering bus service to the city from various locations.

Putting the Pedal to the Metal

▶ **Getting into Manhattan.** When traveling to the city by car, you will find it an excellent idea to invest in a good map and keep it handy in the car. American Automobile Association (AAA) members can use AAA's travel service to determine the most direct route into the city and provide materials on parking options, alternate-side-of-the-street parking information and city maps (they also offer other travel-related services you may want to check out). You can also purchase a good city map in most bookstores or visit one of the websites listed in the resource section of this chapter for directions from your point of origin to a local New York address.

The options for traveling into Manhattan by car from elsewhere are many. Where you are coming from clearly will make some routes more practical than others. Keep in mind though that if you are traveling during rush hour (and note that the driving rush hour is a bit different from the commuter rail rush hour: generally 7–9 a.m. and 4–6 p.m., Monday through Friday) you are bound to encounter heavy traffic at all of the city entry and exit points. Though we cannot provide you with specific directions into the city because the permutations are infinite, we can give you a bit of an overview of the basic access points into Manhattan.

◢ **From New Jersey.** If coming from New Jersey, you will need to go either over or under the Hudson River. You can go under the river through the Holland Tunnel, which takes you to lower Manhattan, or the Lincoln Tunnel, which takes you to West 30th Street. You can go over the Hudson via the George Washington Bridge (GWB), which brings you into upper Manhattan at approximately 178th Street. Having crossed the GWB, you can take the Henry Hudson Parkway or Riverside Drive to the west side of Manhattan or the Harlem River Drive, which becomes the FDR Drive, to the east side.

◢ **From Queens.** If you are approaching from Queens, you will need to cross the East River via one of the many east-side crossings. The Queensborough Bridge (also called the 59th Street Bridge) connects Long Island City (which is within Queens) with Manhattan at

First and Second Avenues between 59th and 60th Streets. The bridge not only delivers motorists to major roadways in Queens, including Queens Boulevard, Northern Boulevard and the Long Island Expressway via Van Dam Street, but it is free. The Queens Midtown Tunnel links Queens with Manhattan on First and Second Avenues in the low 30s and there is a toll in both directions. The Triborough Bridge manages to connect Queens, Manhattan and the Bronx and all three boroughs with Randalls Island. The Triborough Bridge can be a bit confusing to navigate, and there are tolls in all directions.

◤ **From the Bronx.** The Bronx is connected to Manhattan by the Triborough Bridge, the Willis Avenue Bridge, the Third Avenue Bridge, the Madison Avenue Bridge and the Macombs Dam Bridge. These crossings deliver you to northern Manhattan (between approximately 125th and 155th Streets). The Henry Hudson Bridge connects Riverdale, an area in the Bronx, with Manhattan.

◤ **From Brooklyn.** There are four crossings connecting Brooklyn to lower Manhattan. The three bridges are free, but the tunnel is not. The Brooklyn Bridge, which is one of the city's most famous bridges, connects Manhattan with Camden Plaza and the Brooklyn Queens Expressway (BQE). The Manhattan Bridge links Canal Street and Chinatown in Manhattan to Grand Army Plaza and Atlantic Avenue in Brooklyn. The Williamsburg Bridge connects Delancey Street on the Lower East Side of Manhattan with Metropolitan Avenue and the BQE in Brooklyn. Finally, the Brooklyn Battery Tunnel connects the lower tip of Manhattan with the Gowanus Expressway in Brooklyn.

◤ **From Staten Island.** To get to the city from Staten Island you simply have to take the Staten Island Ferry. You can even bring your car. (Note: at various times since September 11, 2001, cars have been prohibited on the ferry, so please check the ferry status before you drive. See the resource section of this chapter for phone numbers and websites.) The ferry arrives and departs from St. George on Staten Island and Whitehall Street adjacent to Battery Park in lower Manhattan. The fare is free, unless you are traveling with a car. If you do not want to travel by ferry, you can get to Staten Island by taking the Brooklyn Battery Tunnel out of Manhattan to Brooklyn and then the Verrazano Narrows Bridge to Staten Island.

▶ **Do I really want a car in New York?** Having a car in Manhattan poses some interesting challenges. While it can be comforting to feel that you are controlling your transportation destiny by having your own vehicle, the reality is that having to deal with traffic and parking can potentially ruin an otherwise pleasant experience. Some things to consider:

◤ **Day trips.** If you live in the New York City vicinity and are visiting the city for all or part of a day, the answer is a definite maybe. We highly recommend leaving the car home when possible, but there are good reasons for taking it on occasion. Your decision will depend on how long you are staying, how many are in your group, the time of day you will be traveling, whether you need to transport things as well as people, your transportation alternatives into the city and how many things you are planning to do while here. For example, if there will be several people in your party, it might be less expensive to drive in and park in a garage than to buy round trip train tickets for everyone, especially if your planned activities are not going to be near a station or terminal and you want to avoid taking many buses and cabs. On the other hand, if your destination for the day is near a train station or bus terminal, it may not be worth bothering with the car.

Your decision will depend on how long you are staying, how many are in your group, the time of day you will be traveling, whether you need to transport things as well as people, your transportation alternatives into the city and how many things you are planning to do while here.

The advantages of using your car include the use of age-appropriate safety seats, convenient transport of a good number of children and all of their gear and not getting stuck without transportation at inopportune times. Areas outside of midtown are generally easier to navigate. Driving works best on weekends, particularly Saturday and Sunday during the summer (watch out for street festivals and parades). Avoid rush hour and midtown weekdays during business hours.

If you do drive in, your main issue will be parking, either once for the day or moving the car as you get through your day's activities. If you are willing to park in the street and you can find a spot, driving can be a downright bargain. If you end up in a garage, note that most garages have required minimum fees, so if you move from garage to garage you may spend a small fortune.

◪ **Longer than a day trip.** If you are vacationing in New York City from out of town and do not specifically need the car for excursions outside of the city, the answer to whether you need a car during your stay is probably not. Unlike other American cities where having a car is either desirable or essential, in New York you will not need or want to drive within the city limits as your primary means of moving around and exploring.

Since getting around on foot, by taxi or by mass transit is not only part of the experience but how the natives do it, if you arrive into the city by car, most likely you will park it and not use it again until it is time to depart. If you are arriving by plane, you will generally not find it necessary to rent a car at the airport and drive in. To the contrary, if you want access to a car for an out-of-city excursion, you will save money and aggravation by just renting one on the day you need it.

▶ **Traffic strategy.** Traffic is endemic to New York City and its constant presence provides another reason to leave the car behind. Despite the many different ways to get into the city, you will rarely find yourself alone on the road. You can count on hitting traffic during rush hour, but there are other traffic obstacles to be on the lookout for, including parades (usually on weekends, but not always), street fairs, visits to the city by the President or other dignitaries, construction and roadwork.

The best time to drive into or out of the city during the week is between 10 a.m. and 3 p.m. Weekend traffic is usually much better, although it is common to hit traffic when driving into the city on Friday or Saturday evenings between 7 p.m. and 9 p.m. Note that particularly during the summer months, leaving Manhattan on Friday (from late afternoon on) and driving into the city on Sunday (from the afternoon on) can put you in heavy traffic with New Yorkers who weekend outside the city. In addition, be aware that no matter how good your planning may have been, you may still be delayed by road work, which is often performed during off-peak traffic hours.

If you are in the car, tune in to WINS (1010 AM dial) or CBS-AM (880 AM dial) for frequent traffic reports and updates, which can help you avoid traffic jams if you are in a position to change your route. If you cannot change your route, at least you will have an explanation for the wait. Another major time-saver for drivers living in the tri-state area is the E-Z Pass, a local electronic toll-collecting system. For information call 800 333-TOLL (800 333-8655) or visit www.e-zpassny.com.

▶ **Everything you heard about parking in New York is true.** Having driven into Manhattan, you are faced with a serious dilemma: what to do with the car. The magnitude of this problem should not be underestimated. You have only two choices. You can either park on the street or park in a garage facility. Neither option is ideal. While parking on the street is cheap (free at unmetered spaces and typically 25 cents for 15 minutes at metered spaces), it is often difficult to find a space that is near where you want to be. While garages are somewhat plentiful, they are expensive and, depending on the time of day you show up, do not always have space available. That said, if you want to drive to New York, do not be dismayed. If you have the time and patience and are prepared to shell out for a garage, you will be able to park.

It is worth noting that if you are coming into the city to explore a particular attraction—for example, one of the museums—call ahead to the place you are visiting (or check their website) to see if they have a garage or a list of local parking garages and other transportation information. Some organizations have very detailed information, which can take the headache out of finding a practical parking solution.

◪ Garages. While there are many garages all over Manhattan, it is inevitable that whenever you need one, there is not one to be found. With all the wonderful contraptions that many cars come equipped with these days, a parking lot locator would be our preference for trips into and around the city. The closest thing to such a tool is the *Parking Guide to New York City* produced by the Department of City Planning, Transportation Division (see the resources at the end of this chapter for more information). The *Guide* provides maps of off-street parking facilities located south of 72nd Street in Manhattan.

For additional parking information, you can visit the Department of City Planning website, www.nyc.gov/html/dcp/html/dcptd/index.html, which offers maps showing the location of over 2,400 licensed parking facilities in the five boroughs. Without the *Guide*, above 72nd Street or without a visit to the Internet, the only way to find a private parking garage is by cruising the streets. The city does operate three Municipal Parking Lots in Manhattan, which are listed at the end of this chapter.

If you are staying in a hotel, your hotel may provide on- or off-site parking (be sure to check the cost of this service). If not, the hotel personnel can surely direct you to the closest parking facility. If you simply do not want to be bothered and want to delegate your parking-lot search to someone else, you can call Auto Baby Sitters of NY (718 493-9800). This service will pick up your car and park it for you in a covered garage near the Brooklyn Museum. Rates vary, depending on the type of car and the amount of time you will be parking the car. A midday pick-up and delivery is the easiest to orchestrate, and you must call during business hours to make the arrangements. Although the garage is open 24 hours, a day's notice is required for pick-up or delivery.

One of the great New York mysteries is understanding how private parking lots calculate their rates. Daily parking rates vary greatly, not only among garages but among neighborhoods, without rhyme or reason. Even more mystifying is that although there is a detailed rate schedule posted by law at every facility, when you go to get your car, the amount you are charged seems to bear no relationship to the rate schedule, and somehow, whatever is up on the board seems not to apply to you. To add insult to injury, an 18.25 percent tax will be added to your bill (outside of Manhattan, 10.25 percent). If you are parking for the day in midtown Manhattan, expect to pay upwards of $25 for the privilege; prices will be lower outside midtown.

If you plan to park a large sports utility vehicle (SUV) or a high-end luxury or sports car (think Rolls Royce or Ferrari), expect to pay a parking surcharge. In fact, the larger SUVs, including the Lincoln Navigator, the Ford Expedition and Toyota Land Cruiser to name a few, are usually not welcome at many garages.

Be sure to inspect your car before leaving a parking lot or garage. If you find that your car has been damaged, request a claim form and, when possible, get a police report. If the matter is not resolved to your satisfaction with the garage owner, you can file a complaint with the Department of Consumer Affairs. Most garages post signage indicating that the management is not responsible for valuables left in the car, and so whenever possible, do not leave anything valuable in the car. If you have separate keys for the engine and the trunk of the car, you can store items in the trunk and take that key with you when you leave the garage.

◤ **Street parking.** Parking on the street is always an option, but you may find it difficult to find a space when and where you need one. If you do park on the street, be sure to read the street signs, since there is not a street in the city where you can park a car for a week without moving it. If you are concerned about your car being stolen or broken into, it is best to park in busy, well-lit areas. Car alarms and other deterrents are a plus in warding off thieves.

Some New York parking basics:

➥ Alternate-side-of-the-street parking requires that at designated times during the day or week, parking is permitted on only one side of the street to allow for street cleaning. On certain holidays this rule is suspended. You can call the Department of Transportation's 24-hour hotline at 212 225-5368 or 718 225-5368 for more information.

➥ A "No Stopping" sign means you are not permitted to wait or stop in that space to pick-up or drop-off people or packages.

- A "No Standing" sign means you can stop to pick-up or drop-off passengers, but you cannot wait or leave the car to stop to pick-up or drop-off packages.

- A "No Parking" sign means that you cannot wait or leave the car, but you can stop to pick-up or drop-off packages or people.

- Double-parking of passenger cars is illegal.

- You may not park within 15 feet of either side of a fire hydrant.

- Pursuant to New York's Vehicle and Traffic Law 1959, all of the city is a tow-away zone. This means that if your car is parked illegally or does not have a current registration or inspection sticker displayed on the windshield, it can be towed.

- Parking tickets begin at around $55 dollars. This is a big source of income for the city, so read the parking signs.

► **It's the law.** Remember, seatbelts save lives, and in New York City, as in the rest of New York State, you are required to wear a seatbelt in your vehicle. Children ages four and under are required to be in age- and size-appropriate car seats. All front-seat passengers and passengers under the age of 16 must be buckled in. It is illegal to turn right at a red light in Manhattan, and never, never "block the box" (get stuck not being able to move completely through an intersection before the light turns red). Blocking the box will cost you money and may result in penalty points on your license. Under state law, the driver of a vehicle may not operate a hand-held cell phone while driving (except in an emergency).

► **Fill 'er up.** Gas stations in Manhattan are few and far between, not to mention expensive. If you have the opportunity, it is worth filling up your tank before you reach the city so you can save yourself the difficulty of locating a gas station and the added expense of paying for gas in the city.

► **On the road *en famille*.** Forget traffic and the cost of parking; it is the whining and fighting in the car that usually makes car trips unbearable. Here are a few tips to ease the pain:

- ◔ Pack the snacks. Pack water, juices, cheese and crackers, fruit and other healthy snacks (in a cooler, if necessary). Avoid choking hazards such as popcorn, nuts or grapes, with small children. Give each child his or her own snack bag to avoid their fighting over the goodies.

- ◔ Bring a small garbage bag and wipes for easy clean up. Hand sanitizer is truly a modern miracle.

- ◔ Make sure that when your child is properly belted into the car, the car-seat straps or seat belt do not chafe skin. Bring pillows or other soft items that can be used to prop a child's head against a locked door for a comfortable nap.

- ◔ Invest in a travel pack of car games.

- ◔ Bring along books on tape. If you are feeling extravagant, you can rent or buy a car video unit which allows passengers in the back seat to view their favorite tapes or even play video games in the car.

- ◔ Travel with lap tables to provide a great surface for drawing and playing games like cards.

- ◔ When traveling with a teen, consider having your son or daughter invite a friend. Generally, teenage company is all that is needed to entertain a teen.

- ◔ Map out the trip. Provide the kids with a spare map and then write out or draw some of the landmarks you will pass on separate pieces of paper. Bring tape and have the kids place the landmarks on the map as you pass them.

- ◔ To the best of your ability, maintain a good sense of humor.

The streets of New York are certainly not paved with gold, so there are many things to watch out for, including potholes, traffic, aggressive drivers, bicycles, emergency vehicles and pedestrians who sometimes dare you to hit them. It can get ugly, so take it easy and do not feel compelled to beat out the taxi drivers.

By Sea

► **New York Harbor.** Passenger ships from the major cruise-ship lines arrive in and depart from New York Harbor at the Passenger

Ship Terminal (246-5450/1) located between 48th and 55th Streets on Manhattan's West Side.

► **Ferries.** Believe it or not, getting to the city by ferry is not only possible but also how thousands of people get to work every day. You can travel by ferry between Manhattan and Staten Island, Brooklyn, Queens and New Jersey. There are also seasonal schedules for ferries between Manhattan and Yankee Stadium and Shea Stadium.

Getting Around Town Once You Are Here

Physically getting around New York requires an understanding of traffic flow and a basic knowledge of the city's ever-changing landscape. Helpful extras, depending on your mode of transportation, might include plenty of quarters, a MetroCard, small bills for taxi fares, a wallet-size street map and a good pair of walking shoes.

Getting from Point A to Point B does not have to be a test of your endurance, thanks to the number of transportation options. There are subways, buses, taxis, car services, or the family car. For the adventurous, bikes, Rollerblades and scooters are available, although the number of individuals you can transport may be severely compromised. Last but not least, there is the most reliable mode, your own two feet. Depending on the time of day you are traveling and how important it is that you be on time, if you are going fewer than ten blocks and your children are good walkers or still in the stroller, it is generally faster to walk. No matter which mode of transportation you choose, if you are toting a tot or shuffling a school-age kid around the city, it is advisable to take the path of least resistance.

► **Yellow Medallion Taxis.** New York City is known for many things: bagels, Central Park, hotdog vendors, the Empire State Building and of course those world-famous yellow cabs. Taxis now come in as many shapes and sizes as their drivers do, but a genuine New York City yellow cab will always have a medallion on the hood of the vehicle. The driver's name, license number and the medallion number must be displayed in the taxi and are usually located

to the right of the meter on the dashboard or on the partition sep-
arating the front and back seats. The medallion number must also
be displayed on the exterior of both rear doors, the roof light, the
hood and the license plates.

Yellow medallion taxis are hailed on the street by pedestrians
(there are also several taxi stands, which are listed at the end of this
chapter). Taxi fares are regulated and set by the Taxi and Limousine
Commission (TLC). Rates are posted on the doors of the taxi, and
meters are required to be calibrated accordingly. There are special
fares for trips to airports and rules governing the fares that may be
charged for trips outside of the five boroughs, which are posted in
the back seat of the taxi. Tipping is customary. The standard tip is
15–20 percent of the fare. Drivers are not required to change bills
over $20. It is wise to travel with small bills, as drivers often do not
have change for a $20 bill, even though they are supposed to.

A yellow cab with its rooftop light illuminated (indicating that it
is for hire) that stops to pick you up must take you to any destination within the five boroughs, although a driver is permitted to
refuse to take you outside New York City. A driver who asks you
where you are going and declines to take you anywhere within city
limits on hearing your destination is in violation of the regulations
governing the operation of yellow cabs.

The TLC has promulgated specific rules governing service,
including the Taxi Riders Bill of Rights. The Taxi Riders Bill of
Rights, which must be posted in the back seat of each medallion
cab, states that as a taxi rider, you have the right to: direct the destination and route used; be taken to any destination in the five boroughs; a courteous, English-speaking driver who knows the streets
in Manhattan and the way to major destinations in other boroughs;
a driver who knows and obeys all traffic laws; air conditioning on
demand; a radio-free (silent) trip; smoke and incense-free air; a
clean passenger seat area and trunk and a driver who uses the horn
only when necessary to warn of danger. Refuse to tip if these basics
are not complied with. State law provides that a driver may not
operate a hand-held cell phone while driving.

The TLC recommends that passengers abide by their suggested
Basic Rules of Common Courtesy. Passengers are encouraged not to
ask the taxicab driver to violate traffic laws (for example, asking the

driver to make a U-turn or exceed the speed limit) and to inform the driver of all stops and destinations at the start of the trip. The TLC asks that all fares be paid before the passenger exits the taxicab. It is illegal for a passenger to remove any stickers or take the passenger information maps from the interior of the cab.

◢ **The rules of the road.** Taxi drivers get a bad rap in part because, from the viewpoint of the passenger, the whole taxi riding experience can be a rather arbitrary one. Some drivers ask you your route preferences, help you with your packages, know their way around town and are polite, while others seem to go out of their way to make your trip as unpleasant as possible. The problem is that no one really seems to know what the rules of the road are, and when the rules are known, they are inconsistently applied. As a result, passengers and drivers alike are not really clear as to what services are required to be provided, a situation that is further complicated by cultural diversity among drivers and passengers and the occasional less-than-perfect manners of some individuals.

According to the TLC, taxi drivers are supposed to follow certain basic operating parameters. Knowledge of these guidelines affords you the opportunity to tip generously when service is above average, not to tip when you are dissatisfied, and to file a complaint against the driver if you are treated inappropriately. And if you want your children to say please and thank you, remember to show them your good manners too.

➲ How many kids can fit in a cab? TLC regulations state that a driver is not allowed to have more than four passengers in a four passenger cab, except that an additional passenger must be accepted if such passenger is under the age of 7 and is held on the lap of an adult. However, according to the TLC, a cab driver is required to take only up to three adults unless the driver determines it is safe to, and he chooses to, allow a passenger to sit in the front seat. There is no formula to calculate how many children fit in a cab. For instance, two children do not necessarily equal one adult. So, if you are traveling by cab and your group includes two adults and two kids you are probably fine. If your gang is more than four, well, hope for an agreeable driver and tip accordingly.

○ Does the safety-belt law apply to taxis? The law requires that there be three back seat belts in working order and available for passengers to use, but strangely, the law does not require that you use them (although the TLC recommends that all passengers be strapped in by a safety belt). Even though you are not in violation of the law if you are not wearing your seat belt, if you are injured in an accident, your not having worn a seat belt may affect your insurance claim or a claim against the driver. Ask your pediatrician for a recommendation on how to transport your small child.

○ How much is too much to ask of a cab driver? As annoying and counterintuitive as it may seem, a taxi driver is not required to assist a passenger or to allow the front seat to be used for cargo such as a stroller, even though the regulations provide that upon request, the driver must help load or unload the passenger's luggage in or from the trunk. So, do not be outraged if a driver merely pops the car trunk open for you but does not help you fold your stroller and get you settled in the back seat. When you are in a situation where you are provided with only the most basic service and when clearly you could have benefited from some assistance, you may want to consider returning the favor and pay the driver only the basic fare and no tip.

◢ **To file a complaint.** Do not hesitate to file a complaint against the driver with the TLC if: the driver was not driving safely, the driver did not know basic thoroughfares, the driver could not communicate in English, the physical condition of the taxi was poor or the driver was discourteous.

To file a complaint, you can either call the TLC Consumer Hotline at NYC-TAXI (692-8294); write to the TLC at 40 Rector Street, Fifth Floor, New York, NY 10006; or file your complaint on-line at www.nyc.gov/html/tlc. You will need this necessary information to file a complaint: the medallion number; the driver's name and license number; the date, time and pickup and destination points of the ride; and your mailing address and daytime phone. All complaints are confidential. Always remember to ask for a meter receipt when in a taxi because it contains the medallion number of the vehicle and the time of the ride.

▶ **Mass Transit.** With one of the largest public transportation systems in the nation, the Metropolitan Transportation Authority (MTA) operates New York City's subways, public buses and railroads and the local bridges and tunnels, moving 2.3 billion commuters via subway, bus or rail and more than 300 million vehicles per year.

The bus and subway systems are so vast that if you are not already familiar with them, the thought of getting acquainted while you are trying to travel with your children may seem overwhelming. Fear not, mass transit does not take much savvy to master and there are advantages to using it. To begin with, taking the bus or subway can create an instant activity for your children, because for most, especially young kids, it is an adventure. If you travel by subway, you do not have to deal with traffic or gridlock and can reach your destination quickly.

Using mass transit can save you a bundle because children under 44-inches tall travel free. There is no official limit to the number of children who can travel for free with a single adult. Note that when boarding a bus, you can use the bar that separates the bus driver's area from the passenger side as a rough height guide since it is approximately 44 inches from the floor of the bus.

There are a few things to keep in mind when using mass transit, to better ensure that you make it to your destination safely. Strollers must be folded to board a bus or subway. On a bus, make sure the child is seated correctly in the seat. If you must stand, hold your child's hand in case of sudden stops and starts. The Department of Buses offers "The Insiders Guide," a free brochure that answers many of the questions you may have about the bus system. To obtain a copy of "The Insiders Guide" call the Bus Customer Relations Center, Monday through Friday between 7 a.m. and 5 p.m. at 718 927-7499.

Using mass transit can save you a bundle because children under 44-inches tall travel free.

When traveling by subway, ride the escalators to and from the subway platform with care. Strollers should be folded and children should hold a grownup's hand, not the handrail. Stand away from the sides because clothing can get caught as can shoes, shoelaces, sneakers, boots or sandals if you fail to step off. Never allow a child to run or sit on the steps or handrail of the escalator. The safest way to travel with your baby on the subway is to hold your child and fold the stroller before you enter the subway. If you do not fold the stroller while riding the subway, make sure to do the following: strap your child into the stroller, never place the stroller between closing subway doors, be aware of the gap between the platform edge and the train, engage the stroller brake while the train is in motion, keep the stroller away from the platform edge, and board the subway at the center of the train, in plain sight of the conductor.

Current fare for bus and subway is $1.50, payable in coins or tokens (available for purchase at subway stations) or by MetroCard. You can buy a MetroCard from any subway station, the St. George Ferry Terminal in Staten Island or at over 3,200 neighborhood newsstands, delis, groceries, banks, pharmacies, check cashiers and other stores. You can also buy a MetroCard on-line at www.mta.nyc.ny.us/metrocard/subcool/index.html. When you use the MetroCard, the fare will be automatically deducted and your remaining balance indicated. If you do not have enough money on your MetroCard to cover the fare, you cannot pay the additional amount needed with change or tokens. You can add money to your card at subway stations and at the St. George Ferry Terminal. As with tokens, the MetroCard cannot be replaced if lost or stolen. A MetroCard can be used until the expiration on the back of the card, after which you can transfer any remaining money to a new card at any subway station or the St. George Ferry Terminal.

You can buy MetroCards in denominations from $3 to $80 or unlimited ride MetroCards (1-, 7- or 30-day cards). For more information about MetroCard, visit www.mta.nyc.ny.us/metrocard or call customer service at METROCARD (638-7622) within New York City or 800 METROCARD (800 638-7622) outside New York City between 9 a.m. and 11 p.m. Monday through Friday or between 9 a.m. and 5 p.m. on weekends and holidays. Reduced-fare benefits are available for senior citizens and customers with eligible disabilities, who can also obtain an application for a personalized photo-identification MetroCard by calling 718 243-4999 between 9 a.m. and 5 p.m. Monday through Friday.

For route and schedule information, you can get maps of the transit system from token booths, bus drivers and at approximately

4,000 other locations around the city, including libraries and museums, or by calling 718 330-1234.

If you are traveling by subway, it is important to be street smart. As a general rule, it is best to travel the subways during the day and avoid deserted stations or traveling in the evenings. While waiting for a train, stand where there are other people and do not stand close to the platform edge. Do not let children wander away from you and always have them within your view. It is best not to open purses or bags in the subway station and always hold your purse or other bags close to your body. Expensive or flashy jewelry is best left at home when you know you will be riding the subways. If you see an unsavory character or feel ill at ease or threatened in any way, seek help or leave the station.

► **Car Services.** While it may seem frivolous to transport your family by hired car, it can be a great convenience. Although car services can be expensive—they are not subject to the yellow-taxi rate schedule and each company sets its own rates—there are many reasons why parents have come to rely on them. You can make reservations for a car to drop off and pick up you and your children at prearranged times, which can be enormously helpful when you need to get to and from hard-to-reach places during busy traffic times. Also car-service drivers typically help you with your stroller and help load and unload your packages.

As a general rule, it is best to travel the subways during the day and avoid deserted stations or traveling in the evenings.

Car services and other for-hire vehicles differ from yellow medallion taxis, because they are not supposed to pick up passengers hailing from the street. The law requires that car-service companies, vehicles and drivers be licensed by the TLC. All licensed car services should have cars displaying a diamond-shaped decal in the windshield. If you do not see the decal, do not get in.

The cars bearing "Livery" plates are registered outside of the five boroughs and can drop passengers off in Manhattan but are not supposed to pick up fares within New York City. There are other cars for hire bearing "TLC" license plates (such as limousines), which are also not supposed to pick up passengers in the street and are subject to regulations of their own. It is often hard to determine if a for-hire car is legitimate or not. Certainly there are plenty of "gypsy" (unlicensed by the TLC) cabs driving the streets, but for your own safety, TLC officials recommend that you take only yellow taxis and prearranged licensed cars.

Names of car services can be found in the telephone book. When you call a car-service company, make sure to confirm that the service is licensed. Unfortunately, there is no governmental office to contact to get a list of licensed car services. Discuss rates, reservations procedures, payment procedures, identification procedures (are you given a car number in advance?) and waiting-time policies. If you are staying at a hotel, you can always inquire with the concierge regarding services they recommend. In addition we have listed some of the services you might try contacting, although we do not recommend individual companies.

All complaints against drivers and services can be filed with the TLC in the same manner as complaints are filed against yellow-cab drivers.

► **A word about bicycles.** Although it is unlikely—and not recommended—that you explore the city on a bicycle, it is possible that the spirit may move you to check out the city on two wheels. If you must, your best bet is to confine your riding to the large parks, such as Central Park, and always to stay on the populated roads. It is not a good idea to explore deserted paths.

If you ride in the street, familiarize yourself with the bicycle traffic laws: ride in the direction of traffic (not against traffic), obey all traffic laws, come to a complete stop at stop signs and red lights, use a bike path or lane if one is available and use hand signals to indicate turns. Bicyclists must ride on the street, not on the sidewalk. The exception is riders under 13 riding a bicycle with wheels smaller than 26", who may ride on the sidewalk. Children must be carried in a properly affixed child carrier, and a child under the age of one is not permitted to be carried on a bicycle. Cyclists under the age of 14 must wear a safety helmet.

RESOURCES

Airports & Airport Transportation

For a complete listing of transportation services, call 800 AIR-RIDE (800 247-7433), a recorded information service provided by the Port Authority of New York and New Jersey concerning all area airports, or visit www.panynj.gov.

John F. Kennedy International Airport

www.panynj.gov/aviation/jfkframe.HTM
General information 718 244-4444
Ground transportation 800 AIR-RIDE (800 247-7433)
Medical services 718 656-5344
Police/Emergency 718 244-4333
Police/Lost & Found 718 244-4335
Travelers aid 718 656-4870

Bus Service

New York Airport Service Express Bus 718 875-8200. Service to and from Grand Central Terminal (hotel transfers available, $2 surcharge), Port Authority Bus Terminal or Penn Station. One-way fare is $13.

Trans-Bridge 800 962-9135. Service to and from Port Authority Bus Terminal. One-way fare is $10.

Mass Transit

From the airport:

MTA Q3 to 169th Street and Hillside Avenue where you can transfer to F and R trains to Manhattan. One-way fare is $1.50.

Q10 Green Bus Lines leaves JFK every 15 minutes for Lefferts Boulevard and Kew Gardens where you can transfer to A, E, J, Z, F and R trains to Manhattan. One-way fare is $1.50.

To the airport:

Take the A train from Manhattan to the Howard Beach Station, where you transfer to a free shuttle bus to the airport. Call 800 247-7433 for departure times for the bus from the station to the airport and the airport to the station.

Taxi Service

Taxi dispatchers at all baggage-claim locations all day and night. From the airport to Manhattan costs a flat rate of $35 plus tolls and tip. From the city, the cost is what the meter says plus tolls and tip. Expect to pay $30–$45 plus tolls and tip.

Van Service (shared mini-bus)

SuperShuttle 800 BLUE-VAN (888 258-3826) One-way fare is $17.

LaGuardia Airport

www.panynj.gov/aviation/lgaframe.HTM
General information 718 533-3400
Ground Transportation 800 AIR-RIDE (800 247-7433)
Medical services 718 476-5575
Lost and found 718 533-3988
Police/Emergency 718 533-3900

Bus Service

New York Airport Service Express Bus 718 875-8200. Service to and from Grand Central Terminal (hotel transfers available), Port Authority Bus Terminal or Penn Station. One-way fare $8–$12.

Mass Transit

MTA M60 bus service between LaGuardia and Morningside Heights and Harlem with connections to the 2, 3, 4, 5, 6, 1, 9, A, C and D trains in Manhattan. One-way fare is $1.50.

Triborough Coach Q33 (from all terminals except Marine Air Terminal), Triborough Coach Q47 (from Marine Air Terminal) 718 335-1000. Services between LaGuardia and Jackson Heights 74th Street subway station with connections to the E, F, R, V and 7 trains to Manhattan. One-way fare is $1.50.

Taxi Service

Taxi dispatchers at all baggage claim locations all day and night. Expect to pay $20–$30 plus tolls and tip.

Van Service (shared mini-bus)

SuperShuttle 800 BLUE-VAN (888 258-3826). One-way fare is $15.

Newark International Airport

www.panynj.gov/aviation/ewrframe.HTM
General Information 973 961-6000
Parking, weather and traffic information 888 EWR-INFO (888 397-4636)
Police/Lost & Found 973 961-6230
Ground Transportation 800 AIR-RIDE (800 247-7433)

Bus Service

Olympia Airport Express 964-6233, 908 354-3330. Service to and from Port Authority Bus Terminal, Grand Central Terminal (connecting service to hotels, $5 surcharge) and Penn Station. One-way fare is $11.

Mass Transit

AirTrain regional transport network operates the Rail Link Station at Newark Airport, which links with NJ Transit, Amtrak and PATH service to Manhattan. The Rail Link Station is linked to airline terminals via the airport Monorail. 888 397-4636 or 800 AIR-RIDE (800 247-7433). www.panynj.gov

Taxi Service

Taxi dispatchers at all baggage-claim locations all day and night. Expect to pay $35–$55 plus tolls and tip. From Manhattan, fare is what is on the meter plus $10 plus tolls and tip.

Van Service

SuperShuttle 800 BLUE-VAN 888 258-3826. One-way fare is $19.

Teterboro Airport (private or charter airplanes)

www.teb.com
Teterboro, New Jersey
201 288-1775

General Airport Transportation Information

Car Rental

Avis 800 331-1212

Budget 800 527-0700

Dollar 800 800-4000

Hertz 800 654-3131

National 800 227-7368

Car Services

Airport Towncar Express
800 945-5316

Carmel 800 924-9954

Dial Car 800 342-5106 or
718 743-8383

Tri-state Limo 777-7171

Helicopters (private charters, cost ranges from $550 to $800 one way)

Liberty Helicopters, Inc. 888 692-4354

Schiavone Helicopter 201 440-5555

Wall Street Helicopters, Inc. 943-5959

Heliports

East 34th Street and the East River 889-2551

JFK Airport 718 244-3501

LaGuardia Airport 718 533-3701

Pier 6 at Wall Street 248-7240

West 30th Street and the Hudson River 563-4442

Limousines (cost ranges from $60 to $110 one way)

Classic Limousine 631 567-5100, 800 666-4949 (outside NY) or www.classictrans.com

Fugazy 661-0100

Limousine.com 800 472-1211, www.limousine.com

Luxury Limo 800 LIMO-NEED (546-6633) or 718 832-2100

Bus Service

Port Authority Bus Terminal, Eighth Avenue at 40th–42nd Streets, 564-8484, www.ny.com/transportation/port_authority.html

George Washington Bridge Station, 178th Street between Fort Washington and Wadsworth Avenue, 800 221-9903

Connecticut

Connecticut Transit (New Haven) 203 624-0151, www.cttransit.com

Connecticut Transit (Stamford) 203 327-7433, www.cttransit.com

Greenwich Shuttle 800 982-8420, www.norwalktransit.com

Inter-Borough Bus Service

General information 212 or 718 CALL-DOT (225-5368)

Command Bus Company 718 277-8100, www.commandbus.com, service to Brooklyn

Liberty Lines Express 718 652-8400, www.libertylines.com, service to the Bronx

New York Bus Service 718 994-5500, www.nybus.com, service to the Bronx

Green Bus Lines 718 995-4700, www.greenbus.com, service to Queens

Jamaica Buses 718 526-0800, www.jamaicabus.com, service to Queens

Queens Surface 718 445-3100, www.qsbus.com, service to Queens

Triboro Coach 718 335-1000, www.triborocoach.com, service to Queens

Long Island

Long Island Bus 516 542-0100, www.mta.nyc.ny.us/libus

National and Regional Buslines

Adirondack Trailways 800 858-8555, www.greyhound.com

Bonanza Bus Lines 800 556-3815, www.bonanzabus.com

Greyhound Lines 800 231-2222, www.greyhound.com

Olympia Trails 212 964-6233, www.olympiabus.com

Peter Pan Trailways 800 343-9999, www.peterpanbus.com

Shortline 800 631-8405, www.shortlinebus.com

New Jersey

New Jersey Transit Information Center 800 772-2222 (within New Jersey) 973 762-5100 (outside New Jersey), www.njtransit.com

New York

Dutchess County 845 485-4690, www.dutchessny.gov

Putnam County 845 878-RIDE (914 878-7433), www.putnamcountyny.com

Rockland County 845 364-3333, www.co.rockland.ny.us

Westchester County 914 813-7777, www.beelinebus.com

Driving Resources

American Automobile Association
Emergency Road Service 800 AAA-HELP (800 222-4357)
www.aaa.com
www.aaany.com (Automobile Club of New York, Inc.)
Executive offices 516 746-7730
Bronx, Brooklyn, Queens 718 224-2222
Long Island 516 746-7141
Manhattan 757-2000
Rockland County and Westchester 914 948-4600

Auto Baby Sitters of NY 718 493-9800

Directions

www.aaa.com

www.mapquest.com

www.survivethedrive.com

E-Z Pass, 800 333-TOLL (8655), www.e-zpassny.com

New York City Department of Transportation
www.nyc.gov/html/dot/home.html
24-hour hotline 212/718 225-5368
24-hour Towed Vehicle Information and Borough Tow Pound
971-0770/1/2/3 (Manhattan tows only). You will need $150 in cash
to retrieve your car.
Parking Violations Helpline 718 422-7800 (800 813-9183 out of state)
or www.nyc.gov/finance to find a towed car

Parking Pal (motorists' rights organization), 800 PARK-PAL (727-5725)

Ferries

Department of Transportation General Information 212/718 CALLDOT (225-5368)

Staten Island Ferry, Information 718 815-BOAT (718 815-2628)

Liberty Landing Marina, 201 985-8000, www.libertylandingmarina.com, Service to Liberty State Park, NJ

New York Fast Ferry, 732 291-2210 or 800 693-6933, www.nyff.com, Service to New Jersey and Shea Stadium

NY Waterway (formerly Port Imperial Ferry), 800 53 FERRY (800 533-3779), www.nywaterway.com, Service to New Jersey, Brooklyn, Queens and Yankee and Shea Stadiums

Seastreak (formerly Express Navigation), 800 BOAT RIDE (800 262-8743), www.seastreak.com, Service to New Jersey and Yankee and Shea Stadiums

Mass Transit

MTA New York City Transit
  www.mta.nyc.ny.us
  Travel Information Center 718 330-1234
  Travel Information for non–English-speaking people 718 330-4847
  Department of Buses "Insiders Guide" 718 927-7499
  Travel Information for people with disabilities 718 596-8585
  Hearing Impaired 718 596-8273
  Lost Property 712-4500
  Elevator/Escalator Hotline 800 734-6772

MetroCard
  www.mta.nyc.ny.us/metrocard
  638-7622 (within New York City)
  800 METROCARD (800 638-7622) (outside New York City).
  M–F, 9 a.m.–11 p.m. Weekends and Holidays, 9 a.m.–5 p.m.
  Reduced fare information 718 243-4999

Port Authority of New York & New Jersey, www.panynj.gov, 435-7000

Subway Directions, www.straphangers.com

Parking Facilities

Municipal parking facilities

Municipal parking facilities are generally open 24 hours a day, seven days a week. Metered parking only. Meters take either quarters (20–30 minutes per 25 cents) or NYC Parking Cards.

www.nyc.gov/html/dot/html/get_around/park/prkintro.html

NYC Parking Card (pre-paid parking meter cards available in values of $10, $20 and $50) can be used at most municipal parking lots and can be purchased by calling 718 786-7042 or downloading an application from www.nyc.gov/html/dot/html/get_around/park/municard.html

Broome and Ludlow Municipal Parking Field, Broome Street, between Ludlow and Essex Streets (4-hour limit)

Delancey and Essex Municipal Parking Garage, 107 Essex Street, just North of Delancey Street

Leonard Street Municipal Parking Field, Leonard Street, between Lafayette and Centre Streets (2-hour limit)

NYC Parking Cards can also be used at special on-street meters on Second Avenue from 30th to 33rd Streets and on 43rd to 59th Streets between Fifth and Broadway, 72nd Street, 8th Street, Battery Park and Orchard Street during specified hours.

Private parking facilities

Visit www.nyc.gov/html/dca/html/parkguide.html for a copy of *The Parking Guide.*

Visit www.nyc.gov/html/dcp/html/dcptd/index.html for information on licensed parking facilities.

Passenger Ship Information

Passenger Ship Terminal, 48th–55th Streets at the Hudson River in Manhattan, 246-5450/1

Taxi Service

Taxi and Limousine Commission,
    40 Rector Street, 5th Floor, New York, NY 10006, 676-1000
    24-Hour Consumer Hotline NYC-TAXI (692-8294)
    www.nyc.gov/html/tlc/
    Complaint Line www.nyc.gov/html/tlc/html/tlccompl.html

Dispatcher-Operated Taxi Stands

Citicorp Center, Lexington Avenue between East 53rd and East 54th Streets

Grand Central Terminal, Vanderbilt Avenue and East 42nd Street

Penn Station,
    Seventh Avenue and West 32nd Street
    Eighth Avenue and West 33rd Street

Peter Minuit Plaza at Staten Island Ferry Terminal

Port Authority Bus Terminal
    Eighth Avenue between West 40th and West 41st Streets
    Eighth Avenue between West 41st and West 42nd Streets

Other Taxi Stands

Taxi stands are located at major transit hubs, hotels, office and retail centers and hospitals in Manhattan. At these stands, drivers are permitted to wait to pick up passengers. Taxi-stand signs are affixed to guide rails and lampposts on the sidewalk.

Train Service

Grand Central Terminal, Park Avenue at 42nd Street, www.grandcentralterminal.com

Pennsylvania Station, Seventh and Eighth Avenues at 32nd Street, www.amtrak.com/stations/nyp.html

Amtrak Information, www.amtrak.com, 800 USA-RAIL (800 872-7245)

Metro-North Information
www.mnr.org
532-4900 (inside New York City)
800 METRO-INFO (800 638-7646) (outside New York City)
Police 878-1001
Lost and Found 340-2555

Long Island Rail Road
www.mta.nyc.ny.us
718 217-LIRR (718 217-5477) (inside New York City)
516 822-LIRR (516 822-5477) (in Nassau County)
631 231-LIRR (631 231-5477) (in Suffolk County)
Special packages and promotions 718 558-7498
Lost and Found 643-5228 M–F 7:20 a.m. to 7:20 p.m.
Police 718 558-3300/3301

NJ Transit
Official website www.njtransit.com
Unofficial website www.nj.com/njtransit
800 772-2222 (inside New Jersey)
973 762-5100 (outside New Jersey)

PATH, www.panynj.gov/path, 800 234-PATH (800 234-7284)

Websites

www.allny.com

www.cityguideny.com

www.citysearch.com

www.digitalcity.com

www.go-newyorkcity.com

www.nyc.com

www.nyc.gov
(official website of New York City)

www.nyctourism.com

www.nycvisit.com

www.nytoday.com

Chapter 4

EAST SIDE, WEST SIDE, ALL AROUND THE TOWN

N ew York City is a great patchwork of colorful, idiosyncratic and diverse neighborhoods. From Chinatown to the Upper East Side to Hunts Point to Fort Greene to Historic Richmondtown, your family can explore the historical roots and cultural variety of a city created by waves of immigrants from all corners of the world.

When planning an itinerary, many visitors focus only on Manhattan. However, the other four boroughs have myriad attractions of historic, artistic and cultural significance well worth investigating. We urge you cross a bridge or two and experience a taste of the entire Apple.

As you follow our virtual tour of this magnificent city, remember that these are just some of the highlights intended to give you a general overview of the more well-known neighborhoods and more popular destinations. In your own travels you are bound to come upon many other locations of historical and cultural importance that are fun to explore, and you may even experience a giggle or two. We encourage you to follow your interests and get lost in the wonders of the city.

Lower Manhattan—Below 23rd Street

Lower Manhattan is a great place to start your tour of Manhattan neighborhoods. It all began here in the early 1600s, when the Dutch established a trading post at the southern tip of the island where the harbor was well suited for sailboats. Since that time, lower Manhattan has been a fort, a center of commerce, a seat of government and a point of entry for millions of immigrants. The narrow winding streets of the financial district (many of which are named after Dutch traders) serve as a reminder of colonial America. The skyscrapers that house many of the world's largest financial institutions reflect the growth of the last century. This area was home to the tallest buildings in New York, the twin towers of the World Trade Center, until September 11, 2001, when a terrorist attack destroyed them and forever changed the lower Manhattan skyline.

► **Battery Park.** Located at the southwestern tip of Manhattan, **Battery Park** is named for the gun batteries built by the British in 1683 to guard the entrance to the Hudson and East Rivers. In nice weather, Battery Park is full of tourists, vendors selling souvenirs and people eating lunch. It offers great views of the Statue of Liberty and Ellis Island, and it is from here that ferries leave for both. The **Staten Island Ferry** (718 727-2508), which leaves from the South Ferry every 20–30 minutes, is free, takes about 30 minutes in each direction, provides fantastic views of Manhattan and is a fun trip for kids.

Battery Park has a number of other important sites, including Castle Clinton, Bowling Green, the U.S. Custom House and Peter Minuit Plaza. **Castle Clinton** (344-7220) is Manhattan's only existing fort. It was built in the late 18th century as a defense post with 28 guns (never fired!) in 8-foot thick walls facing Castle William on Governor's Island, which was held by the British. It was named for DeWitt Clinton, the New York mayor who was responsible for rein-

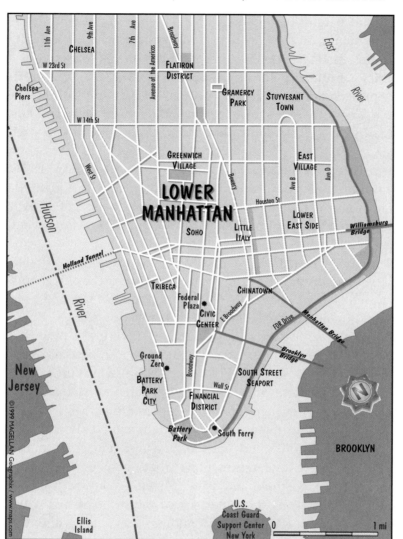

forcing harbor defenses. In 1733, **Bowling Green**, New York City's oldest park, was rented from the city by three rich locals for lawn bowling, at a rate of 1 peppercorn a year. A statue of George III stood there until revolutionary patriots pulled it down in 1776. The park has benches, a fountain and that famous bronze statue of a bull that is featured in many photographs and advertisements.

Just south of Bowling Green is the **U.S. Custom House** (State

Street and Battery Place, 466-2906), a Beaux Arts treasure built in 1907. It stands on the site of Fort Amsterdam, which was built by the Dutch in 1625. One wing houses the **National Museum of the American Indian** (1 Bowling Green, 514-3700), which, as part of the Smithsonian Institution, contains a first-rate collection of Native American art and artifacts, including bison hides and lots of moccasins, as well as rooms from a home on a contemporary reservation.

In a corner of Battery Park, near the ferry building, is **Peter Minuit Plaza**, which is named for the Dutchman who bought Manhattan from the Indians in 1626. The plaza is the site of a flagpole honoring the first Jewish immigrants to New York, who arrived in 1654.

New York Unearthed (17 State Street at Battery Park, 748-8628) preserves and displays objects that were dug up as the city grew. You can watch archeologists at work in their glassed-in lab, and a video display simulates the experience of an excavation site.

To the east of Battery Park is **Fraunces Tavern** (54 Pearl Street, 425-1778), located on a site dating back to 1719. In 1763, Samuel Fraunces, a former steward of George Washington, purchased the building and turned it into a tavern. Washington gave a post-victory farewell dinner here for his officers in December 1783. Only one brick wall from the original building remains. The tavern was reconstructed in 1907 and opened as a restaurant and museum shortly thereafter. The entire block that includes the tavern— bounded by Pearl, Broad and Water Streets—along with Coenties Slip (once a wharf) has been designated a historic district where a number of early 19th-century buildings in Federal and Greek Revival styles still stand.

The plaza next to **Coenties Slip** (55 Water Street) now holds the New York Vietnam Veterans Memorial, a simple glass block commemorating those who died in the war.

▶ **Wall Street.** Just to the northeast of Battery Park is **Wall Street**, the financial capital of the nation. Wall Street actually follows the line of the palisade wall built in 1653 by the Dutch across the northern perimeter of New Amsterdam to protect against attack by

British New Englanders. By 1699 the wall was gone, but the name survived. Although the neighborhood is known for its tall sky-scrapers and fast-moving professionals, it also has sites of historical importance.

At the head of Wall Street is **Trinity Church** (at Broadway, 602-0872). An example of a fine Gothic Revival Church, it dates from the mid-1800s. The first church was built on the site in 1698, burned down in 1776 and was rebuilt in 1787. The building was razed in 1839, and the current edifice was erected. Many prominent New Yorkers, including Alexander Hamilton, are buried in the graveyard. Miraculously, Trinity Church survived the attack on the World Trade Center.

At 26 Wall Street, George Washington was sworn in as our first pres-ident, and a statue of him stands in front of what is now the **Federal Hall National Monument** (825-6888). This Greek Revival–style build-ing dates to the mid-1800s and housed the U.S. Customs Service for a number of years until it became a national monument in 1955. It fea-tures exhibits relating to the first inauguration.

The **New York Stock Exchange** (20 Broad Street, 656-5168) may be the biggest exchange in the world, but it had a small beginning. In 1792, traders met under a buttonwood tree at the corner of Wall and William Streets to buy and sell stocks and bonds among them-selves. In 1903 the Exchange moved into its current building, where you can see thousands of traders waving their arms and shouting out orders—it's really loud! Check out the visitors' gallery to view the action.

The **Federal Reserve Bank** (33 Liberty Street, 720-6130), known as "The Fed," is where other banks get fresh bills in exchange for old, worn-out ones. The Fed has 10,000 tons of gold in under-ground vaults (worth about $100 billion!). Free tours are offered, but you need to reserve in advance.

Finally, **St. Paul's Church** (Broadway at Fulton Street, 269-0014) is a small pre-revolutionary church that has been in continuous use since it opened, having survived the fire of 1776 and other disas-ters. George Washington worshipped here on the day of his inau-guration; his box is roped off.

▶ **South Street Seaport.** To the east is **South Street Seaport** (207 Front Street, 748-8600), a restoration of New York's early 19th-century waterfront. In the 1800s, the streets bustled with ships' captains, sailors and all trades that supported commerce by tall ship. By the end of the 1800s, steamships took over, shipping moved to the deeper Hudson River waterfront and the seaport began to decay. In the 1980s, the area was restored and is now a historic district comprising some 11 blocks filled with museums, a children's center, famous old ships, a marketplace and a working fish market as well as **Schermerhorn Row** (on Fulton between South and Front Streets), a series of 19th-century Federal-style brick buildings that have been converted to boutiques and restaurants.

Among the ships anchored at the Seaport are the ***Peking***, built in 1911 and the second largest sailing ship of its kind in the world (its tallest mast is 17 stories high) and the ***Pioneer***, a 19th-century cargo schooner that makes twilight sails around Manhattan. Don't miss the lighthouse at the pier entrance. It is a memorial to those who drowned on another famous boat, the ***Titanic***, and everyday at noon, a black ball slides down the pole at its top.

Fulton Fish Market is named for Robert Fulton, the developer of the steamboat. Fulton ran a ferry from Manhattan to Brooklyn beginning in 1814, and its landing stood here. This working wholesale fish market has operated since 1834. The real action takes place early—about 4 to 5 a.m.—but you can still get the sense of its workings (smells included) later on in the day.

▶ **Civic Center.** North and west of the Seaport are the courthouses and the local seats of municipal, state and federal governments. When **City Hall** (City Hall Park, 788-3071) was completed in 1811, it stood at the northern end of the city. The building faces south and has marble only on the south side of the building—its architects thought no one would ever see the north side! A statue of Nathan Hale, the patriot, adorns City Hall Park, a reminder that American protests against the British took place here (that is, when it wasn't being used as a cow pasture).

At the top of City Hall Park is a building that many people often mistake for City Hall: the **Tweed Courthouse** (officially known as the Old New York County Courthouse). It is named for William "Boss"

Tweed, the corrupt politician of the late 1800s. Despite its bad name, it has an attractive Italianate design and beautiful interiors.

In the early 1990s, workers excavating at Broadway and Duane Street came upon human remains. What they found turned out to be a 5-acre graveyard containing the remains of about 20,000 African Americans who were buried in the 1700s. The site is now known as the **African Burial Ground** (Duane and Elk Streets). This discovery made the public aware of the large number of African slaves and freed men and women who were living here at that time.

Walking to the north and east you will pass the **Municipal Building** (Centre and Chambers Streets), where you can see people lined up outside to get their marriage licenses and the occasional bride in a white gown going to (or coming from) her wedding. Just north are several courthouses: the **U.S. Courthouse** (40 Centre Street), the **New York County Courthouse** (60 Centre Street) and the **Criminal Courts Building** (100 Centre Street).

▶ **Battery Park City.** Just north of Battery Park is **Battery Park City**, a 92-acre complex built on a landfill, which is home to **The World Financial Center** and a number of high-rise apartment buildings. The Center's Winter Garden Greenhouse, which had palm trees, shops and restaurants, suffered a great deal of damage in the September 11, 2001 attacks, most of which has been restored. Battery Park City also has parks, a fabulous playground, museums and a marina. On weekends, the area is crowded with cyclists, in-line skaters and dog walkers. When in town, the Cirque du Soleil is set up here.

The **Museum of Jewish Heritage** (18 First Place, 509-6130) is a re-creation of Jewish culture over the last century—before, during and after the Holocaust. The first floor explores the richness of Jewish family life in the late 19th to early 20th century, and the second floor focuses on the Holocaust.

▶ **Tribeca.** **Tribeca** stands for the Triangle Below Canal. It was given that acronym in the 1970s, when artists moved from SoHo to this industrial neighborhood with a long history. In 1705, Queen Anne granted this land (part of Queen's Farm) to Trinity Church, which developed much of the area in one of the first grid street patterns in Manhattan. The church built row houses for the middle class, making the neighborhood one of the city's first exclusively residential areas. The **Harrison Street Houses** (25-41 Harrison Street) are the remaining Federal style buildings. In the 1800s, merchants built big warehouses and manufacturing plants, and the area became a hub for the dairy, coffee, tea and spice trades that supplied the city's markets.

As residents and businesses left the area, the big spaces became vacant. Beginning in the 1960s and 1970s, artists moved their studios to the large, inexpensive and open spaces. In the 1980s, trendy restaurants, stores, nightclubs and galleries began to arrive, as did young financial professionals, because of Tribeca's proximity to Wall Street. It also developed a certain celebrity population as a result of Robert DeNiro's involvement in a local restaurant and in the Tribeca Film Center, which houses film production companies.

▶ **SoHo.** SoHo, an acronym for South of Houston Street (pronounced "house-ton"), is a trendy neighborhood famous for its cast-iron buildings, art galleries, restaurants and shops. It comprises the area between Houston and Canal Streets, Sixth Avenue and Lafayette Street. Originally farmland, it was dotted with the country estates of prosperous residents. In the 19th century, townhouses and large, cast-iron warehouse-sized spaces were built, and the area became the city's light industrial and retail center. The warehouses were taken over by artists in the 1960s and 1970s, who were themselves driven out in the 1980s and 1990s by high rents. Their studios were replaced by luxury loft apartments, galleries, shops and restaurants.

Among the sites worth visiting are the **Children's Museum of the Arts** (182 Lafayette Street between Broome and Grand Streets, 274-0986), a hands-on museum where children can create art, dress up or play on the hi-tech computers and in the low-tech "ball pond"; the **New York City Fire Museum** (278 Spring Street between Varick and Hudson Streets, 692-1303), a small converted firehouse and a young child's dream museum filled with antique fire engines (including horse-drawn ones), a stuffed firedog, bells, alarms, pick-axes and all sorts of firefighting mementos; the **Museum for African**

Art (593 Broadway, 966-1313) and the **Cast Iron Historic District** (from West Broadway to Canal Street to Broadway).

▶ **NoHo.** Wedged in between SoHo, the East Village and Greenwich Village lies **NoHo** (North of Houston). It is a small neighborhood that now has trendy bars, shops and restaurants and also its own quirky history. Some of the city's most illustrious families, including the Astors and the Vanderbilts, lived here in the 1830s, building Greek Revival townhouses on "Colonnade Row" on Lafayette Street between Astor Place and Great Jones Street. Only four of the nine mansions remain: one houses the Astor Place Theater (home to "Blue Man Group," a great show for kids) and another, which belonged to John Jacob Astor, houses the Joseph Papp Public Theater. The city designated NoHo a historic district in 1999.

▶ **The Lower East Side: Chinatown, Little Italy and NoLita.** To many, the **Lower East Side** symbolizes the influx of immigrants to New York City in the 1800s and early 1900s. Before the American Revolution, the area was farmland owned by wealthy landholders. (Orchard Street ran through fruit trees.) After the war, middle-class New Yorkers built row houses there. Over time, these prosperous citizens moved north to more spacious and genteel neighborhoods and immigrants took over, crowding into what had become tenements. Poverty and poor health conditions abounded, captured by Jacob Riis in his well-known photographs. For a feeling of what tenement life was like, head to the **Lower East Side Tenement Museum** (90 Orchard Street, 431-0233). In the early 20th century, the city modernized the area, and conditions improved. Today the Lower East Side is home to hip young residents, galleries, restaurants, bars and edgy new stores that exist alongside the established discount shops.

The Lower East Side has always had a large Jewish population, and Jewish businesses still operate there next to newer Asian stores. Many of the Jewish-owned businesses are closed on Friday afternoon and Saturday in observation of the Sabbath. Of note are Guss Pickles and Streit's Matzoh Factory. The **Eldridge Street Synagogue**

(12-16 Eldridge Street, 978-8800), completed in 1887, is a Moorish Revival building that is currently being restored to its original beauty, including lavish stained-glass windows, carved detailing and chandeliers. It was the first large-scale Orthodox synagogue in New York City, and it is a window into Jewish life at the turn of the last century.

Chinatown was not always Asian—check out the street signs reading Mott, Pell, Bayard, and others. It was not until the early 19th century that a small number of Chinese sailors and merchants settled in this neighborhood. After the transcontinental railroad was completed in 1869, thousands of Chinese laborers ended up in Chinatown. By the 1980s, Chinatown had more Chinese residents than San Francisco. Today the area is full of restaurants, stalls and shops selling cheap items and knock-off designer merchandise. Street signs, phone booths and shop signs are in English and Chinese, and pagoda-style roofs are everywhere (even on phone booths). The only remaining wood pagoda roof in Chinatown is at 41 Mott Street. Visit the **Museum of Chinese in the Americas** (70 Mulberry Street at Bayard Street, 619-4785) to see a fascinating collection of photographs and artifacts, including tiny shoes for the bound feet of Chinese women, opera costumes and laundry equipment.

As Chinatown has expanded over the years, **Little Italy** has shrunk. It used to be the heart of New York's Italian cultural life, but not much of this classic tenement neighborhood remains. In the 1850s, Italians arrived in great numbers, and in the first half of the 20th century, nearly everyone in the neighborhood was of Italian descent. Today, Mulberry Street north of Canal is the center of what is left. There are restaurants (touristy), cafes, markets, clubs and alleged "mob" hangouts. In September, Little Italy celebrates the **Festival of San Gennaro**, the patron saint of Naples, and Mulberry Street is closed to traffic for a big fair with rides and games for children, food and live bands.

Old St. Patrick's Cathedral (263 Mulberry Street, 226-8075), built in 1809, is the precursor of the midtown version. Behind its red brick walls is a tiny cemetery where the city's early Roman Catholic bishops are buried, as is Pierre Toussaint, who was born a Haitian slave in 1766 but became a free man and philanthropist.

NoLita, an acronym meaning North of Little Italy, comprises the area just east of SoHo. It has young and trend-setting residents, including artists and professionals, and an up-to-the-minute mix of retail and nightlife.

▶ **Greenwich Village**. Greenwich Village is one of the city's most legendary neighborhoods. It is centered around **Washington Square Park** and extends from Broadway west to the river and from Houston Street north to 14th Street. The area consisted of woodlands until the Dutch West India Company planted tobacco there in the 1600s. When the British captured New Amsterdam, the area became known as Greenwich or "green village" and wealthier New Yorkers moved there, seeking relief from the hubbub and epidemics of the city to the south. As the neighborhood prospered, merchant-class row houses were built, as were more modest homes for marine craftsmen near the water. The area's irregular street layout (based on divisions that once marked farms) survived the 1811 Grid Plan, which divided Manhattan into manageable blocks. Greenwich Village is known for its beautiful tree-lined streets with low-rise houses and courtyards.

By the beginning of the 20th century, Greenwich Village had a diverse ethnic, economic and political population, with a preponderance of writers, intellectuals and artists. It was known for its tolerance of alternative lifestyles and its support for the arts. It was one of the first centers of theatrical experimentation—Eugene O'Neill had his first showcase here. It is still the heart of Off Broadway, with lots of small theaters and performance groups. Famous residents have included Henry James, Edith Wharton, Herman Melville, Edna St. Vincent Millay, Margaret Mead, Cary Grant and William Steig (author of *Shrek*).

After World War II, the beats and bohemians moved in, followed in the 1960s by the flower children and radicals. The Village also became a refuge for gay and lesbian residents, although in recent years much of the gay population has moved north to Chelsea. The Village gay scene is centered around Christopher Street, the site of the 1969 Stonewall Tavern standoff between police and gays.

Washington Square Park, named for George Washington, was a common burial ground in the late 18th century. It was converted to a park in 1827, and beautiful Greek Revival houses were built on its north side. At the northwest corner stands the **Hanging Elm**, a reminder of the public executions of the early 19th century. You can't miss the landmark **Washington Arch**, designed by Stanford White and dedicated in 1895. The park is now surrounded by the campus of **New York University** (the largest private university in the country), and the area is teeming with students. In addition to the students, there are families, dogs, chess players, street performers and, unfortunately, drug dealers.

Bleecker Street has an Italian presence, with food shops selling cheese, sausage and other delicacies. It also has lots of inexpensive ethnic restaurants. The **Meatpacking District**, located in and around Gansevoort Street, was once a seamy, crime-ridden locale, but it has benefited from a crackdown on crime and now boasts restaurants, bars, stores and art galleries.

► **East Village.** The **East Village's** western boundary coincides roughly with the border of what used to be the farms, called "Bouwerji" in Dutch (now Bowery), owned in the late 1600s by Peter Stuyvesant, the last Dutch governor of New Amsterdam. In the 1800s the area grew, and Federal-style row houses were built around St. Mark's Place. Since then, many immigrants have come through the neighborhood via the Lower East Side, including Germans, Ukrainians, Italians and Eastern European Jews (the area was the home of the "Yiddish Rialto," a center for Jewish theater). It became a "village" in the mid-1900s, when high rents and gentrification squeezed artists, musicians and intellectuals east from Greenwich Village, turning it into a center for radical politics and art. Today the East Village has been gentrified, but it retains an urban cool. It is home to young, hip professionals and families, as well as immigrants and artists, with many funky shops, restaurants, bars and galleries.

Tompkins Square Park, named for Daniel Tompkins, a governor of New York, is at the center of the East Village. Once a drug-infested area that was the site of a confrontation between the police and the homeless, it has since been totally cleaned up and now has a wonderful playground. Avenues A, B, C and D, also known as **Alphabet City**, lay mostly to the east of the park and are a bit rougher.

Among the interesting sidelights is **St. Mark's Place**, which was home to the beatniks, hippies and punks in the 1950s, 1960s and 1970s, respectively, and is now home to vintage clothing stores, bookstores and cafes, as well as The Gap. **Little India** is a cluster of Indian restaurants on East 6th Street. The **Hell's Angels** have their headquarters on East 3rd Street—listen for the motorcycles.

An interesting little museum is the **Old Merchant's House** (29 East 4th Street, 777-1089), the preserved former home of the Tredwells, a prosperous middle-class family who lived there continuously from 1835 to 1933. Peter Stuyvesant is buried behind **St. Mark's-in-the-Bowery** (East 10th Street at Second Avenue, 674-6377), and some say that his ghost walks there, tapping his wooden leg. The church has weekly poetry readings.

Cooper Union (30 Cooper Square, 353-4100) was founded in 1859 as the country's first free college by Peter Cooper, the builder of the first steam locomotive. Housed in the city's first steel-frame building, it is a progressive school of architecture, art and engineering. In February 1860, Abraham Lincoln gave the famous anti-slavery speech here that garnered him the Republican nomination.

▶ **Chelsea.** **Chelsea**, which is located on the west side from about 14th to 28th Street, was originally a Dutch farm that Captain Thomas Clarke bought in 1750 and named after London's Chelsea Royal Hospital. Clarke's grandson, Clement Clarke Moore (author of *The Night Before Christmas*), developed the land, dictating the style of houses to be built. His home at Ninth Avenue and 21st Street still stands.

Shipping, lumber and brewery trades flourished in Chelsea, as did retail. Sixth Avenue south of 23rd Street was known as Fashion Row and boasted a number of huge stores. Chelsea was home to the first "Broadway" theater district and Manhattan's silver-screen industry (pre-dating that industry's move to Hollywood) as well as to writers and artists. Today it is known for high rents, art galleries (it is the next SoHo), hip clubs and restaurants, a large gay population and tree-lined streets dotted with churches and brownstones.

To many New York children, Chelsea is synonymous with **Chelsea Piers** (23rd Street at the river, 336-6500). Chelsea Piers was once the main passenger terminal for transatlantic ocean liners (the *Titanic* would have docked at Pier 59) and is now a huge 30-acre sports facility offering roller-skating, ice skating, hockey, golf, basketball, gymnastics, rock-climbing, soccer, batting cages, bowling and several restaurants. It is home to over 1,500 local sports teams as well as several television and film production companies. All in all, it's not to be missed, especially on a rainy day.

On a more offbeat note, the **Chelsea Hotel** (222 West 23rd Street, 243-3700) was the home of many writers and, later, rock stars. Plaques on the hotel's façade honor these literary guests, who include Mark Twain, Dylan Thomas and Tennessee Williams.

▶**Flatiron District.** The **Flatiron District** is named for the unusual wedge-shaped **Flatiron Building**, located at 175 Fifth Avenue (at 23rd Street). Built in 1902, it was the city's tallest building at 20 stories until the Woolworth Building surpassed it. The Flatiron District describes the area between 14th and 23rd Streets, from Park to Sixth Avenues. Today it is another trendy area with stores, restaurants and bars. Of interest to children is the **Forbes Magazine Galleries** (62 Fifth Avenue, 206-5548), which showcases publisher Malcolm Forbes' amazing collection of stuff, in particular toy boats, soldiers, monopoly games, and presidential papers.

Union Square Park (14th to 17th Streets, between Fifth and Park Avenues) is the first of a series of squares along Broadway. Although it was once a rallying spot for organized labor, its name actually derives from the union of Bloomingdale Road (now Broadway) and Bowery Road (now Fourth Avenue). The park has been cleaned up and restored recently and has a big farmers' market on Monday, Wednesday and Saturday.

Ladies' Mile, located between Broadway and Sixth Avenue from Union to Madison Squares, was a fashionable post–Civil War shopping district. Many of the biggest retailers, including Lord & Taylor and B. Altman, were there until they moved uptown.

▶ **Gramercy Park.** Gramercy Park was once part of Peter Stuyvesant's bowery. The Dutch called it "Krom Moerajse" ("little crooked swamp"), which was anglicized to "Gramercy." In 1822 Samuel Ruggles purchased and drained the swamp, laid out the park and sold lots to affluent families, who built elegant row houses. Ruggles named the street that runs south from the park to 14th Street Irving Place, after his friend Washington Irving. (Irving never lived there, contrary to popular belief.)

Gramercy Park is the city's only private park—only residents have keys to the locked gate. Among the area's well-known residents were actors James Cagney, John Barrymore and Margaret Hamilton (the Wicked Witch of the West) and author O. Henry. Teddy Roosevelt was born at 28 East 20th Street, just west of Gramercy Park.

The West Side —
From West 23rd Street to West 60th Street

As the city began to grow, industries moved north from lower Manhattan. Factories, warehouses and rail yards were built in the 1920s, 1930s and 1940s. Although most of the factories are gone, the rail yards remain and the area is home to the U.S. central post office, Madison Square Garden, Pennsylvania Station, the Jacob Javits Convention Center, and such companies as Federal Express and United Parcel Service. Many of the large warehouses in the West 20s are being converted into residential lofts.

▶ **The Garment District and Herald Square.** The **Garment District**, in and around Seventh Avenue in the West 30s, is the nation's fashion capital. It is a bustling commercial district, and on any weekday you can see runners pushing racks of clothing through the streets or carrying fur pelts.

Herald Square, located where Broadway and Sixth Avenue cross 34th Street, isn't really a square at all, but a triangle. It is named for the *New York Herald*, a newspaper that had offices on 35th Street from 1894 to 1921. The only thing remaining from the newspaper's original building is the clock. Every hour, two bronze bell ringers, nicknamed Stuff and Guff, strike the bell. Herald Square was the center of the seamy Tenderloin district, home to brothels and speakeasies, until **Macy's** (151 West 34th Street, 695-4400) opened in 1902 and gave the area new respectability. Macy's is still the world's largest department store and hosts a famed annual Thanksgiving Day parade. Check out the wooden escalators!

▶ **Broadway and Times Square.** At the turn of the century, **Broadway** became known as "The Great White Way," because of its appearance when lit up by its signs, which at that time used only white lightbulbs. Today, spectacular signs use every color of the rainbow. Broadway is New York's theater center, and at any given time theatergoers can choose from 40-odd productions in the neighborhood and eat in a wide variety of restaurants.

Times Square, where Broadway intersects 42nd Street, may be the most recognized intersection in the world. On New Year's Eve, the world watches as the ball is dropped to mark the start of the new year. Times Square takes its name from the *New York Times* building on 43rd Street, which was built in 1904. Before that, the area was known as Longacre Square and was home to blacksmiths and stables. When the *Times* came, the area became a neighborhood. By the 1970s, the area had become sleazy and somewhat dangerous—x-rated movie theaters and sex shops were plentiful and hustlers abounded. After a major redevelopment in the 1990s, it is now clean and visitor friendly. Disney, Toys R Us, Loews and others have taken the place of grimier establishments. Over 230,000 people now work in the Times Square area, and some 27,000 people live there.

Times Square has lots for kids to do and see, including the **New Victory Theater** (229 West 42nd Street, 382-4042), a jewel of a theater dedicated to high-quality children's programming; **Madame Tussaud's** (234 West 42nd Street, 512-9600), a branch of the famed London wax museum; and, for less cultural activities, **XS** (1457 Broadway, 398-5467), a family virtual-game center and **ESPN Zone**, (1472 Broadway, 921-3776), a sports entertainment and high-tech interactive and sports simulation games center. Head west from Times Square towards the river and you will find the **Intrepid**

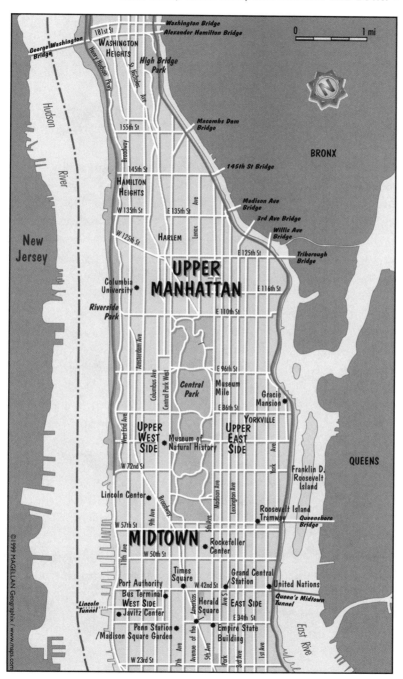

0   1 mi

Washington Bridge
Alexander Hamilton Bridge

181st St
George Washington
Bridge
WASHINGTON
HEIGHTS
High Bridge
Park

Hudson

River

New
Jersey

Henry Hudson Pkwy

St. Nicholas Ave

Broadway

155th St

Macombs Dam
Bridge

145th St

BRONX

145th St Bridge

HAMILTON
HEIGHTS

W 135th St   E 135th St

Lenox Ave

Madison Ave
Bridge
3rd Ave Bridge
Willis Ave
Bridge

W 125th St   HARLEM

E 125th St

Triborough
Bridge

Columbia
University

UPPER
MANHATTAN

E 116th St

Riverside
Park

E 110th St

Amsterdam Ave

Columbus Ave

Central Park West

E 96th St

Central
Park

Museum
Mile

Gracie
Mansion

E 86th St

YORKVILLE

West End Ave

UPPER
WEST
SIDE

Museum of
Natural History

UPPER
EAST
SIDE

QUEENS

W 72nd St

York Ave

Franklin D.
Roosevelt
Island

Lincoln Center

Broadway

9th Ave

Madison Ave

Lexington Ave

Roosevelt Island
Tramway

Queensboro
Bridge

W 57th St

5th Ave

MIDTOWN

Rockefeller
Center

11th Ave   W 50th St

Times
Square

Grand Central
Station

United Nations

Port Authority
Bus Terminal
WEST SIDE
Javitz Center

W 42nd St

Herald
Square

Avenue of the Americas

EAST SIDE

Queen's Midtown
Tunnel

Lincoln
Tunnel

E 34th St

Penn Station
/Madison Square Garden

Empire State
Building

7th Ave

5th Ave

Park Ave

3rd Ave

1st Ave

East River

W 23rd St

© 1999 MAGELLAN Geographix • www.maps.com

Sea/Air Space Museum (Pier 86, West 46th Street and Twelfth Avenue, 245-0072), a decommissioned aircraft carrier that fought in World War II in the Pacific and was badly damaged. It was opened in 1982 as a museum of naval aviation history and has warplanes, fighter jet simulators and NASA space capsules among its exhibits.

▶ **Midtown West.** This area, encompassing the West 30s through the 50s and the western side of Fifth Avenue over to Sixth Avenue, is almost entirely commercial. Skyscrapers abound, and shops, museums, libraries and parks share the space.

The **Empire State Building** (350 Fifth Avenue, 736-3100) was completed in 1931 at the height of the Depression and was nicknamed the "Empty State Building," because at that time, only about one-half of the floor space was rented. It was the tallest building in the world until the World Trade Center opened. It has 102 floors, 73 elevators and over 6,500 windows. At the top of its radio mast and the lightning rod (think King Kong), it is 1,454 feet tall. The top 30 floors have colored lights that are lit to honor different holidays.

A bit further north on Fifth Avenue is the **New York Public Library** (at 42nd Street, 661-7220), one of the world's greatest libraries. It opened in 1911 on what had been the Croton Reservoir, with the donation of the important libraries of John Jacob Astor and James Lenox. The Library now has over 9 million books and over 21 million other items, including manuscripts, recordings, photographs, prints and maps. The Main Reading Room is the size of a football field! Out front, kids love the sculptured lions that guard the steps, named Patience and Fortitude by former Mayor Fiorello LaGuardia. The broad steps that lead up to the entrance are a favorite gathering place for New Yorkers.

Just behind the Library is beautifully restored **Bryant Park**, named for William Jennings Bryant, a poet and longtime editor of the *New York Post*. On Monday nights in the summer, the park serves as an urban drive-in: classic movies are shown outdoors, and people picnic on the grounds.

Between Fifth and Sixth Avenues on 44th Street are a number of impressive buildings, including the **Algonquin Hotel**, home of the literary Round Table, and the **New York Yacht Club**, a great looking building with nautical windows that was home to the America's

Cup from 1857 to 1983. At 43rd Street and Sixth Avenue is the **International Center of Photography** (1133 Sixth Avenue, 857-0000), a museum devoted solely to photography.

Rockefeller Center, a small city within a city, runs from 48th to 51st Streets between Fifth and Sixth Avenues (632-3975). Built in the 1930s by the wealthy Rockefeller family, it has 19 Art Deco buildings that house offices, stores, theaters and television studios. The tallest building is the **General Electric Building**, which houses NBC; you can tour the studios and also see the *Today Show* being filmed in the morning. Behind the skating rink is a golden statue of Prometheus and the Promenade, where the gigantic Christmas tree is lit. At the northwestern end is **Radio City Music Hall** (1260 Sixth Avenue, 632-4041), which was built as the world's most luxurious movie theater in 1932. This Art Deco fantasy is home to the high-kicking Rockettes and hosts top entertainers throughout the year.

Two cultural landmarks in Midtown West not to be missed are the **Museum of Modern Art (MOMA)** (11 West 53rd Street, 707-9400), which showcases the best collection of 20th-century art in the world and has a wonderful sculpture garden designed by Philip Johnson (through 2004, MOMA is undergoing a major renovation and the collection has moved to MOMA Queens, located at 45-20 33rd Street at Queens Boulevard), and **Carnegie Hall** (154 West 57th Street, 903-9629), built by Andrew Carnegie in 1891. Tchaikovsky conducted the inaugural concert, and the world's greatest musical talents have performed there since, including Toscanini, Ella Fitzgerald, Frank Sinatra and The Beatles.

Also worth visiting, especially on a rainy day, is the **Museum of Television and Radio** (25 West 52nd Street, 621-6600) with its collection of thousands of old programs and vintage commercials (and on weekends, special shows for children).

▶ **Hell's Kitchen.** This neighborhood, which runs from the West 30s to the 50s around Ninth and Tenth Avenues, takes its name from an Irish gang that terrorized the neighborhood in the late 1800s. Its tenements were home to workers in the iron foundries, stone yards, lumberyards and abattoirs, all of which supported the railroads. In 1959, in an effort to revitalize the neighborhood, it was renamed Clinton, after DeWitt Clinton.

Today, **Hell's Kitchen** is still socioeconomically diverse, with young professionals and theater people joining immigrant groups. Ninth Avenue is a bazaar of small ethnic restaurants and bars catering to its young population. **Restaurant Row**, 46th Street between Eighth and Ninth Avenues, is a long block of restaurants filled with theatergoers. The Ninth Avenue Food Festival is held on a Saturday in mid-May, featuring foods from all over the world. On the northern end of Hell's Kitchen are Roosevelt Hospital and John Jay College.

The East Side —
East 23rd Street to East 60th Street

The East Side in this part of the city is a mix of commercial and residential areas, slightly more residential than its West Side counterpart. As on the West Side, industry and people moved northward over time.

▶**Madison Square, Kips Bay and Murray Hill.** Madison Square includes the area from 23rd Street to the low 30s, bounded on the east by the restaurant areas on Madison and Park and on the west by the fashion district. Named for President James Madison, **Madison Square Park** was a former military parade ground that opened to the public in 1847. At the end of the 19th century, Madison Square was home to the city's entertainment center and two early incarnations of Madison Square Garden.

Kip's Bay, a residential neighborhood, is the area between Gramercy Park and **Murray Hill**. Before the 1811 Grid Plan, these areas consisted of public open lands and farms owned by significant landowners, for which the areas are now named. Kip's Bay is named for the Kip family, Dutch settlers who established a farm just after the Canarsie Indians had sold Manhattan. Murray Hill, which extends from 34th to 40th Streets and from Madison to Third Avenues, is named for the Robert Murray family, whose estate stood at 37th Street and Park Avenue. Legend has it that Robert's wife, Mary, invited British General Howe to tea in 1776, knowing that he would be too polite to refuse, thereby buying time for Washington to escape up to Fort Tryon.

The tree-lined streets of Murray Hill are a throwback to the time when some of the city's richest and most socially prominent people lived there, including John Pierpont Morgan, who, in addition to being one of the richest men of his era, was a leading collector of rare books and manuscripts, sculpture, paintings, drawings and musical scores. His collection grew so large that he needed a whole building to house it. The building was completed in 1906 and opened to the public in 1924 as the **Pierpont Morgan Library** (29 East 36th Street, 685-0610). The neighborhood is also home to a growing Indian and Korean population, with respective restaurants and stores.

► **Grand Central.** Begun in 1903 and opened in 1913, **Grand Central Terminal** (42nd Street and Park Avenue, 340-3000) is a beautiful Beaux Arts train station through which over 150,000 commuters and thousands of pedestrians pass every day. It underwent a large-scale interior renovation in the 1990s, in which the East Waiting Room was completed and the Main Concourse's vaulted ceilings, painted to look like the constellations, were cleaned and restored. It is home to the famous Oyster Bar (and its Guastavino tiles, which make it possible to whisper into one corner and have someone in the opposite corner hear it).

Across Lexington Avenue is the **Chrysler Building** (405 Lexington Avenue, 682-3070), a beautiful Art Deco landmark. It was built in 1929 for automobile magnate Walter P. Chrysler, who had the façade adorned with automotive detail: wheels, radiator caps and stainless steel gargoyles that resemble hood ornaments. The stainless steel pinnacle is fashioned after a radiator grill.

► **Turtle Bay.** Turtle Bay is the area in and around First and Second Avenues in the East 40s. Authorities debate whether it is named for the turtle-filled cove that existed there in the 19th century or for the cove shaped like a knife blade ("deutal" in Dutch). Turtle Bay is a residential neighborhood with pretty row houses and is home to people in the theater and literary worlds, including Katherine Hepburn, Stephen Sondheim and E. B. White.

The main attraction in Turtle Bay is **United Nations Plaza** (First Avenue and 46th Street, 963-7713). In 1946, John D. Rockefeller gave the United Nations Organization the 18-acre plot on the East River. At that time, the site was home to tenements, slaughterhouses and breweries. The entrance to the U.N. is lined with a colorful array of flags from the 188 member nations. The U.N. actually consists of three connected buildings: the 39-story glass-walled Secretariat Building designed by Le Corbusier, the low-slung General Assembly and the Conference Building, where the Security Council meets. Guided tours are available (led by students from all over the world), and there is an eclectic art collection donated by the member nations. Don't miss the Chagall windows.

Just north of the U.N. are **Beekman Place** and **Sutton Place**, two of the city's most exclusive and expensive neighborhoods. The Beekman family mansion was located at Beekman Place from 1765 to 1874. The British convicted Nathan Hale of spying and executed him there in 1776. In 1875, Effingham Sutton bought the land that is now Sutton Place. At that time, the banks of the East River had factories and tenements. Sutton developed the area, and in the 1920s prestigious families like the Vanderbilts and Morgans moved in.

▶ **Roosevelt Island.** **Roosevelt Island**, a small island in the East River, was at various times a prison, an almshouse, an insane asylum and a smallpox hospital. Today it is a self-contained residential neighborhood with modern apartment buildings, a post office, library, church, deli, bank and school, as well as lots of green areas and playgrounds. It has a racially mixed, middle-class population for whom it represents an escape from the more frenzied pace of Manhattan. If you have time, it's fun to ride the big red tram across the river. It leaves from Second Avenue at 60th Street and offers superb views of the city.

▶ **Midtown East.** **Midtown East** is for many tourists the heart of Manhattan. It is New York's major business and shopping district and has art galleries, hotels, restaurants, museums, churches and synagogues. Despite its current cosmopolitan atmosphere, it was historically open country. Then came farms, estates, factories and tenements to the east. After the Civil War, New York society settled on "Millionaire's Row" on Fifth Avenue from 34th Street to 59th

Street. As businesses arrived in the early 1900s, the millionaires moved north on Fifth Avenue.

Fifth Avenue is home to some of the finest shops in the world, from such jewelry giants as Cartier and Tiffany to major department stores like Bergdorf Goodman and Saks Fifth Avenue to the Disney store and FAO Schwarz. It is also home to **St. Patrick's Cathedral** (Fifth Avenue at 50th Street, 753-2261), the center of American Catholic life. St. Patrick's is the largest Catholic cathedral in the U.S. and has beautiful stained-glass windows that are best viewed on a sunny day.

The **Sony Wonder Technology Lab** (550 Madison Avenue, 833-8100), a techno wonderland, is an interactive exploratorium for children ages four and over, where kids get to experiment with lots of hi-tech equipment, from television cameras to robots.

The Upper West Side — West 61st Street to West 110th Street

The Upper West Side is a popular residential neighborhood characterized by busy avenues with lots of restaurants, bars and shops, and quiet side streets with attractive brownstones. Its residents come from different social and economic backgrounds and are known for their open-mindedness and devotion to their neighborhood.

The area was farmland until the Civil War; then it became a shantytown until the elevated Ninth Avenue line was built. In 1884, the Dakota Apartments went up, so named because the site was so far from the center of the city. Soon other buildings followed, especially after the arrival of the subway in 1904. The area became a haven for New Yorkers engaged in the arts, publishing and advertising. Central Park West is now home to many celebrities, including Jerry Seinfeld and Barbra Streisand.

Central Park West is also home to two of the West Side's important museums, the **New York Historical Society** and the **American Museum of Natural History**. The Historical Society (170 Central Park West, 769-5100), founded in 1804, is the oldest museum in the city and has been an important institution for preserving the city's history and culture. Its eclectic collection includes original Audubon watercolors, a Gilbert Stuart portrait of George Washington, American silver, Tiffany lamps and tons of books. The Museum of Natural History (Central Park West at 79th Street, 769-5000) is one of the world's largest museums—it takes up over four square blocks and has almost 40 million specimens, including such popular attractions as the Dinosaur Hall, the Hall of Minerals and Gems, the Hall of Biodiversity (a new area featuring a rain forest), the North American Indian exhibits, the spectacular new Rose Center for Earth and Space and the Planetarium. Not to be missed.

▶ **Lincoln Center.** Lincoln Center for the Performing Arts (Broadway at 65th Street, 546-2656) is home to New York's most prestigious performing-arts companies, including the New York Philharmonic, the Metropolitan Opera, the New York City Opera, the New York City Ballet, the American Ballet Theater and the Lincoln Jazz Orchestra. Over five million people a year attend performances here, and thousands of others visit or attend open-air dances and other free events in the summer. The Juilliard School of Music is here and so is Damrosch Park, home to the Big Apple Circus, a manageable and appealing circus for younger children on Lincoln Center's southern end.

▶ **Broadway and Columbus Avenue.** Broadway was originally an Indian trail that ran north from the southern tip of Manhattan. Today Broadway runs from the Battery up to the Bronx. Its name comes from the Dutch "Breede Wegh," which describes the width of the thoroughfare. Columbus Avenue (also known as Ninth Avenue below 65th Street) is named, of course, for Christopher Columbus. In the 1890s the city's growing Italian American community dedicated a statue of Columbus (now in the center of Columbus Circle) to commemorate the 400th anniversary of his ocean voyage.

Both Broadway and Columbus Avenue are lined with large chain stores (like The Gap and Barnes & Noble) as well as smaller boutiques. Restaurants and bars are plentiful, as are movie theaters. The **Children's Museum of Manhattan** (212 West 83rd

Street, 721-1234) is an engaging spot with cool stuff to look at, play with or touch. Some exhibits are based on children's books, while others teach about art, science or theater. There is even a television studio where kids can record their own shows.

The Upper East Side —
East 61st Street to East 110th Street

The Upper East Side has been New York's "Gold Coast" since the late 19th century. In the early 1800s, the area was pastureland. Later in the century, Central Park was opened, mansions sprung up on Fifth and Park Avenues and brownstones were built on the side streets. On these thoroughfares, the apartment buildings are stately and the gardens manicured. You see exquisitely dressed matrons, uniformed children going to private schools, dog walkers and door-men. In and around Madison Avenue are expensive boutiques, art galleries, elegant hotels and restaurants.

► **Carnegie Hill**, the area from 86th Street to 96th Street between Fifth and Park Avenues, is named for millionaire Andrew Carnegie, who built a mansion at 91st and Fifth Avenue (now the Cooper-Hewitt Museum). **Lenox Hill**, the area around Park Avenue in the 70s, is named for Robert Lenox, who had a 30-acre estate there.

Further east, Lexington, Third and Second Avenues are home to families and young urban professionals. High-rise apartment build-ings are mixed in with a multitude of lively bars and restaurants. In an earlier time, this part of the Upper East Side was home to immi-grants. Elevated trains carried workers downtown, and tenements underneath the train tracks housed them. The elevated train tracks were torn down in the 1950s.

The Upper East Side is home to numerous museums (see Chap-ter 8 for more details), including **The Abigail Adams Smith Museum** (425 East 61st Street, 838-6878); the **Frick Collection** (1 East 70th Street, 288-0700), housed in the former home of steel magnate Henry Clay Frick (children under ten are not admitted); and the **Whitney Museum of American Art** (945 Madison Avenue,

570-3676), devoted to 20th-century American art and housed in a Marcel Breuer–designed building.

▶ **Museum Mile.** Many of the museums found on **Museum Mile**, which runs from 80th Street to about 106th Street on Fifth Avenue, are housed in what were once millionaires' mansions. See Chapter 8 for details. Starting at the southern end of Museum Mile and working north are the **Metropolitan Museum of Art** (Fifth Avenue at 81st Street, 535-7710), which is perhaps the largest museum in the Western Hemisphere; the **Solomon R. Guggenheim Museum** (1071 Fifth Avenue at 88th Street, 423-3500), housed in a famous streamlined, round building designed in the 1940s by Frank Lloyd Wright (his only building in New York City); **The Cooper-Hewitt National Design Museum** (2 East 91st Street, 849-8300), housed in the former home of Andrew Carnegie (a "modest" 64-room mansion) and the only design museum in the U.S.; the **Jewish Museum** (1109 Fifth Avenue, 423-3200), located in the former home of financier Felix Warburg and containing a rich collection of Judaica, including coins, ceremonial objects, paintings and archeological treasures, representing 4,000 years of history; the **Museum of the City of New York** (1220 Fifth Avenue, 534-1672), created in 1923 to collect and preserve the history of the city and displaying a great diversity of wonderful objects dating from colonial times to the present, including toys, Currier & Ives prints, firefighting memorabilia, furniture and lots of other "stuff"; and **El Museo del Barrio** (1230 Fifth Avenue, 831-7272), which houses a small but distinguished collection of Latin American art and culture as well a hands-on children's room.

▶ **Yorkville.** Yorkville is the area from approximately 79th Street to 96th Street, east of Lexington Avenue. Immigrants from Germany, Ireland and Hungary moved there from the Lower East Side as they prospered. The German center of Yorkville was located on 86th Street around Second Avenue, with restaurants, stores, theaters and beer halls with oompah bands. After World War II, many Germans moved out of the city and numerous establishments closed, but you can still find restaurants and delicatessens that sell authentic German food.

▶ **Gracie Mansion.** Gracie Mansion, a 1799 Federal-style house built by Archibald Gracie on the site of a revolutionary fort (88th Street and East End Avenue, 570-4751), is the official mayoral residence, although the current mayor, Michael Bloomberg, doesn't live there. Gracie Mansion sits in the northern end of **Carl Schurz Park**, a quiet 10-acre park (with a very popular playground) on the East River, named for a prominent 19th-century German immigrant who was a newspaper editor and reform politician.

Upper Manhattan — Above 110th Street

▶ **Spanish Harlem.** Spanish Harlem, also known as "El Barrio," was not always Hispanic. The area was agricultural until the mid-19th century when mass transport connected the area to the city. Tenements were built for its working-class inhabitants, including Germans, Irish, Italians, Jews, and then African Americans. Puerto Ricans and other Latin Americans came after World War II. Today it is lively area, with bodegas, restaurants and cafes.

▶ **Morningside Heights.** The island of Manhattan narrows at its northern end, and rises to its greatest elevation of 267.75 feet! Ridges, hills, plateaus, bluffs and rocks are all part of the landscape there, hence the descriptive "Heights" in various neighborhoods' names. **Morningside Heights** is the neighborhood from West 110th to West 125th Streets. It was first known as Vandewater Heights, after a 17th-century Dutch settler, Harmon Vandewater. By the late 1800s, a number of educational and religious institutions had set up shop there.

Morningside Heights boasts several important attractions. **Columbia University** (Broadway and West 116th Street, 854-4902) was chartered as King's College in 1754 and was originally located downtown in Trinity Church. Graduates included Alexander Hamilton and John Jay. In the 1950s, Columbia was home to beatniks, and during the Vietnam War, it was the site of televised student protests. Over 20,000 students attend Columbia and its sister school, Barnard College. Together with those attending other neighborhood schools like the Jewish Theological Seminary and the Union Theological Seminary, there are so many students that the area feels like Manhattan's college town, with lots of academic bookstores and old coffee shops.

Cathedral Church of St. John the Divine (Amsterdam Avenue at West 112th Street, 361-7540) was begun in 1872 and is still not finished. It is so big that the Statue of Liberty could fit under the central dome, and it is second in size only to St. Peter's Basilica in Rome. Do not miss the biblical garden and children's sculpture garden. **Riverside Church** (Riverside Drive at West 122nd Street, 870-6700) is also a mammoth Gothic-style church. Its bell tower is 355 feet high and offers great views of the city. The church was inspired by the Cathedral at Chartres and has beautiful stained-glass windows as well as a giant working carillon given by the Rockefeller family.

To find out who is really buried in **Grant's Tomb**, go to the General Grant National Memorial (Riverside Drive at West 122nd Street, 666-1640). The largest mausoleum in the U.S., it is modeled after Napoleon's Tomb in Paris. President Grant and his wife are, in fact, interred there.

▶ **Harlem.** **Harlem** stretches from 125th Street up to 145th Street. In the 18th century, Harlem was an upper-Manhattan getaway for wealthy downtowners. After the Civil War, prosperous merchants, in particular German Jews, built beautiful row houses there. In the early 20th century, Harlem became a magnet for African American city dwellers who came from the southern U.S. and the Caribbean. By the 1920s, the Harlem Renaissance was underway. African American artists, writers and musicians such as Langston Hughes, Zora Neale Hurston, Count Basie and Billie Holiday gathered in Harlem, and a proud cultural movement blossomed. Hot spots included the **Apollo Theater** (253 West 125th Street, 749-5838), which is still going strong, and the Cotton Club, which is no longer.

The Crash of 1929 and the Depression effectively ended the Harlem Renaissance. Unemployment skyrocketed, the middle class moved out, and Harlem decayed. Recently, Harlem has undergone a second Renaissance. Prosperous residents are buying and renovating brownstones, and West 125th Street has once again become a commercial center anchored by **Harlem USA**, a huge mall with movie theaters and big stores.

The **Abyssinian Baptist Church** (132 Odell Clark Place, 862-7474) may be best known for its former minister, Adam Clayton Powell, Jr., who was also the first African American congressman from New York. The Gothic church dates from 1923, though the congregation goes back to 1808. People line up today to hear the magnificent choir and organ on Sundays.

The **St. Nicholas Historic District** consists of four blocks along West 138th and 139th Streets. Formerly known as Striver's Row, its 19th-century homes were designed by well-known architects (including Stanford White), and many prominent African Americans lived there. Another historic district worth visiting is the **Mount Morris Park Historic District** (tours 369-241), a Victorian enclave that has some of the finest brownstones in the city, built by German Jewish families moving up from the Lower East Side. The park in the center was renamed **Marcus Garvey Park** in 1973, after the black nationalist leader.

▶ **Hamilton Heights.** Situated on Harlem's western edge, **Hamilton Heights** runs north from Morningside Park to about 155th Street. It takes its name from Alexander Hamilton, who had his country home, which still stands, at Convent Avenue and West 141st Street. He lived there until he died in 1804 after that infamous duel with Aaron Burr. The **Hamilton Grange National Memorial** (287 Convent Avenue at West 141st Street, 283-5154) stands on the site of his estate and offers drama, music and colonial craft-making, as well as seasonal activities for children.

In the late 19th and early 20th centuries elegant row houses sprung up between 141st and 145th Streets on land once belonging to Hamilton. Known as **Sugar Hill** (home of the sweet life), its residents included such celebrated African Americans as Thurgood Marshall and Cab Calloway. In the 1940s, the population shifted, and Latin Americans arrived to join African Americans living there. Today the neighborhood is home to Dominicans, Ecuadoreans and Chinese, among others.

The **Audubon Terrace** (Broadway between West 155th and 156th Streets) was built in 1904 and was once part of the naturalist John J. Audubon's estate. It houses several cultural institutions, including the **American Academy and Institute** of Arts and Letters, the **American Numismatic Society** and the **Hispanic Society of America**.

▶ **Washington Heights and Inwood.** The neighborhood of **Washington Heights** begins at about 155th Street and runs north about 40 blocks. Washington Heights, which is primarily Dominican today; has a lively "marqueta" atmosphere where shops are "bodegas" and Spanish is spoken. Just north of Washington Heights is **Inwood**, Manhattan's northernmost tip. Native Americans and then Dutch settlers originally resided there. Some scholars believe that Inwood is where Peter Minuit purchased Manhattan from the Native Americans, whose artifacts were still being found there in the 20th century.

Wealthy New Yorkers had country estates here, and the area remained undeveloped until the early 19th century. When the Broadway subway line opened in 1906, middle-class apartment complexes were built, as were single-family homes. Jewish and Irish immigrants (Henry Kissinger among them) moved to Inwood, and today it is an ethnically diverse neighborhood that is home to young professionals seeking housing in its Art Deco apartment buildings.

These neighborhoods are home to several important cultural and historical institutions. On the river, between 155th and 160th Streets, is where the former Polo Grounds once stood, the home of the New York Giants before the team moved to San Francisco. **Fort Tryon Park** is a pre–Revolutionary War fort where Washington's troops made a last stand against the British before being driven from the island and retreating in 1776. The fort was captured by the British and named for William Tryon, the last British governor of New York. Fort Tryon Park is also home to **The Cloisters** (193rd Street and Fort Washington Avenue, 923-3700). Opened in 1938, it is the medieval art annex of the Metropolitan Museum of Art and offers a unique, transporting and peaceful experience.

The **Morris Jumel Mansion** (65 Jumel Terrace at 160th Street, 923-8008) is an elegant mansion built in 1765 by Roger Morris, a British military officer. George Washington used the building as his headquarters in 1776 during his retreat. A wine merchant, Stephen

Jumel, and his wife, Eliza Bowen, restored it in 1810. After Jumel died, Bowen, who was briefly married to Aaron Burr, continued to live there. The house has noteworthy architecture and interiors.

Also in Inwood is the Dyckman Farmhouse Museum (4881 Broadway at West 204th Street, 304-9422), a reminder that Manhattan was once all farms. The house originally belonged to the Dyckman family, who then owned Manhattan's largest farm. It is a Dutch-style home with a gambrel roof and fieldstone walls; rebuilt in 1783, it was opened as a museum in 1916, with five period rooms and a smokehouse.

Central Park

Central Park is New York's backyard. Over 20 million people a year use the park to run, bicycle, skateboard, sketch, sunbathe, play softball, sail boats, ice skate and much more. It is hard to believe that if this 700-acre parcel had not been bought by the city fathers in the 1850s, the park would not exist. For America's first major park, Frederick Law Olmsted and Calvert Vaux devised a naturalistic plan based on popular English garden design. It took more than 20,000 workers over 20 years to construct its open meadows, dense woods and formal areas. Recently the Park has undergone major renovations, and it looks better than ever.

Starting from the southern end of the Park, some of the attractions that should not be missed include the **Carousel** (mid-Park at 65th Street), a 1908 merry-go-round with elaborately carved wooden horses, and the **Dairy** (mid-Park at 65th Street), a charming 19th-century gingerbread-style house that was actually a dairy when people grazed cows on the Park's meadows but is now a visitor information center with roomfuls of displays about the Park.

The **Central Park Wildlife Center** and the nearby **Tisch Children's Zoo** (5th Avenue at 64th Street, 861-6030) keep their animals in natural settings instead of in cages. Different climates are represented, including the Polar Circle, the Temperate Zone, the Tropical Zone, Monkey Island and the Sea Lion Pool, where feeding is always fun. The Children's Zoo is a petting zoo. At the **Loeb**

Boathouse (74th Street) overlooking the Lake, boats and bikes can be rented.

Belvedere Castle (79th Street) is a Gothic-fantasy building (adjacent to a turtle pond) housing an interactive nature center and offering great views. The **Great Lawn** (80th to 84th Streets) is where kids play softball and adults attend free summer concerts. **Cleopatra's Needle** (behind the Metropolitan Museum) is a 65-foot tall granite obelisk dating from about 1475 B.C. that was given by Egypt to the U.S. in 1885.

Finally, at the Park's northern end is the **Harlem Meer** and the **Charles A. Dana Discovery Center**, a nature-study center offering hands-on nature exhibits and weekend family workshops.

The Bronx

The Bronx is located to the north and east of Manhattan and is the only borough that is attached to the mainland. It is the second smallest borough in size and population and the home of the "Bronx cheer." Although there are some troubled areas of the borough, there are a number of interesting and delightful spots as well.

In 1639, the Dutch West India Company bought the land that was to become the Bronx from the Native Americans. Jonas Bronck, one of the area's first Dutch inhabitants, bought acreage along the river, and it soon became known as the Bronck's river, and people went up to visit the Broncks. From the end of the Revolution to the mid-19th century, the area was rural, inhabited by both modest farmers and large landowners. Over time, villages arose along the post roads. The early 20th century was the golden age of the Bronx, and it was divided into tightly-knit ethnic neighborhoods that were home to German, Irish, Jewish, Italian, Polish and Greek immigrants seeking open space. By the mid-20th century, things began to deteriorate, hitting bottom in the 1970s. The Bronx is now undergoing a rebirth and, with it, acquiring a new sense of vibrancy and pride.

▶ **Grand Concourse.** The **Grand Boulevard and Concourse** is the great boulevard of the Bronx and runs up toward the Botanical Gar-

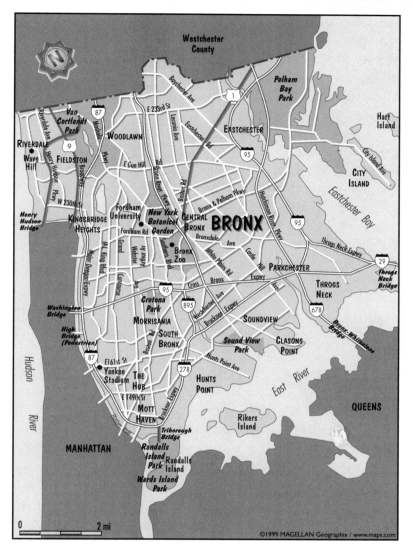

den. It was laid out in 1892 with separate lanes for carriages, cyclists and pedestrians. In the 1920s and 1930s, it was known as the Park Avenue of the Bronx: mostly wealthy Jewish families lived in large Art Deco apartment buildings with beautiful façades. Although neighborhoods to the east and west of the Grand Concourse deteriorated as the middle class moved out, the Grand Concourse withstood the stresses.

The **Bronx Museum of the Arts** (1040 Grand Concourse at 165th Street, 718 681-6000) is the Bronx's fine-arts museum. Established in 1961, it exhibits high-quality, well-curated exhibits of contemporary and historical art, particularly by Bronx artists.

Edgar Allan Poe Cottage (Grand Concourse and East Kingsbridge Road, 718 881-8900) was home to the author and his wife, Virginia, from 1846 to 1848. They moved there hoping that the country air would cure Virginia of tuberculosis, but she died shortly thereafter. While there, he wrote *Annabel Lee* and *Ulalume*. The house was turned into a museum in 1917 and has three period rooms, as well as photographs of, and a film on, Poe's life.

Along the Grand Concourse are many of the borough's civic buildings, including the bold Art Deco **Bronx County Courthouse** and the huge **Bronx Post Office**, with its murals depicting labor and industrial programs.

▶ **South Bronx.** The **South Bronx** is bounded by the Harlem River on the west, the Bronx River on the east and Fordham Road on the north. Also known as "Fort Apache" in the 1970s, it was full of looted, burned and abandoned buildings on bleak open lots. Even then, however, the destruction was not uniform; there were still stable neighborhoods with a strong sense of community pride. That sense has grown today, and much of the area has been rehabilitated.

Highbridge takes its name from the aqueduct crossing the Harlem River. Its most famous landmark is **Yankee Stadium** (River Avenue at 161st Street, 718 293-6000), home to the Bronx Bombers and also known as "the House That Ruth Built." It is said that the stadium was designed with a short right field so that it would be easier for Babe Ruth to hit homers. In fact, the Babe hit a game-winning homer in the first game that was played there, on April 18, 1923. The stadium was renovated in 1976. Although the area is not a particularly good one, Yankee fans make it safe around game time.

University Heights, north of Highbridge, took its name from the NYU campus on University Avenue at 180th Street. It is now Bronx Community College, which is part of the City University of New York. McKim, Mead and White designed the older buildings on the campus, including the **Hall of Fame for Great Americans** (University Avenue at West 181st Street, 718 220-6003), a long semi-circular arcade with bronze busts of great American scientists, writers, inventors and statesmen.

Belmont, just west of the Bronx Zoo, is the Bronx's Little Italy. An enclave of colorful shops, cafes and Italian restaurants line Arthur Avenue. Italians settled there when the Botanical Garden was developed, working there as tradesmen. The neighborhood weathered the 1970s and today is predominantly, but not exclusively, Italian.

▶ **Central Bronx.** The **Central Bronx** is home to two of the Bronx's main attractions, the **Bronx Zoo** and the **New York Botanical Garden**. The **Zoo** (Fordham Road at Bronx River Parkway, 718 367-1010) is the country's largest urban zoo, sitting on 265 acres with over 7,000 animals representing hundreds of species. The Zoo opened in 1899, and its innovative design—keeping animals in their natural habitats, rather than in cages—has been copied worldwide. In recent years the Zoo has become a breeding center for endangered species. Some of its exhibits include the **World of Darkness** (a bat colony), the **Butterfly Zone** (free-flying butterflies), **Wild Asia** (a 40-acre outdoor exhibit viewed by monorail), **Jungle World** (an indoor tropical rain forest), and the **Children's Zoo** (with Prairie Dog Town and a giant spider web). The newest addition is the **Congo Gorilla Forest**, which has over six acres of green play land for African rain-forest animals. The Zoo can be crowded, especially on summer weekends, so plan accordingly.

The **Botanical Garden** (200th Street and Southern Boulevard, 718 817-8700), opened in 1891, was created on 250 acres that the city purchased from the Lorillard family. The Garden's design is based on the Royal Botanical Gardens at Kew, outside London. The **Enid A. Haupt Conservatory** is a spectacular greenhouse inspired by London's Crystal Palace of 1851, a palm court and ten other galleries, including a rain-forest display. The **Everett Children's Adventure Garden** offers many different areas with a variety of activities, including a nature lab to study plants and animals, the Wild Wetland Trail to follow, and gardens with mazes, topiaries and fanciful sculptures to explore. Also on the grounds is the restored

1840 **Snuff Mill**, built by the Lorillard family to grind tobacco with millstones, using the Bronx River's waterpower.

► **Eastern Bronx. Throg's Neck**, a modest residential neighborhood that sits on a peninsula reaching out into Long Island Sound, is named for John Throckmorton, who arrived with a band of followers in 1643 and was chased out by the Native Americans. In the 19th century, wealthy New Yorkers had summer homes here. **Fort Schuyler**, located at the end of Pennsylvania Avenue, was built in 1812 to protect the Sound but was abandoned in 1870; in 1934 it was restored and turned into a maritime college.

Pelham Bay Park was created by the city in 1883. It has over 2,000 acres of salt marsh, lagoon, forest, meadow and seashore, and it is part of the land that Englishman Thomas Pell bought from the Siwanoy Indians in 1654. The **Bartow-Pell Mansion** (895 Shore Road North, 718 885-1461), a Greek Revival stone house, was built there in 1842 by Robert Barton Pell and opened by the city as a museum in 1915. It has ten rooms of period furniture, most of which is on loan from various museums, and a great view of the Sound. **Orchard Beach**, created with sand brought from the Rockaways, is the area's most famous recreational facility. Decades ago, the colonnaded bathhouses of Orchard Beach were dubbed "the Riviera of the Bronx."

Connected to Pelham Bay Park by a bridge is **City Island**, a small (1 1/2 miles long by 1 mile wide!) island with a maritime flavor. It is a quiet village of about 4,000 residents with one main street, many boatyards and marinas, some new condominiums and many seafood restaurants. In 1761, locals built this port to rival New York, and though the scheme failed, the island prospered, supported by the solar saltworks, oystering and shipbuilding industries. Many of the America's Cup defenders have been built by City Island boatyards. The island is also home to the **North Wind Undersea Institute** (610 City Island Avenue, 718 885-0701), which is devoted to preserving marine environments. It is known for its dramatic animal rescues of harbor seals and whales, and its exhibits include whaling artifacts, a mock coral reef and a huge shell collection.

▶ **Riverdale and Wave Hill.** Sometimes called the "Gold Coast" of the Bronx, **Riverdale** is an upper-middle-class neighborhood with old estates and mansions. It runs from the eastern bank of the Hudson River to Van Cortlandt Park, and the Henry Hudson Parkway cuts through it lengthwise. Less expensive high-rise apartment buildings now line the Parkway.

Wave Hill (675 West 252nd Street, 718 549-3200) is a 28-acre estate with two mansions and vast gardens in Riverdale. The mansions were built in the mid-19th and early 20th centuries, and many famous people have lived there, including Theodore Roosevelt, Mark Twain and Arturo Toscanini. Wave Hill was once the official residence of Great Britain's ambassador to the U.N. It offers great views across the Hudson River as well as various cultural events.

▶ **Northern Bronx.** **Van Cortlandt Park** is a huge park with facilities for tennis, golf, running, and other sports. On weekends there are people playing soccer, baseball, cricket and rugby. British sports predominate because the area is home to many West Indians. The Van Cortlandt family, one of New York's first families, lived there from 1646 until 1889, when they donated it to the city. Their home, the **Van Cortlandt House Museum** (718 543-3344), is a 1748 stone manor house and one of the Bronx's oldest buildings. It was used briefly by George Washington as a headquarters during the Revolutionary War. The house is furnished with authentic period Dutch and American pieces.

Woodlawn Cemetery (Jerome Avenue at Bainbridge Avenue, 718 920-0500), located on 400 acres next to Van Cortlandt Park, is where many wealthy New Yorkers are buried. Established in 1863, its elaborate mausoleums are the resting place of Woolworths, Macys, Goulds, and Pulitzers, amongst others.

Norwood, the neighborhood bounded by the Bronx Park, Mosholu Parkway, Woodlawn and Van Cortlandt Park, is also known as "St. Brendan's Parish," because of its mostly Irish population. The **Museum of Bronx History** (3266 Bainbridge Avenue, 718 881-8900) is housed in the Valentine-Varian House, a 1775 fieldstone farmhouse built by Isaac Valentine, a blacksmith. It has prints, paintings, photographs and other artifacts of Bronx history.

Brooklyn

To many people, Brooklyn is a strange place whose residents speak a different, and to some a comic, dialect, pronouncing New York as "Noo Yawk." Brooklynites have strong feelings of pride, nostalgia and chauvinism, their borough being the original home of the Brooklyn Dodgers as well as such famous Americans as Mickey Rooney, Mae West, Woody Allen and Barbra Streisand. In addition to a long and interesting history, Brooklyn has some of the city's loveliest residential areas and worthwhile cultural institutions.

The name Brooklyn comes from the Dutch "Bruecklen," or "broken land." The Dutch West India Company, having purchased the land from the Canarsie Indians, chartered the original town, near Fulton and Smith Streets, in 1646 and incorporated it into Kings County in 1683. The British occupied the area during the Revolutionary War. By 1800, Brooklyn's population had grown to over 4,500, and over 30 percent of its inhabitants were African Americans. Some of the first towns settled by freed slaves were in Brooklyn, which later became a center of the abolitionist movement.

Until 1898, when all of New York City's boroughs were combined into one city, Brooklyn was the third largest city in the country. During Brooklyn's golden years from the late 1800s to the 1920s, the borough had thriving industries, cultural institutions and public works projects. The Depression hit Brooklyn's immigrant residents hard, and many of the more established middle-class families moved further east. Many neighborhoods deteriorated but are now enjoying better times.

►**Fulton Ferry.** Before the Brooklyn Bridge was built, the only way to get from Manhattan to Brooklyn was by boat. As early as 1642, Cornelius Dickerson operated a regular rowboat service, and the Brooklyn landing became a commercial center with taverns,

slaughterhouses and a brewery. After the Battle of Long Island in August 1776, Washington and his troops were ferried across the river from this spot, then known as "Old Ferry," in rowboats. The area was subsequently renamed after Robert Fulton, who introduced steamship service in 1814. Today, **Fulton Ferry** is a lively historic district with a park, refurbished office buildings and restaurants.

The **Brooklyn Bridge** is best experienced by walking across it. Designed by John A. Roebling, a Prussian immigrant, it was the first steel-wire suspension bridge in the world when it opened in 1883. It took 16 years to build, and 21 people died in its construction. The bridge stands 135 feet above the East River and is almost 6,000 feet long. The **Anchorage**, a tall, vaulted space holding the 120,000,000-pound counterweight for the Brooklyn side of the Bridge, is a cool sight, but the only way to see the inside is to go to a performance there.

DUMBO, or Down Under Manhattan Bridge Overpass, is the area between the Brooklyn and Manhattan Bridges. It has big industrial buildings full of crafts workshops and artists' lofts as well as some small businesses. It offers a cool, upward view of the bridge.

▶**Brooklyn Heights.** Brooklyn Heights, an area that became popular shortly after Fulton's ferries made commuting to Manhattan possible, is a beautiful residential area that remains almost exactly as it was built. With over 600 houses and many churches that predate the Civil War, it was designated the city's first historic district in 1965. The section closest to the Bridge, called the North Heights, is a quiet, well-maintained area with sweet street names like Cranberry and Orange. Walt Whitman, W. H. Auden and Arthur Miller were some of its famous residents. Montague Street, a four-block street that runs between the Promenade and the Civic Center, is Brooklyn Heights' commercial center, with cafes, restaurants and shops.

The **Brooklyn Historical Society** (128 Pierrepont Street, 718 624-0890), founded in 1683, has a huge collection of Brooklynalia (including Brooklyn Dodgers memorabilia) in a landmark building.

While some of the Heights' many historic churches have wonderful Tiffany stained-glass windows, a simpler one worth visiting is the **Plymouth Church of the Pilgrims** (Orange Street at Henry Street, 718 624-9385). Lincoln worshipped there, and its preacher, Henry Ward Beecher, was a well-known abolitionist and the brother of Harriet Beecher Stowe. It was also known as the "Grand Central Terminal of the Underground Railroad."

The **Brooklyn Promenade** offers one of the best city views—the Manhattan skyline, the Brooklyn Bridge, the Statue of Liberty—as well as some great people watching. People who work on Montague Street come to eat lunch there; senior citizens chat on benches; Jehovah's Witness bible students stroll. The **Pierrepont Playground** also sits on the Promenade end of Montague Street.

▶ **Civic Center and Downtown.** The Civic Center, devoted to borough affairs today, was formerly the seat of government of the independent city of Brooklyn. **Borough Hall** (209 Joralemon Street at Court Street, 718 875-4047) was built in 1845 as the Brooklyn City Hall and renamed Borough Hall after Brooklyn was consolidated with Manhattan. A marble Greek Revival building, it was renovated in the 1990s. The plaza is a greenmarket on Friday and Saturday. Also visit **Fulton Mall**, a pedestrian shopping area on Fulton Street between Boerum Place and Flatbush Avenue.

▶ **Cobble Hill and Carroll Gardens.** Cobble Hill is a newly gentrified, quiet neighborhood that is north of Red Hook and south of Brooklyn Heights. In colonial times there was a steep hill, "Cobleshill," at Court Street and Atlantic Avenue that was a lookout for American forces during the Revolutionary War. In 1879, a businessman named Alfred Tredway White built 44 homes to house workmen and their families on **Warren Place** (between Warren and Baltic Streets). These landmarked, elaborately ornamented yet compact brick houses line a pedestrian mews with gardens and are now very sought after.

Throughout the years, this area was the home of English, Irish, Swedish, Italian and most recently, Middle Eastern immigrants. Atlantic Avenue, between Court and Hicks Streets, is the center of Brooklyn's Arab population, and Arab bakeries, falafel stands and food and music stores abound, including two of the oldest and most well known establishments, **Sahadi Importing** and **Damascus Bakery**.

Carroll Gardens is not the biggest Italian neighborhood in Brooklyn—Bensonhurst is—but it may be the most well known: *Moonstruck* was filmed there. Even though the area has been gentrified, it is still very Italian. The oldest part of Carroll Gardens, First to Fourth Places between Henry and Smith Streets, was laid out in 1846 in deep blocks so that the houses had both front and back gardens.

In warm weather, you can see elderly residents sitting in folding chairs in their well-maintained gardens and children playing on the quiet streets. **Carroll Park** has bocce games and a playground. You can have coffee at **Sinatra's Museum Caffe Nostalgia**, a shrine to Ol' Blue Eyes.

▶ **Red Hook.** In 1636 the Dutch settled "Roode Hoek" or **Red Hook**, so named for the land's shape and the color of its cranberry bogs. At the beginning of the 20th century, it was a bustling, lively shipping center, populated mostly by Italian and Irish immigrants who worked as longshoremen or ship chandlers. It was on Red Hook's mean streets that Al Capone earned the nickname "Scarface." After World War II, the Brooklyn waterfront began to fade as new container ships went to New Jersey, taking jobs with them. Then, in the 1950s the newly built Brooklyn-Queens Expressway separated Red Hook from shops, subways and the rest of Brooklyn. The neighborhood withered.

Red Hook is now undergoing a resurgence. Artists arrived, attracted by the low rents and loft space, and began to restore the beautiful Civil War–era warehouses. It is particularly festive to visit in summer and is home to the Brooklyn Waterfront Artists Coalition. **The Red Hook Play Center**, built in 1936 and renovated in the 1980s, is a nice playground with a pool.

▶ **Fort Greene.** Fort Greene is bounded by the Navy Yard, Clinton Avenue, Atlantic Avenue and Flatbush Avenue. It is named for Nathanial Greene, a general who supervised the building of Fort Putnam for the Battle of Long Island, and many of its streets are named for Revolutionary War heroes. It is one of Brooklyn's oldest African American neighborhoods; the Hanson Place Baptist Church was a stop on the underground railroad and the Coloured School No. 1 opened in 1847. Currently enjoying a cultural renaissance, the area is home to artists, writers, musicians and movie people. African American–inspired restaurants and stores are plentiful.

Fort Greene Park (formerly Washington Park) sits on the site of a Revolutionary War battle. The park was built in 1850 at the urging of Walt Whitman. **The Prison Ship Martyrs' Monument** was erected there in 1907 to commemorate the awful deaths of 11,500 American soldiers who were imprisoned on wrecked British ships moored just off the shoreline during the Revolutionary War. The park splits Fort Greene in half; to the south are nice, renovated brownstones dating from the 1850s, and to the north are massive public housing projects.

The **Brooklyn Academy of Music**, also known as **BAM** (30 Lafayette Street at Ashland Place, 718 636-4100), provides a cultural focus for the neighborhood. Established in 1861 in Brooklyn Heights, it is the oldest performing arts center in the U.S. BAM moved to its current location in 1907. It is edgy and avant-garde and is home to the Next Wave Festival, the Brooklyn Philharmonic, the BAM Opera and the Cinematheque.

▶ **Sunset Park and Bay Ridge.** **Sunset Park** is named after the park that lies along the Gowanus Bay. In the 1800s Irish Catholics, Poles and especially Scandinavians came for the waterfront economy. It became known as "Little Norway" or "Finntown," and it had public saunas and clean sidewalks. Ralph Kramden of "The Honeymooners" lived there. Fifth, Sixth and Eighth Avenues are the area's business district, which houses many ethnic stores and restaurants, representing the multitude of cultures that live there now.

Greenwood Cemetery was opened in 1840 as an alternative to the city's grim, crowded burial grounds. Amongst some of the famous folk buried in its 478 acres are Louis Comfort Tiffany, Leonard Bernstein, Jean-Michel Basquiat, the Brooks brothers and Boss Tweed.

Bay Ridge is a vast middle-class enclave bounded by the Gowanus Expressway, the Narrows and Gravesend Bay. It was settled by the Dutch in 1662, having been purchased from the Nyack Indians. In the late 1800s the wealthy folks built residences on the high land overlooking the Narrows, and Scandinavians working in the shipbuilding industries built more modest homes. After World War II, Irish and Italian immigrants came, but today there are still numerous Scandinavian stores on Fifth Avenue and on Eighth Avenue between 55th and 59th Streets. Bay Ridge is also known as the setting for the movie *Saturday Night Fever*. The disco scenes were filmed in a disco located at Eighth Avenue and 64th Street.

Fort Hamilton (Shore Road), named after Alexander Hamilton, was built facing Fort Wadsworth on Staten Island in 1825 to protect the entrance to the New York harbor. On the grounds is the **Harbor Defense Museum** (Fort Hamilton Parkway and 101st Street, 718 630-4101), which offers changing exhibitions on military history and is the only military museum in the city.

Named for Giovanni da Verrazano, the Florentine explorer who discovered the New York Bay in 1524, the **Verrazano-Narrows Bridge** may be best known as the start of the New York City Marathon. It was opened in 1964. At that time it was the longest suspension bridge in the world—at 4,260 feet, it is 60 feet longer than the Golden Gate Bridge—and its towers are 70 stories high.

►**Park Slope.** Bordering Prospect Park, **Park Slope** is one of Brooklyn's most popular neighborhoods. It is, actually, three separate neighborhoods. The first and best known, North Slope, between the Park and Sixth Avenue, has great brownstones built by the wealthy during the late 1800s when the Brooklyn Bridge eased commuting to Manhattan. A gentrified, kid-friendly neighborhood, it has a small-town feel, especially around Seventh Avenue, its main shopping street, which is loaded with bakeries, bookstores, toy stores and tony coffee shops. The second area is a "no-man's land" of somewhat dilapidated industry west of Fifth Avenue, and the third is South Slope, near 3rd Street, a working-class district developed in the 19th century for dockworkers.

The **Old Stone House** (J. J. Byrne Park at 3rd Street and Fourth Avenue) has had much history. It was built by the Dutch in 1699, fought over during the first battle of the Revolutionary War, used as a clubhouse by the original Brooklyn (Trolley) Dodgers in 1883 and is now a story-telling place for children.

► **Prospect Park.** Laid out in 1866–67 by Olmsted and Vaux, **Prospect Park** is Central Park's Brooklyn cousin. It is an irregular-shaped 526-acre landscape that offers wonderful activities, outdoor space and a peaceful haven. Although there were some rocky years when crime was a problem, the park is now safer than ever.

All the playgrounds have been recently renovated, including **Tot Spot** (at Garfield Place) and the **Imagination Playground** (at Ocean Avenue).

The northern entrance to the park is at **Grand Army Plaza**, a large oval that has a huge memorial arch honoring the Union dead in the Civil War. From there, you can go to the **Long Meadow**, which, at 75 acres, is the largest open space in any urban park—it is six times bigger than Central Park's Sheep Meadow! Washington's troops camped there in August 1776 during the Battle of Brooklyn, and today people use the space for barbecuing, playing catch, and hanging out.

The **Prospect Park Carousel** (near Empire Boulevard and Flatbush Avenue, 718 965-8999) is one of twelve remaining carousels designed by Charles Carnel. Near the carousel is the **Lefferts Homestead** (Flatbush Avenue, 718 965-6505), an 18th-century Dutch colonial farmhouse that belonged to Peter Lefferts, an affluent farmer who was a delegate to the New York Constitutional Convention in 1788. It is full of exhibits for children, including period rooms and old-fashioned toys and books. It offers workshops, craft demonstrations and storytelling.

The **Prospect Park Wildlife Center** (450 Flatbush Avenue, 718 399-7339) is great for pre-schoolers and young grade-schoolers. There are abstract sculptures, an "Animals in Our Lives" petting zoo, an outdoor Discovery Trail, a small theater where baboons run around, and a prairie dog space, where dogs (and kids) get to go in and out of gopher holes.

▶ Brooklyn Museum of Art, Brooklyn Public Library and Brooklyn Botanic Garden.

A triangle of land bounded by Flatbush Avenue, Eastern Parkway and Washington Avenue, originally named Institute Park, is home to the Brooklyn Museum, the Public Library and the Botanic Garden.

The **Brooklyn Museum of Art** (200 Eastern Parkway, 718 638-5000) was designed by McKim, Mead and White in 1893 as one pavilion of a much larger plan that was never completed. The museum could have used the space, though, because the collection is so large that only six percent of the museum's collection can be exhibited at any given time. The museum's African and Egyptian holdings (fabulous mummy cases) are world famous, as are its 18th and 19th-century American painting collection, which has works by Gilbert Stuart (portraits of Washington) among others. In addition, it has an excellent collection of 19th-century French art. Don't miss the 28 reconstructed rooms from the New York City area, going back to the 17th century and up to the Gilded Age, including John D. Rockefeller's Moorish smoking room. The outdoor sculpture garden is a popular summer spot for jazz concerts.

The **Brooklyn Children's Museum** (145 Brooklyn Avenue, 718 735-4400) is located several blocks to the west of the Brooklyn Museum. The entrance leading to this underground playground is under a 1907 trolley kiosk. The museum, established in 1899, is the world's oldest children's museum and is well known for its pioneering interactive exhibits. Everything in the museum is hands-on and all the exhibits are reached through various passageways, or "people tubes."

Completed in 1941, the **Brooklyn Public Library** (Flatbush Avenue and Eastern Parkway, 718 230-2100) is a wonderful Art Deco structure that is the largest of 53 Brooklyn branches. It has an extensive collection of photographs of Brooklyn and Brooklynites dating back to 1870 and also houses the morgue of the *Brooklyn Eagle*, a newspaper that stopped publication in 1955. Between the Library and the Museum is a playground.

The **Brooklyn Botanic Garden** (1000 Washington Avenue at Eastern Parkway, 718 623-7200) was founded in 1910 as a department of Brooklyn's Institute of Arts and Sciences. It has over 13,000 species of plants in 13 specialized gardens on 52 acres, so there is always something blooming! Its various gardens include the **Cherry Esplanade** (cherry trees from Japan), the heavily perfumed **Fragrance Garden**, the **Shakespeare Garden** (plants mentioned in his plays), the **Japanese Hill and Pond Garden** (a winding garden with a pond that is home to a giant turtle named Godzilla) and the **Children's Garden** (where schoolchildren learn to grow vegetables and flowers). There are several conservatories, including the **Victorian Palm Conservatory** and the **Steinhardt Conservatory**, which houses the Bonsai Museum and the Trail of Evolution. It is best to visit the Garden during the week, when it is less crowded.

▶ **Crown Heights and Bedford-Stuyvesant.** Crown Heights, located between Park Slope and Bedford-Stuyvesant, is home to a longstanding African American population as well as to two other very visible ethnic groups, Hasidic Jews and West Indians. The area has the largest enclave of Lubavitch Hasidim in the city; their headquarters is at 770 Eastern Parkway, and Kingston Avenue is their shopping strip. There are many West Indian restaurants, bakeries and shops along Nostrand and Utica Avenues, and each year there is a West Indian carnival along Eastern Parkway.

Crown Heights is either a corruption of the 19th-century place name "Crow Hill," or a racial slur directed at **Weeksville**, a thriving free-black community of the 19th century. Named for James Weeks, an African American stevedore who bought the land from the Lefferts family in 1838, nine years after slavery was outlawed in New York, Weeksville was a calm and comfortable community and a haven for runaway slaves. Its main street was Hunterfly Road, a colonial highway on which the **Hunterfly Road Historic Houses** (718 756-5250 for an appointment), the only remaining vestiges of Weeksville, are located. These four small, wood-frame houses were saved from demolition in 1968, and supporters are trying to create a historical museum.

By the late 1800s, Crown Heights had also become an upper-middle-class suburb. Its main street, Eastern Parkway, was designed by Olmsted and Vaux in 1866 to be a sister boulevard to Ocean Parkway. Beautiful row houses were built along President Street between Brooklyn and New York Avenues, known as "Doctors' Row." For a good part of the 20th century, the area was a middle-class Jewish neighborhood. Until 1956, Crown Heights was the home of the Brooklyn Dodgers; **Ebbets Field** was situated on the block bounded by Montgomery Street, Sullivan Place and Bedford Avenue. After the Dodgers left, there was some deterioration, but since then the area has been reborn and become vibrant again.

Bedford-Stuyvesant used to be two separate neighborhoods—Bedford and Stuyvesant Heights. Bedford had a large African American population going back to colonial times. After World War I, other ethnic groups joined its African American population, which today is the nation's second largest African American community after Chicago's South Side.

The neighborhood has some carefully maintained brownstones, as well as some unsightly areas. It also has a number of cultural venues, including the **Billie Holiday Theatre** (1368 Fulton Street, 718 636-0918), which produces shows written and performed by African Americans. With 12,000 congregants, the **Concord Baptist Church of Christ** (833 Marcy Avenue, 718 622-1818), which was founded in 1847 by six freed slaves and was the first African American Baptist church in Brooklyn, is the largest African American congregation in the country.

Don't miss the **Magnolia Tree Earth Center** (677 Lafayette Avenue, 718 387-2116), a landmark cultural center. In the 1960s, Hattie Carthan mobilized the neighborhood against deterioration by taking care of a rare 40-foot magnolia tree that had been brought from North Carolina in 1885 and saving the brownstones behind it from demolition.

► **Williamsburg.** **Williamsburg** is a cool, hip neighborhood with a gentrified main street (Bedford Street between North 5th and North 9th Streets) that has cafes, bars, music stores, edgy fashion and antique shops. It is home to many Hispanics (South Williamsburg), Hasidic Jews and young designers, musicians and artists, who came for the cheap loft space available in what were previously small manufacturing or warehousing buildings.

The neighborhood is named for Colonel Jonathan Williams, who surveyed it in 1810; in 1855, it became part of the city of Brooklyn. At that time, it was a fashionable resort area with hotels, clubs and beer gardens, attracting wealthy industrialists and professionals, who built mansions and row houses. When the Williamsburg Bridge opened in 1903, the neighborhood changed—working-class Jews, Italians and Eastern Europeans came from the Lower East Side and wealthy families moved away. Later, Hispanic immigrants came. In 1957, the Brooklyn-Queens Expressway opened and sliced up the area. It wasn't until the 1990s that the neighborhood became revitalized.

The **Williamsburg Art and Historical Center** (135 Broadway, 718 963-1150) offers an eclectic mix of art shows, lectures and concerts. Not to be missed, for those who love their beef, is the historical **Peter Luger Steakhouse** (178 Broadway, 718 387-7400), founded in 1887.

► **Gravesend, Coney Island and Brighton Beach.** Gravesend has the historical distinction of being the only colonial settlement founded by a woman and the only one of Brooklyn's original six towns not founded by the Dutch. The story goes that Lady Deborah Moody Van Sicklen fled England seeking religious freedom and founded Gravesend in 1643, naming it after her hometown. She is buried in a tiny cemetery on Gravesend Neck Road near her house at No. 27 (available to visit by appointment only). Today Gravesend has a large Italian community as well as a close-knit Sephardic Jewish community. The main street, Avenue U, has many ethnic restaurants.

No doubt about it, **Coney Island** is tacky. It has a boardwalk, a beach, a pier, the **New York Aquarium** and a world-famous, old-fashioned amusement park, which actually consists of two separate parks, **Astroland** and **Deno's Wonder Wheel**. The area had its heyday in the early 20th century and declined after World War II, but today its history is attracting renewed interest.

The heart of Coney Island ("Konijn Eiland" or "Rabbit Island" in Dutch) is Surf Avenue. At 1208 Surf Avenue, **Sideshows by the Seashore** offers daily performances by snake charmers, fire-eaters, sword-swallowers and tattooed people. At 1237 Surf Avenue stands **Philip's Candy Store**, which has made candy for over 40 years. At 1310 Surf Avenue is the original **Nathan's Famous Frankfurters**, opened in 1916.

The **Aquarium** (Surf Avenue at 8th Street, 718 265-3474) has more than 10,000 fish, sea mammals and sea birds. Opened in 1896, it is the oldest aquarium in the country and features beluga whales and dolphin and sea lion shows. Recent additions include Discovery Cove, where the water tanks can be touched and a wave crashes overhead, and Sea Cliffs, where penguins, seals and otters can be viewed from below the waterline.

The main attraction at **Astroland** (Surf Avenue at West 12th Street, 718 265-2100) is the **Cyclone**, a landmarked 70-year-old wooden roller coaster, and at **Deno's Wonder Wheel** (Surf Avenue at West

12th Street, 718 372-2592), a 150-foot Ferris wheel opened in 1920. Both parks have lots of other rides. In and around the area are other remnants of the past: the somewhat decrepit elevated subway, the B&B Carousel below it, the dilapidated Thunderbolt roller coaster and the rusted Parachute Jump, built for the World's Fair of 1939.

On Brooklyn's south shore is **Brighton Beach**, or "Little Odessa by the Sea," the home of New York's Russian community since the 1970s. Although it is now a booming enclave with many nightclubs, restaurants and sidewalk cafés offering everything from blintzes to sushi, the area has had its ups and downs. The boardwalk bustles year round with men playing dominoes, children in strollers and cyclists. The main street is Brighton Beach Avenue, located under the elevated subway. Look for the landmark eatery **Mrs. Stahl's Knishery** (1001 Brighton Beach Avenue, 718 648-0210), which sells 20 flavors of this traditional Jewish snack and has been in the same location since the 1940s (and feels and looks that way!).

▶ **Flatlands.** One of the original Dutch towns in Brooklyn dating back to 1666, **Flatlands** takes its name from its terrain, the low coastal plains adjoining salt marshes. It is a primarily residential area with some light industry and is home to several historical structures as well as **Gateway National Recreation Area** (718 338-3338). **Gateway** was established in the 1970s as one of the nation's first urban recreational parks and is the site of **Floyd Bennett Field**, an abandoned airfield with Art Deco buildings. The field is named for the pilot who flew Admiral Byrd over the North Pole in 1926. Other famous aviators who flew from here were Amelia Earhart, Howard Hughes, Beryl Markham and Eddie Rickenbacker. Recently the park was home to various Coast Guard and New York Police Department divisions, and each August it hosts the Brooklyn County Fair. It is one of the few places in Brooklyn where camping is allowed.

Flatlands Dutch Reformed Church (3931 Kings Highway, 718 252-5540) dates back to 1654 and is one of three churches in Brooklyn established by Peter Stuyvesant. The **Pieter Claesen Wyckoff House** (5902 Clarendon Road, 718 629-5400) one of the oldest wooden buildings in the country, was built in 1652 by an indentured servant who later became a magistrate and rose to wealth and prominence. The Dutch Colonial farmhouse remained in the family until 1902 and was restored by the city in the 1980s.

Queens

To the east of Manhattan is Queens, the city's great middle-class borough, where hardworking immigrant groups have colonized its mostly residential neighborhoods. It is the city's largest borough, occupying one-third of the city's total area, and the second most populous borough (after Brooklyn). Queens' neighborhoods are still identified by the names of the various villages that existed before they were merged into New York City in 1898. Some areas have a very suburban feel, with detached houses, nice gardens and garages, while others are at the poorer end of the economic scale.

The first inhabitants of Queens were the Rockaway Indians. The Dutch arrived in 1635 and purchased the land from the Rockaways in 1639. In 1863, the county was named Queens in honor of Queen Catherine, the wife of King Charles II. The area was mostly farmland until the Queensboro Bridge was built in 1909, whereupon commercial centers grew up throughout the borough at the crossroads of earlier towns.

▶ **Long Island City**. Long Island City was a manufacturing area and transportation hub, with rail yards and factories. Local workers lived in the Queensbridge Houses, a large public housing project with 3,161 apartments in 26 buildings on 62 acres. Today the area's industrial buildings have been rehabilitated and are now home to design-oriented businesses, cultural centers and young artists. One such center, the **P.S. 1 Contemporary Art Center** (22-25 Jackson Avenue, 718 784-2084), housed in a 100-year-old schoolhouse with a large outdoor courtyard, supports artists who are producing art that is not traditionally shown in museums. Long Island City is also the home of the **Museum of Modern Art** while the Manhattan location undergoes a renovation (see page 91).

The peaceful **Isamu Noguchi Garden Museum** (32-7 Vernon Boulevard at 33rd Road, 718 204-7088) holds over 300 of Noguchi's works, including his well-known light sculptures (which look like Japanese paper lanterns), his theatrical sets and his stone sculptures, which are set in a serene garden. Not far away is the **Socrates Sculpture Park** (31-42 Vernon Boulevard at Broadway, 718 956-1819), a four-acre park on the East River. Formerly a shipyard, the site was converted to an outdoor sculpture park in the 1980s and offers changing exhibits of public sculpture in a variety of media, as well as a terrific view of Manhattan.

▶ **Astoria.** Long home to a large Greek community, **Astoria's** population has in recent years become more diverse. Today, many ethnic groups call this neighborhood home, but Greek restaurants, delis and shops still dominate 31st Street, the area's main commercial street.

Astoria was the movie capital of the country until the industry headed west to Hollywood in the 1920s. Not only is the **Kaufman-Astoria Studio** (35th Avenue at 36th Street, 718 392-5600) a working film and television studio, but the complex is also the site of the **American Museum of the Moving Image** (718 784-0077). Housed in an old silent-movie studio once used by Paramount, the museum offers displays of still photos, posters, movie-related collectibles and objects used in making films. In addition, "Tut's Fever" Movie Palace is a little theater playing vintage films. Not to be missed is "Behind the Screen," a hands-on experience in creating movies.

▶ **Steinway.** Steinway, just east of Astoria, is named for William Steinway of piano fame. The **Steinway Piano Factory** (19th Avenue and 38th Street, 718 721-2600), opened in the 1880s, is still making pianos. Make an appointment to tour the factory for a close-up view of the craftsmen at work. Steinway created a company town, with low-income housing, a park, a library, a school and ball fields.

The 1726 **Lent Homestead** (78-03 19th Road at 78th Street) is one of the oldest dwellings in Queens. Built by Abraham Lent, the grandson of Abraham Riker (who owned Riker's Island), it is a Dutch-style farmhouse that has been modernized. The bridge to

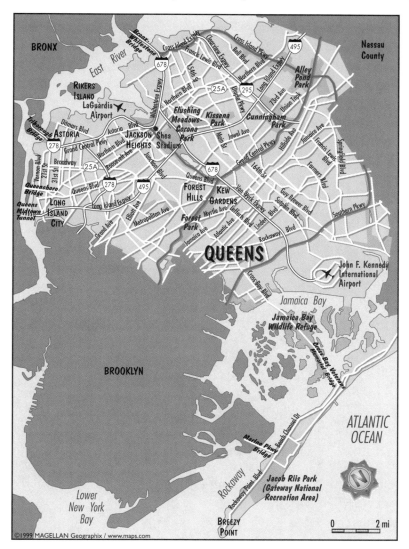

©1999 MAGELLAN Geographix / www.maps.com

Riker's Island, the site of several penal institutions, is located at 19th Avenue and Hazen Street, but it is not accessible to the public.

► **Ridgewood.** Founded by Dutch farmers in the 17th century, **Ridgewood** was industrialized in the early 1900s. A number of Ridgewood's brown and yellow brick townhouses have been placed on the National Register of Historic Places. The **Vander-Enke Onderdonk House** (1820 Flushing Avenue, 718 456-1776) is a 1709 stone farmhouse that has been restored and turned into a museum and cultural center.

► **Corona.** Some of Queens' most popular attractions are in **Corona**. Settled in the 17th century by Dutch and English farmers, it took its name in 1870. The **Flushing Meadows-Corona Park** sits on over 1,200 acres of what was once salt marsh, along what was once the Flushing River. It was the site of two World's Fairs, in 1939–40 and 1964–65. Some of the structures from those fairs remain, including the **Unisphere**, built by U.S. Steel as the 1964–1965 fair's symbol and still the largest globe in the world and the remnants of the fair's New York Pavilion (featured in the film *Men in Black*).

The old New York City Building, used for both fairs, now houses the **Queens Museum of Art** (718 592-9700), which boasts a large collection of 20th-century art by New York artists, including some great Tiffany lamps. The museum's most famous exhibit is the **Panorama of New York City**, a huge, 3-D recreation of the New York skyline that is kept up-to-date. It is the world's largest scale model, filling a room the size of two basketball courts, and kids love to pick out familiar landmarks.

The **New York Hall of Science** (47-01 111th Street, 718 699-0005) is housed in what was once the World's Fair Space Center and is one of the top hands-on science centers in the U.S. It has more than 185 exhibits on physics, biology and technology and is full of really fun, quick activities. Near the Hall is the **Queens Wildlife Center** (718 271-1500), a smart little zoo with a focus on North American species. It has a geodesic dome by Buckminster Fuller that is now the aviary, a pretty walking trail and a mini-farm with domestic animals that kids can feed.

Another Corona attraction is **Louis Armstrong's House** (65-30 Kissena Boulevard, 718 478-8274), where Louis and his wife, Lucille, lived from 1943 until their deaths. The house and furnishings have been preserved as a museum.

▶ **Whitestone.** Whitestone, located on Long Island Sound, was named for a big white boulder that stood at the landing place. It was settled in 1645 by Dutch farmers who paid the Indians one axe for each 50 acres of land. In 1735 a large clay deposit was discovered, and the area became a manufacturing site for pottery and clay pipes. Today, it is a pleasant residential neighborhood with a nice park, **Francis Lewis Park**, at the footings of the Whitestone Bridge. The **Hammerstein House** (168-11 Powell's Cove Road) was built by Arthur Hammerstein, an uncle of Oscar's, in 1923. He named it "Wildflower," after a hit Broadway musical that he produced.

▶ **Little Neck.** Little Neck, a small residential town on Long Island Sound, is where the clams got their name. It is also home to the **Queens County Farm Museum** (73-50 Little Neck Parkway, 718-347-3276), a working 18th-century farm. There are fields, orchards, barns and a three-room frame house built in 1772, which has period rooms and changing exhibitions on agriculture. The museum has daily demonstrations of farm life from that time.

▶ **Flushing** is a bustling, stable community that is home to a large Asian population. First settled in 1642, its name is a corruption of the Dutch "Vlissingen," a town in Holland from which some of the earliest settlers came, seeking religious freedom. In the 19th century it was a summer colony and pleasant residential area until the subway and then the highways built for the 1939 World's Fair led to rapid development.

Historic sites are plentiful in Flushing. The **Bowne House** (37-01 37th Avenue, 718 359-0528), an English-style farmhouse built by John Bowne in 1661, is the oldest house in Queens. Bowne lived there, using it as a Quaker meeting house in defiance of Peter Stuyvesant and the Dutch Reform Church. Stuyvesant had him arrested, but the Dutch West India Company ordered him to be freed, upholding the principle of religious freedom. Nine generations of Bowne's family lived there until 1945, when it became a museum, offering visitors a view of period rooms and changing exhibits.

Nearby is the **Friends Meeting House** (137-16 Northern Boulevard, 718 358-9636), a simple wooden structure built in 1694. It has been used for Quaker services continuously since then, except during the British occupation from 1776 to 1783. Another Quaker, Charles Dougherty, built the 1785 **Kingsland Homestead** (143-35 37th Avenue, 718 939-0647), which now houses the **Queens Historical Society**. The Society exhibits memorabilia from the home's residents, including photos, a Victorian period room and changing exhibits on Queens history. Next to the house is Queens' most famous tree, a weeping beech planted in 1847.

The **Queens Botanical Garden** (43-50 Main Street, 718 886-3800) comprises 39 acres, including a 22-acre arboretum. It has a Wedding Garden for marriage ceremonies, a rose garden and an ethnic garden, with plants from the various countries represented in this diverse community.

▶ **Jamaica.** Originally settled by the English, most of southern Queens was originally within the boundaries of **Jamaica**. The origin of its name is unknown, although the accepted source is the Algonquin name for beaver. In the early 18th century, Jamaica was at the intersection of major roads and became a trading center for Long Island farmers taking their produce to Brooklyn and Manhattan. With the arrival of the railroad and the subways by 1920, the area really started to develop, hitting its commercial peak in the 1930s and 1940s. After that, the middle class moved east, and Jamaica began to deteriorate a bit. South Jamaica still suffers from bad economic conditions while North Jamaica, in particular Jamaica Estates, a wealthy neo-Tudor community developed in 1903, is prospering.

The main commercial district is on Jamaica Avenue, between Sutphin Boulevard and 171st Street. The **Jamaica Arts Center** (161-04 Jamaica Avenue at 161st Street, 718-658-7400) is a community gallery for local artists, offering changing exhibits. The **Prospect Cemetery** (159th Street and Beaver Road) was established in 1669 and is the oldest public burial ground in Queens. **St. John's University** is a Roman Catholic college founded in 1870 by Vincentian fathers.

⅏ Staten Island

Staten Island, measuring 13.9 miles long and 7.3 miles wide, is perhaps the most suburban of New York City's boroughs. Geographically, it is more like part of New Jersey, because it is only 500 feet across the river from Linden and Perth Amboy and over 20 miles from Manhattan. In 1609 Henry Hudson, who was on a voyage for the Dutch West India Company, named it "Staaten Eylandt."

For many years the island remained very rural. After the ferry service was started, Staten Island grew as a seaside resort, especially New Brighton, where the hotels attracted prominent New Yorkers. Then, when the Verrazano Narrows Bridge was built in the 1960s, the island became more accessible, and low-income apartment complexes and houses were built. Staten Island's population topped 400,000 in the 1990s, and its minority and immigrant populations have grown tremendously, especially on the more urban northern shore.

► **St. George.** The Staten Island ferry docks at **St. George.** The terminal was moved there in 1883 by Erastus Wiman, a businessman who thought the new location would shorten the commute to Manhattan. Wiman named the village after George Law, from whom he bought the land. Once a seaside boomtown, St. George is the seat of borough government. Just past the ferry terminal is **Borough Hall**, a 1906 Carrere and Hastings building that houses courts as well as historical exhibits. Near the police station is the **Staten Island Institute of Arts and Sciences** (75 Stuyvesant Place, 718 727-1135), which has more than two-million items in its collection, some dating back to 1881, including photos, paintings, sculpture and examples of the decorative arts.

► **New Brighton.** In the 1880s **New Brighton** was a beautiful seaside resort dotted with impressive Greek Revival mansions that stood along Richmond Terrace (which borders the northern shoreline, overlooking the Kill van Kull). One of these mansions, the John Neville residence, later became a home for aged sailors and, more recently, the **Snug Harbor Cultural Center** (1000 Richmond Terrace, 718 448-2500). The center has several cultural attractions: the **Newhouse Center for Contemporary Art** (718 448-2500), a community gallery; the **Staten Island Children's Museum** (718 273-2060), an interactive kids' museum; and the **Staten Island Botanical Garden** (718 273-8200), which has a number of specialized gardens (including a traditional Chinese Scholar's Garden) and a lush orchid greenhouse.

A bit further inland is the **Staten Island Zoological Park** (614 Broadway, 718 442-3100), which is known for its great reptile collection. It also has an aquarium, an aviary and a special program called "Breakfast with Beasts."

▶ **Rosebank.** Rosebank is bounded by the Staten Island Expressway, Hylan Boulevard, Vanderbilt and Bay Streets. Its first settlers were Dutch farmers, and beginning in the 1830s it became a summer community for wealthy Manhattanites. In the late 1800s, Irish immigrants fleeing the potato famine arrived. It has long been a predominantly Italian, blue-collar neighborhood. The **Garibaldi-Meucci Museum** (420 Tompkins Avenue, 718 442-1608) is located in an 1845 farmhouse that was home to two famous Italians: Antonio Meucci, the inventor of a prototype phone, lived here with Giuseppe Garibaldi, the Italian hero who was exiled here after the collapse of the Republic in 1845. The museum has exhibits on their lives, including photos, letters and memorabilia.

A reminder of Rosebank's earlier prosperity can be found at the **Alice Austen House** (2 Hylan Boulevard, 718 816-4506), a Gothic Revival cottage located on the waterfront and presenting a beautiful view of the Narrows. Austen was one of America's finest early women photographers. She began taking photos at age ten and never stopped. The museum preserves her home and her work.

▶ **Dongan Hills**. Bounded by Richmond Road and Todt Hill Road, **Dongan Hills** is one of the most affluent residential areas on the island; its large houses supplant what were once grand estates. In the 17th century it was a mining town named for Thomas Dongan, then governor of New York. The **Billiou-Stillwell-Perine House**

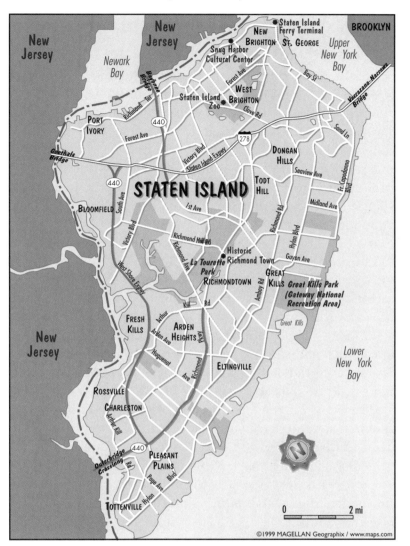

©1999 MAGELLAN Geographix / www.maps.com

(1476 Richmond Road, 718 987-9336, by appointment) is the oldest surviving building on Staten Island and one of the oldest house museums. The original stone farmhouse was built in the 1660s, and additions were constructed over the next 150 years.

The **Jacques Marchais Museum of Tibetan Art** (338 Lighthouse Avenue, 718 987-3500) actually resembles a Tibetan monastery and contains the largest private collection of Tibetan art outside Tibet. Jacques Marchais is really Mrs. Harry Klauber, a dealer in Oriental art.

▶ **Historic Richmond Town.** Historic Richmond Town (441 Clarke Avenue, 718 351-1611) is like a "mini-Williamsburg" of the north, with 28 restored buildings encompassing a 100-acre area in La Tourette Park. The village dates back to 1690 when it was called "Cocclestown," probably because of the oysters and clams found nearby. In 1729 this centrally located village became the seat of county government. The British occupied it during the Revolutionary War during which time its name was changed to Richmondtown.

In the 1830s New York City experienced rapid growth and Staten Island became a desirable suburban retreat as well as a site for new industries. A civic center was built in Richmondtown to accommodate this development. Its buildings include a Greek Revival courthouse (now the **Visitor Center**) and the Richmond County Clerk's and Surrogate's Office (now the **Staten Island Historical Museum**, whose permanent exhibition shows the evolution of the borough).

A number of the buildings lining the village's small streets have been brought from other parts of the island, but most were original to the site. Among the structures are the 1695 **Voorlezer House** (the oldest surviving elementary school in the country), the 1670 **Britton Cottage**, the 1740 **Guyen-Lake-Tysen House** (a beautiful Dutch colonial home), the 1839 **Bennet House** (now a museum of childhood—visit the toy room), the 1860 **Ettingville Store** (a one-room country store with a printing press), the 1810 **Basketmaker's House** and many others. There are costumed staffpersons and craft demonstrations, and kids can run in and out of the houses.

▶ **Tottenville.** At the southernmost tip of New York is **Tottenville**, a working class, mostly Italian neighborhood of about 5,000. Home to many city workers, including police officers and firefighters, it sometimes takes up to two hours to get to Manhattan. Today the wooded blocks are lined with old bungalows, and its streets are named after families who still live nearby. Main Street is a throwback to an earlier, quieter time, with tree-lined, 19th-century houses with gingerbread ornamentation.

Tottenville played an important part in American history. In September 1776 Benjamin Franklin, John Adams, Edward Rutledge and Sir William Howe, the Commander of the British troops, held what was ultimately an unsuccessful peace conference there. The meeting took place in a stone house by the sea, the **Billop House** (7455 Hylan Boulevard, 718 984-2086), originally named for its first owner, Christopher Billop, who built it in 1680. After the meeting, the house became known as **Conference House**. It fell into disrepair but has been restored, and guided tours are available.

▶ **Charleston, Rossville and Travis.** These sections are in the western lowlands of Staten Island. In the 19th century, **Charleston** was called Kreischerville, after Balthazar Kreischer, who discovered clay deposits in 1854 and built a brick-making factory. The **Kreischer House** (4500 Arthur Kill Road), a Victorian Gothic structure built in 1885, still stands. The Kreischer family also built housing and a church for its employees. The clay pits are to the east of Arthur Kill Road and are now part of the **Clay Pits Ponds State Park** (718 967-1976), a 250-acre preserve.

RESOURCES

Tours

Guided Walking Tours

92nd Street Y, 996-1100. Huge selection of different walks.

A La Carte New York, 410-2698. Customized, special walking tours.

Adventures on a Shoestring, 265-2663. Ninety-minute tours of New York and surrounding areas, like the "Hell's Kitchen Hike" and the "World of Edith Wharton."

Architectural City Tours, 800 557-2176, www.artandarchitecture.com. Educational tours led by architectural historians and local writers.

ARTime, 718-797-1573. Walking tours focused on exploring the fine arts, going to museums, galleries and other showcases. Good for children who are interested in art.

Big Apple Greeter, 669-8159, www.bigapplegreeter.org. Non-profit volunteer group that operates through the Manhattan Borough President's Office offers personalized tours based on visitor request, matching knowledgeable New Yorkers with visitors.

Big Onion Walking Tours, 439-1090, www.bigonion.com. Variety of tours from simple neighborhood tours to in-depth historic and ethnic surveys to multiethnic eating tours of particular neighborhoods led by graduate students. For children 8+.

Bravo New York, 718 834-8655. Customized tours.

Central Park Conservancy, 360-2727. One-hour tours that explore the history, ecology and design of Central Park, guided by New York City Park Rangers, skilled birders and other park experts.

ChinatownNYC.com Walking Tours, 571-2016, www.chinatownnyc.com. Tours of Chinatown, which can be customized to include a feast in a Chinese restaurant.

CityWalks, 989-2456. Private tours focusing on the history and architecture of lower Manhattan, especially Chelsea, Greenwich Village, the Lower East Side and the Financial District. It is highly regarded and expensive and may not be interesting to small children.

Discovery Tour, 665-8363. Various tours of historic districts and trendy areas in Harlem, Brooklyn, the Bronx and Queens.

Foods of New York Walking and Eating Tours, 732 636-4650. Two-hour tours of the food, landmarks, music and culture of Greenwich Village. Participants visit 18 eating establishments and sample food from six.

Harlem Heritage Tours, 280-7888, www.harlemheritage.com. Variety of tours of Harlem including Sunday church-service tours.

Harlem Spirituals, 391-0900, www.harlemspirituals.com. Multilingual tours of all boroughs, specializing in tours focused on historical sites in Harlem, African American culture, jazz and gospel, Sunday church-service tours and Saturday night soul-food tours. Its New York Visions division offers tours of various ethnic neighborhoods outside Manhattan.

Harlem Your Way, 690-1687. Tours of Harlem focusing on African American culture, jazz and gospel, including Sunday church-service tours.

Hassidic Tours, 718 953-5244, www.jewishtours.com. Tours of Crown Heights conducted by Hassidic guides, including a visit to a synagogue and a meal in a kosher eatery.

I'll Take Manhattan Walking Tours, 732 270-5277, www.nycwalks.com. Two- to three-hour tours of various Manhattan neighborhoods.

Joyce Gold History Tours of New York, 242-5762, www.nyctours.com. Variety of tours of New York City neighborhoods. Customized tours available.

Lower East Side Shopping Tours, 888 VALUES 4 (800 825-8374). Tour of the discount shopping area of the Lower East Side. Departs from Katz's

Deli (Ludlow and East Houston Streets) at 11 a.m. Sundays from April to December.

Mainly Manhattan Tours, 755-6199. Weekend tours of Greenwich Village, the Upper West Side and the theater district.

Municipal Art Society, 439-1049, www.mas.org. "Discover New York" program, a diverse year-round roster of tours examining the history and culture of various neighborhoods.

Museum of the City of New York, 534-1672. Occasional and fascinating arts-oriented tours of historic Harlem, etc.

New York City Discovery Tours, 465-3331. Choice from among some 60-odd tours, ranging from "Historic Taverns" to "John Lennon's New York."

New York Historical Society, 673-3400. Summer weekend walking tours through Central Park.

New York Talks and Walks, 888 377-4455, www.newyorktalksandwalks.com. Ethnic and historical tours, such as "Hidden Treasures of Chinatown" and the "Jewish Gangster Tour." Child-friendly tours are also available.

NYC Cultural Walking Tours, 979-2338. Architecture and design tours of Manhattan neighborhoods. A popular tour is "Gargoyles in Manhattan."

Rock and Roll Tours of New York, 807-7625. Customized nostalgia tours, showing where the Beatles, for example, stayed, ate and sang.

Sidewalks of New York, 517-0201. Tours of the haunts and homes of famous writers and artists.

Small Journeys, Inc., 874-7300. Customized, expensive ($250+), walking or driving tours.

Times Square Tours, 226 West 42nd Street. Tours of the Times Square area led by actor/guides. Tours start at noon on Fridays at the Times Square Visitors Center.

Townhouse Tours, 347 693-1484, www.townhousetours.com. Various scheduled and customized tours.

Urban Park Rangers, 427-4040. Weekend walking tours through Central Park and other green areas in all five boroughs. Known for their great guides.

Wildman Steve Brill's Food and Ecology Tours, 718 291-6825. Four-hour tours of parks focusing on plant life. Brill was once arrested for eating dandelions in New York.

Self-Guided Tours

Chinatown History Project, 70 Mulberry Street, 619-4785. Publishes a walking tour guidebook of the neighborhood and offers the occasional guided tour.

Heritage Trails, 26 Wall Street, 466-3600, 888 4-TRAILS (800 487-2457), www.heritagetrails.org. This non-profit state foundation publishes a $2 booklet full of interesting historical information. Colored dots on the sidewalk define pedestrian routes past landmarks discussed in the booklet.

Bus Tours

As Scene on TV Tours, 410-9830. Visits places used as exterior settings for television shows. Tours depart from Times Square Visitors Center.

Gray Line Tours, 800 669-0051, 397-2600, www.graylinenewyork.com. Variety of different tours lasting from two hours to all day, including the Grand Tour, the Lower Manhattan Loop, the Upper Manhattan Loop and the "Total New York," a 2-day tour with free admission to the Statue of Liberty and the Empire State Building. Participants can hop on and off. The buses pick up at major hotels as well as near the Port Authority.

Hasidic Tours, 718 953-5244. Tours designed to familiarize people with the Crown Heights area of Brooklyn and to educate them about Hasidic Jews.

Kramer's Reality Tour, 800 KRAMERS (800 572-6377), www.kennykramer.com. Three-hour multimedia tour offered by Kenny Kramer, the real life person on whom the "Seinfeld" character is based, of the "Seinfeld" universe, including the Soup Nazi, Monk's Restaurant and Joe's Produce.

New York Apple Tours, Eighth Avenue and 53rd Street, 800 876-9868, www.nyappletours.com. Variety of narrated tours on red London-style double-decker buses, offering hop on–hop off service.

New York Double Decker, 967-6008, www.nydecker.com. Variety of tours run like a shuttle service, leaving from various hotels every half hour.

Boat Tours

Chelsea Screamer, Pier 62 at West 23rd Street, 924-6262. One hour speed-boat cruise around lower Manhattan.

Circle Line, Pier 83 at West 42nd Street, 563-3200, www.circleline.com, www.ridethebeast.com. Three-hour tour around Manhattan—down the Hudson River past the Statue of Liberty, back up the East River along the Upper East Side, through the Spuyten-Duyvil Creek and back down the Hudson. One-hour Liberty Cruise (great for kids) past the monuments. The Circle Line also runs "The Beast" speedboat, which travels at over 50 miles per hour.

Express Navigation Cruises, 800 262-8743. Seventy-five-minute tours of the harbor.

NY Waterways, Pier 78 at 38th Street or Pier 17 at the South Street Seaport, 800 533-3779, www.nywaterway.com. Ninety-minute tour, offering views of the Statue of Liberty and other sights. It also runs special baseball cruises to Yankees and Mets games and music cruises featuring disco and show tunes. Its boats are new and clean. Free bus pick-up from various sites around town.

Pioneer, Pier 16 at the South Street Seaport, 748-8590. Two-hour harbor cruise leaving several times a day on a historic schooner.

Seaport Liberty Cruises, Pier 16 at the South Street Seaport, 630-8888. Narrated one-hour harbor cruises (good for smaller children) and jazz cruises around the Statue of Liberty and Ellis Island.

Spirit Cruises, Chelsea Piers, 201 867-8307. Various packages touring the major sites.

World Yacht Cruises, Pier 81 at West 41st Street, 630-8100, 800 498-4270, www.worldyacht.com. Have dinner (three hours) or Sunday brunch (two hours) while cruising around Manhattan.

Helicopter/Seaplane Tours

Island Helicopter Sightseeing, 564-9290. Tours from Monday through Friday, weather permitting, including occasional night flights. Multilingual staff.

Liberty Helicopter Tours, 967-6464, www.libertyhelicopters.com. Various tours of Manhattan.

Sea Air, 684-5959. Thirty-minute seaplane tour of Manhattan.

Websites

General

www.allny.com

www.citidex.com

www.citysearch.com

www.cityguideny.com

www.digitalcity.com

www.go-newyorkcity.com

www.fieldtrip.com/ny/index

www.nps.gov
(national parks service)

www.nyc.com

www.nyc.gov
(official website of New York City)

www.nyc-arts.org

www.nycparks.org

www.nyctourism.com

www.nycvisit.com

www.nytoday.com

www.preserve.org

Manhattan

www.centralpark.org

www.columbusavenuebid.org

www.downtownnny.com

www.grandcentralpartnership.org

www.greenwich-village.com

www.lincolnbid.com

www.morningsideheights.com

www.orchardstreet.org

www.rioc.com
(Roosevelt Island info)

www.timessquare.com

www.unionsquarenyc.org

www.villagealliance.org

The Bronx

www.ilovethebronx.com

www.bronxarts.org

Brooklyn

www.astroland.com

www.brooklynart.org

www.brooklynonline.com

www.brooklynx.org

www.coneyislandusa.com

www.tasteofbrooklyn.com

www.wonderwheel.com

Queens

www.noguchi.org

www.nyhallsci.org

www.ps1.org

www.queensmuse.org

Staten Island

www.si-web.com

www.statenislandonline.com

www.statenislandusa.com

Chapter 5

THAT'S ENTERTAINMENT

W hile visitors are certainly often entertained by the theater that presents itself daily on the streets of New York, most will want to attend a professional performance at some point. Indeed, it is hard to imagine being in New York City without sampling its theater, dance, music or film. At the top of the list for most visitors are Broadway shows and concerts or performances at the major institutions such as Lincoln Center and Carnegie Hall. These are wonderful places to start, but they are by no means the only offerings available in a city that is home to an amazing and varied creative community.

Among the entertainment options for grownups are many which are appropriate also for children. Older children and teenagers in particular will both enjoy and understand a wide variety of performances that are primarily geared to adults. Younger children on the other hand, who may enjoy being taken to a performance, especially if it is in the evening and will extend their bedtimes, may not actually appreciate the content of what they are attending and become easily bored and cranky.

Happily, there is something for everyone in New York City. In addition to Manhattan's 39 Broadway theaters, there are at least 125 Off-Broadway performance venues and countless Off-Off-Broadway performance spaces hosting more than one-thousand annual productions. From marathon esoteric performance art happenings to 20-minute puppet shows for the pre-verbal, if it can be done on stage, on film or outdoors, it is probably here.

There is no magic to finding entertainment in New York City that will be suitable for the kids and pleasant for you. Like most other aspects of planning your time in the Big Apple, the answer lies in doing your research and being realistic about what you and your young charges can handle and will enjoy. In this chapter, we will help you do just that and direct you to a variety of arenas for theater, dance, music, film, seasonal attractions, circuses and other performances. What is not included in this chapter is information about sporting events, museum programs, arcades and other "boredom busters," all of which can be found in Chapter 6.

At the end of this chapter, you will find everything indexed by category. Now, let's put on a show!

Tripping the Light Fantastic

New York City has a huge selection of shows performed by professionals and geared for audiences of children, presenting wonderful opportunities to expose children to the arts. There is a vast array of alternatives, including puppet shows, plays, dance performances, storytelling, films, all kinds of music, mime and even stand-up comedy by and for children. In addition to providing an introduction to cultural pursuits, taking your children to a performance provides a wonderful opportunity to introduce them to many new concepts, such as being in a dark theater, focusing on a performance, listening and observing, doing without food and drink for a period of time, keeping quiet and, when they need to talk, remembering to whisper.

New York has an abundance of talented performers who mount children's productions. The beauty of these performances is that they are created to appeal to the younger set. They are typically short, the stories are not too complex, they are scheduled at child-appropriate times and they often include elements of audience participation or interaction. While children's shows are not always the most interesting to parents, they are usually very appealing to your children and provide a great introduction to various forms of performing arts.

In addition to the performances created specifically for children, there are many other performances put on by the major adult-oriented cultural institutions of the city (such as opera and dance companies) exclusively arranged for children. Sometimes, productions that are otherwise primarily directed at adult audiences may offer tickets to dress rehearsals or other less formal previews that are suitable for children to attend. These options represent a perfect transition from the purely child-oriented performances to big-time city culture, which can otherwise often create culture shock for your children. Generally the harsh reality of grownup show protocol and the length of grownup performances can be quite difficult for kids and parents alike without some advance preparation.

▶ **Theater etiquette for kids.** Gone are the days when children were to be seen and not heard. In those times, a conversation about children's behavior at a performance was academic as there were so few performances at which children were permitted. Today, however, we have become quite accustomed to introducing our children to the arts ever earlier, and more and more performances are accessible to the younger set.

That said, it is important to make sure that when children attend performances they know the basics, such as not talking during the performance, using the restroom before the show begins or during intermission, not eating in theaters where food is not permitted and so forth. Adults taking children to performances should also try to remember to be considerate of other audience members and deal with noisy, unhappy, scared, tired, crying or overly fidgety children by promptly taking them out of the theater. While of course it is difficult to deal with an unhappy child you have brought to a show, your audience neighbors are far less likely to be tolerant if their own enjoyment of the show is disrupted.

The best way to insure a successful trip to a performance is to be sensitive to the suggested age recommendations. Your preschool child may indeed enjoy pieces of *A Midsummer Night's Dream*, but the attention span of a three-year-old rarely holds for the number of hours required to sit through the entire performance. Even a child who seems mature is likely not to understand or appreciate a performance that is above his or her head. It is useful to familiarize yourself with the content of a performance you plan on attending so that you do not end up at a show that is not appropriate for your child.

The best way to insure a successful trip to a performance is to be sensitive to the suggested age recommendations.

While age-appropriate children's programming is the most likely to provide a positive experience for adult and child alike, if you are considering taking your child to an event or performance not particularly geared to children, your child will most likely be welcome as long as you are respectful and considerate of others. This requires a lot of effort because it is often difficult to contain an active, curious child or keep his or her interest during an activity not inherently interesting to children. At the same time, it is not fair to others to let your child run wild in an adult environment.

So what do you do when you want to take your child to something more adult? The most important thing is to be realistic about both what you think your child can handle and how hard you are prepared to work to make the outing pleasant for you and your child. It is no fun to spend your leisure time and dollars trying to keep your unhappy children in their seats, and it is no fun for your children to be yelled at for doing what kids do. Even an activity that is family oriented, such as the circus, can make you feel as if you are being fed to the lions if the children get bored.

You can also call in advance of attending to find out whether it is appropriate to bring children at all, and if you are told no, listen to that advice. If your child cannot make it through the entire performance, the grownups in the group can take turns watching the show while one takes the children outside. You can also bring distractions, in the form of food, toys, books, or anything else your child will enjoy and that will buy you some time, provided that they are not prohibited in the theater and will not disturb other patrons. If your child is not doing well and is becoming disruptive and unhappy, be prepared to leave, regroup and try again another time.

When you do venture beyond the kid-oriented selection of performances to bring your child to a grownup show, a few tricks may keep potential disaster at bay. Children under eight usually do not last more than an hour and a half, so be prepared to leave at intermission. Unless your children are quite used to staying up late, when possible get tickets for a matinee rather than an evening performance. If you must go in the evening, try to avoid Friday and Saturday nights. Try to get aisle seats so that if you have to get up, you can escape without requiring the entire row to get up with you. Bring lifesavers or other "quiet" candy that can buy you some time until intermission or the end of the show.

Parents often ask whether children need to dress up when attending live performances. When attending children's shows, your kids will definitely find informal, casual dress appropriate. When taking children to Broadway shows, evening performances or other special events, it is always nice to recognize the occasion by having the children dress in other than playclothes. While there are typically no official dress codes for theaters and other performance spaces, it helps children understand that there is a standard of behavior and attention required at performances if they dress for the event.

A final word—do not forget to turn off your cell phones and beepers during the performance!!

▶ **How to find out what is going on around town.** To find out about concerts, theater, and other performances or cultural activities geared to children, the best sources are the local newspapers. The *New York Times* Friday Weekend section contains listings of family activities. You can also check the other local papers, the *Daily News*, the *Post* and the weekly *Observer*, for listings. Even the *Wall Street Journal* may contain information about particular local events for kids. The city's weekly magazines, *New York*, *Time Out New York* and the *Village Voice*, contain family entertainment listings. The weekly *New Yorker* occasionally contains listings for families.

The local parent publications, *New York Family, Big Apple Parent Paper, PARENTGUIDE* and *Family Entertainment Guide*, all contain extensive listings of activities and events for children. These free publications can be found in bookstores, children's stores and libraries. You can subscribe to these publications, order copies of particular issues or visit their websites if you are unable to obtain copies elsewhere. Information about these and other publications is in the resource section at the end of this chapter.

The museums frequently organize children's programs, as do other metropolitan cultural institutions (for example, Carnegie Hall, Lincoln Center, City Center). Some programs are single-performance events and others are part of longer series. See Chapter 6 for a list of city museums.

To find out about special events in the city's parks, you can call the City Parks and Recreation Special Events Hotline at 888 NY-PARKS (888 697-2757) or 360-3456 or visit www.nyc.gov/parks. Find out about jazz performances by visiting www.jazzfoundation.org or call Jazzline (presented by the Jazz Foundation of America) at 479-7888.

Discover what is happening on Broadway and learn about special ticket offers by calling The Broadway Line at 888-BROADWAY (888 276-2392) from outside Manhattan or 302-4111 within Manhattan or by visiting www.broadway.org, the website of Live Broadway. Find out what is happening Off-Off-Broadway at www.offoffbway.com. You can also peruse theater listings (as well as reviews and lots of other theater information and news) at www.playbill.com and www.nytheatre.com

For a listing of Lincoln Center events and other information about Lincoln Center, you can call the Lincoln Center Information Hotline at LINCOLN (546-2656) or visit the website at www.lincolncenter.org. You can learn about a variety of performances and special cultural and educational events and institutions by visiting www.nyckidsarts.org, the website of the Alliance for the Arts, a not-for-profit organization that gathers and publishes information about the arts in New York City. The Alliance also publishes the *Kids Culture Catalog*, which contains comprehensive listings of things cultural for kids.

▶ **Broadway, Off-Broadway, Off-Off-Broadway and beyond.**
Broadway theater generally refers to the major theaters located in the Times Square vicinity, from 42nd Street to around 56th Street and between Broadway and Eighth Avenue. Broadway theaters are denominated as such in theater listings and connote more a state of mind than an actual Broadway address. Broadway shows are typically the blockbuster, celebrity-studded, big-ticket musicals and plays. Tickets sell for between $40 and $75 dollars or even higher. Occasionally, theaters will offer standing-room tickets for $20 or less (note though that standing-room tickets would not be appropriate for children).

Off-Broadway theaters, which can be located anywhere around the city (including in the Broadway theater district), tend to seat 500 patrons or fewer. Productions may be less mainstream and casts may contain lesser known actors, although many major performers like to do more "artistic" or less mainstream work in Off-Broadway shows. Off-Off-Broadway performances typically feature "non-equity" (non-union) actors and are held in much smaller venues. It is to Off-Off-Broadway you head when you are interested in more experimental theater.

For music, dance, opera and theater, Lincoln Center is a great destination. The Lincoln Center complex, located on Manhattan's West Side on Broadway between 62nd and 66th Streets, includes several theaters and recital halls, an opera house and an outdoor band shell. Avery Fisher Hall is home to the New York Philharmonic. The Metropolitan Opera House is home to the Metropolitan Opera and American Ballet Theatre. The New York City Opera and New York City Ballet reside at the New York State Theater. Alice Tully Hall hosts the Lincoln Center Chamber Music Society and the annual International Film Festival. The New York Film Festival and other films are featured at the Walter Reade Theater. The Repertory Company of Lincoln Center, Wynton Marsalis' Jazz Orchestra, the Chamber Music Society, and a variety of additional programming can also be found at Lincoln Center. In addition, the Vivian Beaumont Theater and the Mitzi Newhouse Theater stage plays of all types. The plaza to the rear of the complex hosts various arts-and-crafts shows and the Big Apple Circus.

Carnegie Hall, located at 57th Street and Seventh Avenue, is an architectural landmark as well as the host to musical performances of all types. Another important concert hall is the Brooklyn Academy of Music (BAM), which hosts the Brooklyn Philharmonic, concerts and performances of all types as well as cutting-edge performance festivals.

Venues for dance include City Center, the Joyce Theater and the Sylvia and Danny Kaye Theater. Musical performances can be found at the Juilliard School located at Lincoln Center and The Tisch Center at the 92nd Street Y. The 92nd Street Y also hosts many performances specifically geared to or otherwise appropriate for children.

Madison Square Garden, which serves as the home court for several athletic teams, is also a major venue for pop-music concerts and the ever-popular ice shows. The Theater at Madison Square Garden hosts many children's shows (including "Sesame Street Live" and "A Christmas Carol").

▶ **Getting tickets.** You do not have to have special connections to get tickets to a performance in New York. You can purchase full-price tickets to most performances with your credit card through one of the ticket agencies serving New York City or at the theater box office.

The ticket agencies are:

- CenterCharge, 721-6500 or www.lincolncenter.org for Lincoln Center events only

- CityTix, 581-1212/7907 or www.citycenter.org for City Center events only

- Madison Square Garden, 465-MSG1 (465-6741) or www.thegarden.com for Madison Square Garden events only

- NYC/On Stage, 768-1818 to hear recorded listings of various performances and have your call transferred to the ticket agency handling the tickets for that event

- Tele-charge, 800 432-7250 from outside New York City, 239-6200 or 563-2929 (Broadway Inner Circle) within New York City or www.telecharge.com

◆ Ticket Central, 279-4200, www.ticketcentral.org

◆ Ticketmaster, 800 755-4000 from outside New York City, 307-4100 or 307-7171 within New York City or www.ticketmaster.com

It is also possible to get tickets for certain productions on eBay and other auction websites. If you are commuting into the city by one of the local rail services, check their websites for special promotions featuring tickets to Broadway shows and other performances (see Chapter 3 for resource listings).

If you are unable to get tickets for a particular show through the usual routes, it is sometimes possible to get what are known as "house seats." House seats refer to tickets that are reserved by the theater to be used for VIPs or other special guests of the production. Often, these tickets will be released to the public for sale. House seats can be released at any time from weeks before a performance to the day of. When checking with one of the ticket services for tickets, be sure to inquire whether there are any house seats or "released" tickets available. You can also get house seats from Care-Tix (840-0770, ext. 229 or 230), run by Broadway Care/Equity Fights AIDS, www.broadwaycares.org. Tickets can be purchased from Care-Tix at twice their face value, but 50 percent is donated to charity and is therefore tax deductible.

For smaller productions and many of the children's productions, tickets are generally purchased directly from the box office. In most cases, you can call the box office and either reserve tickets, which are picked up and paid for at the time of the performance, or pay for tickets in advance by credit card over the phone. If you are staying in a hotel with a concierge service, the concierge can typically arrange tickets for you.

You can also purchase same-day theater tickets at TKTS, a discount ticket seller. Tickets to most shows are half-price, but some shows are discounted by 25 percent, and you will pay a $3 surcharge per ticket. TKTS does not accept credit cards but takes only cash or travelers checks. Information concerning the tickets available for the day is posted on a board. You must go in person to get the tickets, and you should be prepared to stand in line. Visit www.tdf.org for more information.

The TKTS outlet is located at 47th Street and Broadway on a little traffic island called Duffy Square. It is open from 3 p.m. to 8 p.m. Monday through Saturday, from 10 a.m. to 2 p.m. on Wednesday and Saturday (matinee days) and 11 a.m. to 8 p.m. on Sunday. There is also a downtown location at the corner of John and Front Streets at the South Street Seaport. It is open from 11 a.m. to 6 p.m. Monday through Saturday and 11 a.m. to 3 p.m. on Sunday. At the downtown location, matinee tickets can be purchased one day in advance.

If you are willing to pay a premium for tickets, you can usually purchase tickets, particularly hard to get ones, from tickets brokers (also known as ticket resellers). Some ticket brokers are Theatre Direct International at 800 334-8457 (outside New York) or 541-8457 (in New York), www.theaterdirect.com; Prestige Entertainment at 800 243-8849, www.prestigeentertainment.com; Manhattan Entertainment 382-0633; Applause Theatre & Entertainment Service at 307-7050, www.applause-tickets.com; or you can check the listings in the Yellow Pages of the telephone book under Tickets. By law, ticket brokers are not supposed to sell tickets for the greater of 10 percent or $5 more than their face value, but this law is routinely flouted. If you elect to buy through a ticket broker, it is wise to get price quotes from more than one broker.

Ticket brokers should not be confused with "scalpers." Scalpers are individuals offering tickets to theaters, concerts, sporting events and other performances, who typically hawk their tickets in front of or near the entrance to the theater or arena. Scalpers are not licensed or authorized to sell their tickets and usually charge a big premium above the price of the tickets. Beware of purchasing tickets from scalpers, because the tickets they hand you may very well be counterfeit; if so, you will have no recourse.

If you have an American Express Card, you can purchase theater tickets on the American Express website through its Playbill Online service at www.americanexpress.com. If you have a Gold or Platinum American Express Card, you may also be able to get tickets to special events from the AmEx special events programs. Visit www.americanexpress.com/gce to find out what events are available in New York for the time you will be visiting.

Visa cardholders can visit www.visa.com to explore their ticket-purchase opportunities. Having recently become the sponsor of the renowned Broadway Tony Awards and entering into partnerships with various organizations, Visa card may have special offers for advance tickets and priority seating for various theater events. MasterCard also offers ticket-purchase opportunities on its website at www.mastercard.com. Gold and Platinum MasterCard holders may have special access to various performances through Master-Card's Preferred Seating program.

Some theaters and the major cultural institutions offer discounts for children, students and senior citizens for certain performances. Be sure to bring identification for students and seniors.

Junior high school and high school students can purchase special discounted tickets to performances (and discounted museum admissions) through the High Five Tickets to the Arts programs. Participating arts organizations donate tickets to the program. The tickets are then sold to students for $5.00 each. Tickets can be purchased at Ticketmaster and some can be purchased on the High Five website. Students must show valid student identification to purchase tickets. For more information and listings of events for which High Five tickets are available, you can call HI5-TKTS (445-8587) or visit the website at www.high5tix.org. High Five also sponsors special Teen Scene events.

If your preferred form of family entertainment is going to the movies, you can avoid standing in line and get guaranteed admission to the film of your choice by ordering advance tickets from Moviefone at 777-FILM (777-3456), www.moviefone.com; or Fandango at 800-555-TELL (8355), www.fandango.com. Tickets are available over the phone or Internet for credit-card purchase, and some theaters even offer reserved seating. If you are not sure whether a film is kid friendly, visit the family movie guide at www.nytoday.com.

▶ **A word about subscriptions.** If you live near New York or tend to visit on a regular basis, you may want to consider theater subscriptions or series tickets for various venues or companies. Besides potentially saving you some money on tickets (many subscriptions feature a discount) and supporting a performance center or group, you are guaranteed tickets to popular performances and have the added benefit of a scheduled event around which to build your day in the city.

Performances, Concerts, Theater and More

We have compiled a list of popular performance groups and venues to help you find your way to performances that will please and entertain the children. Keep in mind that this list is merely a starting point, that it does not include every possible venue in town and that the groups and venues listed may not stage exclusively children's or family events or may not have any children's or family events scheduled for when you will be in New York.

As soon as you know when you will be in town, be sure to check newspapers and other publications and websites (see the resources at the end of this chapter) for special, seasonal or holiday events. If you will be staying in a hotel with a concierge, you can call ahead to arrange for advance ticket purchases. For any performance in which you are interested, be sure to check the age for which the performance is recommended.

Aaron Davis Hall
West 135th Street and Convent Avenue (on the campus of City College of New York), 650-6900, www.aarondavishall.org
This performing-arts center in the heart of Harlem, located on the campus of The City College of New York, is the host to a variety of programming throughout the year. For more than 15 seasons, the multicultural International Series has presented 20 to 30 performances per year featuring music, dance, theater and film from African, Caribbean, Asian, Latino, African American and European cultures. Some performances are part of the Dialogue Series where the artists speak with the audience after the show. Performances are on weekdays at 10:30 a.m. and 12:30 p.m. The Saturday afternoon Family Series, which usually runs approximately five times each year, features programming for children and their parents and often includes ancillary programs connected to the performance.

Abrons Arts Center
Henry Street Settlement at Pitt Street, 466 Grand Street, 598-0400, www.henrystreet.org
This multifunctional arts center boasts three professional theaters as well as classrooms, art studios and gallery space and hosts professional and student theater and music performances for all ages. Throughout the

school year, the Abrons Arts Center offers an Arts for Families series (usually one weekend a month), featuring a variety of performances for children. Reservations are recommended, and do not forget to check the age recommendation for the show.

Alvin Ailey American Dance Theater
767-0590, www.alvinailey.org
This renowned modern dance troupe is in residence for six weeks during December and early January at City Center. While most of its work is geared to mature audiences and young adults, during the New York City season they schedule several Family Matinee performances. The junior company, Ailey II (formerly the Alvin Ailey Repertory Ensemble), is in residence at Aaron Davis Hall for a brief season during March or April. Students from the Ailey School usually perform in May.

American Ballet Theatre
477-3030, www.abt.org
ABT is in residence in New York for an eight-week season April through July at Lincoln Center. Though its repertoire is geared to mature audiences and young adults, your young ballet fan (age 10+) may be able to sit through a portion of a regular program. For the past several years, ABT has had an annual Saturday matinee Family Day gala once each spring. ABT also conducts a unique Family Series program once each fall and each spring during which you and your child can attend studio visits, tours, education workshops and performances over a two-afternoon period. Although the Family Series is an expensive proposition, it may be appropriate for a serious ballet fan or student.

Apollo Theater
253 West 125th Street, 531-5305; events hotline 531-5301,
www.apollotheater.com
This legendary theater in the heart of Harlem showcases a variety of musical performances, amateur shows, and standup comedy featuring African American performers. Call ahead to determine whether the programming for the dates you are in town is age appropriate. Every Wednesday evening is Amateur Night and children are welcome. There is a free film for kids program featuring first-run, G-rated movies. Tours of the theater are available.

ArtsConnection
520 Eighth Avenue, Suite 321, 302-7433, www.artsconnection.org
Housed in a historic landmark building in the theater district, ArtsConnection operates its Saturdays Alive! Program from October through May, hosting performances, readings and hands-on arts workshops. The Family Performance series features dance, theater and music from cultures all around the world. The Family Workshop series allows children and parents to participate in projects led by professional artists. The Books Alive! series includes readings by, and activities with, children's authors. Artsplay! features performances for children between the ages of three and five.

Big Apple Circus
Lincoln Center, 268-2500, www.bigapplecircus.org
This popular one-ring circus sets up its heated tent at Lincoln Center each year (from October through January). The Big Apple Circus, a not-for-profit performing-arts institution that is committed to children and families, is unusually child friendly and manages to thrill and delight young audiences with a variety of clowns, acrobats, jugglers, animals large and small and other annual surprises. No seat is more than 50 feet from the action. Fun for the parents, too.

Bronx Arts Ensemble
Bronx, 718 601-7399, www.bronxartsensemble.com
The Bronx Arts Ensemble, in residence at Fordham University, features music from many cultures and styles, including classical, salsa and jazz. The Ensemble features an annual children's performance series and includes family-friendly programming in its general performance schedule. The Music Circus Children's Concerts are part of the Ensemble's regular season.

Brooklyn Academy of Music (BAM)
30 Lafayette Avenue, Brooklyn, 718 636-4100, www.bam.org
BAM is one of the oldest performing arts centers in the U.S. and is host to a variety of performing arts throughout the year, including contemporary and classical dance, theater, performance art, repertory and first run films, music performances (including the resident Brooklyn Philharmonic and BAM Opera) and theater for young people. While often associated with avant-garde performances, BAM showcases many traditional and contemporary works as well. BAM features BAMfamily music and theater performances for the entire family.

Brooklyn Center for the Performing Arts at Brooklyn College
Flatbush Avenue and Avenue H, Brooklyn, 718 951-4500,
www.brooklyncenter.com
This performing-arts complex in the heart of Brooklyn contains the 2,450-seat Walt Whitman Hall, the 500-seat Gershwin Theatre as well as several other performance and rehearsal venues. The Center hosts an array of music, dance and theater performances as well as film events and the Jewish Gems (Yiddish theater), Music Masters, World of Dance and Caribbean Celebrations series. The Family Fun Sunday matinee series offers several annual productions (between October and May) especially for children and a *Nutcracker* each December.

Carnegie Hall
57th Street and Seventh Avenue, 247-7800, www.carnegiehall.org
World-class musicians look forward to performing in this landmark concert hall. From the top orchestras of the world to contemporary singers, there is a variety of programming throughout the year. While much of the pro-

gramming is not specifically child friendly, there is a great deal that would be appropriate for older or more mature children and particularly for young (10+) musicians. In addition, Carnegie Hall hosts occasional Saturday matinee Family Concerts, which are accompanied by pre-performance family activities, and weekday CarnegieKids concerts for preschoolers. Carnegie Hall also sponsors an annual series of Neighborhood Concerts in various locations throughout the five boroughs. Tours of the facility are available.

Chamber Music Society of Lincoln Center
Alice Tully Hall at Lincoln Center, 875-5775,
www.chambermusicsociety.org
The Chamber Music Society of Lincoln Center performs chamber music of all periods during its annual concert season. The Meet the Music! series features three short concerts per year to introduce children to chamber music.

City Center
130 West 55th Street, 581-1212, 581-7907, www.citycenter.org
Since 1943, City Center has been a venue for music, dance and theater. Companies that perform annually at City Center include Alvin Ailey, American Ballet Theatre, American Dance Theater and Paul Taylor Dance Company. City Center also houses Manhattan Theatre Club and City Center Encores! Great American Musicals in Concert. Others who have recently performed at City Center include the Australian Ballet, Ballroom Fever, the Dance Theatre of Harlem and the Moscow Chamber Orchestra. Although the productions are not aimed at children, particular perform-ances may be appropriate for your older (10+) child.

City Lights
300 West 43rd Street, Suite 402, 262-0200, www.clyouththeatre.org
This non-profit educational organization provides quality theater-arts pro-grams for children ages 7 to 18. Performances are held at various locations in the city.

Colden Center for the Performing Arts
65-30 Kissena Boulevard (Queens College of the City University of New York), Flushing, Queens, 718 544-2996, www.coldencenter.org
The Colden Center for the Performing Arts has hosted many of the world's leading artists in music, dance, theater and other performing arts as well as innovative and entertaining children's programming. Especially for kids are the KidsClassics and Family Theater series, many of which feature audi-ence participation or interaction. Different series will have age recommen-dations. In addition, there are many special events that are appropriate for children of all ages.

Community Works Theater Connections
459-1854

This not-for-profit community arts organization brings a rich variety of affordable, multicultural performing arts events to more than 65,000 students per year (grades K–12) via its Theater Connections program. Their four major presenting sites are Hostos Center for the Arts & Culture (Bronx), Pace University Downtown Theater (lower Manhattan), Marcus Garvey Park Amphitheater (Harlem) and LaGuardia Mainstage Theatre (Queens). Performances are primarily geared to school groups, held on weekdays during school hours and generally open to the public.

Czechoslovak–American Marionette Theatre
777-3891, www.czechmarionettes.org

Since 1990, this company has produced traditional and original puppet plays for adults and children (generally 5+) using a troupe of antique marionettes. The Czechoslovak–American Marionette Theatre performs in various venues in New York as well as nationally and internationally. Reservations recommended.

Dance Theater Workshop
219 West 19th Street, 924-0077, www.dtw.org

Dance Theater Workshop is a not-for-profit organization that provides artist sponsorship programs, production facilities and support services to independent artists in New York City and across the country. Dedicated to identifying and nurturing contemporary artists working in diverse cultural contexts, DTW offers a Family Matters series of performances for children ages 5 to 12 and their parents on selected weekend afternoons at its Beside Schoolbag Theater. Artists who have worked with DTW include Mark Morris, Bill Irwin, Bill T. Jones and Whoopi Goldberg.

Dance Theatre of Harlem
466 West 152nd Street, 690-2800, www.dancetheatreofharlem.org

This world-famous multicultural dance company has an exciting repertory of many works. Though the performances are not specifically geared to children, your older dance fan (10+) will find a lot here to enjoy. For families, the Dance Theatre of Harlem offers an Open House Series on the second Sunday of each month between November and May. Open House performances feature a variety of performers, such as jazz and gospel musicians, other dance companies and Dance Theatre of Harlem students. Performances are followed by a reception.

Film Society of Lincoln Center
Walter Reade Theater at Lincoln Center, 875-5610; ticket orders at
496-3809, www.filmlinc.com

The Film Society of Lincoln Center hosts Movies for Kids on various Saturdays and Sundays at 2:00 p.m. The Reel to Real series, offered over several weekends spaced out over the school year, features "silver screen classics on

double bills with dynamic live performances and audience participation."
A true New York experience.

Growing Up with Opera
Metropolitan Opera Guild, 362-6000, www.operaed.org
Growing Up With Opera, presented by the Metropolitan Opera Guild
(769-7022), the organization behind the Metropolitan Opera, is a unique
program that introduces children (and adults, too!) to opera. Classic works
are sung in English and performed in child-friendly venues. Backstage tours
of the Opera House are available for children nine and older (769-7020).

Hostos Center for the Arts & Culture
**450 Grand Concourse (at the Hostos Community College of the City
University of New York), Bronx, 718 518-4455, www.hostos-cuny.edu**
Containing an art gallery, theater and concert hall, this facility showcases
drama, folk arts, dance and music, including strong Spanish-language
theater programming and works from cultures from around the world. For
children, there are performances including everything from puppets,
merengue, poetry reading and a rhythm-and-blues Christmas concert.
Performances reflect the concerns and traditions of the local Latino and
African American communities.

Ice Theatre of New York
929-5811, www.icetheatre.org
This professional skating group, which is the nation's first not-for-profit
artistic ice dancing ensemble, is the "PBS of figure skating." Not to be confused with ice extravaganzas, the Ice Theatre of New York performs original
choreographed pieces every year between October and May. You can catch
their unique works in October at the Chelsea Piers Skyrink and can watch
for free at Rockefeller Center on the third Wednesdays of January, February
and March at 1:00 p.m. and at Riverbank State Park on the third Thursdays
of January, February, March and April. Ice Theatre is great for any child
who loves skating and dance.

Jazz at Lincoln Center
Alice Tully Hall, Lincoln Center, 258-9800, www.jazzatlincolncenter.org
Jazz at Lincoln Center features a series of jazz concerts, films, lectures and
other programming under the artistic direction of Wynton Marsalis. The
Jazz for Young People series, offered several times between October and
May, is a unique series of one-hour concerts led by Wynton Marsalis
exploring different forms of jazz. It is fun for the kids and educational for
the grownups, too, but it is not recommended for children under six.

Joyce Theater
175 Eighth Avenue, 242-0800, www.joyce.org
Founded in 1982, The Joyce Theater was created by dancers as a home for
all types of dance, from contemporary to the avant-garde. The Joyce The-

ater building was converted from a 1941 movie house into an intimate theater seating 472. The Joyce's Family Matinee Series consists of six to eight family-oriented performances followed by Meet the Artists gatherings each year. The Joyce Junior Membership Program offers children (ages 6 to 14) who see four Family Matinees a 40 percent discount on the price of their tickets as well as discounts at local restaurants and bookstores.

Lenny Suib Puppet Playhouse
Mazur Theater at Asphalt Green, 555 East 90th Street, 369-8890
Every Saturday at 10:30 a.m. and noon from September to April, the Lenny Suib Puppet Playhouse stages a puppet show for children between the ages of two and seven in the intimate Mazur Theater. Stories are drawn from fairy tales, folk tales and original pieces and are very kid friendly. Plays usually last about 45 minutes. Performances are diverse and can include hand, shadow and rod puppets, marionettes, magicians, clowns, storytellers and more. There is a different show each weekend.

Lincoln Center

70 Lincoln Center Plaza, 875-5000; customer service 875-5456,
Hotline LIN-COLN (546-2656), www.lincolncenter.org
Situated on 15 acres on Manhattan's Upper West Side, Lincoln Center is one of the world's largest cultural complexes, offering an array of programming for all ages and tastes. Through its Department of Programs and Services for People with Disabilities, Lincoln Center has made a major commitment to providing access to patrons, visitors and artists with disabilities (875-5375). Lincoln Center consists of Alice Tully Hall (875-5050), Avery Fisher Hall (875-5030), The Juilliard School (799-5000), Lincoln Center Theater (362-7600), Metropolitan Opera House (362-6000), New York Public Library for the Performing Arts (870-1630), New York State Theatre (870-5570), and the Walter Reade Theater (875-5601).

At Lincoln Center, you can find

- American Ballet Theatre, 477-3030, Metropolitan Opera House, www.abt.org (see listing above)

- The Chamber Music Society of Lincoln Center, 875-5775, Alice Tully Hall, www.chambermusicsociety.org (see listing above)

- The Film Society of Lincoln Center, 875-5610, Walter Reade Theater (see listing above), www.filmlinc.org

- Jazz at Lincoln Center, 258-9800, www.jazzatlincolncenter.org (see listing above)

- Juilliard School, 799-5000, www.juilliard.edu.
This famed college invites the public to the school's free public recitals by advanced students on Saturdays during the academic year. A treat for your aspiring musician.

- Lincoln Center Theater, 362-7600, www.lct.org.
  The Vivian Beaumont and Mitzi E. Newhouse Theaters have a year-round schedule of programming. While not particularly geared to children, certain of the productions may be appropriate for older children (10+) or teenagers.

- Metropolitan Opera, 362-6000, www.metropera.org (and see www.operaed.org, Growing Up with Opera listing above)

- New York City Ballet, 870-5570, New York State Theatre, www.nycballet.com (see listing below)

- New York City Opera, 870-5600, New York State Theatre, www.nycopera.org (see listing below)

- New York Philharmonic, 875-5656, www.nyphilharmonic.org (see listing below)

Little Orchestra Society
971-9500, www.littleorchestra.org
For the past 50 years, the Little Orchestra Society has been introducing the youngest audiences to orchestral music in a delightful, fun-filled way. For three- to five-year-olds, the weekend Lollipop Concerts, three of which are offered in the fall, winter and spring, use friendly characters, each representing a section of the orchestra, to teach the ABCs of music at Kaye Playhouse at Hunter College. Happy Concerts for 6- to 12-year-olds are offered at Avery Fisher Hall at Lincoln Center three times a year (including a rousing *Amahl and the Night Visitors*, complete with live animals!). A New York tradition.

Los Kabayitos Puppet & Children's Theater
Society of the Educational Arts (SEA), CSV Cultural & Educational Center, 107 Suffolk Street, 260-4080 ext. 14, www.sea-ny.org
Voted one of the "10 Best Latino Theater Companies in New York," The Society of the Educational Arts, Inc./Sociedad Educative de las Artes, Inc. is a not-for-profit Hispanic/Bilingual Arts in Education organization founded in Puerto Rico in 1985. In addition to an array of community- and school-based programming, Los Kabayitos Puppet & Children's Theater offers year-round general audience performances in both Spanish and English. Their original productions explore educational themes as well as Latino arts and culture.

Madison Square Garden
Seventh Avenue between 31st and 33rd Streets, 465-MSG1 (465-6741), www.thegarden.com
More than five million fans pass through the turnstiles every year at Madison Square Garden. Located in the heart of Manhattan above Pennsylvania Station, this newly renovated landmark sports-and-entertainment complex is home to the NY Knicks, Rangers and WNBA and hosts ice

shows, Ringling Brothers Barnum & Bailey Circus, horse shows, dog and cat shows, rock concerts and more. The facility consists of the 20,000-seat Arena, the 5,600-seat Theater and the 40,000-square-foot Expo Center. Annual favorites at the Theater include "Sesame Street Live" and "A Christmas Carol." Tours of the facility are available.

Manhattan Children's Theatre
380 Broadway, 4th floor, 252-2840, www.manhattanchildrenstheatre.org
This not-for-profit organization is committed to producing "affordable, high-quality theatrical experiences for children and families" by offering "professional writing, compelling stories and exceptional production values" in its brand new family-friendly space located in the heart of Tribeca. Audiences will also have the ability to see the production and technical team do their magic. Some productions will offer activities after the performance.

Marionette Theater
Swedish Cottage in Central Park (near 81st Street), 988-9093, www.centralpark.org

Originally built as a schoolhouse in 19th-century Sweden, the cottage made its way to Central Park via the 1876 Philadelphia Centennial Exposition. Marionette performances run between September and June and are at 10:30 a.m. and noon on weekdays and 1:00 p.m. on Saturdays. Each autumn, a new production of a classic fairy tale is presented. Performances last about an hour and are great for children between the ages of 4 and 11. Reservations are recommended.

New Victory Theater
209 West 42nd Street between Seventh and Eighth Avenues, 646 223-3020, www.newvictory.org
This gem of a theater located in the heart of Times Square is totally dedicated to children's programming. The VicTeens programs allow 13 to 18 year olds to mingle with cast members and go behind the scenes. Throughout the year, the New Victory hosts an incredible array of high quality and often unique performances by artists from around the world, including circuses, mime, plays, music, puppeteers, dance and even performance art for the younger set. All programs have specific age recommendations (which are very accurate) and are reasonable in length. Should not be missed!

New York City Ballet
New York State Theater at Lincoln Center, 870-5570, www.nycballet.com
This world-renowned ballet company highlights works by George Balanchine, Jerome Robbins, Peter Martins and new choreographers. While not particularly geared to young children, your older ballet fan (10+) will enjoy this wonderful dance company. For children ages eight and older, NYCB offers Family Matinee Insights, a pre-performance program (usually offered four times a year) designed to enhance the ballet experience for young audience members and their families. The NYCB's *Nutcracker* is an institution.

New York City Opera
New York State Theatre at Lincoln Center, 870-5600, www.nycopera.com
This company is decidedly more accessible than the Met, without any diminution in quality. Foreign-language operas are presented with supertitles projected above the stage. For children ages 6 to 12, the New York City Opera offers hour-long programs designed to introduce youngsters to opera. Prior to selected matinees during the regular season, there are also several pre-performance young people's workshops during which a City Opera teaching artist conducts a brief interactive program introducing audience members to the opera being performed that day.

New York Philharmonic
Avery Fisher Hall at Lincoln Center, 875-5656,
www.newyorkphilharmonic.org
Under the direction of Lorin Maazel, this world-famous orchestra, the oldest in the United States, presents numerous concerts each year. Its famed Young People's Concerts (usually four per year on Saturday afternoons between September and June) introduce children ages 6 to 12 to orchestral music. Concerts are preceded by an hour-long Children's Promenade where children are invited to meet members of the Philharmonic and make their own music. Children from 12 to 17 can participate in Philharmonic Teens and attend a Rush Hour Concert (Wednesdays at 6:45 p.m.) preceded by a pre-concert event at 5:30 p.m. The youngest music lovers (ages three to six) can attend a free half-hour musical storytime with members of the Philharmonic at Barnes & Noble at Broadway and 66th Street.

92nd Street Y
1395 Lexington Avenue, 415-5500, www.92ndstY.org
The 92nd Street Y, located on Manhattan's Upper East Side, offers a full range of performance programming and activities for families. The "Y" has a long history of serving as a community cultural center presenting concerts, dance performances, lectures, films and other special events and family activities throughout the year. The Bronfman Center for Jewish Life (415-5765) offers a variety of programming for adults and families.

Paper Bag Players
362-0431, www.paperbagplayers.org
Since 1958, the award-winning Paper Bag Players has been delighting young audiences with their rousing songs, freewheeling dances and sets and props fashioned from cardboard boxes and paper bags. Perfect for children ages four to eight. They can be found at the Sylvia and Danny Kaye Playhouse from January through March and at other locations during the rest of the year.

Poppy Seed Players
Elaine Kaufman Cultural Center, Merkin Hall, 129 West 67th Street, 501-3360, www.ekcc.org

Since 1990, the Poppy Seed players have been staging family musicals with Jewish cultural themes. Professional actors perform about five productions per year. Productions are based on various stories, including those of Isaac Bashevis Singer. There are also special holiday productions during Chanukah, Passover and Purim, all of which feature a children's chorus comprising students from the Lucy Moses music school. Performances are usually at 11:00 a.m. on Sunday. Recommended ages vary based on productions, although the holiday shows are fine for kids four and up.

Puppetworks
338 Sixth Avenue, Brooklyn (Park Slope), 718 965-3391, www.puppetworks.org

The Puppetworks Company stages weekend afternoon performances with hand-carved wooden marionettes. These original productions are based on children's literature, folk and fairy tales and other familiar stories. Perfect for children between the ages of 5 and 12.

Radio City Music Hall
1260 Sixth Avenue at 50th Street, 247-4777; for tickets 307-7171, www.radiocity.com

This dazzling landmark Art Deco masterpiece, located in the heart of Rockefeller Center and having the largest proscenium stage in the world, is a must-see for all visitors. Radio City is perhaps best known for the annual Christmas Spectacular featuring the famed Rockettes (seen by more than one-million people each year), but it is also the venue for concerts, television events and other special events. You can find live family entertainment shows such as Barney and the Rugrats at Radio City as well as family movie premieres. Tours of Radio City are available.

Ringling Brothers and Barnum & Bailey Circus
Madison Square Garden, 800 755-4000, www.ringling.com

The Greatest Show on Earth comes to New York every spring (usually sometime in March) for a six-week run at Madison Square Garden. With three rings, clowns, daring tumblers, aerialists, live animals and a menagerie, the circus is bound to delight and thrill your children. Be advised that your littlest ones may be overwhelmed by the action, so plan accordingly.

Shadow Box Theater
YWCA of Brooklyn, 30 Third Avenue, Brooklyn, 724-0677, www.shadowboxtheatre.org

This award-winning, not-for-profit company has been presenting "puppet and people" musicals and storytelling performances for more than 30 years. Its mission is to reach children "with important messages of multicultural awareness, self-esteem, preservation of the earth's environment, health and safety and the simple joy of artistic expression." Shadow Box Theater is the resident children's theater of the YWCA of Brooklyn. Performances are on weekdays, usually at 10:30 a.m., between November and May.

Sony IMAX Theatre
Broadway and 68th Street, 800 555-8355
Feel as if you are in the movie when you experience a 3D IMAX film in this theater with an eight-story-high screen. The kids will love the cool head-gear they wear to get the full 3D effect. Films typically run about one hour. IMAX may be a bit much for kids under five or six.

Symphony Space
Broadway at 95th Street, 864-5400, www.symphonyspace.org
This Upper West Side performing-arts center features a broad array of diverse music, dance, film, theater and other arts programming. One Saturday per month from November through April, Symphony Space presents Just Kidding, a series intended to introduce children between the ages of 5 and 12 to the arts and excite them about its possibilities. Performances tend to be lively and often interactive. A great opportunity to get a taste of the Upper West Side!

Tada! Theater
15 West 28th Street, 3rd Floor, 252-1619, www.tadatheater.com
This not-for-profit youth theater company presents original musicals, plays and dance productions performed by the multiethnic members of the TADA! Company, all of whom are between the ages of 8 and 17. Your kids will love seeing kids perform.

Theater for a New Audience
229-2819, www.tfana.org
Since 1978, TFANA has been staging the works of Shakespeare and other works from the world's classic repertoire and has been committed to "bonding the diverse community of New York to the language, pleasures and issues of classical drama." While the performances are not particularly geared to children, your older child (10+) and your teens will enjoy these works. At certain performances, TFANA features a pre- or post-performance event with the actors that will give your older child a window into the pro-duction. The Sunday afternoon New Deal events (offered several Sundays during the year) bring a scholar or person involved with the production to meet with the audience about the day's show.

Theatreworks/USA
647-1100, www.theatreworksusa.org
Theatreworks/USA is the nation's largest professional not-for-profit theater company for children performing all over the U.S. and reaching an annual audience of almost four million people. In New York, Theatreworks/USA presents its October–April weekend series at the Equitable Tower (787 Sev-

enth Avenue between 51st and 52nd Streets). Theatreworks mounts approximately 14 shows each season from a body of work of more than 90 plays and musicals that fall into three categories: history and biography, literary adaptations and "issue" shows. The shows feature such themes as discrimination, peer pressure, friendship, illiteracy and perseverance. While Theatreworks entertains children from pre-school through high school, each show has a (very accurate) recommended age level. These high quality and entertaining shows should not be missed.

Thirteenth Street Repertory Company
50 West 13th Street , 675-6677, www.13thstreetrep.org
For the past 28 years, this Greenwich Village repertory company has been delighting young audiences with original children's theater. Throughout the year, the Thirteenth Street Theater offers entertaining shows for the younger set on Saturday and Sunday at 1:00 p.m. and at 3:00 p.m. The early show is usually for kids three and up and the later show is for kids five and up. Audience participation is definitely part of the program!

Tribeca Performing Arts Center
199 Chambers Street, 220-1460, www.tribecapac.org
This downtown performing arts center produces a variety of multicultural dance, theater and music programming. For children, it offers a popular weekend Family Folk and Fairy Tale series from October to June. Works are performed by American and international companies.

UniverSoul Big Top Circus
Downing Stadium, Randalls Island, www.universoulcircus.com
This unique and exciting circus brings hip-hop, rhythm and blues, jazz and gospel to traditional circus acts performed by people of color from around the world. UniverSoul is usually in New York during April and May each year.

Wave Hill
675 West 252nd Street, Bronx, 718 549-3200, www.wavehill.org
This picturesque public garden located in the Riverdale section of the Bronx offers a variety of performing arts (primarily concerts) in addition to spectacular views of the Hudson River and Palisades, green lawns and magnificent gardens. For children, Wave Hill hosts Nature Stories and Songs for Families between October and March. A great break from the hustle and bustle of the city.

Weekend Family Films
Metropolitan Museum, 1000 Fifth Avenue, 570-3932,
www.metmuseum.org
In conjunction with the Museum's Look Again! and Hello, Met! family programs (sketching and discussion programs conducted at the Museum for children between 5 and 12 with accompanying adults), short films are

presented in the Museum's Uris Auditorium on Saturdays and Sundays from 12:30 p.m. to 1:00 p.m. and Tuesday through Friday from noon to 12:30 p.m.

World Financial Center Arts & Events Program
The Winter Garden, West Street, Battery Park City, 945-2600, www.worldfinancialcenter.com
This vaulted glass and steel dome overlooks the Hudson River from the heart of the World Financial Center (WFC), which was severely damaged by terrorist attacks on September 11, 2001. It has been painstakingly restored and features an "innovative series of free performances and visual and sound installations created to showcase emerging as well as established artists." Summer events are frequently staged on the outdoor Plaza on the Hudson River. Since 1988, the program, which is one of the largest privately funded ongoing free performing- and visual-arts programs in the country, has hosted more than 800 performances, including works commissioned for the WFC and previews of works headed for the city's major cultural venues.

Long Running Shows

Beauty and the Beast
Lunt-Fontanne Theatre, 205 West 46th Street, 575-9200.
A big musical stage version of the Disney movie about the beautiful Belle, the scary Beast (really a handsome prince under a wicked spell), the enchanted castle (where the Beast's loyal staff have been turned into household objects) and a happy ending. (2 hours, 30 minutes)

Blue Man Group: Tubes
Astor Place Theatre, 434 Lafayette Street, 254-4370.
Three guys painted blue, a lot of noise, a lot of silliness and a lot of fun. Since 1991, Blue Man Group has been entertaining audiences with its own brand of irreverent performance art and physical and intellectual comedy. While some of the humor is above kids' heads, the show is so entertaining that everyone has a good time. Audience members in the front row risk getting wet or "goo-ed." The grand finale involves a lot of toilet paper. OK for kids over five, but note, there are a few "bad" words in the show. (1 hour, 45 minutes)

Les Miserables
Imperial Theatre, 249 West 45th Street, 239-6200.
Based on the epic novel by Victor Hugo, "Les Mis" tells the stories of Jean Valjean, the policeman Javert and a host of other memorable characters set in the backdrop of 19th-century France. Beautiful music and some amazing theater moments (particularly the barricade scene) create a special theater outing for the family (as well as a chance to discuss good and evil and some history). Best for older kids. Closing in 2003. (3 hours, 10 minutes).

The Lion King
New Amsterdam Theatre, 214 West 42nd Street, 282-2900.
Based on the Disney movie, "The Lion King" tells the story of Simba, Mufasa, Scar and Nala. Notwithstanding the underlying issues of fratricide, greed and the like, this is still a show for kids. What distinguishes this show from others are the incredible costumes, masks, puppets and staging. The opening scene is truly unforgettable and pure magic. For kids four and older. (2 hours, 40 minutes)

The Phantom of the Opera
Majestic Theatre, 247 West 44th Street, 239-6200.
The story of a young beautiful opera singer and the disfigured Phantom who haunts the Opera House makes for a romantic tale set to a wonderful score. With lavish costumes and sets, including a very realistic chandelier that descends over the audience to crash onstage, this is a spectacle your older children will enjoy. (2 hours, 30 minutes)

Rent

Nederlander Theatre, 208 West 41st Street, 921-8000.
Set in New York's East Village and loosely based on "La Bohème," this energetic rock musical explores love and friendship in the age of AIDS. This show is definitely not for kids, but your teen will not forgive you if you do not at least try to get tickets. (2 hours, 45 minutes)

Seasonal Events

Big Apple Circus
October through January.

A Christmas Carol
The Theater at Madison Square Garden. November and December.

The Nutcracker
New York City Ballet. Christmastime.

Radio City Holiday Shows
Christmas Show—November, December and the beginning of January. Spring Spectacular—April.

Ringling Brothers Barnum & Bailey Circus
Six-week run usually commencing in March.

RESOURCES

Outings with Your Children

The Cool Parents Guide to All of New York by Alfred Gingold and Helen Rogan (City & Company, 1996)

Kids Culture Catalog by the Alliance for the Arts, distributed by Harry N. Abrams, Inc., www.nyckidsarts.org

Kids Take New York by Christine C. Moriarty (Book Happy Books, 2nd ed., 1999)

New York's 50 Best Places to Take Children by Allan Ishac (City & Company, 1997)

Publications

Big Apple Parent. Monthly. Free. Widely distributed throughout the city. Produces an annual Parents' Source Book. Subscriptions available. 889-6400. www.parentsknow.com

City Guide. Weekly. Distributed free in hotels. www.cityguidemagazine.com

Family Entertainment Guide. Five issues per year (seasonal plus holiday). Free. Available at schools, libraries and family facilities. 787-3789. www.familybuzzguide.com

IN New York. Monthly. Distributed free in hotels. www.in-newyorkmag.com

iNew York Quick Guide. Distributed free in hotels. www.cityspin.com

New York Daily News. Daily newspaper. www.nydailynews.com

New York Family. Monthly. Free. Available at pediatricians' offices, schools, libraries and stores. Subscriptions available. Produces an annual Family Resource Guide. 914 381-7474. www.nyfamily.com.

New York Magazine. Weekly magazine. www.metronewyork.com

New York Post. Daily newspaper. www.nypost.com

New York Times. Daily newspaper. www.nytimes.com

New Yorker. Weekly magazine. www.newyorker.com

PARENTGUIDE. Monthly. Free. Available at pediatricians' offices, schools, libraries and stores. Subscriptions available. 213-8840. www.parentguidenews.com

Time Out New York. Weekly magazine. www.timeoutny.com

Village Voice. Weekly magazine. Free. www.villagevoice.com

Wall Street Journal. Newspaper, Monday through Friday. www.wsj.com (paid subscription)

Where. Distributed free in hotels. www.wheremagazine.com

Websites

www.allny.com

www.applevision

www.citidex.com

www.cityguideny.com

www.citysearch.com

www.digitalcity.com

www.go-newyorkcity.com

www.fieldtrip.com/ny/index

www.lasroomfinders.com/newyork
/kids.htm

www.nyc.com

www.nyc.gov
(official website of New York City)

www.nyckidsarts.org

www.nyc-arts.org

www.nyctourism.com

www.nycvisit.com

www.nytoday.com

www.stayinnewyorkcity.com

Tickets

Ticket brokers

Applause Theatre & Entertainment
Service, 307-7050,
www.applause-entertainment.com

Manhattan Entertainment, 382-0633

Prestige Entertainment,
800 243-8849,
www.prestigeentertainment.com

Theatre Direct International,
800 334-8457,
www.theaterdirect.com

Ticket and special event information

City Parks and Recreation Special
Events Hotline, 888 NY-PARKS
(888 697-2757) or 360-3456

Jazzline (presented by the Jazz
Foundation of America), 479-7888

League of American Theatres &
Producers, www.broadway.org

Lincoln Square Business Improvement District, www.lincolnbid.com

New York Theatre Experience,
757-7200, www.nytheatre.com

Off Broadway Theater Information
Center, 251 West 45th Street, 575-
1423, www.offbroadway.com

Off-Off Broadway information,
www.offoffbway.com

www.broadway.com

www.broadwaynewyork.com

www.dealsonbroadway.com

Ticket services

American Express,
www.americanexpress.com/gce

Broadway Hotline, 888-BROADWAY
(888 276-2392) outside NYC,
302-4111 within NYC

Care-Tix, 840-0770,
www.broadwaycares.org

CenterCharge, 721-6500
Lincoln Center events only

CityTix, 581-1212
City Center events only

Fandango, 800 555-TELL
(800 555-8355), www.fandango.com

High Five Tickets to the Arts,
HI5-TKTS, www.high5tix.org

Lincoln Center Information Hotline,
LINCOLN (546-2656),
www.lincolncenter.org

Madison Square Garden, 465-MSG1
(465-6741), www.thegarden.com

MasterCard, www.mastercard.com

Moviefone, 777-FILM (777-3456),
www.moviefone.com

NYC/On Stage, 768-1818

Tele-charge, 800 432-7250 outside
NYC, 239-6200 or 563-2929
within NYC, www.telecharge.com

Ticket Central, 279-4200

Ticketmaster, 800 755-4000 outside
NYC, 307-4100 and 307-7171
within NYC, www.ticketmaster.com

Ticketweb, 269-4TIX (269-4849),
www.ticketweb.com

TKTS, 47th Street and Broadway on
Duffy Square, South Street Seaport,
www.tdf.org

Visa Card, www.visa.com

ENTERTAINMENT INDEX

Folk Arts and Multicultural Events
Aaron Davis Hall
ArtsConnection
Bronx Arts Ensemble
Brooklyn Center for the Performing
  Arts at Brooklyn College
City Center
Community Works Theater
  Connections
Czechoslovak–American Marionette
  Theatre
Dance Theater Workshop
Dance Theatre of Harlem
Hostos Center for the Arts & Culture
Los Kabayitos Puppet & Children's
  Theater
92nd Street Y
Poppy Seed Players
Shadow Box Theater
Tribeca Performing Arts Center
UniverSoul Big Top Circus

Ice Shows
Ice Theatre of New York
Madison Square Garden

Music
Aaron Davis Hall
Abrons Arts Center
Apollo Theatre
ArtsConnection
Bronx Arts Ensemble
Brooklyn Academy of Music (BAM)
Brooklyn Center for the Performing
  Arts at Brooklyn College
Carnegie Hall
Chamber Music Society of Lincoln
  Center
City Center
Colden Center for the Performing Arts
Growing Up with Opera
Hostos Center for the Arts & Culture
Jazz at Lincoln Center
Lincoln Center
Little Orchestra Society
Madison Square Garden
New Victory Theater
New York City Opera
New York Philharmonic
92nd Street Y
Radio City Music Hall
Symphony Space

Tribeca Performing Arts Center
Wave Hill

Puppet Shows
Czechoslovak–American Marionette
  Theatre
Hostos Center for the Arts & Culture
Lenny Suib Puppet Playhouse
Los Kabayitos Puppet & Children's
  Theater
Marionette Theater
New Victory Theater
Puppetworks
Shadow Box Theater

Readings
ArtsConnection
Wave Hill

Special Events
World Financial Center Arts & Events
  Program

Theater
Aaron Davis Hall
Abrons Arts Center
ArtsConnection
Brooklyn Academy of Music (BAM)
Brooklyn Center for the Performing
  Arts at Brooklyn College
City Center
City Lights
Colden Center for the Performing Arts
Community Works Theater
  Connections
Hostos Center for the Arts & Culture
Lincoln Center
Los Kabayitos Puppet & Children's
  Theater
Madison Square Garden
Manhattan Children's Theatre
New Victory Theater
Paper Bag Players
Poppy Seed Players
Shadow Box Theater
Symphony Space
Tada! Theater
Theater for a New Audience
Theatreworks/USA
Thirteenth Street Theater
Tribeca Performing Arts Center

Chapter 6

WHAT'S A CHILD TO DO?

ultivating culture is serious fun in the Big Apple. Since New York is home to some of the world's greatest museums, zoos, parks and libraries as well as a thriving creative community in almost any discipline you can imagine, even the youngest visitors to the city have a unique opportunity to explore just about anything their hearts desire. With literally hundreds of possibilities—from fine art, historical houses and famous landmarks to bowling, sports and laser tag—the abundance of choices can render even the most competent, resourceful and energetic parent helpless. The challenge is to spend time in ways that prove both meaningful and fun.

Mastering the ABCs of cultural exposure and enrichment for youngsters in New York City does not have to be the first step on the road to insanity, although we can guaranty that the number of things kids can do in Manhattan is indeed mind boggling. The first step to introducing your children to a variety of New York experiences is to get a handle on what is actually out there for children to do. In this chapter, we have endeavored to do just that by providing you with our ABC guide to child-friendly activities that includes **A**ttractions and **B**oredom Busters—drop-in activities, excursions, landmarks, parks, public libraries and sporting events—and **C**ultural institutions—galleries, gardens, historic sites, museums and zoos.

▶ **Creating a culture connection.** Since New York is one of the world's premier destinations for culture hounds, many adults look forward to immersing themselves in the city's cultural attractions immediately upon arrival. Unfortunately, most kids do not share that sentiment, and getting the children to log in hours, or even minutes, in museums, galleries, historic houses or other attractions or to admire the local architecture and landmarks can provoke battles of epic proportions.

Fortunately for the culture-hungry parent, New York has numerous attractions geared specifically to children that are designed to engage the younger set and present material (be it science, history, art, architecture or another field) in an age-appropriate and interesting way. While children's venues are not always the most entertaining for parents, they are usually very appealing to children and provide a great introduction to cultural pursuits.

In addition, cultural institutions have responded to parents' desires to provide their children with an early introduction to cultural and educational resources by presenting a wealth of programming, events and exhibits intended to draw a family audience. Such programming enables parents to lure their kids into big-time cultural destinations with child-sized portions of things of interest to the grownups in the group. And, if you're lucky, once the kids are engaged, you may even be able to continue your exploration and expand your visit.

While children's programming is the most likely to provide a positive experience for adult and child alike, that is no reason to shy away from New York's more grown-up cultural landmarks. The key to a successful encounter of the cultural kind is to be realistic about both what you think your child can process and how hard you are prepared to work to make the experience pleasant for everyone. Having to stuff the kids with cookies or reprimand, chase or restrain them to get through an exhibit you really want to see leaves both the adults and kids cranky, frustrated and unsatisfied.

▶ **Making it fun.** Deciding how to spend your city time involves a reasonable assessment of the various attention spans, energy levels and interests of the kids and adults; a realistic determination of the total amount of time you are allocating to sight-seeing; and, if the children in the group are old enough to express a point of view, a major negotiation among all parties and points of view to come to a viable decision. Have fun, this is your leisure time. Enjoy it!

◪ **Keep it short.** There is an old adage that it is best to leave a party while you are still having fun. The same is true for sightseeing. Children generally do not have the ability to spend hours in a museum. By the same token, parents generally do not have the ability to spend hours at a children's attraction (think hours of arcade games). A good rule of thumb is to allocate one to two hours to a particular place, leaving room to stay longer if it is going well. Your family will have a better time loving half of the exhibits at a major museum than dragging itself through every last gallery.

◪ **Do different kinds of things in a day.** The best way to keep the group happy is to keep the day varied. For example, organizing your day for a visit to a museum and including a stop in a playground for some physical activity (not to mention the ability to make a lot of noise) or some shopping will take the pressure off a day of "museum manners."

◪ **Divide and conquer.** The whole group does not have to be together 24/7. Splitting up throughout the day or even for an entire day allows everyone to get to do the things he or she wants to do. Sightseeing also offers an excellent opportunity for each adult to spend one-on-one quality time with each child while other grownups in the group do something else with other children or even have some alone time. Moreover, if you find yourself grappling with uncooperative kids, the grownups can take turns alternately minding the kids and going through the exhibit or attraction.

◪ **Check it out first.** Whenever possible, do a little research in advance of your visit. For example, see whether there is a special kid-friendly exhibit, an interesting short film or a guided tour geared to families. If you are in doubt, call ahead to find out whether it is appropriate to bring children at all.

◪ **One from column A...** Engage the family in the planning process by having each person make a list of what he or she wants to do while in New York. Then, review the lists as a group and let everyone select a top choice or two. This exercise in negotiation and deal making will not only ensure that everyone gets to do what is most valued, but it will provide a hands-on experience in cooperation, collaboration and respecting the wishes of others.

◪ **Keep moving.** If you get to a place and it is a complete bust for your group, move on . . . even if it is a famous place and you may not get a chance to return. Particularly if your child is becoming disruptive and unhappy, it may be best to leave and try again another time. With all the choices in this city, there is always something else to do.

◪ **Bring distractions.** It is always worth packing a small bag with a variety of distractions in the form of food, toys, books, electronic games, drawing materials, workbooks or anything else your child will enjoy that will buy you some time, provided that the distraction is not prohibited in the facility and will not disturb other patrons. An instant form of entertainment is to give each child a disposable camera with which to document the excursion.

◪ **Take breaks.** Sightseeing can be very exhausting, both physically and mentally. Everyone is taking in a lot of information and is not on a regular schedule. When the troops get pooped, stop and rest. Everyone will welcome a chance to stop for a snack, sit in the park or even go back to the hotel for a hit of cartoons to let the group have a break from activity.

◪ **Bribery.** Most parents balk at the concept of outright bribery, but in some instances, a modest bribe can be a good thing. For example, if you really want to get to the Museum of Modern Art and your kids are whining about seeing another painting, perhaps the offer of a ride on the Screamer (a speedboat tour of the Hudson River), a fast food meal or an hour of television may create a little more cooperation.

► **From culture to kitsch.** As you plan your itinerary, it is helpful to consider the range of available sights and activities. Some thoughts:

◢ **Boredom busters.** New York has a wealth of everyday activities that visitors can drop in on, as well as lots of in-and-around-town adventures, such as drop-in sports, computer and art activities, arcade games, outdoor experiences, boat rides and tours of popular destinations. While not all such activities necessarily rise to the level of "culture," they are still part of the fabric of the city and can provide a memorable family experience

◢ **Campuses.** More than 75 colleges, universities and other centers of higher learning call New York home, including Columbia, New York, Fordham, Yeshiva, New School and Rockefeller Universities; specialty schools such as Parsons School of Design, Fashion Institute of Technology, Juilliard and Cooper Union; and seminaries and medical schools. Some schools have oasis-like campuses while others offer a glimpse into urban college life, and all have within their facilities interesting buildings, research facilities and sometimes even exhibits.

◢ **Historical houses.** The Historic House Trust of New York, a not-for-profit organization, preserves and promotes the 20 historic houses located within New York City parks. In addition, many other homes of famous (or in some cases not so famous) New Yorkers are operated by other organizations. These homes can give children a window into the lives of celebrated personalities or just to life in other times.

◢ **Landmarks.** It would be impossible to chronicle the myriad landmarks dotting the city, but is entirely possible to avail yourselves of the various vistas, views, bridges, famous intersections (think Times Square, Wall Street, the tony shops of Fifth Avenue), styles of architecture and amazing skyscrapers and residences just by strolling around town.

◪ **Libraries.** The New York Public Library System has over 85 branches, millions of books and a variety of specialty research facilities. Many libraries feature children's programming as well as children's collections.

◪ **Museums.** New York is home to literally hundreds of museums, from world class to the virtually unknown, so you can likely find an institution that will inspire a child's natural creativity and curiosity.

◪ **Parks.** There is no lack of opportunity for outdoor fun in the city. The New York City Department of Parks and Recreation operates more than 1,700 parks, playgrounds and recreation facilities (614 ball fields, 13 golf courses, 6 ice rinks and so on) covering 28,000 acres, as well as 14 miles of beaches. Not to be missed are the Vaux and Olmstead–designed Central Park and Prospect Park and Flushing Meadows Corona Park (home to the 1939 and 1964 World's Fairs). The United States Park Service also operates national parks, including the Gateway and Statue of Liberty sites.

◪ **Sports.** Sports fans visiting New York have come to the right place. With professional basketball, baseball, hockey, football and other teams and extremely devoted fans, sports lovers have many choices for attending spectator sports events. For the more active, New York even offers opportunities to play a variety of outdoor and indoor sports.

◪ **Zoos and gardens.** New York City's Wildlife Conservation Society, which has for over a hundred years encouraged visitors to care about our natural resources and heritage, is also responsible for managing four zoos throughout the city and a terrific aquarium: The Bronx Zoo, Prospect Park Wildlife Center, Central Park Wildlife

Center & Tisch Children's Zoo, Queens Wildlife Center and the Aquarium for Wildlife Conservation (in Brooklyn).

▶ **How to use this chapter.** While we have listed more than 200 destinations of interest to kids and grownups alike, it is by no means a list of every possible New York attraction. In addition to listing the major "don't miss" sights for which the city is famous, we have included other places that are generally popular with children, focus on some particular subject matter, are reasonably accessible geographically or are just plain fun.

Entries are listed in alphabetical order and include the location, phone number, website (where applicable) and a brief description. For your reference, we have also noted the ages for which the destination is most suitable. This designation does not mean you cannot bring children who are outside the recommended age range. Rather it is to assist you in figuring out the age group for which the particular place is likely to be most interesting or fun (or, in some cases, even comprehensible).

Most facilities offer some level of handicapped accessibility. Because this designation will mean different things with respect to different organizations and may in fact be somewhat limited (for example, only certain areas may be wheelchair accessible) and because the particular accessibility needs of individuals will differ, it is crucial to call ahead to discuss particular circumstances in order to avoid wasted excursions or disappointment. In addition, even if a facility is not officially handicapped accessible, the staff may be able to offer assistance or make an alternative entrance available to disabled individuals in order to make possible a visit to the facility.

Specifics such as operating hours and admission charges have been omitted because that sort of information tends to change frequently (and often seasonally). We urge you to call for and confirm details for all programs, events and facilities in advance and, when appropriate, to make reservations. To find out about particular events, exhibits or programs, see the list of resources at the end of this chapter and the list of useful publications and websites in the Chapter 2 appendix.

Attractions and Boredom Busters

Asphalt Green
All ages
555 East 90th Street at York Avenue, 369-8890, www.asphaltgreen.com
Open swimming sessions in Olympic and Delacorte (smaller and warmer) pools. Call for hours and rates.

Basketball City
6+
Pier 63 at West 23rd Street and Twelfth Avenue, 924-4040, www.basketballcity.com
Open playtime weekdays and weekends.

Beaches
All ages
The City Parks & Recreation Department operates 14 miles of public beaches in four boroughs as well as 53 public outdoor swimming pools and a number of indoor swimming pools.

- ☛ GENERAL PARKS & RECREATION DEPARTMENT INFORMATION: Manhattan, 718 408-0243; Bronx 718 430-1858; Brooklyn, 718 965-8941; Queens, 718 520-5936; Staten Island 718 390-8020; www.nycparks.completeinet.net

- ☛ BRONX: Orchard Beach and Promenade (Long Island Sound), 718 885-2275

- ☛ BROOKLYN: Brighton Beach and Coney Island (Atlantic Ocean), 718 946-1350, www.coneyislandusacom; Manhattan Beach (Atlantic Ocean), 718 946-1373

- ☛ QUEENS: Rockaway Beach and Boardwalk (Atlantic Ocean), 718 318-4000; Jacob Riis Beach and Boardwalk (Atlantic Ocean), 718 318-4300

- ☛ STATEN ISLAND: South and Midland Beaches and Franklin D. Roosevelt Boardwalk (Lower New York Bay), 718 816-6804, 718 987-0709; Wolfe's Pond Beach (Raritan Bay), 718 984-8266

- ☛ The United States National Park Service operates Gateway National Recreation Area, a 26,000-acre recreation area extending through Brooklyn, Queens, Staten Island and New Jersey, which includes several beaches. 718 338-3688, www.nps.gov, www.rockawaychamberofcommerce.com

- ☛ Jones Beach State Park, Wantagh, Long Island, 516 785-1600. Located 33 miles from Manhattan, this famous local beach offers 6.5 miles of ocean beach, a bay beach, two swimming pools, a boardwalk, deck games and miniature golf.

Bowlmor Lanes 4+
110 University Place between 12th and 13th Streets, 225-8188,
www.bowlmor.com
Bumper bowling for beginners, regular bowling for older children and
adults.

Broadway City 4+
241 West 42nd Street, between Seventh and Eighth Avenues, 997-9797,
www.broadwaycity.com
Arcade with pinball, basketball and video games with prizes. Best to visit
before 5 p.m.

Bryant Park All ages
42nd Street and Sixth Avenue, 719-3434
Various activities for kids during the summer months. Call for details.

Carl Schurz Park All ages
86th Street and East End Avenue
Beautiful park overlooking the East River with a playground, dog run and
areas for biking and rollerblading.

Carnegie Hall Individual Tours 4+
57th Street at Seventh Avenue, 247-7800 (box office), 903-9765
(tour schedule), www.carnegiehall.org
Weekday tours of behind-the-scenes Carnegie Hall. (Note that tours are not
offered during the summer.) Visit the small museum on the second floor to
see changing exhibits of mementoes. Carnegie Hall also holds a number of
educational events, including concerts for families.

Central Park All ages
From 59th Street (or Central Park South) to 110th Street and from
Central Park West to Fifth Avenue, 360-3444; Emergencies 570-4820;
Urban Park Rangers 988-4952; www.centralparknyc.org
Covering over 840 acres with many playgrounds and special spots within
it, the park is available to visitors for most activities with the exception of
barbecuing. To find out more about the park, programs and events, pick up
a free copy of the Central Park Conservancy's quarterly publication, "Central Park Views," at any of the park's visitor centers: The Charles A. Dana
Discovery Center, The Dairy, Belvedere Castle and The North Meadow
Recreation Center (locations listed below). Copies of "Central Park Views"
are also mailed to Central Park Conservancy members free (call 310-6641
for membership information or visit www.centralparknyc.org).

Some of the special spots in Central Park of particular interest to children:

   ♦ Alice in Wonderland Sculpture. Near Fifth Avenue at 75th Street.
   ♦ Balto the Sled Dog Statue. East side of the park at 67th Street.

- Belvedere Castle. Mid-park at 79th Street. A 19th-century stone castle, it houses the Henry Luce Nature Observatory, a learning center with exhibits and programs (772-0210). Sign out a free "Discovery Kit," a backpack with binoculars, sketching materials, guidebook and map.

- The Carousel. Mid-park at 64th Street, 879-0244, 369-1010.

- Carriage Rides. Located on 59th Street between Fifth and Sixth Avenues or at Tavern on the Green (67th Street and Central Park West).

- The Charles A. Dana Discovery Center. At 110th Street between Fifth and Lenox Avenues, 860-1370. Nature classes, arts and crafts, family workshops and fishing (photo ID required for fishing).

- Conservatory Garden. At 105th Street and Fifth Avenue.

- Conservatory Water. Enter the park at 72nd Street and head north along Fifth Avenue.

- The Dairy. Mid-park at 65th Street, 794-6564. Displays, interactive computer programs and models provide visitors with information on the design, architecture and history of Central Park.

- Delacorte Clock. North of the Central Park Zoo at 65th Street.

- Hans Christian Andersen Statue. On the east side of the park at 72nd Street.

- Lasker Rink. Mid-park at 110th Street, 534-7639. Typically from November through March, the rink is open for outdoor private and group skating and ice hockey instruction. From July 4th to Labor Day, the rink is converted to a swimming pool.

- Loeb Boathouse. East Drive at 74th Street, 517-2233 for reservations for the restaurant. Rent boats with lifejackets; available mid-March through October. ID required.

- North Meadow Recreation Center. Mid-park at 97th Street, 348-4867. Youth center offering a variety of outdoor activities, including basketball and handball courts, and new indoor and outdoor climbing walls. Some activities are available on a drop-in basis; others require registration.

- Strawberry Fields. On the west side of Central Park at 72nd Street. John Lennon memorial.

- Trolley Tours of Central Park. Grand Army Plaza at Fifth Avenue and 60th Street, 360-2727 or 397-3809 for reservations.

- Wollman Rink. South of the 65th Street transverse in the center of the park, 396-1010. During the winter months the rink is prepped for ice skating. In warmer weather, Wollman transforms into a rollerblading rink with a special area dedicated to a basketball challenge course

- Zoo/Central Park Wildlife Center/Tisch Children's Zoo. 64th Street near Fifth Avenue, 861-6030.

Some helpful hints

- When in Central Park, it is easy to forget you are in the center of one of the world's largest and busiest cities. Even though the park is well patrolled, use the same safety rules for your family as you would elsewhere in the city, such as staying away from isolated areas and being aware of your surroundings.

- Becoming geographically disoriented in the park is not an uncommon problem. Note that some lamp posts are marked with the cross street to help identify your location.

Playgrounds within Central Park:

EAST SIDE

- Billy Johnson Playground. Fifth Avenue between 67th and 68th Streets

- Fifth Avenue between 71st and 72nd Streets

- James Michael Levin Playground. Fifth Avenue between 75th and 76th Streets

- Three Bears Playground. Fifth Avenue between 79th and 80th Streets

- Ancient Playground. Fifth Avenue between 84th and 85th Streets

- Fifth Avenue between 95th and 96th Streets

- Bernard Playground. 108th and 109th Streets; enter on 110th Street and walk south

- 110th Street between Fifth and Lenox Avenues

WEST SIDE

- Heckscher Playground. Central Park South and 62nd Street; enter at Seventh Avenue and Central Park South and walk north

- Adventure Playground. Central Park West and 67th Street

- Diana Ross Playground. Central Park West and 81st Street

- Belfer Playground. Central Park West between 84th and 85th Streets

- Ross Pinetum. Central Park West and 84th Street; enter at 84th Street and walk east

- Spector Playground. Central Park West between 85th and 86th Streets

- Safari Playground. Central Park West between 90th and 91st Streets

- Wild West Playground. Central Park West between 93rd and 94th Streets

- Rudin Playground. Central Park West between 96th and 97th Streets

- Robert Bendheim Playground. Central Park West between 99th and 100th Streets

- Central Park West and 110th Street

Chelsea Piers Sports and
Entertainment Complex   Depends on ability/activity
Piers 59-62 at West 23rd Street and the Hudson River, 336-6666,
www.chelseapiers.com
Batting cages, ice skating, rollerblading, golf, rock climbing, basketball, extreme skating/skateboarding/bmx biking and bowling available on a drop-in basis during scheduled times.

Circle Line   4+
Pier 83 at West 42nd Street; Pier 16 at the South Street Seaport,
563-3200, www.circleline.com
Three-hour cruise around the island of Manhattan leaving from Pier 83. Toddlers and very active children might find this too long an adventure. Bring lap activities to provide additional entertainment. The Pier 16 cruise is approximately one hour in length and tours lower Manhattan.

Claremont Riding Academy   6+
175 West 89th Street between Columbus and Amsterdam Avenues,
724-5100
Private horseback riding instruction for all levels by appointment.

Coney Island   All ages
Surf Avenue, Brooklyn, 718 372-5159, www.coneyisland.com
Attracting locals and tourists alike for many decades, this famous waterside attraction includes Astroland, Coney Island USA and Deno's Wonder Wheel amusements parks, the renowned Cyclone Rollercoaster, tons of rides for adults and kids, sideshows, freak shows, the New York Aquarium, Nathan's Famous Hot Dogs, a museum and a boardwalk.

The Craft Studio   3+
1657 Third Avenue between 92nd and 93rd Streets, 831-6626
Drop-in projects include painting plaster molds, flower pots and watering cans and decorating chocolate with edible paints.

Creatability   2+
500 East 88th Street between York and East End Avenues, 535-4033,
www.creatibility.us
Walk-in "craftshops," including drawing, painting, decorating, beading and other crafts projects.

Dieu Donne Papermill   5+
433 Broome Street between Crosby and Broadway, 226-0573,
www.papermaking.org
Tour a genuine paper mill and see how paper is made. Papermaking workshops are also held here.

Empire State Building Observatory   All ages
350 Fifth Avenue between 33rd and 34th Streets, 736-3100,
www.empirestatebuilding.com
Two observation decks offer great views of the city and surrounding areas.
Don't miss the Guinness Exhibition of World Records. (See also New York
Skyride.)

ESPN Zone   5+
1472 Broadway at Times Square, 921-3776, www.espn.go.com
Sports entertainment complex, including a restaurant, lots of televisions
for watching the big games and high-tech interactive and sports simulation
games.

Extra Vertical Climbing Center   5+
61 West 62nd Street in the Harmony Atrium, 586-5718
Climb the walls, literally.

14th Street Y   3+
Sol Goldman YM-YWHA of the Educational Alliance, Inc.
344 East 14th Street at First Avenue, 780-0800, www.edalliance.org
Indoor playground available at scheduled weekly times.

French Institute/Alliance Française   5+
22 East 60th between Park and Madison Avenues, 355-6100,
www.fiaf.org
Occasional dance, films and other events geared to young audiences.

Frozen Ropes   3+
207 West 74th Street between Broadway and Amsterdam Avenue,
362-0344, www.frozenropesnyc.com
This national network of baseball and softball training centers offers training, professional instruction and an assortment of batting cages for all skill
levels on a drop-in basis. Reservations for batting cages recommended.

Fulton Fish Market Tour   10+
165 John Street near the South Street Seaport, 748-8590
The country's oldest wholesale fish market. Tours are offered through the
South Street Seaport Museum and require a minimum of eight people or
the tour is canceled. Call for scheduled dates; reservations required.

Galactic Circus   7+
1540 Broadway at 46th Street, 869-9397
Entertainment complex with games, motion ride simulators, live performers,
prizes and a café.

Gracie Mansion 11+
East End Avenue at 88th Street, 570-4751,
www.nyc.gov/html/om/html/gracie.html
Weekday tours of the official residence of the Mayor of New York available by reservation only.

Horse Drawn Carriage Rides All ages
A quintessential New York experience. Carriages are available at 59th Street and Fifth Avenue, along Central Park South and at Tavern on the Green (inside Central Park at 67th Street and Central Park West). Fare is $34 for the first half-hour, $10 for each additional 15 minutes.

Ice Rink at Rockefeller Plaza 3+
49th and 50th Streets between Fifth and Sixth Avenues, 332-7654
Experience the magic of skating in one of the most recognized spots in the world. Skate rentals available. Call for public skating hours.

Institute of Culinary Education 6+
50 West 23rd Street between Fifth and Sixth Avenues, 847-0700,
www.iceculinary.com
Single-session cooking classes include pizza-making, baking and others.

Kids on Wheels 5+
Joel Rappelfeld's Rollerblading, 744-4444
In-line skating instruction offered after school and on weekends.

Lazer Park 7+
163 West 46th Street between Broadway and Sixth Avenue, 398-3060,
www.lazertag.com
Laser tag for the intrepid.

Leisure Time Bowling 4+
625 Eighth Avenue and 40th Street in the Port Authority Bus Terminal,
268-6909
Bumper bowling for beginners, regular bowling for older children and adults.

Liberty Helicopters Parental discretion
West 30th Street Heliport, 967-6464, www.libertyhelicopters.com
Aerial tours of the Hudson, lower Manhattan and up to Central Park.

Libraries All ages
The New York Public Library system (www.nypl.org) contains a wealth of literary works for even the youngest readers. The library branches listed below have children's areas and even entire children's floors. Programs vary but can include films, story hours, workshops, computer games and instruction. The Donnell Library on West 53rd Street has the honor of being the permanent residence of Winnie-the-Pooh and his friends. Call

the branch you wish to visit for specific hours. A monthly calendar of city-wide activities and events can be obtained at any branch.

- New York Public Library Offices of Children's Services. 340-0904
- 58th Street Branch. 127 East 58th Street, 759-7358
- 67th Street Branch. 328 East 67th Street, 734-1717
- 96th Street Branch. 112 East 96th Street, 289-0908
- 115th Street Branch. 203 West 115th Street, 666-9393
- Chatham Square Branch. 33 East Broadway, 964-6598
- Columbia Branch. 514 West 113th Street, 864-2530
- Donnell Library Center. 20 West 53rd Street, 621-0615
- Early Childhood Resource and Information Center. 66 Leroy Street, 929-0815
- Epiphany Branch. 228 East 23rd Street, 679-2645
- Harlem Branch. 9 West 124th Street, 348-5620
- Jefferson Market Branch. 425 Sixth Avenue, 243-4334
- Kips Bay Branch. 446 Third Avenue, 683-2520
- Lincoln Center. 127 Amsterdam Avenue, 870-1633
- Muhlenberg Branch. 209 West 23rd Street, 924-1585
- Ottendorfer Branch. 135 Second Avenue, 674-0947
- Riverside Branch. 127 Amsterdam Avenue, 870-1810
- St. Agnes Branch. 444 Amsterdam Avenue, 877-4380
- Tompkins Square Branch. 331 East 10th Street, 228-4747
- Webster Branch. 1465 York Avenue, 288-5049
- Yorkville Branch. 222 East 79th Street, 744-5824

Lincoln Center Tours   6+
**Broadway and 64th Street, 546-2656, 875-5350 (tour desk information),
www.lincolncenter.org**
Behind-the-scenes look at New York City's famous cultural center. Rehearsals viewed weekdays. Meet at the Metropolitan Opera House on the Concourse level next to the gift shop. Call for weekly schedules.

Little Shop of Plaster   4+
431 East 73rd Street between First and York Avenues, 717-6636
Paint plaster molds of your choice.

Madame Tussaud's   All ages
**234 West 42nd Street between Broadway and Eighth Avenue,
800 246-8872, www.nycwax.com**
View replicas of more than 150 of your favorite celebrities, including Lady

Diana, Elton John, Jacqueline Kennedy Onassis, George W. Bush and more, at this 85,000 square foot New York location of the world-famous wax museum.

Madison Square Garden Tour   9+
Seventh Avenue between 31st and 33rd Streets, 465-5800,
www.thegarden.com
See what's behind the bleachers, visit a corporate box, check out the locker rooms and more. Tickets available at the box office.

My Favorite Place   6 mos.–4 yrs; age specific
265 West 87th Street between Broadway and West End Avenue, 362-5320
Indoor playroom and toy store offering toddler and after-school drop-in programs at scheduled times, including a "Toddler Sing-Along" each week-day morning.

NBC Studio Tour   Children under 6 not permitted
GE Building, 30 Rockefeller Center between 49th and 50th Streets,
664-3700, www.nbc.com
See what happens on television from the other side of the screen. Tickets are sold on a first-come, first-served basis and can be purchased on the website. Reservations are recommended. Call 664-3056 for tickets to NBC shows taped in New York.

Nelson A. Rockefeller Park (formerly Hudson River Park)   All Ages
Battery Park City, 267-9700
Enter at the end of Chambers or Vesey Streets or at the World Financial Center and walk north along the river. This site offers a fabulous playground with breathtaking views. Special events are organized for all ages, including recreational and arts programs, music and storytelling, after-school programs, drawing classes, fishing and walking tours. May through October.

New York Skyride   3+
350 Fifth Avenue at 34th Street (in Empire State Building), 2nd floor,
800 975-9743, www.skyride.com
Big-screen flight simulator takes you for a ride over Manhattan.

New York Stock Exchange   8+
Interactive Education Center, 20 Broad Street between Wall Street and
Exchange Place, 656-5168, www.nyse.com
Self-guided tours weekdays at no charge. See what makes the ticker tape tick.

New York Waterway Cruises   4+
Pier 78 at 38th Street and Twelfth Avenue, 800 533-3779,
www.nywaterway.com
A number of cruise opportunities available for various lengths of time. Toddlers and very active children might find some excursions too long an adventure. Bring lap activities to provide additional entertainment.

Our Name is Mud   4+
1566 Second Avenue between 81st Street and 82nd Streets, 570-6868
506 Amsterdam Avenue between 84th and 85th Streets, 579-5575
59 Greenwich Avenue at Seventh Avenue, 647-7899
Glaze the clay piece of your choice on a drop-in basis.

Parades, street festivals and other happenings   All ages
The Mayor's Street Activity Office, 788-7439
Calendar of community events delivered by automated voice system. See
also Chapter 2 appendix for calendar listings.

Parks   All ages
www.nyc.gov (city agencies, Parks & Recreation) or
www.nycparks.completinet.net; Special Events Hotline, 888 NY PARKS
(888 697-2757) or 360-3456 or 800 201 PARK (800 201-7275)
The City Parks & Recreation Department operates 35 recreation centers;
hundreds of parks; playgrounds; playing fields (including softball, cricket,
football and soccer fields); basketball, tennis, volleyball and bocce courts;
golf courses; ice skating rinks; roller hockey rinks; marinas; running tracks;
skate parks (inline skating, roller hockey and skateboarding) and bike
paths. Visit the website for locations and operating hours.

The Parks & Recreation Department operates 10 Urban Park Ranger Nature
Centers that offer walking tours, workshops, educational programs and
recreation facilities.

6

- ✪ BRONX. Pelham Bay Nature Center, 718 885-3467; Crotona Park, 718
  378-2061; Orchard Beach Nature Center, 718 667-6042 or 718 967-
  3542; Van Cortlandt Nature Center, 718 548-0912.

- ✪ BROOKLYN. Salt Marsh Nature Center, 718 421-2021.

- ✪ MANHATTAN. Inwood Hill Nature Center, 304-2365; Belvedere Castle
  Visitor Center (Central Park), 628-2345; Dana Discovery Center (Central Park), 860-1370.

- ✪ QUEENS. Alley Pond Nature Center, 718 217-6034 or 718 846-2731;
  Forest Park Nature/Visitor Center, 718 846-2731.

- ✪ STATEN ISLAND. Blue Heron Nature Center, 718 967-3542; High Rock
  Nature Center, 718 967-3542.

The Parks & Recreation Department operates 20 Historic Houses. For details
of these and other houses, see www.nyc.gov, City Agencies, Parks & Recreation, or www.nycparks.completeinet.net.

- ✪ BRONX. Bartow-Pell Mansion Museum, Van Cortlandt House Museum.

- ✪ BROOKLYN. Leffert Homestead Children's Historic House Museum, Old
  Stone House Historic Interpretive Center, Pieter Claesen Wyckoff
  House Museum.

- ✪ QUEENS. King Manor Museum, Kingsland Homestead.

- ✪ STATEN ISLAND. Conference House, Seguine Mansion.

Playgrounds
All ages

With more than 200 playgrounds in Manhattan alone, you are never too far from a "play break" as you wend your way through the city. The most popular playgrounds are found in Central Park, Riverside Park (from 72nd to 100th Streets, along the Hudson River) and along the East River. However, there are many playgrounds, small and large, tucked within most residential neighborhoods. For a complete list of playgrounds in all boroughs, visit www.nyc.gov, City Agencies, Parks & Recreation, or www.nycparks.completeinet.net.

Some favorites:

- Bryant Park. 42nd Street and Sixth Avenue behind the Public Library
- Hippo Park. In Riverside Park at 91st Street
- Hudson River Playground. Chambers Street at Greenwich Street
- John Jay Playground. 76th Street and the FDR Drive
- Mercer Street Playground. Mercer Street between Bleecker and West 3rd Streets
- Union Square Park. Union Square between 14th and 17th Streets
- For older kids interested in extreme skating, Owls Head Park in Bay Ridge Brooklyn

Post Office Tour—The Morgan Mail Facility
7+ only

341 Ninth Avenue between 29th and 30th Streets
Tours on weekdays of the Post Office's automated mail processing. Generally, a two-week advance reservation is required.

Public Spaces
All ages

These areas, which are open to the public, offer a nice place to stop and rest while touring midtown Manhattan. All offer seating and some have food concessions at certain hours or seasonally.

- Citicorp Center. 53rd Street with entrances on Lexington and Third Avenues. Shopping arcade.
- Crystal Pavilion. 50th Street at Third Avenue. Atrium with waterfalls.
- IBM Plaza. 56th Street at Madison Avenue. Atrium.
- Olympic Tower. 51st Street at Fifth Avenue. Atrium with waterfall.
- Paley Park. 53rd Street from Fifth to Madison Avenues. Passageway with waterfall.
- Park Avenue Plaza. Park Avenue from 52nd to 53rd Streets. Passageway with waterfall and shopping arcade.
- Water Tunnel. From 48th to 49th Streets between Sixth and Seventh Avenues. Passageway with waterfall.

Radio City Music Hall Tours   10+
1260 Sixth Avenue between 50th and 51st Streets, 632-4041,
www.radiocity.com
Backstage tours of this world-famous theater.

Rain or Shine   6 mos.–6 yrs.
115 East 29th Street between Park and Lexington Avenues, 532-4420
Indoor play space that resembles a natural rain forest.

Riverdale Equestrian Center   5+
West 254th Street and Broadway in Van Cortlandt Park, Riverdale, Bronx,
718 548-4848
Private riding lessons by appointment, pony rides on weekends from 1 to
3 p.m.

Rockefeller Center Tour   6+ only
GE Building, 30 Rockefeller Center between 49th and 50th Streets,
664-3700, 664-3700, www.nbc.com
Tour NBC, Radio City, the skating rink, gardens and more in this Art Deco
jewel in the heart of Manhattan.

Sports   Depends on event
Arenas

- Madison Square Garden. Seventh Avenue between 31st and 33rd
  Streets, 465-6741, www.thegarden.com. The Garden hosts basketball
  (professional, college and even high school championships), hockey,
  tennis, wrestling; the circus; dog, cat and horse shows; concerts and
  more. The teams that call the Garden home are the Knicks, the
  Rangers and the Liberty.

- Nassau Veterans Memorial Coliseum. Uniondale, Long Island, 516
  794-9300, www.nassaucoliseum.com. Long Island's sports and entertainment complex is home to the Islanders, New York Saints La Crosse
  and New York Dragons football.

- Meadowlands Sports Complex. East Rutherford, New Jersey, 201 935-
  3900, www.njsea.com. Consisting of the Continental Airlines Arena,
  Giants Stadium and the Meadowlands Race Track, this sports/enter-
  tainment complex is home to the Giants, Jets and Metrostars.

- Shea Stadium. Flushing, Queens, 718 507-8499, www.ballparks.com.
  Home to the Mets.

- USTA National Tennis Center, Flushing Meadows–Corona Park
  Queens, 718 760-6200, tickets 888 673-6844, www.usta.com,
  www.usopen.org. Home to the U.S. Tennis Open.

- Yankee Stadium. Bronx, 718 293-6000, www.ballparks.com. Home to
  the Yankees.

6

Teams

BASEBALL

- New York Mets. Shea Stadium, 718 507-8499, www.newyorkmets
- New York Yankees. Yankee Stadium, 718 293-6000, www.yankees.mlb.com
- Brooklyn Cyclones. Keyspan Park, Coney Island, 718 449-8497, www.brooklyncyclones.com
- Brooklyn Kings. www.brooklynkings.com
- Staten Island Yankees. Richmond Country Bank Ballpark, Staten Island, 718 720-9265, www.siyanks.com

BASKETBALL

- New York Knicks. Madison Square Garden, 465-5867, www.nba.com/knicks
- New York Liberty. Madison Square Garden, 564-9622, www.wnba.com/liberty

FOOTBALL

- New York Giants. Meadowlands, 201 460-4370, www.giants.com
- New York Jets. Meadowlands, 201 935-3900, www.newyorkjets.com

HOCKEY

- New York Islanders. Nassau Coliseum, www.newyorkislanders.com
- New York Rangers. Madison Square Garden, www.newyorkrangers.com

SOCCER

- New York Metro Stars. Meadowlands, 201 583-7000, www.metrostars.com
- New York Power. Mitchel Athletic Complex, Uniondale, Long Island, 372-0440, 866 769-7849 (tickets), www.nypower.com

Television show tapings   Depends on show

While most television shows are taped in Los Angeles, quite a few are taped in New York. Dramatic shows typically do not allow visitors on the set, but talk shows, sitcoms and game shows tape before a studio audience. Audiences Unlimited, 818 753-3470, www.tvtickets.com, offers free tickets to tapings. Most are in LA, but occasionally New York tickets are available for specific shows. See also www.nycvisit.com (look at visitors, things to do) for a list of shows that tape in the city as well as shows that can be seen from outside the studio (such as *The Early Show* at Fifth Avenue and 59th Street, *Good Morning America* at 44th Street and Broadway, *The Today Show* at 30 Rockefeller Plaza, and *Total Request Live* at 1550 Broadway between 44th and 45th Streets). Visit www.abc.com, www.nbc.com (or call 664-3056), www.fox.com, www.thewb.com and www.upn.com to see if your favorite New York–based shows have live tapings or studio visits.

Tennis Courts
Depends on ability

There are a number of courts located in and around the city where you can pay a court fee and play or even arrange a lesson. The following is an abbreviated listing. See also www.parksnyc.completeinet.net for a list of public courts.

- Columbus Tennis Club. 795 Columbus Avenue at 98th Street

- Crosstown Tennis. 31st Street between Fifth Avenue and Broadway

- HRC Tennis and Yacht. Piers 13 and 14 at the Seaport, 422-9300

- HRC Village Courts. 110 University Place between 12th and 13th Streets, 989-2300

- Manhattan Plaza Racquet Club. 450 West 43rd Street between Ninth and Tenth Avenues

- Midtown Tennis Club. 341 Eighth Avenue at 27th Street, 989-8572

- Roosevelt Island Racquet Club. 280 Main Street (next to the tram)

- Stadium Racket Club. 11 East 162nd Street (across from Yankee Stadium)

- Sutton East Tennis Club. 488 East 60th Street, 751-3452

- USTA National Tennis Center. Corona Park, Flushing Meadows, Queens, 718 760-6200

Tin Pan Alley Studios
5–13

One East 28th Street between Fifth and Madison Avenues, 3rd floor

Make your own CD. Studio musicians accompany child's performance of a collection of songs and/or instrumental selections.

United Nations
Children under 5 not permitted on tours

First Avenue between 42nd and 48th Streets; visitors' entrance at 46th Street

45-minute tours given daily.

World Financial Center
Depends on program

Battery Park City between Vesey and Liberty Streets, 646 772-6885, www.worldfinancialcenter.com

The Center's Winter Garden is a most amazing indoor public space that hosts shows, concerts, dance programs and other family activities.

XS New York
6+

1457 Broadway with entrances on Broadway and Seventh Avenue in Times Square, 398-5467

Virtual Game arena, laser tag.

Cultural Institutions, Galleries, Gardens, Museums and Zoos

Abigail Adams Smith Museum 7+
421 East 61st Street between First and York Avenues, 838-6878
Experience New York City as it once was in this restored 18th-century carriage house that was built for President John Adams' daughter and her husband, even though they never got to live there. Evening and weekend programs for families. Special annual events for children. The museum contains nine period rooms furnished with American antiques.

Abyssinian Baptist Church 8+
132 Odell Clark Place between Adam Clayton Powell Jr. and Malcolm X Boulevards, 862-7474, www.abyssinian.org
This well-known church is one of the oldest in Harlem.

Alice Austen House 7+, programs for 5+
2 Hylan Boulevard, Rosebank, Staten Island, 718 816-4506, www.aliceausten.8m.com
Alice Austen was famous for her contribution to early photography. This one-room farmhouse originally built in 1690 was home to the Austen family.

Alley Pond Environmental Center 3+
228-06 Northern Boulevard, Douglaston, Queens, 718 229-4000, www.alleypond.com
A 700-acre park is the setting for this center's many learning opportunities. The indoor facility, wetlands and many exploration trails allow visitors to study environmental history and science. An extensive educational department offers programs including weekend, summer and special clubs.

American Craft Museum 7+, programs for younger children
40 West 53rd Street between Fifth and Sixth Avenues, 956-3535, www.americancraftmuseum.org
This was the first museum dedicated to the work of fine American craft artists. Exhibitions include works from both established and emerging artists. The museum also holds workshops, demonstrations and lectures.

American Museum of the Moving Image 5+
36-01 35th Avenue at 36th Street, Astoria, Queens, 718 784-0077, www.ammi.org
Located near the Kaufman Astoria Studios complex at 36th Street, this museum houses a wonderful collection of films and all kinds of artifacts from the industry. Hands-on exhibits allow first-hand testing of the principles and techniques used by filmmakers.

American Museum of Natural History   All ages, programs age-specific
Central Park West between 77th and 81st Streets, 769-5100, 769-5200
for reservations and program information, www.amnh.org
One of the world's largest museums, this amazing institution houses an
extensive range of exhibits that cover the history of human life and natural
evolution, including over 40 million natural specimens. Favorites include
Dinosaur Hall, the Hall of Minerals and Gems, the Hall of Biodiversity (a
new area featuring a rain forest) and the North American Indian exhibit.
There is a Discovery Room for children that requires tickets but is free of
charge. The Natural Science Center is also open to children for exploration
at specified times.

American Museum of Natural History – Hayden Planetarium,
Rose Center for Earth and Space   All ages
81st Street between Central Park West and Columbus Avenue, 769-5100,
www.amnh.org
Now housed in a sleek new glass box, the Rose Center for Earth and Space
and the Planetarium provide a virtual journey through time–space and the
mysteries of the universe.

American Numismatic Society   8+
Broadway at 155th Street in the Audubon Terrace Museum Complex,
234-3130, www.amnumsoc.org
The exhibition galleries have extensive collections of coins, medals and
paper money. An appointment can be scheduled for a tour with a curator.

Anne Frank Center, USA   10+
584 Broadway between Houston and Prince Streets, 431-7993,
www.annefrank.com
This exhibit explores the life of Anne Frank, her family and other Jewish
families during WWII in Europe.

The Aquarium for Wildlife Conservation   All ages, programs age-specific
West 8th Street and Surf Avenue, Coney Island, Brooklyn, 718 265-
FISH(3474), 718 265-3448 for program information,
www.nyaquarium.com
Observe an abundance of sea life. Daily performances. Programs for children and families throughout the year plus summer and holiday programs,
including lectures, beach walks, and "get wet" workshops.

The Asia Society   10+
725 Park Avenue at 70th Street, 288-6400, 517-NEWS for events informa-
tion, www.asiasociety.org
Permanent and changing exhibitions create an awareness and understanding of Asian cultures.

The Bard Graduate Center for Studies in the Decorative Arts   6+
18 West 86th Street between Central Park West and Columbus Avenue, 501-3000, www.bgc.bard.edu
Interactive programs including gallery tours, artisan demonstrations, theatrical role-playing, book readings and arts-and-crafts projects. Educational programs are keyed into current exhibits.

Bronx Museum of the Arts   5+
1040 Grand Concourse at 165th Street, Bronx, 718 681-6000, www.bronxview.com/museum/
Founded in 1971 to serve the culturally diverse population of the Bronx and the rest of New York, the museum focuses on modern and contemporary art. There are Sunday family programs.

The Bronx Zoo/Wildlife Conservation Park   All ages, programs age-specific
Bronx River Parkway at Fordham Road, Bronx, 718 367-1010 general information, 718 220-6854 program information, www.bronxzoo.com, www.wcs.org
Natural habitats house hundreds of species live at this world-class zoo. Rides, shows, feedings and a special Children's Zoo. Seasonal exhibits, programs, lectures and workshops.

Brooklyn Botanic Garden   All ages, programs age-specific
1000 Washington Avenue, Brooklyn, 718 623-7200, 718 623-7220 for tour information, www.bbg.org
Explore 59 acres and over 12,000 kinds of plants, and participate in a variety of special programs. Tours are given on weekends.

Brooklyn Children's Museum   2–13
145 Brooklyn Avenue at St. Mark's Avenue, Brooklyn, 718 735-4432/4400, www.brooklynkids.org
The exhibitions and many hands-on activities here provide the materials for children to learn about the world and different cultures around them. Many different kinds of children's programs are offered.

The Brooklyn Historical Society   5+
128 Pierrepont Street at Clinton Street, Brooklyn Heights, 718 222-4111, www.brooklynhistory.org
These exhibitions on Brooklyn history include permanent exhibits on the Brooklyn Bridge, Coney Island, the Dodgers, the Navy Yard and Brooklynites. Note: the Historical Society Building is closed for renovation until early 2003, and the Society is temporarily located at 45 Main Street, Suite 617; only the photo archives are available by appointment.

The Brooklyn Museum of Art   4+, programs age-specific
200 Eastern Parkway, Brooklyn, 718 638-5000, www.brooklynart.org
Some of the museum's permanent exhibits include traditional art of Africa, the South Pacific and the Americas. Paintings, sculpture, costumes, decora-

tive arts and period rooms are on display. The museum is also home to pre-eminent collections of Egyptian, Classical, Middle Eastern and Asian art. "Arty Facts" is a weekly series of workshops and gallery visits for families. The museum offers many other programs for all different ages and interests. Note: The Museum is under renovation until the end of 2002.

Cathedral Church of St. John the Divine   8+
Amsterdam Avenue at 112th Street, www.stjohndivine.org
Begun in 1892 and home to the Episcopal Church, this is one of the world's largest cathedrals.

Central Park Wildlife Center, Wildlife Gallery and
The Tisch Children's Zoo   All ages, programs age-specific
Fifth Avenue at 64th Street behind the Arsenal Building in Central Park, 861-6030, www.wcs.org
View this collection of habitats within various climate zones. Shows, activities, workshops and special events. Adjacent to the Central Park Wildlife Center is the Children's Zoo, which is filled with opportunities to "walk with the animals."

Central Synagogue   6+
55th Street and Lexington Avenue, www.centralsynagogue.org
This is the oldest Jewish house of worship in the city in continuous use. Serving a Reform congregation, the magnificent Moorish-style Sanctuary Building is a National and New York City historic landmark.

The Children's Interactive Jewish Museum   4+
14th Street Y, Sol Goldman YM-YWHA of the Educational Alliance
344 East 14th Street at First Avenue, 780-0800, extension 254, www.edalliance.org
This museum is set up for families to learn about Jewish feasts, fasts, celebrations and holidays in an interactive and educational way.

Children's Museum of the Arts   2–10
182 Lafayette Street between Broome and Grand Streets, 274-0986, www.cmany.org
The museum offers many types of programs for children and families, including dance and theater workshops.

Children's Museum of Manhattan   All ages
212 West 83rd Street between Amsterdam Avenue and Broadway, 721-1224, www.cmom.org
Wonderful, original, interactive exhibits provide a unique setting for children and adults to learn about art, science and the world around them. The museum offers classes, workshops and many programs for children.

China House Gallery/
China Institute in America   12+, programs for younger children
125 East 65th Street between Park and Lexington Avenues, 744-8181,
www.chinainstitute.org
The gallery hosts special exhibits of Chinese art and other cultural items and offers accompanying special workshops, which can range from exploring Chinese languages to instruction in calligraphy.

City Hall/Governor's Room   9+
City Hall, 788-6865, www.nyc.gov
Get a hands-on lesson in local government via a self-guided tour of City Hall and the Governor's Room (available for parties of ten or fewer). Larger groups can tour the facility with a sergeant. Requires a two-week advance reservation.

The Cloisters   4+
Fort Tryon Park, Upper Manhattan, 923-3700, www.metmuseum.org
The Cloisters, on a hilltop overlooking the Hudson River, is a branch of the Metropolitan Museum of Art and is devoted to the art and architecture of medieval Europe. Special workshops are offered for families, typically on Saturdays.

Cooper-Hewitt National Design Museum   Depends upon exhibits
2 East 91st Street at Fifth Avenue, 849-8300, www.si.edu/ndm
The Smithsonian Institution's National Museum of Design offers changing exhibits focusing on various aspects of contemporary and historical design, including anything from buttons to jewelry to kitchen utensils.

Dahesh Museum   10+
601 Fifth Avenue at 48th Street, 759-0606, www.dasheshmuseum.org
Visit this small museum dedicated to exploring 19th-century European academic art.

DIA Center for the Arts   10+
548 West 22nd Street, 431-9232, www.diacenter.org
The center shows large-scale installations of contemporary art, usually by a single artist.

The Dyckman Farm House   7+
4881 Broadway at 204th Street, 304-9422, www.dyckman.org
The last remaining Dutch colonial farmhouse in Manhattan contains period artifacts depicting life in colonial New York. Demonstrations can be scheduled in advance.

Edgar Allan Poe Cottage   10+
2460 Grand Concourse and East Kingsbridge Road, Bronx, 718 881-8900
The 1812 cottage where Edgar Allan Poe settled in 1846 has been restored

and is dedicated to one of America's greatest literary masters. Tours by appointment during the week.

Eldridge Street Project 5+
12 Eldridge Street near Canal and Allen Streets, 978-8800,
www.eldridgestreet.org
Tours of this historic landmark synagogue are available. Programs offered include storytelling.

Ellis Island Immigration Museum All ages will enjoy the boat ride,
otherwise 6+
Ellis Island, by way of the Statue of Liberty ferry, 363-3200,
ferry schedule 269-5755, www.ellisisland.org
The Ellis Island immigration station, which operated from 1892 to 1954, has been restored as a museum. Among its many exhibits, the museum displays countless artifacts belonging to the individuals who passed through years ago. Explore the passenger record archive (culled from arriving ships' manifests) for information on the individuals who entered this country at Ellis Island.

El Museo del Barrio 5+
1230 Fifth Avenue at 104th Street, 831-7272, www.elmuseo.org
Through paintings, sculpture, graphics, photography, archaeology, films, music and theater, the museum highlights the cultural heritage of Puerto Ricans and all Latin Americans living in the United States. Traditional folk art and contemporary urban art of the barrio are displayed. El Museo is one of the city's foremost Hispanic cultural institutes, offering concerts, workshops and other programs, some of which are appropriate for children.

Fashion Institute of Technology 8+
Seventh Avenue at 27th Street, 217-5800, www.fitncy.suny.edu
With a huge collection of costumes, textiles and clothing, this museum, dedicated to the social and cultural contexts of style and fashion, will delight fashion-conscious kids.

The Forbes Magazine Gallery 7+
60 Fifth Avenue between 12th and 13th Streets, 206-5548,
www.forbes.com
The galleries display 300 pieces of Fabergé art, 12,000 toy soldiers, 500 toy boats, an assortment of historical documents and other memorabilia and paintings from the permanent collection.

Fraunces Tavern Museum 3+
54 Pearl Street, 425-1778, www.frauncestavernmuseum.org
Tucked in the historical Fraunces Tavern, the museum has a permanent collection of artifacts, decorative arts, paintings and prints from 18th-century America. One weekend each month, the museum conducts programs for families and children.

The Frick Collection   Children under 10 not admitted
One East 70th Street at Fifth Avenue, 288-0700, www.frick.org
Formerly a single-family residence and now a museum, this grand mansion houses an incredible collection of 18th- and 19th-century art, transporting visitors into the grandeur of turn-of-the-century high society.

Guggenheim Museum (Solomon R. Guggenheim Museum)
                       Activity guide for 7 and under, programs age-specific
1071 Fifth Avenue at 88th Street, 423-3500, www.guggenheim.org
A diverse collection of contemporary art that grew out of the private collection of millionaire Solomon Guggenheim. The building has an upward spiraling ramp around a large atrium—a manageable space that is kid-friendly. The museum offers programs for children and conducts family workshops at scheduled times throughout the year. (Note that advance registration for these workshops is generally required; call 423-3587.) A family activity guide is available and relates to current exhibitions.

Hispanic Society of America   10+
613 West 155th Street at Broadway, at the Audubon Terrace, 926-2234,
www.hispanicsociety.org
The diverse collection of work housed at this reference library and museum represents the arts, literature and culture of Spain, Portugal and Latin America.

Historic Richmond Town   6+
441 Clark Avenue, Staten Island, 718 351-1611,
www.historicrichmondtown.org
This authentic village of historic buildings, including a museum, takes you back in time. There is a story time for young children.

International Center of Photography   11+
1133 Sixth Avenue at 43rd Street, 857-0000, www.icp.org
ICP is Manhattan's only museum dedicated solely to photography. Great photographic works are restored and on permanent display and in special exhibits. Educational opportunities, lectures and other events take place year round.

Intrepid Sea, Air and Space Museum   4+
Intrepid Square, Pier 86, West 46th Street and Twelfth Avenue, 245-0072,
www.intrepidmuseum.com
A decommissioned aircraft carrier houses a museum of naval history. In addition to the aircraft carrier, other vessels are available to tour, including a submarine. Talks and workshops are offered occasionally.

Islamic Cultural Center of New York   8+
1711 Third Avenue at 96th Street, 288-3215
This modern (completed in the 1990s) mosque was built at an angle to face Mecca.

Jacques Marchais Museum of Tibetan Art 6+
338 Lighthouse Avenue, Staten Island, 718 987-3500,
www.tibetanmuseum.com

Tibetan and Asian works of art are housed in a building designed by Jacques Marchais to look like a Buddhist mountain temple. Surrounded by gardens, this museum seeks to promote a better understanding of Tibetan culture, art, philosophy and history. Weekend workshops, family programs, concerts, dances, performances and storytelling are scheduled.

The Jewish Museum 4+
1109 Fifth Avenue at 92nd Street, 423-3200, 423-3337 for family program information, www.thejewishmuseum.org

This museum houses the largest collection of Judaica in America. Contemporary and folk art exhibits depict Jewish culture throughout history. It has Sunday drop-in programs for children, story time and gallery talks.

Judaica Museum of the Hebrew Home for the Aged at Riverdale 6+
5961 Palisade Avenue, Bronx, 718 581-1787,
www.hebrewhome.org/museum

This educational center houses objects, paintings, and textiles from the Jewish religion and culture.

The Liberty Science Center 2+
251 Phillips Street, Liberty State Park, Jersey City, New Jersey, 201 200-1000, www.libertysciencecenter.org

This huge world-class science-oriented museum features an Omni Max Theater, interactive activities, demonstrations, hands-on exhibits, classes, workshops, special events and more. You can get there by car or by taking a ferry from the World Financial Center to the Colgate Center in Jersey City (call 800 53 FERRY) and then a short shuttle bus to the museum.

Little Red Lighthouse 5+
Fort Washington Park, 178th Street and the Hudson River

This lighthouse, officially known as Jeffrey's Hook Lighthouse, is the star of the 1942 classic children's book *The Little Red Lighthouse and the Great Gray Bridge* by Hildegarde H. Swift.

Lower East Side Tenement Museum 6+
90 Orchard Street at Broome Street, 431-0233, www.tenement.org

The museum draws the visitor to America's urban immigrant roots through tours of its 1863 tenement building, neighborhood walking tours, exhibits, performances and media presentation. The Confino family apartment is open on weekends for viewing and provides an interactive experience for families with children.

Metropolitan Museum of Art   6+, programs age-specific
1000 Fifth Avenue at 82nd Street, 535-7710, www.metmuseum.org
One of the premier museums in the United States, its permanent and special exhibits are devoted to representing 5,000 years of human expression in over 32 acres of exhibition space and through more than 3.5 million pieces of art from all over the world. Special museum guides are available for children, to facilitate interaction between adults and children during a self-guided tour. There is so much to see, it's best to pick and choose a few areas. Favorites for kids include exhibits on ancient Egypt, Arms and Armor and ancient Greece and Rome. Programs for children, families and teens are run through the membership and education departments.

Morris-Jumel Mansion   5+
65 Jumel Terrace at 160th Street in Washington Heights, 923-8008,
www.morrisjumel.org
This restored building was built in 1765 as a summer house and in 1776 established by George Washington as the headquarters for the Continental Army. The museum highlights New York history, culture and the arts, and has 12 period rooms. Summer and after-school programs are occasionally arranged. Annual Washington's Birthday Celebration.

Museum for African Art   5+
593 Broadway between Houston and Prince Streets, 966-1313,
www.africanart.org
Celebrate African history and culture via concerts, exhibits, lectures, workshops, films, family and weekend programs that bring African art to life. Note: The museum has temporarily moved to 36-01 43rd Avenue in Long Island City, Queens (718 784-7700), while its new permanent home is being constructed at the northern end of Museum Mile in Manhattan.

Museum of American Financial History   10+
28 Broadway across from Bowling Green Park, 908-4519,
www.financialhistory.org
This very small museum contains a "wealth" of information and is a neat place to visit in conjunction with a look around the Stock Exchange.

Museum of American Folk Art   5+
45 West 53rd Street between Fifth and Sixth Avenues, 265-1040
Eva and Morris Feld Gallery, 2 Lincoln Square on Columbus Avenue
between 65th and 66th Streets, 595-9533, www.folkartmuseum.org
Changing exhibitions explore the work of three centuries of American folk artists and their culture. Sunday workshops for families are scheduled periodically, generally requiring reservations.

Museum of American Illustration   Depends upon exhibit
128 East 63rd Street between Park and Lexington Avenues, 838-2560,
www.societyillustrators.org
Changing exhibitions feature the work of illustrators from around the
world.

Museum of Bronx History/Valentine–Varian House   10+
3266 Bainbridge Avenue at East 208th Street, Bronx, 718 881-8900,
www.bronxhistoricalsociety.org
The Museum of Bronx History is contained within the Valentine–Varian
House, which is a restored farmhouse built in 1758. The museum hosts special exhibitions on Bronx culture, history and well-known residents.

Museum of Chinese in the Americas   4+
70 Mulberry Street at Bayard, 2nd floor, 619-4785, www.moca-nyc.org
Housed in a century-old school building, the museum is dedicated to preserving the history and culture of Chinese immigrants and their descendents
in the Western hemisphere. It features exhibits, children's book readings,
walking tours of Chinatown. Specially scheduled family programs.

The Museum of the City of New York   4+
1220 Fifth Avenue at 103rd Street, 534-1672, www.mcny.org
The museum collects, preserves and features original artifacts, documents,
prints, maps and other items relating to the history of Manhattan. Various
programs for children and several annual family events.

Museum of Jewish Heritage—A Living Memorial to the Holocaust   7+
18 First Place, Battery Park City, 509-6130, www.mjhnyc.org
The museum is dedicated to teaching all ages and backgrounds about 20th-
century Jewish life. Exhibits include photographs, artifacts and narratives
of life during the Holocaust.

The Museum of Modern Art   5+
11 West 53rd Street between Fifth and Sixth Avenues, 708-9400,
www.moma.org
This pre-eminent museum houses one of the world's largest collections of
19th- and 20th-century painting, sculpture, photography and design.
Workshops, lectures, films, performances and special events are offered for
children and their families, including Saturday morning tours. "Art Safari,"
a guide created especially for children, is available for sale in the gift shop.
MOMA is undergoing a major renovation and is temporarily located at
45-20 33rd Street at Queens Boulevard in Long Island City, Queens. The
museum offers Queens Artlink, a free weekend bus shuttle service to
MOMA, P.S. 1 Contemporary Art Center, The Noguchi Museum, Socrates
Sculpture Park and the American Museum of the Moving Image.

The Museum of Television and Radio
Depends upon exhibit
25 East 52nd Street between Fifth and Madison Avenues, 621-6600,
www.mtr.org
The museum's collection of over 90,000 radio and television programs offers everything from news, public affairs programming and documentaries to the performing arts, children's programming, sports, comedy shows and advertising. There are special events for children during the International Children's Festival, typically in the fall and spring.

National Academy of Design
5+
1083 Fifth Avenue at 89th Street, 369-4880, www.nationalacademy.org
One of the largest collections of American art in the country is displayed in a former home of a philanthropist. The Academy offers after-school programs, seminars, weekend and family programs, workshops, lectures, art classes and concerts. Family Fun Days are held on Saturday.

National Museum of the American Indian
5+
One Bowling Green, across from Battery Park, 514-3700, 514-3888 for
program information, www.nmai.si.edu
Past and present Native American cultures are celebrated. Cultures from the Arctic to the Antarctic are represented. One Saturday each month, the museum features a Traditional Native American Performance program.

New Museum of Contemporary Art
7+
583 Broadway between Prince and Houston Streets, 219-1222,
www.newmuseum.org
Founded in 1977, the museum has changing exhibits of contemporary art and offers talks and workshops.

The New York Botanical Garden
5+, although at any age a stroll
through the gardens can be enjoyable
200th Street and Southern Boulevard near the Bronx Zoo, Bronx,
718 817-8700, www.nybg.org
Located on 250 acres in the Bronx, the New York Botanical Garden offers educational programs and seasonal displays to teach visitors about the plant world.

The New York City Fire Museum
2+, programs age-specific
278 Spring Street between Varick and Hudson Streets, 691-1303,
www.nycfiremuseum.org
This renovated 1904 firehouse displays equipment used to battle fires throughout history. Programs for children and their families.

The New York City Police Museum
7+
100 Old Slip, 480-3100, www.nycpolicemuseum.org
This museum is located in the Police Academy Training School and offers the opportunity to view badges, counterfeit money, fingerprinting equip-

ment, firearms and uniforms. Weekend family activities. Open weekdays by appointment only.

New York Hall of Science   3+
47-01 111th Street, Flushing Meadows, Queens, 718 699-0005,
www.nyhallsci.org
Designed to improve the public understanding of science and technology through exhibits, programs and media, and ranked as one of the 10 top science museums, the hall features the largest collection of interactive exhibits in New York City. A variety of programs for children (including sleepovers!) are offered. The Discover Room and Bubble Area are designed for preschoolers.

New York Historical Society   8+
2 West 77th Street at Central Park West, 873-3400, www.nyhistory.org
The permanent collection includes everything from American paintings to sleighs. Changing exhibits highlight the history of the city and state.

The New York Transit Museum   4+
Boerum Place and Schermerhorn Street, Brooklyn Heights, Brooklyn,
718 694-5100, www.mta.nyc.ny.us
The Transit Museum is located in a decommissioned 1930s subway station. Learn about the history of our rapid transit system. Weekend family workshops. Note: The museum is currently closed for renovation but is scheduled to reopen in 2003.

New York Unearthed   7+
17 State Street at Pearl Street, 748-8628.
This archeology museum features dioramas filled with actual artifacts excavated from beneath New York City and a functioning glass-enclosed laboratory where you can view conservators at work.

Newseum/NY   10+
580 Madison Avenue between 56th and 57th Streets, 317-7596,
www.newseum.org
Newseum is a media educational and cultural institute aimed at improving public understanding of journalism and First Amendment issues. Good for budding reporters.

North Wind Undersea Institute   6+
610 City Island Avenue, Bronx, 718 885-0701
Explore this environmental museum with its many ongoing and hands-on exhibits of marine life, deep-sea diving equipment, scrimshaw and sunken treasures. Weekend tours given on the hour.

The Old Merchant's House   10+
29 East 4th Street between Lafayette and Broadway, 777-1089,
www.merchantshouse.com
This restored Greek Revival row house, built in 1832, was once owned by
the merchant Samuel Treadwell. It provides an example of living conditions in 19th-century New York.

The Paine Webber Art Gallery   Depends upon exhibit
1285 Sixth Avenue between 51st and 52nd Streets, 713-2885,
www.ubspainewebber.com
This gallery features changing art exhibits. Closed on weekends.

The Pierpont Morgan Library   4+
29 East 36th Street at Madison Avenue, 685-0610,
www.morganlibrary.org
J.P. Morgan's vast collection of rare books, sculpture, paintings, manuscripts
and musical scores is housed here, and special exhibits are displayed as well
(past exhibits have included the works of Beatrix Potter, for example). Each
year the library hosts annual family days in the spring and winter with readings, events, performances and activities.

Queens Botanical Garden   4+
43-50 Main Street, Flushing, Queens, 718 886-3800,
www.queensbotanical.org
Over 39 acres of gardens to explore, including a Victorian wedding garden.
Workshops for families are conducted, including seed planting for children.

Queens County Farm Museum   3+
73-50 Little Neck Parkway, Floral Park, Queens, 718 347-FARM (3276),
www.queensfarm.org
This unique museum is a historical, full-size, working farm. Special events
for families are offered on weekends. Note that this is primarily an outdoor
experience.

The Queens Museum of Art   4+
New York City Building, Flushing Meadows – Corona Park, Queens,
718 592-9700, www.queensmuse.org
The museum hosts fine-arts exhibitions and the "Panorama of New York,"
an exact scale model of the five boroughs that was designed originally for
the 1964 World's Fair and is updated as needed. Weekend drop-in programs
are held year round.

The Riverside Church   8+
Riverside Drive at 122nd Street, www.theriversidechurchny.org
This interdenominational Gothic church was modeled after the 13th-century
Gothic cathedral in Chartres, France, known for its 392-foot-high tower. The
Labyrinth on the floor of the chancel is quite interesting for kids.

Rose Center for Earth and Space.
See American Museum of Natural History

St. Patrick's Cathedral 8+
Fifth Avenue at 50th Street, www.ny-archdiocese.org
Begun in 1858 and renovated as recently at 1989, this is the largest (seats 2,200) decorated, Gothic-style Catholic Cathedral in the United States.

Schomburg Center for Research in Black Culture 6+
515 Malcolm X Boulevard at 135th Street, 491-2200, www.nypl.org
Part of the New York Public Library, this widely used research facility preserves materials relating Africa and the African Diaspora. It presents changing exhibits on African American culture and various programs.

Skyscraper Museum 10+
44 Wall Street, 968-1961, www.skyscraper.org
The museum is dedicated to the study of high-rise buildings. Note: The museum is closed until 2003, when it will open in its new permanent home in Battery Park City.

Sony Wonder Technology Lab 7+
550 Madison Avenue between 55th and 56th Streets in Sony Plaza, 833-8100, www.sonywondertechlab.com
This one-of-a-kind interactive science and technology center was designed to showcase the latest in communication technology. The lab holds after-school, weekend and family programs.

The South Street Seaport Museum 5+
207 Fulton Street and the 11-square block historic district including Fulton Street, South Street and 17 State Street, 748-8600, www.southstseaport.org
Exhibits explore the workings of the waterfront district from colonial times to the present. Family and children's programs as well as workshops are offered. "NY Unearthed," a satellite exhibit of the Museum, is located at 17 State Street. Also visit the Whitman Gallery at 209 Water Street to see ship models on display.

The Spanish Institute 2+ (language classes)
684 Park Avenue between 69th and 70th Streets, 734-4177, www.spanishinstitute.org
The museum was founded to promote an understanding of Spanish culture and its influence on the Americas. It offers changing exhibits and language classes for children.

Staten Island Botanical Garden
All ages
1000 Richmond Terrace, Snug Harbor Cultural Center, Staten Island, 718 273-8200, www.sibg.org
Explore 15 acres of wetlands and 13 acres of various gardens. Junior Green Team and family programming.

Staten Island Children's Museum
3–12
718 273-2060, www.snug-harbor.org
The museum offers many opportunities for children to explore and learn by doing and an outdoor area for picnics. Weekend workshops and activities are offered for parents and children, including performances, storytelling, films, concerts and craft projects. No strollers in the museum.

The Staten Island Institute of Arts & Sciences
7+
75 Stuyvesant Place, Staten Island, 718 727-1135, www.siiasmuseum.org
A two-block walk from the ferry terminus, this institute features changing and permanent exhibits as well as the Staten Island Ferry Collection, which explores the history of, and includes large-scale models of, the Ferry Line.

The Statue of Liberty National Museum
All ages
Liberty Island, 363-3200, www.nps.gov.stli

Reach Liberty Island by boat from Battery Park North (for ferry information call 269-5755). View New York from the crown or visit the museum in the base, which features the history and development of the famous statue. Note: The Statue itself is currently closed; only the grounds are open for visiting.

The Studio Art Museum in Harlem
5+
144 West 125th Street between Lenox and Seventh Avenues, 864-4500, www.studiomuseum.org
This museum showcases African American artists. Special exhibits feature a diversity of work produced by new and established talent. Classes, workshops, concerts and various programs are conducted on a regular and special-events basis.

Temple Emanu-El
8+
Fifth Avenue at 65th Street, 744-1400, www.emanuelnyc.org
Mingling Moorish and Romanesque architectural styles and completed in the late 1920s, this synagogue is home to the largest Reform congregation in the world. The Herbert and Eileen Bernard Museum houses an extraordinary collection of Judaica.

Theodore Roosevelt Birthplace, National Historic Site
8+
28 East 20th Street off Broadway, 260-1616, www.nps.gov/thrb
The boyhood home of Theodore Roosevelt features artifacts from Roosevelt's life and presidency.

Trinity Church Museum   10+
74 Trinity Place – Trinity Church at Broadway and Wall Street, 602-0872, www.trinitywallstreet.org
Exhibits highlight the Church's history and the history of the city and nation throughout the Dutch, British and American eras.

The Ukrainian Museum   5+
203 Second Avenue between 12th and 13th Streets, 228-0110, www.ukrainian.org
Family workshops are typically conducted around major holidays such as Christmas and Easter.

Wave Hill   3+
675 West 252nd Street and Independence Avenue, Riverdale, Bronx, 718 549-3200, www.wavehill.org
Twenty-eight acres of public gardens feature an incredible number of plants from around the world. The Kerlin Learning Center offers workshops for visitors to gain a better understanding the natural history of Wave Hill, the Bronx and the world we live in. Family art projects are offered on the weekends.

Whitney Museum of American Art   4+
945 Madison Avenue at 75th Street, 570-3676, www.whitney.org
Founded by Gertrude Vanderbilt Whitney, a sculptor herself, the Whitney is devoted to 20th-century art featured in permanent and changing exhibitions. The museum offers a Saturday gallery tour and conducts a Family Fun program once a month.

Yeshiva University Museum   Depends upon exhibit
15 West 16th Street between Fifth and Sixth Avenues, 294-8330, www.yu.edu/museum
Changing exhibitions highlight Jewish life, history and culture. Throughout the year, the museum offers special family workshops relating to Jewish holidays.

RESOURCES

www.culturefinder.com   www.nyc-arts.org

www.museumstuff.com   www.nyckidsarts.org

www.newyorkled.com   www.nymuseums.com

Chapter 7

THE ULTIMATE
SHOPPING GUIDE

Manhattan is a magnet for shoppers. From bargain to bespoke, you can find it, have it made or order it from here. Depending on whether you are a born consumer or hate to shop, the scope and variety of merchandise available in New York City is either a blessing or a curse. Wherever you fall on the buying spectrum, there is no question that if you want it, in all likelihood you can have it without ever leaving the borough.

Shopping for children in Manhattan is a unique experience. The vast selection of clothing, shoes, toys and other children's products and services can unnerve even the hardiest of shoppers. Our goal is to help you find your way to the products you want, both in terms of price and location of the shops convenient to you. In this book, you will find a list of stores specializing in children's clothing, shoes, books, toys and supplies as well as clothing and accessories for teens, tweens and expectant mothers.

Please note that we do not attempt to chronicle every shop that sells something for or related to children. In a city with an ever-changing landscape of hundreds of thousands of square feet of retail space, to do so would be virtually impossible. Therefore, we have not included every neighborhood candy store, pharmacy or stationery store that carries some children's items; adult clothing or gift stores that carry a few items of children's clothing, accessories or baby paraphernalia; bookstores that carry a small selection of children's books; furniture stores that carry a few pieces either designed or suitable for children's rooms; or sporting-goods stores that carry a few items for kids. Rather, we have focused on those businesses that are devoted primarily to children's goods or carry a significant or particularly unique inventory of products for children.

Each entry contains information about what is carried in the store, the general price range of merchandise and where exactly the store is located. At the end of the chapter, you will find the stores indexed by the type of goods sold and a neighborhood locator. Happy shopping!

🏙

The Shopping Landscape

There are basically three categories of stores in Manhattan: department stores, multi-unit stores and boutique/specialty stores. Department stores are large institutions that carry many types of goods for men, women, children and the home. Multi-unit stores are those that are individual locations of larger businesses, whether regional, national or even international in scope. Boutique or specialty stores are usually single-location businesses, although occasionally there may be an additional location in the city or in the tri-state area. Boutique and specialty stores, big or small, carry unique merchandise individually selected by the store's management.

▶ **Department Stores.** Several department stores in Manhattan carry children's merchandise. Department stores at the highest end of the spectrum, such as Bergdorf Goodman and Barney's, tend to carry exclusive, imported and expensive items for infants and young children as well as luxury accessories for the layette and nursery. Stores such as Bloomingdales, Saks Fifth Avenue, Macy's

and Lord & Taylor have much more extensive children's departments, typically going up to pre-teen or teen sizes, stocking both
premium or designer (i.e., more expensive) labels as well as more
moderately priced labels and a respectable selection of accessories,
stuffed animals and perhaps dolls. The discount department stores
such as Kmart carry nationally known clothing labels as well as toys
and baby supplies.

▶ **Multi-unit Stores.** Multi-unit stores range from the discount to
luxury categories. Included within this group would be moderately
priced stores you are likely to find in shopping malls, such as the
Gap, Talbots Kids or Gymboree or national chains such as Toys R
Us, as well as stores (in either the moderate or expensive price
ranges) that have boutiques in various other cities in the U.S. or
even around the world. For example, Manhattan is home to a number of higher-end European chains such as Jacadi, Catimini and
Oilily. For us, these stores feel more like the boutique or specialty
category by virtue of the unique merchandise they carry, but in fact
they are not stand-alone stores. Also in this group are discount
stores such as Daffy's.

▶ **Boutiques and Specialty Stores.** The plethora and variety of
boutique and specialty shops are, to many, what New York shopping is all about. It is in these individually owned and operated
stores that one can often find amazing merchandise. Some are big
and well known while others are tiny retail spaces crammed full of
goodies and good ideas. These stores can carry anything from
antique toys to environmentally correct products and everything
you could possibly need for your new baby or older child, from
luxury layette to funky downtown clothes, from handmade play-
things to science-fiction toys. Prices range from bargain to the
stratosphere, depending on the nature of the merchandise carried.
Some boutiques are known only to neighborhood cognoscenti while
others are magnets for shoppers from all over. The boutiques and
specialty stores of Manhattan truly offer something for everyone.

▶ **Malls.** New York is not really a mall town. However, there are a
few containing stuff for kids and teens, for those who prefer a con-

centrated dose of shopping. The South Street Seaport Marketplace (732-7678), located in lower Manhattan, is an outdoor mall with a nautical theme. It includes a pedestrian mall at Fulton Street, the Fulton Market Building (the site of the original Fulton Fish Market) and the shops at Pier 17. Expect to find mall regulars such as the Gap, Ann Taylor, J. Crew, Victoria's Secret as well as a host of small and specialty stores and a food court. The Seaport tends to attract many tourists, especially on beautiful weekend afternoons.

The Manhattan Mall (465-0500), located in the garment district on Sixth Avenue and 33rd Street is a glass-encased vertical mall featuring an atrium and food court and 55 stores, mostly in the moderately priced category. The Herald Center (634-3883), located at 1 Herald Square, just across from Macy's, also features lower-priced merchandise. Rockefeller Center, bordered by Fifth and Sixth Avenues and 48th and 51st Streets has a shopping plaza just off Fifth Avenue worthy of visiting as you stroll down Fifth Avenue and take in the sights of Rockefeller Center—Art Deco buildings, the skating rink and Radio City. Shops your older kids and teens may want to visit include Kenneth Cole, J. Crew, Banana Republic, Brookstone and the Sharper Image.

▶ **What you will find in this chapter.** We confess that putting together this listing of stores was not an entirely scientific process. Our list was culled from advertising sources, word of mouth and pounding the pavement. We have endeavored to be as current as possible, keeping in mind that small businesses tend not to advertise and do tend to open and close without much fanfare, all of which makes it difficult to be totally comprehensive.

The goal is to provide you with a broad range of shopping options, both in terms of price, location and type of merchandise, to assist you in finding what you need when and where you need it. To be sure, there will be stores that we may have missed or that you think should have been included, but we think you will agree that this list, containing over 400 establishments, is by far the most comprehensive list of its type to date.

Please remember that we do not list every store that carries some children's items. We have focused on those businesses that either cater entirely to the younger set, carry a meaningful selection (in our subjective opinion!) of children's merchandise, or offer merchandise so unique or special (even if only in a limited quantity) that we thought you would want to be aware of them. For teens, we have focused on stores that carry adult-sized clothing but whose merchandise is cool, trendy and youthful for maximum appeal to this savvy clientele.

▶ **How to use this directory.** All entries are listed in alphabetical order together with their addresses and cross streets and a brief description of what is carried in the store. The intention is to give you an objective listing of the merchandise carried and a general indication of the price point at which the majority of the goods in the store are sold. In compiling this information we developed a list of categories of children's merchandise, which we share with you.

Please note that these are the broadest descriptions of each category and not every store listed as carrying a certain type of merchandise will have each item we included in our definition. Additionally, even if a store does carry most of the items on our list for a particular category, quantities of particular items will vary among stores. The definitions are here mainly to serve as a very general guideline as to what you can expect, not an inventory of each individual store. Therefore, if you are shopping for a very specific item in a certain category, we urge you to call first and make sure that the store carries it.

- ↪ ACCESSORIES AND NOVELTIES—all types of trendy, popular, fun, cool, generally inexpensive personal accessories, small room accessories and little toys such as costume jewelry, mirrors, picture frames, inflatable and bean-bag pillows and furniture, lava lamps, charms, key chains, travel accessories, "bunk junk" for summer camp, purses, beads, pens, little desk toys and other items kids covet.

- ↪ ACTIVEWEAR—clothes and accessories for sports and dance, leotards, bathing suits, sports shorts, warm-ups and sweats.

- ↪ BABY GIFTS—special, usually expensive, gifts for new babies, including fine china and silver items such as frames, rattles, porringers, spoons, comb and brush sets, boxes and other engraved items.

🔾 **BOOKS**—all types of books for children, hard and soft cover, board and/or fabric books for infants. Larger bookstores will also carry books for young readers (chapter books, series, classics, etc.).

🔾 **CLOTHING AND ACCESSORIES**—all types of children's clothing, which generally also includes undergarments, pajamas, seasonal clothing (e.g., snowsuits and bathing suits) and outerwear. Stores that carry clothing also typically carry a variety of accessories such as hats, gloves, scarves, socks and tights, slippers, hair ornaments (bows, headbands), belts, ties, suspenders, bags (backpacks, children's purses), and sometimes water shoes (jellies, flip-flops). Stores that carry baby clothes often carry some stuffed animals and crib toys (and sometimes even a few baby books) to package with baby gifts. Most clothing stores carry clothing up to sizes 12–16 children's (fitting children between the ages of 10 and 12). Most stores organize merchandise by numerical sizes, while others categorize their merchandise by the age of the child it is meant to fit. For our purposes, if an entry does not contain a size or an age range, you can assume that the store carries items for infants up to 10- or 12-year-olds. When a particular store carries a more limited range of sizes (or only fits up to a certain age range), that information is specifically indicated.

🔾 **COMICS/TRADING CARDS**—current, vintage and collectible comic books, sports cards and other types of trading cards and related merchandise, which usually consists of action figures, T-shirts and other collectible character representations and toys.

🔾 **COSMETICS/BATH ACCESSORIES**—products for the bath including soaps, shampoos, bubble bath and bath oils, lotions; hair products; aromatherapy products; candles and potpourri and accessories such as sponges, washcloths, loofahs and bath toys. Cosmetics refer to products appropriate for teens or tweens such as lip gloss, glitter gel, cologne and accessories such as mirrors, cosmetic bags, hair brushes and so forth. Note that stores referenced may also carry full lines of adult makeup and products which may not be appropriate for young girls.

🔾 **DECORATIVE ACCESSORIES**—accessories for the nursery or older child's room, such as toy boxes, grow sticks, hat/coat racks, easels, child-sized furniture (tables, chairs, miniature sofas), rocking toys, bulletin boards, decorative storage boxes and units, baskets, step stools, storage cabinets, hampers, decorative pillows, picture frames, wall hangings and throws. Many of these items are hand wrought, handpainted/decorated or personalized. Some stores will have a modest selection of lamps and perhaps even small area rugs. Decorative accessories for tweens and teens might include such things as inflatable furniture, kitschy lamps or desk accessories and storage units (CD holders, storage boxes, etc.).

↷ EQUIPMENT—merchandise for infants and toddlers (typically up to preschoolers) such as strollers, baby carriers, prams, car seats, playpens and portable cribs, swings, cloth diapers and burp cloths, crib sheets and accessories, toddler bedding, crib toys and mobiles, baby bathtubs, diaper bags, nursery monitors, gadgets, child-proofing and child-safety items, bottles, first cups, cutlery and dishes.

↷ FURNITURE—cribs, rockers, kid-sized tables and chairs, beds, changing tables, bureaus, armoires and upholstered furniture. Some stores carrying furniture may also include lamps and decorative accessories, window treatments and floor coverings (area rugs) for the nursery or child's room. Some stores may offer design services and customized furniture.

↷ GADGETS AND ELECTRONICS—CD players, boomboxes, video games (hardware and/or software), computers, computer software and accessories, and all sorts of other cool (and, your children will insist, much needed) gadgets designed to make life easier (or more complicated, depending on your point of view) and more interesting.

↷ GAMES AND HOBBIES—model kits, merchandise specific to particular games such as chess or relating to collectibles or hobbies such as electric trains.

↷ LAYETTE—bedding for cribs, cradles and bassinettes, newborn clothing, hats, booties, receiving blankets, bibs, crib toys and stuffed animals, decorative pillows, quilts and blankets and accessories for the newborn. Bedding can consist of basic sheets and blankets or can include bumpers, bed skirts, wall hangings and coordinating window treatments.

↷ LINENS—a number of higher-end imported fine linen stores carry some bedding and bath accessories (towels, robes) for children.

🜂 **MAGIC**—merchandise for the budding magician including tricks, gags and props. Magic stores often have personnel on-site to demonstrate tricks.

🜂 **MATERNITY**—everything for the mother-to-be including clothing, undergarments, sleepwear, pantyhose, nursing paraphernalia and accessories. Many maternity shops also stock some items for the newborn and usually offer pregnancy and new baby books.

🜂 **MUSEUM STORES**—stores operated by museums. These stores typically carry not only merchandise related to particular exhibits but items— toys, games, stuffed animals, souvenirs, books, videos, T-shirts, novelties—more generally related to the subject of the museum (art, history, animals, science, etc.) Museum gift shops range from modest little stores to full-blown emporia with extensive inventory, handcrafted items, furniture and decorative accessories and a wide range of unique merchandise.

🜂 **OUTERWEAR**—coats, jackets and foul-weather gear. Some stores carry gear for particular activities such as skiing or camping.

🜂 **SHOES**—casual shoes, dress shoes, sandals, sneakers and athletic shoes and water shoes.

🜂 **SPORTING GOODS**—sports equipment, rackets, balls, skates, rollerblades, helmets, bats, gloves and gear for water sports. Sporting goods stores usually also carry athletic shoes and activewear.

🜂 **STATIONERY**—writing papers and supplies, notebooks, desk accessories, photo albums, journals, gift wrapping supplies, writing implements and art supplies.

🜂 **TEENS**—clothing and accessories for teens and, if you dare, tweens. The stores referenced in this category are not necessarily "teen" stores per se, but rather adult stores that because of their cool merchandise, trendy style, petite sizes and high concept presentation have become destinations for teens and teen wannabes. Clothing in the teen category is sized in adult sizes although some stores may have some junior sizes. Be aware that the stores that cater to teens are likely to have very adult prices!

🜂 **THEME STORES**—stores with merchandise relating to particular brands or themes such as Disney, as well as stores devoted to particular sports or teams.

🌜 Toys—anything kids play with, including games, puzzles, dolls, stuffed animals, educational toys, building toys, arts and crafts supplies, models, cars and trucks, ride-on toys (which may include bicycles and tricycles), project kits, puppets, action figures, character figures (for example, Sesame Street, Pooh), classic toys, handmade toys, some sports toys, dress-up, crib and baby toys, etc. Some toy stores carry computer software, electronic toys, audio and/or video tapes and a few books.

▶ **Consumer information.** It is useful to be aware of your rights under local consumer law. You have the right: to know the price of any item, which must be clearly marked either on the item or on a display sign; to know the store's refund policy before you make your purchase (if there is no posted policy, you have the right to a full refund if you return the goods within 20 days of purchase); to obtain a receipt for all purchases over $20, which includes the price, description, tax, date, and name and address of the store; to know what you are purchasing (if the product is used or reconditioned, it must say so).

NYC Consumer Affairs urges visitors to beware of the these practices at electronics stores: bait and switch—you are lured in with an advertisement for a low-priced item but told it is sold out when you arrive and you are offered something higher priced or of lower quality; Manufacturer's Suggested Retail Price—by law, the store must tell you this price; tourist traps—be wary of salespeople who ask you where you are from and how long you are staying as they may be setting you up for a scam on the theory that you will not be here long enough to complain or return the item. Be wary of buying expensive items from street vendors; note that their products are usually knock-offs (imitations) rather than the real thing.

If you have a consumer problem, call Consumer Affairs at 487-4444 or 718 286-2994 Monday through Friday from 9:30 a.m. to 4:30 p.m. or file a complaint on-line at www.nygov.com/consumers.

▶ **Sales tax.** There is a sales tax of 8.25% (4% for New York State, 4.25% for New York City) on all purchases of clothing and shoes in excess of $110 per item. In other words, if you purchase a pair of shoes for $60, pants for $125 and a blouse for $80, you will pay tax on only the $125 pants. Note that the exemption does not apply to jewelry, watches, handbags or other accessories. If you ship your purchases out of state, meaning that you do not take possession of them in the store, you will have to pay shipping charges, but no New York sales tax will be charged on the items. You will, however, be charged the sales tax, if any, levied by the jurisdiction to which the item is being shipped. Unlike the VAT in Europe, tourists do not receive any sales-tax refund when they leave the United States.

► **A word about price.** Indicating the price range of merchandise carried in a store is extremely complicated. While it is easy to identify stores in the discount and luxury categories, the vast majority of stores sell somewhere in the middle or sell merchandise at multiple price points. To attempt to quantify price points specifically is an exercise in futility. As a result, we came up with a not-quite-perfect three-point system for looking at prices: $ for discount or value-priced goods, $$ for moderately priced goods and $$$ for expensive or luxury goods. It is best to think of these valuations as relative rather than as absolute—a way of distinguishing among choices when you are faced with a shopping expedition. For example, you may want to seek stores in the $ or $$ category for play-clothes and the $$$ category for party clothes and baby gifts.

In addition, it is our experience that many of the stores in the $$ category stock inventory at the top and bottom of the range, or even into the next range. It is, for example, quite common to find a clothing store that carries great value leggings and T-shirts next to $200 hand-knit sweaters and $95 imported jeans. In such cases, we have indicated the store's price range as $$ to $$$. Also, even stores at the top of the $$$ category may have incredible blow-out sales for which you should be on the lookout.

Stores that sell items other than clothing, shoes or items for the home (decorative accessories and furniture) are extremely difficult, if not impossible, to differentiate in terms of price. For example, most toy stores carry an assortment of toys, small to large, inexpensive to expensive. Bookstores, too, may carry an array of inexpensive paperback books as well as full-price hardbound books. Stores that sell games, hobbies, comics, sports cards, and cosmetics/bath accessories will also have a range of merchandise at different price points. For that reason, in general we have noted price ranges only for stores purveying clothing, accessories, shoes and items for the home and not for stores selling toys, books, games/hobbies or theme stores unless the store is clearly in a particular category.

In order to help you figure out where in the spectrum stores fall when no price range is indicated, here are some general rules.

- ↪ Boutique toy stores carrying unique, specialty, educational, imported and handmade toys will generally have a selection of merchandise more expensive than those carrying more commercial brands (such as Fisher Price) or national chains such as Toys R Us or Kmart.

- ↪ Books at the smaller specialty bookstores or neighborhood stores will likely not be discounted as they may be in the chain superstores.

- ↪ Stores carrying unique, exclusive lines of cosmetics, bath products, electronics, furniture or decorative accessories will be higher priced than chain stores or stores carrying widely available national brands.

- ↪ Wherever possible, we indicate in the store description the general nature of the merchandise, from which you can deduce whether it is of the pricier more exclusive variety or of a more commercial and mass merchandise nature.

Remember, prices are relative and identifying the prices of goods is a highly subjective process. A bargain to one family can be a luxury to another, while for other families price is not the top priority in making a purchase. The system we have used is neither foolproof nor perfect, but we hope it will help you identify, at least generally, the stores you want to start with when you need or want to shop.

Let's Go Shopping

ABC Carpet and Home $$ to $$$
888 Broadway at 19th Street, 473-3000, www.abchome.com
A huge, full-service home furnishings, carpet, fabric, furniture and decorative accessories emporium that carries beautiful linens and specialty and gift items (such as cashmere baby blankets). Design services available. Definitely worth a visit downtown.

Abercrombie & Fitch $$ to $$$
199 Water Street at Fulton Street, South Street Seaport, 809-9000
www.abercrombie.com
This popular brand delivers trendy casual clothes and accessories for kids ages 7 to 16 and adults. It is very popular among teens and tweens.

Abracadabra
19 West 21st Street between Fifth and Sixth Avenues, 627-5194
www.abracadabra-superstore.com
This magic superstore, complete with a stage and a café, also stocks costumes and novelties, theatrical makeup and props.

Adidas Originals $$
136 Wooster Street between Prince and Houston Streets, 777-2001
www.adidas.com
Sporty teens and tweens will love the Adidas footwear, clothing and accessories in this store that seeks to create a "fusion of sport authenticity and global street style."

Albee's $$
715 Amsterdam Avenue between 94th and 95th Streets, 662-8902/5740
www.albeebaby.com
This Upper West Side institution carries everything you need for the new baby and young child, including equipment, layette, furniture, toys, books and some clothing (basics only for ages 0–12 months).

Alex's MVP Cards
256 East 89th Street between Second and Third Avenues, 831-2273
This shop has a very good selection of vintage and new comics, sports cards and some non-sports toys.

Alphabets
47 Greenwich Avenue between Perry and Charles Streets, 229-2966
115 Avenue A between 7th and 8th Streets, 475-7250
2284 Broadway between 82nd and 83rd Streets, 579-5702
www.alphabetsnyc.com
Your kids will enjoy browsing among the unique retro toys, novelties, cards and reproductions of goodies from yesteryear.

Alphaville
226 West Houston Street between Sixth Avenue and Varick Street,
    675-6850, www.alphaville.com
This store/gallery specializes in vintage toys, games and collectibles (think wind-up toys and ray guns) with an emphasis on toys made from the 1940s through 1960s, including a large collection of 3D toys and flickers (plastic images which change as you move them). Prices start at 95 cents. Alphaville also carries a small line of "retro contemporary" new toys inspired by their vintage predecessors.

Alskling $$
228 Columbus Avenue between 70th and 71st Streets, 787-7066
"Alskling," which means sweetheart in Swedish, carries a unique selection of Swedish designs for women and handknitted infant cardigans, dresses for girls 0–3 and some casual playclothes.

American Craft Museum Shop
40 West 53rd Street between Fifth and Sixth Avenues, 956-3535
www.americancraftmuseum.org
This well-stocked museum gift shop carries a large assortment of creative kits, small toys and some children's books.

American Museum of Natural History Store
Central Park West between 77th and 81st Streets, 769-5100
www.amnh.org
This 8,500-square-foot shop is a treasure trove of educational toys and books, many relating to current exhibits in the museum and planetarium, as well as souvenirs, stuffed animals and T-shirts.

America's Hobby Center
146 West 22nd Street between Sixth and Seventh Avenues, 675-8922
www.ahc1931.com
This is the place for "vehicular hobbies": model cars, trains, planes, boats and radio-controlled vehicles. For children ages 8+.

April Cornell $$ to $$$
487 Columbus Avenue between 83rd and 84th Streets, 799-4342
www.aprilcornell.com
This shop offers a large selection of quality classic clothing for girls ages 1–12 and women, including mother–daughter outfits.

Art & Tapisserie $$ to $$$
1242 Madison Avenue between 89th and 90th Streets, 722-3222
www.artandtapisserie.com
This neighborhood boutique stocks a unique selection of decorative accessories and some furniture (much of which can be personalized), toys and books.

Astor Place Hair Designers
2 Astor Place at Broadway, 475-9854
Downtown's own trendy, but basic, barbershop. Cash only.

Au Chat Botte $$$
1192 Madison Avenue between 87th and 88th Streets, 722-6474
This French shop is a great source for classic and elegant European layette, equipment, furniture and clothing for girls and boys up to size 2.

Avon Salon & Spa
725 Fifth Avenue at 57th Street, Trump Tower, 755-2866
This spa and salon featuring Avon products offers a full line of products (shampoo, soap and other items) for babies and children.

A/X Armani Exchange $$ to $$$
568 Broadway at Prince Street, 431-6000
645 Fifth Avenue at 51st Street, 980-3037
www.armaniexchange.com
Come here for Italian designer Giorgio Armani's less expensive casual clothes for men and women. Many of the items, often bearing the company logo, will appeal to your teens.

Baby Depot at Burlington Coat Factory $
707 Sixth Avenue at 23rd Street, 229-1300/2247
www.burlingtoncoatfactory.com
Discount department store for the whole family. The children's department carries clothing, equipment, layette and furniture for the nursery.

The Balloon Man
209 West 80th Street between Broadway and Amsterdam Avenue,
  874-4464, www.tshirtexpress.com, www.selectagram.com
On the West Side for 25 years, this shop creates party and event decorations, including helium balloons, and will customize t-shirts and hats for your special occasion or to commemorate your visit.

Bambini $$$
1367 Third Avenue at 78th Street, 717-6742, www.bambininyc.com
This lovely boutique has a unique selection of classic imported, mostly Italian, clothes (up to size 8–10 for girls and boys), layette and a good selection of unique imported shoes.

Bambi's Baby Center $

2150 Third Avenue at 117th Street, 828-8878

This is upper Manhattan's source for everything you need for the new baby and young child, including equipment, layette, furniture, toys, books and some clothing (basics only for ages 0–12 months).

Banana Republic $$

205 Bleecker Street at Sixth Avenue, 473-9570

528 Broadway at Spring Street, 334-3034

550 Broadway between Prince and Spring Streets, 925-0308

111 Eighth Avenue between 15th and 16th Streets, 645-1032

89 Fifth Avenue between 16th and 17th Streets, 366-4630

114 Fifth Avenue at 17th Street, 366-4691

107 East 42nd Street at Vanderbilt Avenue, Grand Central Terminal, 490-3127

130 Lexington Avenue at 59th Street, 751-5570

1110 Third Avenue at 65th Street, 288-4279

17 West 34th Street between Fifth and Sixth Avenues, 244-3060

626 Fifth Avenue at 50th Street, Rockefeller Center, 974-2350

1136 Madison Avenue between 84th and 85th Streets, 570-2465

1529 Third Avenue at 86th Street, 360-1296

215 Columbus Avenue at 70th Street, 873-9048

2360 Broadway at 86th Street, 787-2064

888 BRSTYLE (277-8953) for automated listing of stores

www.bananarepublic.com

This national chain, offering stylish, modern, basic clothing, accessories and shoes for men and women at reasonable prices, has a large selection appropriate for your teen.

Bank Street Bookstore

610 West 112th Street at Broadway, 678-1654, 877 676-7830

www.bankstreetbooks.com (links to Barnes & Noble College Bookstore)

The knowledgeable, helpful staff will guide you through this bookshop's extensive selection of children's books, educational toys, games and books on education, learning and parenting.

Barnes & Noble Superstores

4 Astor Place at Broadway, 420-1322

396 Sixth Avenue at 8th Street, 674-8780

33 East 17th Street at Union Square North, 253-0810

105 Fifth Avenue at 18th Street, 807-0099

675 Sixth Avenue at 22nd Street, 727-1227

385 Fifth Avenue at 36th Street, 779-7677

750 Third Avenue at 47th Street, 697-2251

160 East 54th Street at Third Avenue, Citicorp Building, 750-8033

600 Fifth Avenue at 48th Street, 765-0590

240 East 86th Street between Second and Third Avenues, 794-1962

1280 Lexington Avenue between 86th and 87th Streets, 423-9900

1972 Broadway at 66th Street, 595-6859

2289 Broadway between 82nd and 83rd Streets, 362-8835
www.bn.com
Books for all ages, many discounted. Some stores have specific B & N Jr.
departments, music departments and cafés.

Barney's New York $$$
660 Madison Avenue between 60th and 61st Streets, 826-8900
236 West 18th Street between Seventh and Eighth Avenues, 593-7800 (Co-op)
116 Wooster Street between Prince and Spring Streets, 965-9964 (Co-op)
www.barneys.com
This high-end department store with a charming children's department
carries unique, stylish, mostly imported clothing (up to size 6), decorative
accessories and some nursery furniture and linens. Barney's Co-op (within
the main store and two downtown locations) has a great selection of
trendy clothing and accessories for teens at less than stratospheric prices.

Bath & Bodyworks $ to $$
Pier 17, South Street Seaport, 349-1561
693 Broadway at West 4th Street, 979-2526
141 Fifth Avenue between 20th and 21st Streets, 387-9123
304 Park Avenue South at 23rd Street, 674-7385
441 Lexington Avenue at 44th Street, 687-1231
7 West 34th Street between Fifth and Sixth Avenues
    (in the Express Store), 629-6912
1240 Third Avenue at 72nd Street, 772-2589
www.intimatebrands.com
The Bath & Bodyworks chain carries a full line of moderately priced bath,
body, hair- and skin-care products and accessories. Young girls will enjoy
the line created especially for them, including body and hair glitter, lip
gloss, fragrances and bath products (which make great inexpensive party
favors or gifts to bring home to friends).

Bath Island $$
469 Amsterdam Avenue between 82nd and 83rd Streets, 787-9415,
    877 234-3657, www.bathisland.com
This fragrant oasis on the Upper West Side offers natural and biodegradable
bath and aromatherapy products and accessories. Parents and kids will love
their all-natural Bath Island Baby products.

A Bear's Place Inc. $$ to $$$
789 Lexington Avenue between 61st and 62nd Streets, 826-6465
This stocked-to-the-rafters boutique carries a varied selection of unique
toys as well as decorative accessories and some children's furniture.

Bebe $$
100 Fifth Avenue at 15th Street, 675-2323
805 Third Avenue at 50th Street, 588-9060
1127 East 66th Street at Third Avenue, 935-2444

1044 Madison Avenue between 79th and 80th Streets, 517-2323
www.bebe.com
Very trendy high-fashion clothes and accessories for your teen. Although
some of the clothing tends towards the skimpy (think bare midriffs, tight
fitting and low cut) and is for a more mature clientele, the pants, suits and
dresses are quite popular among the (ladies) size 0–4 set.

Bebe Thompson $$ to $$$
1216 Lexington Avenue between 82nd and 83rd Streets, 249-4740
This boutique carries a unique selection of clothing, contemporary to classic, much of it imported (European), accessories, layette, some toys and
handmade items.

Bed Bath & Beyond $ to $$
620 Sixth Avenue between 18th and 19th Streets, 255-3550
410 East 61st Street between York and First Avenues, 215-4702
www.bedbathandbeyond
Discount department store for all things for the bed, bath and kitchen. For
children, look for bedding, bath accessories (towels, robes, accessories for
the sink and tub), toys, some books, dishes, storage units and closet organizers, decorative accessories and gadgets galore.

Bellini Juvenile Designer Furniture $$ to $$$
1305 Second Avenue between 68th and 69th Streets, 517-9233
www.bellini.com

A good selection of higher-end furniture, decorative accessories and bedding for the nursery and older children.

Benetton (United Colors of Benetton) $$
10 Fulton Street, South Street Seaport, 509-3999
749 Broadway at 8th Street, 533-0230
597 Fifth Avenue between 48th and 49th Streets, 593-0290
188 East 78th Street at Third Avenue, 327-1039
555 Broadway between Prince and Spring Streets, 941-8010
666 Third Avenue at 42nd Street, 818-0449
120 Seventh Avenue between17th and 18th Streets, 646 638-1086
www.benetton.com
Contemporary, well-priced sportswear and casual clothing with the Italian
Benetton label for teens, tweens and adults.

Ben's For Kids $$ to $$$
1380 Third Avenue between 78th and 79th Streets, 794-2330
This Upper East Side institution carries everything for the new baby and
young child, including equipment, layette, furniture, toys (for babies to age
5/6), books, art supplies and clothing for ages 0–2.

Bergdorf Goodman $$$
754 Fifth Avenue at 57th Street, 753-7300

This high-end department store now has an in-store Best & Co. department offering classic imported layette, furniture for the nursery, linens and clothing and accessories for children up to size 8.

Berkley Girl $$$
410 Columbus Avenue between 79th and 80th Streets, 877-470

This boutique for tween girls specializes in up-to-date, stylish clothing and accessories for girls sizes 7–16 as well as a good selection of special-occasion dresses (including Nicole Miller), separates and suits.

Betsey Johnson $$
138 Wooster Street at Houston and Prince Streets, 995-5048
1060 Madison Avenue between 80th and 81st Streets, 734-1257
248 Columbus Avenue between 71st and 72nd Streets, 362-3364
251 East 60th Street between Second and Third Avenues, 319-7699
www.betseyjohnson.com

Avant-garde designer Betsey Johnson, known for her "exuberant, embellished and over the top" fashion, offers very trendy and funky clothes for your teen (and you, if you dare!).

Betwixt $$ to $$$
245 West 10th Street between Hudson and Bleecker Streets, 243-8590

Especially for tween girls, this boutique features cool, stylish casual clothes (for example, Monkey Wear, Roxy, Juicy) for girls sizes 7–16 and junior sizes 0–13. They have a good selection of accessories as well as special-occasion dresses, sportswear for kids and juniors, party/dressy outfits, school clothes and accessories (bags, jewelry).

Big City Kite Company
1210 Lexington Avenue at 82nd Street, 472-2623, 888 476-5483
www.bigcitykites.com

This tiny store specializes in all types of kites and other airborne toys.

Big Fun Toys
636 Hudson Street at Horatio Street, 414-4138, www.bigfuntoys.com

This toy emporium, where you are urged to "shop yourself silly," is full of cool stuff for kids of all ages.

Blades Board & Skate $$
659 Broadway between 3rd and Bleecker Streets, 477-7350
Roller Rink at Chelsea Piers, at 23rd Street and the Hudson River, Pier 62, 336-6299
Sky Rink at Chelsea Piers, at 23rd Street and the Hudson River, Pier 61, 336-6199
160 East 86th Street between Lexington and Third Avenues, 996-1644

120 West 72nd Street between Columbus Avenue and Broadway, 787-3911
www.blades.com
These shops have the latest in ultra-cool skates (in-line, roller and ice),
skateboards, snowboards and gear.

Bloomers $$
1042 Lexington Avenue between 74th and 75th Streets, 570-9529
This local shop, which has a great selection of women's nightgowns, paja-
mas and robes, also carries cute playwear for boys and girls up to size 6x
and girls' sleepwear up to size 14.

Bloomingdales $$ to $$$
1000 Third Avenue at 59th Street, 705-2000, www.bloomingdales.com
This full-service department store boasts a large (two floors) children's
department that carries clothes, layette and trendy accessories, featuring
many popular brands and designer labels. Your teens and tweens will love
the second floor, which is stocked with popular sportswear labels. Bloomies
also features Belly Basics and Babystyle clothing for the fashionable expec-
tant mom.

The Body Shop $ to $$
16 Fulton Street, South Street Seaport, 480-9876
747 Broadway at Astor Place, 979-2944
135 Fifth Avenue at 20th Street, 254-0145
479 Fifth Avenue between 40th and 41st Streets, 661-1992
509 Madison Avenue at 53rd Street, 829-8603

714 Lexington Avenue between 57th and 58th Streets, 755-7851
901 Sixth Avenue at 33rd Street, Manhattan Mall, 268-7424
1270 Sixth Avenue and 51st Street, Rockefeller Center, 397-3007
142 West 57th Street between Sixth and Seventh Avenues, 582-8494
2151 Broadway at 76th Street, 721-2947
1 East 125th Street at Fifth Avenue, 348-4900
1145 Madison Avenue between 85th and 86th Streets, 794-3046
www.thebodyshop.com
This international company with a conscience produces naturally inspired
products from traditional recipes for the skin, hair and bath. The company
creates "sustainable trade relationships with communities in need around
the world," does not believe in animal testing and actively promotes protection of the environment and human rights internationally.

Bombalulu's $$ to $$$
101 West 10th Street at Sixth Avenue, 463-0897
244 West 72nd Street between Broadway and West End Avenue, 501-8248
www.bombalulus.com
This is a great shop to find unique contemporary clothing for girls and
boys up to size 8, toys and wonderful handmade quilts.

Bonne Nuit $$$
30 Lincoln Plaza at 62nd Street and Broadway, 489-9730
Enjoy this charming boutique stocked with fine imported classic clothing for girls up to size 10 and boys up to size 6, as well as layette and some crib and baby toys.

Bonpoint $$$
811 Madison Avenue at 68th Street, 879-0900
1269 Madison Avenue at 91st Street, 722-7720
www.bonpoint.com
Your children will fit in on the Champs Élysées in the fine, elegant imported classic clothing, shoes and layette from this French company. The 68th Street store carries up to size 12 for girls, up to size 8 for boys. The 91st Street store carries up to size 16 for girls, up to size 12 for boys. It's just the place to splurge for that perfect party dress.

Bookberries
983 Lexington Avenue between 71st and 72nd Streets, 794-9400
Bookberries is a fine neighborhood bookstore with a good selection of children's books.

Books of Wonder
16 West 18th Street between Fifth and Sixth Avenues, 989-3270
www.booksofwonder.com
This downtown institution houses an extensive selection of children's books and related items, such as dolls and puzzles, and a knowledgeable staff.

Borders Books and Music
550 Second Avenue between 31st and 32nd Streets, 685-3938
461 Park Avenue at 57th Street, 980-6785
www.borders.com
Books and music for all ages, some of it discounted.

Brooklyn Museum of Art Shop
200 Eastern Parkway, Brooklyn Museum, Brooklyn, 718 638-5000
www.brooklynart.org
The Brooklyn Museum of Art carries a large selection of toys, art materials, activity kits, books and other cool stuff for kids.

Brooks Brothers $$ to $$$
346 Madison Avenue at 44th Street, 682-8800
666 Fifth Avenue at 53rd Street, 261-9440
LaGuardia Airport, US Air Terminal, 718 779-6300
www.brooksbrothers.com
This store, famous for its classic business attire and casual clothing for men (and classic fashions for women), also carries traditional clothing, including suits and formalwear, for boys sizes 6–20.

Brookstone $$ to $$$
16 West 50th Street at Rockefeller Center, 262-3237
20 West 57th Street between Fifth and Sixth Avenues, 245-1405
JFK Airport, domestic terminal, Concourse D, 718 553-6306
JFK Airport, international terminal, Concourse level, 718 244-0192
LaGuardia Airport, departure level, Concourse D, 718 505-2440
LaGuardia Airport, departure level, center section, 718 505-2415
www.brookstone.com
This national chain (found in many shopping malls) carries a variety of gadgets and electronics, many of which are intriguing to kids of all ages. Kids (and their weary parents!!!) are drawn like magnets to the massage chairs.

Bu and the Duck $$ to $$$
106 Franklin Street at Church Street, 431-9226, www.buandtheduck.com
Unique, funky, original casual clothing for infants and children up to age 8 and European shoes, including those made for the store in Italy, for children up to age 6. This charming store also carries vintage furniture and decorative accessories and a selection of handmade Raggedy Ann/Andy dolls.

Bunnies Children's Department Store $
100 Delancey Street between Essex and Ludlow Streets, 529-7567
www.bunnies.com
Discount children's department store that carries clothing for girls up to size 14 and boys up to size 20, equipment, layette and furniture.

Burberry $$$
9 East 57th Street between Madison and Park Avenues, 371-5010
131 Spring Street between Wooster and Greene Streets, 925-9300
www.burberry.com
This venerable British label has transformed itself into a very hip shopping destination. For children, you can find outerwear and some clothing for ages 18 months to 7 years. The ubiquitous plaid scarves and accessories are popular among the prep-school set.

Cadeau $$$
254 Elizabeth Street between Prince and Houston Streets, 674-5747
www.cadeaumaternity.com
Created by two former Barney's executives, this new line of maternity wear is made in Italy and reflects the owner's philosophy that pregnant women need not sacrifice their style. The line includes both casual basics and dressy pieces in a range of stretch and luxury fabrics.

Calypso $$$
280 Mott Street at Houston Street, 965-0990
424 Broome Street at Lafayette Street, 274-0449
935 Madison Avenue at 74th Street, 535-4100
This unique store houses a collection of clothing that incredibly manages to blend French style with an island flair. Calypso is best known for its

women's collection of brightly colored silk bustle skirts, sarongs, silk and cotton dresses, delicious sorbet-colored cashmeres and Navajo-inspired summer sandals. The Madison Avenue store carries miniature versions of its adult line for girls up to size 8 and Vilebrequin bathing suits and some other items for boys. Teens will love the selection at all stores but especially the Mott Street shop, which specializes in small sizes.

Calypso Enfants & Bébé $$$
426 Broome Street between Crosby and Lafayette Streets, 966-3234
This Calypso location is just for kids and carries clothes for girls and boys up to size 10. You can find Calypso classics for kids (the tiny sarongs and bustle skirts are particularly adorable), imported clothing, layette and baby cashmere, handcrafted wooden toys, European toys and books and stuffed animals.

Canal Jean Co. $
504 Broadway between Spring and Broome Streets, 226-1130
www.canaljean.com
Dress the whole family from three levels of discount casual clothing (mostly Levis) for children and adults starting at size four months. The upper levels carry popular designer labels for your teen.

Capezio $$
1650 Broadway at 51st Street, 2nd floor, 245-2130
1776 Broadway at 57th Street, 586-5140
136 East 61st Street between Lexington and Park Avenues, 758-8833
1651 Third Avenue between 92nd and 93rd Streets, 3rd floor, 348-7210
www.capeziodance.com
Not just for ballerinas, Capezio is a great source for dance and activewear for dancers of all ages.

Cartier $$$
653 Fifth Avenue at 52nd Street, 753-0111, www.cartier.com
This renowned jeweler is the perfect gift source for luxurious traditional silver baby gifts such as rattles, combs, brushes, porringers, cutlery and picture frames.

Cashmere Cashmere $$$
965 Madison Avenue between 75th and 76th Streets, 988-5252
If you can get past the stacks of cashmere sweaters for men and women, you will find luxurious cashmere sweaters for infants 6 to 18 months and cashmere baby blankets.

Catimini $$$
1284 Madison Avenue between 91st and 92nd Streets, 987-0688
www.catimini.com
This charming boutique has a great selection of adorable and distinctive European (mostly casual) clothing and layette with the Catimini

label, many items featuring characters and animals from French children's stories.

CBS Store
1697 Broadway at 53rd Street, 975-8600, www.cbs.com
Visit this store for memorabilia, novelties, collectibles and T-shirts relating to your favorite CBS shows and personalities.

Century 21 $
22 Cortlandt Street between Broadway and Church Streets, 227-9092
472 86th Street between Fourth and Fifth Avenues, Bay Ridge, Brooklyn,
    718 748-3266
www.c21stores.com
Many seasoned shoppers consider this discount department store to be "New York's best kept secret." The children's department carries discounted major brands and designer-label clothing for kids up to 8 years old, shoes and layette. There is also plenty for your tweens and teens. You need a bit of patience to work through the merchandise, and the inventory can be hit or miss, but you can luck out with incredible designer bargains.

Chameleon Comics
3 Maiden Lane between Nassau Street and Broadway, 587-3411
A great source for new comics, sports cards and all kinds of trading cards, sports memorabilia, T-shirts, model kits, figures and related toys.

Chelsea Kids Quarters $$
33 West 17th Street between Fifth and Sixth Avenues, 627-5524
www.chelseakidsquarters.com
If you are furnishing a child's room, you will appreciate the large selection of solid wood furniture, decorative accessories and some linens (no crib sizes) for older children's rooms. Some custom furniture and design services available.

Chess Forum
219 Thompson Street between 3rd and Bleecker Streets, 475-2369
www.chessforum.com
For the chess lover, this chess club, store and café provides an opportunity for play. The store carries chess boards, books and magazines as well as other board games. It is possible to arrange for private instruction.

Chess Shop
230 Thompson Street between 3rd and Bleecker Streets, 475-9580
www.chess-shop.com
This chess emporium carries more than 1,000 chess sets as well as other board games. You can play a game here or arrange for private instruction.

Children's General Store
91st Street between Second and Third Avenues, opening in 2003
Grand Central Terminal, 628-0004
This store features a good selection of unique and educational toys.

Children's Museum of Manhattan Store
212 West 83rd Street between Amsterdam Avenue and Broadway,
    721-1223, www.cmom.org
Whether or not you visit this excellent, hands-on children's museum, the shop has a good selection of unique and educational toys and books, many tied in to current exhibitions.

Children's Place $ to $$
901 Sixth Avenue at 33rd Street, Manhattan Mall, 268-7696
22 West 34th Street between Fifth and Sixth Avenues, 904-1190
1460 Broadway at 41st Street, 398-4416
1164 Third Avenue at 68th Street, 717-7187
173 East 86th Street between Lexington and Third Avenues, 831-5100
2039 Broadway at 70th Street, 917 441-2374
2187 Broadway at 77th Street, 917 441-9807
36 Union Square East between 16th and 17th Streets, 529-2201
650 Sixth Avenue between 19th and 20th Streets, 917 305-1348
248 West 125th Street between Seventh and Eighth Avenues, 866-9616
877-PLACEUSA (752-33872) for other locations
www.childrensplace.com
This national chain features a good selection of reasonably priced basics for school and play as well as some trendier items.

Children's Resale $
303 East 81st Street between First and Second Avenues, 734-8897
This consignment shop sells a wide variety of "pre-owned" clothing, accessories, toys, books and shoes for children up to about eight years old.

Chimera $$
77 Mercer Street between Spring and Broome Streets, 334-4730
This cute shop stocks fun stuff for kids—everything from stuffed animals and hand puppets to umbrellas, animal-motif rainboots and slippers, hats, accessories and onesies for infants. A fun place for the kids to visit.

Chocks $
74 Orchard Street between Broome and Grand Streets, 473-1929
www.chockcatalog.com
In this shop located on the famed Orchard Street in the heart of the Lower East Side, you will find discount layette, sleepwear, underwear and hosiery for children and adults as well as some wooden toys.

Christofle Pavilion $$$
680 Madison Avenue at 62nd Street, 308-9390
This purveyor of fine silver, crystal and china has a collection of beautiful silver baby gifts, including cutlery, cups, figurines, picture frames, trays and baby china.

City Store
1 Centre Street, North Plaza Municipal Building, 669-8246
1560 Broadway between 46th and 47th Streets (in the Times Square
    Visitors Center)
www.nyc.gov/citystore
Run by the city government, this store carries books (everything from official publications to coffee-table books) about or relating to the city as well as novelty and souvenir items.

C. J. Laing
30 East 74th Street between Park and Madison Avenues, 819-0248
www.cjlaing.com
This store, well known in Locust Valley, has landed in Manhattan and is known for its trademark "delightfully unique collection" of whimsically embroidered classic clothing for children in sizes 2–14.

Claire's Accessories $
Pier 17, South Street Seaport, 566-0193
755 Broadway at 8th Street, 353-3980
720 Lexington Avenue at 57th Street, 644-8665
1385 Broadway between 37th and 38th Streets, 302-6616

This shop features trendy, very inexpensive accessories for girls, including jewelry (from earrings, bracelets, necklaces to belly chains), walls of hair accessories, some cosmetics (lip gloss, glitter gel and the like), novelty home accessories (picture frames, pillows, pillow covers), boas, cute p.j.s, sunglasses and more. Most items are under $10. Beware, some locations offer ear piercing!

Classic Toys
218 Sullivan Street between Bleecker and West 3rd Streets, 674-4434
www.classictoysnyc.com
This unique shop features classic toys for children and adults, including puppets, tin toys, lead soldiers, classic cars, small character figures and novelties, some books and magazines, die-cast toys, classic games and some vintage toys.

Club Monaco $$
121 Prince Street between Wooster and Greene Streets, 533-8930
520 Broadway at Spring Street, 941-1511
160 Fifth Avenue at 21st Street, 352-0936
Fifth Avenue and 57th Street, opening in 2003
1111 Third Avenue at 65th Street, 355-2949

2376 Broadway at 87th Street, 579-2587
www.clubmonaco.com
Your fashion-forward teens (boys and girls) will love the trendy, current, casual fashions available here at reasonable prices.

Clyde's
926 Madison Avenue at 74th Street, 744-5050
www.clydesonmadison.com
This tony pharmacy and department store offers high-end bath and skin-care products (for kids and adults), cosmetics and some toys (including a good selection of Steiff stuffed animals).

Collector's Universe
31 West 46th Street between Fifth and Sixth Avenues, 922-1110
www.cunyc.com
Visit this shop for a wide selection of sports cards (both vintage and new), comic books, action figures, all types of trading cards and collectible figures.

Compleat Strategist
11 East 33rd Street between Fifth and Madison Avenues, 685-3880
www.compleatstrategist.com
If your family loves board games, then do not miss this shop, which features games (including role-playing and strategy games) and toys for children ages 3+ and adults.

Contempo Casuals $
65 East 8th Street between Broadway and Mercer Street, 228-6188
www.wetseal.com
Teens flock to this shop for trendy, inexpensive, fun clothes, many of which come in junior sizes.

Conway Stores $
151 William Street at Fulton Street, 374-1072
45 Broad Street at Exchange Place, 943-8900
201 East 42nd Street at Third Avenue, 922-5030
11 West 34th Street between Fifth and Sixth Avenues, 967-1370 (no kids department)
225 West 34th Street between Seventh and Eighth Avenues, 967-7390
450 Seventh Avenue between 34th and 35th Streets, 967-1371
1333 Broadway at 35th Street, 967-3460
General Information, 967-5300
The children's department in this discount department store for all ages carries clothing and layette. Some stores may have a modest selection of toys.

Cooper-Hewitt National Design Museum Shop
2 East 91st Street at Fifth Avenue, 849-8355, www.si.edu/ndm
The gift shop carries some children's books and a modest selection of toys and puzzles.

Corner Bookstore
1313 Madison Avenue at 93rd Street, 831-3554
This friendly neighborhood bookstore with a knowledgeable and friendly staff has books for all ages.

Cosmic Comics
10 East 23rd Street between Park Avenue and Broadway, 460-5322
Come here for new and vintage comics as well as action figures, trading cards and models.

Cozy's Cuts for Kids
1125 Madison Avenue between 84th and 85th Streets, 744-1716
448 Amsterdam Avenue at 81st Street, 579-2600
www.cozyscutsforkids.com
Haircuts for children up to age 12 in a totally child-friendly and fun setting. The store also carries a good selection of hair accessories and is well stocked with unique toys. Appointments are recommended.

Cradle & All $$ to $$$
1384 Lexington Avenue between 91st and 92nd Streets, 996-9990
This Upper East Side shop offers beautiful things for the new baby and young child, including layette, some furniture, linens, decorative accessories for the nursery and bath and clothing for infants up to 6 months. Some items can be hand painted or personalized.

Crate & Barrel $$
650 Madison Avenue at 59th Street, 308-0011
611 Broadway at Houston Street, 780-0004
www.crateandbarrel.com
While this huge home-furnishings store does not cater particularly to kids, there are plenty of fabulous, well-priced items that are very kid friendly, including furniture that is perfect for your older child's room, linens, melamine and plastic dishes and glasses, colorful bath accessories and kid-friendly decorative accessories. During the holiday season, the store offers specific gift items for kids and some child-sized furniture, such as table and chair sets.

Crawford Doyle Booksellers
1082 Madison Avenue between 81st and 82nd Streets, 288-6300
A fine neighborhood bookstore with a selection of quality children's books.

Crembebe
68 Second Avenue between 3rd and 4th Streets, 979-6848
This tiny shop offers a good selection of mostly imported stylish casual clothing for boys and girls up to size 4T as well as some toys for young children.

Crush—Hip Stuff You'll Want $$
860 Lexington Avenue between 64th and 65th Streets, mezzanine level,
    535-8142, www.crushstore.com
Your tween or teen will love all the goodies this store—formerly located in
Brooklyn—has to offer. Not only is there cool vintage stuff, but there is
plenty of Hello Kitty merchandise, bags of all sorts, novelties and Power-
puff Girl goodies.

Daffy's $
462 Broadway and Grand Street, 334-7444
111 Fifth Avenue at 18th Street, 529-4477
335 Madison Avenue at 44th Street, 557-4422
125 East 57th Street between Park and Lexington Avenues, 376-4477
1311 Broadway at 34th Street, 736-4477
www.daffys.com
The children's department of this discount department store carries major
brand clothing, shoes, layette and some toys. The inventory changes fre-
quently and the selection is hit or miss, but a patient shopper can find
some great bargains.

Danskin $$
159 Columbus Avenue between 67th and 68th Streets, 724-2992
www.danskin.com
Not just for dancing, this store carries dance and activewear for leisure and
for serious dancers.

Dave's Army & Navy Store $
581 Sixth Avenue between 16th and 17th Streets, 989-6444
This store offers a broad selection of play clothes and Levis for adults and
children (starting at size 4).

David Z $$
655 Sixth Avenue at 21st Street, 807-8546
1384 Fifth Avenue between 35th and 36th Streets, 917 351-1484
821 Broadway at 12th Street, 253-5511
This shoe store for adults, featuring comfort shoes (for example, Birken-
stock, Mephisto, Ecco, Dansko), also carries Timberland and some sneakers
for children sizes 3 and up.

Details $$
347 Bleecker Street at West 10th Street, 414-0039
142 Eighth Avenue at 17th Street, 366-9498
188 Columbus Avenue between 68th and 69th Streets, 362-7344
This eclectic home-accessories shop carries a unique selection of items for
the home and bath that would appeal to kids, including a good selection
of bath products and accessories (from animal-shaped sponges to cute
shower curtains), totes and messenger bags for your school-age kids, cards,
candles and lots of other fun stuff.

Diesel   **$$ to $$$**
StyleLab, 416 West Broadway between Prince and Spring Streets, 343-3863
1 Union Square West at 14th Street, 646 336-8552
770 Lexington Avenue at 60th Street, 308-0055
www.diesel.com
For a totally cool shopping experience, your older kids will love these funky, hip, casual clothes and accessories with the Diesel label (think club- and streetwear) for men and women. The Lexington Avenue store has a kid's department that carries clothing with the signature look for toddlers to size 16. Neither the brand-new Union Square store, which features the new sports (think skates and skateboards) line, nor the SoHo StyleLab, which features the higher priced, more cutting-edge merchandise, has a kids' section, but your teens will love them.

Dinosaur Hill   **$$ to $$$**
306 East 9th Street between First and Second Avenues, 473-5850
www.dinosaurhill.com
This Village shop is a great source for quality educational toys (many hand-made or hand finished) and unique casual clothes in sizes 0–6, including hand-knit sweaters and one-of-a-kind items, baby blankets, infant shoes, hats and other accessories.

Disney Store
711 Fifth Avenue at 55th Street, 702-0702
218 West 42nd Street between Seventh and Eighth Avenues, 302-0595
147 Columbus Avenue at 66th Street, 362-2386
www.disney.com
This national chain offers clothing, toys, books and gift and novelty items with Disney themes for the whole family.

Dollhouse
400 Lafayette Street at East 4th Street, 539-1800
This downtown shop has a treasure trove of stylish, trendy casual clothing for tweens and teens featuring Italian and French labels as well as their own Dollhouse jeans. Skinny moms will have fun here, too.

DKNY   **$$$**
655 Madison Avenue at 60th Street, 223-DKNY (3569)
420 West Broadway between Prince and Spring Streets, 646 613-1100
www.dkny.com
These stores carry the DKNY line for women, men and the home. Your teens (girls and boys) will covet these stylish, pricey clothes and acces- sories. DKNY for kids can be found at Bloomingdales and Macy's.

Dylan's Candy Bar
1011 Third Avenue at 60th Street, 646 735-0078
This brand-new, two-level candy store opened by Dylan Lauren is a candy- lover's dream. You can satisfy your sweet tooth with everything from Pez

to M&Ms and pick your own personal favorites from walls of candy choices. Custom orders available.

Earl Jeans   **$$$**
160 Mercer Street between Prince and West Houston Streets, 226-8709
www.earljean.com
They are expensive, but teen girls can not seem to live without these low-rise tight jeans.

East Side Kids   **$$ to $$$**
1298 Madison Avenue at 92nd Street, 360-5000
This Upper East Side institution stocks a full selection of children's shoes from classic to trendy as well as sneakers and dance shoes.

Eastern Mountain Sports   **$$ to $$$**
591 Broadway between Prince and Houston Streets, 966-8730
20 West 61st Street between Columbus Avenue and Broadway, 397-4860
www.EMSonline.com
This outdoor specialist carries everything for the outdoors for all ages, including outerwear and camping supplies for children.

E.A.T. Gifts   **$$ to $$$**
1062 Madison Avenue between 80th and 81st Streets, 861-2544
This pricey boutique features a unique, eclectic selection of toys, books, decorative accessories, some furniture, party goods, high-end novelties, seasonal items (rain boots, flip-flops), accessories (umbrellas, tote bags) and dishes. Your children can spend hours in here and it is hard to leave empty-handed.

E. Braun & Co., Inc.   **$$$**
717 Madison Avenue between 63rd and 64th Streets, 838-0650
This venerable boutique offers imported luxury linens, including child-sized sheets, duvet covers, silk comforters and cashmere blankets.

Eclipse   **$$**
400 Lafayette Street at 4th Street, 539-1800
Teens love the casual, funky clothing for teen girls, including tank and tube tops, jeans, sweaters, some dresses, jackets and accessories.

Economy Handicrafts   **$**
50-21 69th Street off Queens Boulevard, Woodside, Queens, 800 216-1601
www.economyhandicrafts.com
If you love projects, do not miss this store, which stocks everything you could possibly need for arts-and-crafts projects, all at a discount. Mail/telephone ordering available.

Enchanted Forest
85 Mercer Street between Spring and Broome Streets, 925-6677
www.sohotoys.com
This charming shop carries unique nostalgic toys and books in an incredible setting.

Ethan Allen $$
192 Lexington Avenue at 32nd Street, 213-0600
1107 Third Avenue at 65th Street, 308-7703
103 West End Avenue at 64th Street, 201-9840
www.ethanallen.com
No longer just the home of reproduction colonial furniture, Ethan Allen has morphed into a very stylish and well-priced home furnishings store with lines for all tastes and budgets. They feature several well-priced lines just for kids, including beds, storage and media units, desks and dressers. The stores offer design services and can even dress the bed and windows.

Exploration Station
1705 First Avenue between 88th and 89th Streets, 426-5424
www.explorationstation.net
This store offers a "full line of teacher supplies for the classroom and also carries fun and educational games and kits for the home and school." A great source for math tools, geography games, puppets, anatomy models, science kits, dinosaur digs and arts-and-crafts supplies.

Express $ to $$
Pier 17, South Street Seaport, 693-0096
130 Fifth Avenue at 18th Street, 633-9414
733 Third Avenue at 46th Street, 949-9784
477 Madison Avenue at 51st Street, 644-4453
722-728 Lexington Avenue at 58th Street, 421-7246
584 Broadway at Prince Street, 625-0313
901 Sixth Avenue at 33rd Street, Manhattan Mall, 971-3280
7 West 34th Street between Fifth and Sixth Avenues, 629-6838
321-327 Columbus Avenue at 75th Street, 580-5833
www.expressfashion.com
This national chain has a broad selection of trendy, casual, well-priced clothes based on the season's hottest fashions, along with accessories perfect for your teen.

FAO Schwarz $$ to $$$
767 Fifth Avenue at 58th Street, 644-9400, www.fao.com
This huge toy store (and popular tourist destination) houses an extensive selection of toys (from commercial brands to unique items), stuffed animals, dolls, art supplies, party goods, books, costumes, entire departments dedicated to Barbie, Madame Alexander dolls, Lego and Star Wars, video games and accessories, a new FAO Baby shop and some clothing, all in an amazing setting.

Farmers Daughter and Son　　　　　　　**$$ to $$$**
1001 First Avenue at 55th Street, 421-0484
This neighborhood ladies' boutique carries onesies and sweaters, some hand knitted, for infants.

Filene's Basement　　　　　　　　**$ to $$**
620 Sixth Avenue at 18th Street, 620-3100
2222 Broadway at 79th Street, 873-8000
www.filenesbasement.com
This discount department store does not have a children's department, but your tween (if he or she fits into adult sizes) or teen can find well-priced clothing, accessories and shoes.

Fire Zone
34 West 51st Street, 50 Rockefeller Plaza, between Fifth and Sixth Avenues,
　　698-4520, www.fdnyfirezone.com
Operated by the FDNY's Fire Safety Education Fund, this location houses both a store that sells officially licensed and trademarked products of the Fire Department and terrific hands-on and multi-media presentations about fire safety (including a firehouse, fire scene and empowerment zone).

First & Second Cousin　　　　　　　**$$**
142 Seventh Avenue South between 10th and Charles Streets, 929-8048
This shop offers mostly casual and some party clothes for boys and girls (including such labels as Flapdoodles and OshKosh) up to size 10 as well as toys.

Forbidden Planet
840 Broadway at 13th Street, 473-1576
This unusual store features a wide selection of science-fiction toys, action figures, video games, role-playing games, comic books, fantasy literature and some accessories and T-shirts. For ages 5+.

Fossil　　　　　　　　　　**$$**
530 Fifth Avenue between 44th and 45th Streets, 997-3978
103 Fifth Avenue at 17th Street, 243-7296
www.fossil.com
The source for very cool watches, sunglasses, messenger bags and other accessories with the Fossil label for your tweens and teens.

Freed of London　　　　　　　**$$**
21-01 43rd Avenue, Long Island City, Queens, 718 729-7061
www.freedoflondon.com
This shop is the place to go for serious dancewear and supplies for dancers ages 2 to adult.

French Connection $$
435 West Broadway between Prince and Spring Streets, 219-1139
700 Broadway at 4th Street, 473-4486
1270 Sixth Avenue at 51st Street, 262-6623
304 Columbus Avenue between 74th and 75th Streets, 496-1470
   (women's only)
www.frenchconnection.com
Teens are drawn to the current and trendy styles based on runway looks, which are found here at quite reasonable prices.

Fresh $$$
57 Spring Street between Lafayette and Mulberry Streets, 925-0099
1061 Madison Avenue between 80th and 81st Streets, 396-0344
388 Bleecker Street between Perry and 11th Streets, 917 408-1850
www.fresh.com
Your teenage girl will love the luxurious natural products for skin, hair and body and some products and accessories for the home (they also make great gifts). Fresh also carries a line of lovely all-natural children's bath products.

Frette $$$
799 Madison Avenue between 67th and 68th Streets, 988-5221
www.frette.com
Indulge in imported luxury linens from this Italian company. For kids, you will find fine crib bedding and blankets.

Funny Business Comics

660B Amsterdam Avenue between 92nd and 93rd Streets, 799-9477
This shop is packed full of collectible comics.

Galo Shoes $$$
895 Madison Avenue at 72nd Street (opening in 2003)
825 Lexington Avenue at 63rd Street, 832-3922
1296 Third Avenue between 74th and 75th Streets, 288-3448
www.galoshoes.com
This women's shoe boutique carries a good selection of fashionable, mostly European shoes for boys and girls from one year up.

Game Show
474 Sixth Avenue between 11th and 12th Streets, 633-6328
1240 Lexington Avenue between 83rd and 84th Streets, 472-8011
If your family enjoys games, then this store is a great source for all kinds of games for adults and children ages 4+.

Games Workshop
54 East 8th Street between Broadway and University Place, 982-6314
www.games-workshop.com
This downtown outpost of the Games Workshop organization is dedicated to serious role-playing and battle simulation games. For ages 8+.

Gap $$

113 Front Street, South Street Seaport, 374-1051 (adults, kids, baby)
1 Astor Place at Broadway, 253-0145 (women)
345 Sixth Avenue at 4th Street, 727-2210 (adults)
750 Broadway at 8th Street, 674-1877 (men)
122 Fifth Avenue between 17th and 18th Streets, 917 408-5580 (adults, kids, baby)
1466 Broadway at 42nd Street, 382-4500 (adults, kids, baby)
657-659 Third Avenue at 42nd Street, 697-3590 (adults, kids, baby)
757 Third Avenue at 47th Street, 223-5140 (adults, kids)
900 Third Avenue at 54th Street, 754-2290 (adults)
527 Madison Avenue at 54th Street, 688-1260 (adults)
734 Lexington Avenue between 58th and 59th Streets, 751-1543 (adults)
277 West 23rd Street at Eighth Avenue, 646 336-0802 (adults)
60 West 34th Street at Broadway, 760-1268 (adult, kids, baby)
1212 Sixth Avenue at 48th Street, 730-1087 (adult, kids, baby)
680 Fifth Avenue at 54th Street, 977-7023 (adult, kids, baby)
250 West 57th Street at Broadway, 315-2250 (adults, kids, baby)
1131-1149 Third Avenue at 66th Street, 472-4555 (adults, kids, baby)
1037 Lexington Avenue at 74th Street, 327-2614 (baby)
1066 Lexington Avenue at 75th Street, 879-9144 (adults, kids)
1511 Third Avenue at 85th Street, 794-5781 (adults)
1535 Third Avenue at 87th Street, 423-0033 (kids, baby)
1988 Broadway at 67th Street, 721-5304 (adults, kids, baby)
335 Columbus Avenue at 76th Street, 873-9270 (women)
341 Columbus Avenue at 76th Street, 875-9196 (baby)
2373 Broadway at 86th Street, 873-1244 (adults)
Visit www.gap.com or call 800 GAP-STYLE to locate the store nearest to you.

This phenomenon is the epitome of American casual, offering stylish, contemporary, reasonably-priced basics for babies to adults.

The Gazebo $$$

306 East 61st Street between First and Second Avenues, 6th floor, 832-7077, www.thegazebo.com

This charming home-accessories shop offers country-inspired bedding, handmade quilts, decorative accessories for the nursery and some lovely hand-knit sweaters and crib blankets.

G. C. William $$$

1137 Madison Avenue between 84th and 85th Streets, 396-3400

Personal service is emphasized at this very chic Upper East Side boutique, which carries a variety of fashion-savvy classic and contemporary clothing for children ages 6–16, junior sizes for girls and husky sizes for boys. While there is a terrific assortment of cutting-edge casual clothes and accessories of all kinds, this is also the place to buy elegant, fashionable dress clothes (including Armani Jr. and Burberry), such as boys' suits and tuxedos and chic dresses for girls. Petite moms who fit into the junior sizes will appreciate the selection of Juicy, Petit Bateau and other hip T-shirts. You can also find Roxy and Kenneth Cole shoes for girls and Kenneth Cole shoes for boys.

Geiger $$$
505 Park Avenue at 59th Street, 644-3435, www.geiger-fashion.com
This boutique is the US home of the original Austrian boiled wool jacket (with or without appliqués) for children ages 18 months to 8 as well as jackets and clothing for women.

Geppetto's Toybox
10 Christopher Street at Greenwich Avenue, 620-7511, www.nyctoys.com
This downtown toy store offers a great selection of higher-end quality and educational toys (some handmade) and books.

G-Factory $$
458 West Broadway between Houston and Prince Streets, 260-4570
www.casio.com
This store is the place to go for the latest and best selection of Casio G-Shock and Baby-G watches.

Girlprops.com $
153 Prince Street between West Broadway and Thompson Street,
    505-7615
203 Spring Street between Sullivan Street and Sixth Avenue, 625-8323
33 8th Street between University Place and Broadway, 533-3240
www.girlprops.com
For girls 3 to 83, very cool, fun, trendy accessories including hair accessories, "house props" such as picture frames and pillows, jewelry, makeup, sunglasses, wigs and bags. The price is right, too: Girlprops' motto is "inexpensive. . .we never say cheap."

Good Byes Children's Resale Shop $
230 East 78th Street between Second and Third Avenues, 794-2301
This resale shop is packed with clothing (sizes 0–6), equipment, toys and books.

Gotham City Comics
800 Lexington Avenue between 61st and 62nd Streets, 2nd floor,
    980-0009
This East Side shop has a large selection of new and collectible comics, sports and other trading cards, action figures and toys.

Gracious Home $$$
1217 Third Avenue between 70th and 71st Streets (hardware), 988-8990
1220 Third Avenue between 70th and 71st Streets (bed and bath),
    517-6300
1992 Broadway at 67th Street, 231-7800
www.gracioushome.com

This housewares store carries everything from hardware, home appliances, gadgets, organizers and everything for the kitchen to home furnishings and now a high-end baby department, too. The baby department carries furniture for the nursery, layette, linens, decorative accessories as well as wall and window coverings. Custom design services available.

Granny Made $$ to $$$
381 Amsterdam Avenue between 78th and 79th Streets, 496-1222
www.granny-made.com
This charming shop, known for its excellent selection of hand-knit sweaters, has quality clothing (including handmade items) for adults and children up to size 8/10. For kids, there are casual clothes (including such labels as Heartstrings, Sweet Potatoes and My Boy Sam), layette, decorative accessories, soft sculpture wall hangings, decorative quilts and a particularly good selection of boy stuff.

Granny's Rentals
876-4310, 410-9464
If you do not want to cart your own supplies to New York or you are hosting out-of-town guests, you can rent baby furniture (cribs, changing tables, rocking chair for mom) and equipment (strollers, high chairs, etc.) for your stay as well as kid-size party supplies. A week's notice is usually sufficient, except around major holidays when advance reservations are crucial.

Great Feet $$
1241 Lexington Avenue at 84th Street, 249-0551, www.striderite.com
This popular children's shoe store has a full selection of shoes, from classic to trendy, and sneakers along with toys to play with while you wait. The salespeople are real pros.

The Green Onion $$
247 Smith Street between Sackett and Degraw Streets, Brooklyn,
   718 246-2804
Proprietor Shelley Kruth has created a charming shop filled with cool, funky, fun, upscale stylish clothing and shoes for kids 0 to 7 (some items for girls up to size 10), featuring a terrific layette selection, hand-knit sweaters, unique shoes, educational toys, books and some decorative accessories.

Greenstone's $$ to $$$
442 Columbus Avenue between 81st and 82nd Streets, 580-4322
Greenstone's, too, 1184 Madison Avenue between 86th and 87th
   Streets, 427-1665
This boutique offers fun, contemporary and unique clothing, including a large selection of hand-knit sweaters and very cute hats.

Gryphon Bookshop
2246 Broadway between 80th and 81st Streets, 362-0706
This neighborhood used-book store has a modest children's section.

Gucci $$$
685 Fifth Avenue at 54th Street, 826-2600
840 Madison Avenue between 69th and 70th Streets, 717-2619
www.gucci.com
This high-end Italian leather goods, accessories and clothing store for adults carries signature soft infant shoes for the well-heeled baby.

Guess? $$
23 Fulton Street at South Street Seaport, 385-0533
537 Broadway between Prince and Spring Streets, 226-9545
www.guess.com
Teens love these trendy casual clothes and accessories.

Guggenheim (Solomon R.) Museum
1071 Fifth Avenue at 89th Street, 423-3615, www.guggenheim.org/store
This fabulous museum gift shop has a good selection of educational toys and books and some decorative accessories.

Gymboree Store $$
1049 Third Avenue at 62nd Street, 688-4044
1332 Third Avenue between 76th and 77th Streets, 517-5548
1120 Madison Avenue between 83rd and 84th Streets, 717-6702
2015 Broadway at 69th Street, 595-7662
2271 Broadway between 81st and 82nd Streets, 595-9071
www.gymboree.com
This national chain offers colorful, reasonably priced basic clothing and some shoes up to age 7.

H & M $
558 Broadway between Prince and Spring Streets, 343-8313
640 Fifth Avenue at 51st Street, 489-0390
Herald Square at 34th Street and Sixth Avenue, 646 473-1165
www.hm.com
Sweden's answer to the Gap offers inexpensive, up-to-the-minute, stylish clothes and accessories for men, women and kids. Only the Herald Square store has a kids' department (sizes 0–14), but tweens and teens will love the clothes and accessories in all of the stores. Inventory is constantly changing in these huge stores, so do not pass up that item you fall in love with, because it may be gone by next week.

H2O+ $$
460 West Broadway between Houston and Prince Streets, 505-3223
650 Madison Avenue between 59th and 60th Streets, 750-8119
www.h2oplus.com
Well-priced, water-based natural products for skin, hair and body, which your teens and tweens will love (and they make great gifts and party favors). H2O+ also stocks some great bath products and accessories just for kids.

Halloween Adventure
104 Fourth Avenue between 11th and 12th Streets, 673-4546
www.halloweenadventure.com
Not for the timid, this unusual store stocks magic tricks, gag gifts, costumes, wigs, disguises, makeup, novelties and decorations. A magician is often on the premises to demonstrate the magic tricks.

Hammacher Schlemmer $$ to $$$
147 East 57th Street between Lexington and Third Avenues, 421-9000
www.hammacher.com
This lifestyle store, famous for its catalogue and "best of" products, carries items, tools, retro-inspired novelties, electronics and gadgets for the home, recreation and personal care, designed to make life easier, more fun or more interesting. Kids will definitely enjoy visiting the showroom and testing the merchandise.

Harry's Shoes $$
2299 Broadway at 83rd Street, 874-2035, www.harrys-shoes.com
This Upper West Side institution is a full-service shoe store for children and adults, featuring a large selection of comfort shoes (Birkenstock, Mephisto, Rockport, Dansko, Timberland and others). The children's department carries everything from basics to party shoes. The salespeople are real pros.

Henri Bendel $$$
712 Fifth Avenue at 56th Street, 247-1100, www.bendels.com
This tony, fashion-forward department store has a tiny children's boutique tucked away on the second floor (near the housewares) with a selection of charming items for children 0–2 such as high-end onesies, bathrobes, silver baby accessories and a few items of clothing.

Hermes $$$
691 Madison Avenue at 62nd Street, 751-3181, www.hermes.com
This famed shopping destination of very high end—and high priced—luxury leather goods, clothing and accessories offers a truly extravagant selection of luxe blankets, robes, towels, china and silver accessories for babies and toddlers.

HMV
234 West 42nd Street between Seventh and Eighth Avenues, 302-1451
565 Fifth Avenue at 46th Street, 681-6700
308 West 125th Street between Fredrick Douglas Boulevard and Eighth
     Avenue, 932-9619
www.hmv.com
This British import has a huge selection of music of all types as well as some videos and DVDs.

Homboms
1500 First Avenue between 78th and 79th Streets, 717-5300
This well-stocked neighborhood store has a good selection of toys (from Barbie and Playskool to games and more unique toys) and a large section of crafts and art supplies.

Hoofbeats $$ to $$$
232 East 78th Street between Second and Third Avenues, 517-2633
This little boutique specializes in gifts for new babies: stuffed animals, pillows, diaper bags, robes, tote bags, hooded towels and decorative nursery accessories, many of which can be personalized or monogrammed.

Hoyt & Bond $$ to $$$
246 Smith Street between Degraw and Douglas Streets, Brooklyn, 718 596-5089
This charming shop for women and children offers a varied line of mostly European clothing for children up to 8 years old, featuring such labels as Marimekko and Petit Bateau and kilts from Scotland and Johnson Woolen Mills (American-made logger jackets). You'll also find original designs by owner Elizabeth Beer, hand-knit sweaters and some books, toys and shoes (such as Sonnet shoes from England).

Hyde Park Stationers
1060 Madison Avenue between 80th and 81st Streets, 861-5710
This friendly neighborhood stationers offers a great selection of school supplies, some toys and books, cards, invitations and custom stationery.

Ibiza Boutique $$ to $$$
42 & 46 University Place between East 9th and East 10th Streets, 533-4614
This very cool Village shop features hip European and eclectic clothing, handmade and unique goods, toys and books and whimsical accessories.

Infinity $$ to $$$
1116 Madison Avenue at 83rd Street, 517-4232
This packed shop is literally stuffed with fashion-forward trendy clothing, small toys, accessories (to wear and for your daughter's room) and novelties for girls and women. There is a terrific selection of casual and dressy clothing for tweens and teens.

Integral Yoga Bookstore
227 West 13th Street between Seventh and Eighth Avenues, 929-0586
This store is a great source for books for the New Age parent and yoga accessories.

Iris Brown's Victorian Doll Shop
253 East 57th Street between Second and Third Avenues, 593-2882

This shop houses a treasure trove of vintage and collectible dolls and doll-house accessories.

It's a Mod, Mod World $$
85 First Avenue between East 5th and East 6th Streets, 460-8004
Lovers of kitsch will have a field day in this cool downtown shop packed to the rafters with collectible tin toys, unique toys and games (think Magic 8 Balls), candles, cards, items with pop images, as well as a line of unique fabricated items such as clocks made out of detergent boxes and lamps made out of vintage toasters.

It's "A" Nother Hit
131 West 33rd Street between Sixth and Seventh Avenues, 564-4111
www.itsanotherhit.com
Your little sports fan will want to check out the new and vintage baseball and other sports and trading cards, memorabilia, comics, action figures and collectibles.

J & R Music World
15-33 Park Row between Beekman and Ann Streets (just south of City
    Hall), 238-9000, www.jandr.com
This huge electronics store offers a large selection of computers, electronics, music (equipment and CDs), video games and more.

J. Crew $$
203 Front Street, South Street Seaport, 385-3500
99 Prince Street between Mercer and Greene Streets, 966-2739
91 Fifth Avenue between 16th and 17th Streets, 255-4848
30 Rockefeller Plaza at 50th Street, 765-4412
www.jcrew.com
Known originally for its catalogue, this store offers up the quintessential American preppy look with a cool twist. Teens will love the selection of basics for school, play and dressing up.

Jacadi $$$
787 Madison Avenue between 66th and 67th Streets, 535-3200
1296 Madison Avenue at 92nd Street, 369-1616
1260 Third Avenue between 72nd and 73rd Streets, 717-9292
www.jacadiusa.com
This popular French boutique offers a high-quality line of fine imported classic clothing, shoes, equipment, layette, furniture for the nursery and linens.

Jane's Exchange $
207 Avenue A between East 12th and East 13th Streets, 674-6268
A great source for resale kids' clothing and accessories, books, some toys and tapes, as well as maternity clothing and nursery furniture.

Jan's Hobby Shop
1557 York Avenue between 82nd and 83rd Streets, 861-5075
This shop specializes in models—wood, metal and plastic—for all ages, including airplanes, cars, ships. An on-site restorer is available to restore and repair old models and toys.

Jay Kos $$$
986 Lexington Avenue between 71st and 72nd Streets, 327-2382
This purveyor of fine men's clothing has recently added a complete boys' department featuring private-label classic, stylish casual and formal attire for boys sizes 1–16.

Jewish Museum Store
1109 Fifth Avenue at 92nd Street, 423-3200, www.jewishmuseum.org
This museum store (one part within the museum and one part next door) has a wonderful selection of Judaica and educational toys and books.

Jim Hanley's Universe
4 West 33rd Street between Fifth Avenue and Broadway, 268-7088
www.jhuniverse.com
One of the largest comic book stores in the city, this store stocks vintage and new comics, trading cards (except sports cards), action figures, statues, novels, comic-related apparel and books and supplies for comic artists.

Jodi's Gymwear $$
244 East 84th Street between Second and Third Avenues, 772-7633
Housed within Jodi's Gym (a popular venue for children's classes), this shop carries dance, gymnastics, ice-skating wear and activewear for girls through young junior sizes.

Joyce Leslie $
20 University Place at 8th Street, 505-5419, www.joyceleslie.com
Your teen-age girl will be able to find up-to-the-minute trendiness—clothing, accessories and shoes—all in junior sizes, without spending a fortune.

Judy's Fancies $$$
By appointment only, 689-8663
Judy Correa specializes in christening gowns and custom-made clothing for children of all ages. Special-occasion clothes are available for girls through size 8 and boys through size 6. Other clothing goes up to size 6 for girls and boys. Judy, who uses only natural fabrics and favors a Victorian-inspired look, will create her own designs or work with your ideas.

Julian & Sara $$$
103 Mercer Street between Prince and Spring Streets, 226-1989
This SoHo boutique features fine European clothing and accessories (such as Kenzo and Jean Bourget), baby cashmeres, shoes, mobiles, music boxes

and some toys. The look ranges from classic to cool. The layette selection includes some handmade items.

Jumpin' Julias $$$
240 Seventh Avenue between 4th and 5th Streets, Brooklyn, 718 965-3535
This boutique carries a good assortment of classic, fine European clothing and shoes for children up to size 8.

Juno $$$
550 Broadway between Prince and Spring Streets, 925-6415
www.junokids.com
This downtown shop features cool, hip fashionable shoes for the whole family.

Just for Tykes $$$
83 Mercer Street between Spring and Broome Streets, 274-9121
This upscale children's boutique located in the heart of SoHo is one-stop shopping for kids 0–4. In addition to a large selection of cool European and American clothing, you will find unique bedding (custom and pre-made), furniture, equipment, decorative accessories, toys and a new-mother section. The play area keeps the kids busy while you shop.

Kar'ikter $$ to $$$
19 Prince Street between Elizabeth and Mott Streets, 274-1966
www.karikter.com
This shop is chock full of decorative accessories, dishes, backpacks and other accessories and small toys inspired by popular European characters such as Tintin, the Little Prince, Babar and Noddy. You will also find a colorful selection of modern European home furnishings.

Kate Spade Store $$$
454 Broome Street at Mercer Street, 274-1991, www.katespade.com
These cool, clean-lined, pricey fabric handbags have become de rigueur for the well-dressed teen. Moms may prefer the luxury leather versions, although the large fabric totes have been known to make hip, elegant diaper bags.

Kate's Paperie
561 Broadway between Prince and Spring Streets, 941-9816
8 West 13th Street between Fifth and Sixth Avenues, 633-0570
1282 Third Avenue between 73rd and 74th Streets, 396-3670
www.katespaperie.com
This stationer offers a broad variety of items for the serious writer—paper (from handmade to computer friendly), pens, stationery, wrapping papers and writing and desk accessories. A children's section features some books, arts-and-crafts supplies and kids' stationery. The stores offer periodic events (such as papermaking and crafts activities) for children and adults.

KB Toys
1411 St. Nicholas Avenue at 181st Street, 928-4816
901 Sixth Avenue at 33rd Street, Manhattan Mall, 629-5386
2411 Broadway at 89th Street, 595-4389
www.kbtoys.com
Come here for a large selection of commercial toys and art supplies. Don't miss the huge new flagship store at Rockefeller Center.

Kenneth Cole $$
597 Broadway between Houston and Prince Streets, 965-0283
95 Fifth Avenue at 17th Street, 675-2550
130 East 57th Street at Lexington Avenue, 688-1670 (Reaction)
107 East 42nd Street at Park Avenue, 949-8079
610 Fifth Avenue at 49th Street, 373-5800
353 Columbus Avenue between 76th and 77th Streets, 873-2061
www.kennethcole.com
This hip young label, popular among older teenagers, features shoes, bags and accessories, jackets and some clothing for men and women.

Kidding Around $$
60 West 15th Street between Fifth and Sixth Avenues, 645-6337
This shop offers a good selection of educational and unique toys, books and fun and unique clothing and accessories (up to size 8). A good source for handmade quilts and baby blankets.

Kids Cuts
201 East 31st Street between Second and Third Avenues, 684-5252
Haircuts for children in a totally child-friendly and fun setting. The store also carries a selection of hair accessories and unique toys. Haircuts available for adults too.

Kids Foot Locker $$
120 West 34th Street between Sixth and Seventh Avenues, 465-9041
1504 Second Avenue between 78th and 79th Streets, 396-4567
www.footlocker.com
This national chain offers a large selection of sneakers and activewear (warm-ups, windbreakers, T-shirts) for babies on up.

Kids Supply Co. $$ to $$$
1343 Madison Avenue at 94th Street, 426-1200, www.kidssupplyco.com
This well-stocked shop offers children's higher-end furniture, some decorative accessories and linens. Custom design services available.

Kidstown $
10 East 14th Street between Fifth Avenue and University Place, 243-1301
This store is literally piled high with value-priced clothing, layette, furniture, equipment and toys.

Kiehl's $$

109 Third Avenue between 13th and 14th Streets, 677-3171, www.kiehls.com

Kiehl's natural products for skin, hair and body have been around since 1851. The Village flagship store is worth a visit just to see the collection of memorabilia. In addition to all kinds of products for adults, there is a line of baby products (many swear by the diaper cream) and great products for "problem" skin. Kiehl's products are also available at Barney's, Bergdorf Goodman, Saks Fifth Avenue and Zitomer's.

Kirna Zabete $$$

96 Greene Street between Prince and Spring Streets, 941-9656

www.kirnazabete.com

This high-end, cutting-edge designer boutique for women has a unique, seasonal selection of tiny luxurious infant cashmere sweaters and accessories.

Kmart Stores $

770 Broadway at Astor Place, 673-1540

One Penn Plaza at 34th Street between Seventh and Eighth Avenues, 760-1188

www.bluelight.com

The New York branches of this famed discount department store have large children's departments that carry major brand-name clothing, shoes, equipment, toys and books.

La Layette et Plus $$$

170 East 61st Street between Lexington and Third Avenues, 688-7072

www.lalayette.com

This boutique offers a treasure trove of fine imported layette, custom linens, baby cashmeres, clothing (up to size 2), hand-knits, silver and customized porcelain gift items and handpainted and carved furniture.

La Petite Etoile $$$

746 Madison Avenue between 64th and 65th Streets, 744-0975

www.LaPetiteEtoile.com

This elegant boutique features charming, fine imported classic clothing, layette and equipment, featuring labels such as Cacherel, Sonia Rykiel, I Pinco Pallino, La Perla and Floriane.

Lacoste $$$

551 Madison Avenue between 54th and 55th Streets, 800-4-Lacoste (800 452-26783), www.lacoste.com

Best known for the classic piqué crocodile-emblemed tennis shirt, this once-again trendy boutique offers up candy-colored cotton sportswear for adults and kids sizes 2–16. The logoed tops are very popular among teens and tweens. A flagship store on Fifth Avenue at 49th Street is due to open in 2003.

Laura Ashley   **$$ to $$$**
398 Columbus Avenue at 79th Street, 496-5110, www.laura-ashleyusa.com
Best known for home furnishings, this shop also sells traditional, classic clothes for girls sizes 2–9.

Laura Beth's Baby Collection   **$$**
By appointment only, 717-2559
This former department-store buyer helps expectant moms design the perfect nursery by offering a collection of high-end designer linens and decorative accessories at prices below retail. Custom orders can be accommodated.

Le Chateau   **$$**
611 Broadway at Houston Street, 260-0882
704 Broadway at Washington Place, 674-5560
34 West 34th Street between Fifth and Sixth Avenues, 967-0024
www.le-chateau.com
This Canadian import, which caters to young adults, is known for well-priced trendy clothes, many of which are done in rayon. Great for teens.

Le Sportsac   **$$**
176 Spring Street between Thompson Street and West Broadway,
    625-2626
1065 Madison Avenue between 80th and 81st Streets, 988-6200
www.lesportsac.com

A terrific source for distinctive, reasonably priced nylon bags in all shapes, colors, prints and sizes. Young girls particularly love the tiny shoulder bags. Moms enjoy the light-weight travel and tote bags, which make convenient diaper bags.

Leeper Kids
79 Grand Central Terminal, Lexington Passage, 499-9111
Located in the heart of Grand Central Terminal, this small shop offers trendy, colorful and fun casual clothing and accessories for children up to age 10.

Lee's Art Shop   **$$**
220 West 57th Street between Broadway and Seventh Avenue, 247-0110
This huge full-service art supply store has not only everything the serious artist needs in the way of supplies, but also materials suitable for arts-and-crafts projects, school projects and other kids' art activities (non-toxic paint, crayons, big brushes, modeling clay, and lots more).

Lenox Hill Bookstore
1018 Lexington Avenue between 72nd and 73rd Streets, 472-7170
www.lenoxhillbooks.com
This wonderful neighborhood bookstore has a fine selection of children's and parenting books

Leron   **$$$**
750 Madison Avenue at 65th Street, 753-6700, www.leron.com
In this shop, known for fine luxury linens for the bed, bath and table and customized embroidery, you can also find beautiful quilts, sheets, towels, robes (for all ages) and embroidered pillows for your child.

Lester's   **$$ to $$$**
1534 Second Avenue at 80th Street, 734-9292
This recently expanded Upper East Side boutique is popular for its selection of up-to-the-minute contemporary-to-classic clothing, accessories, shoes, and layette as well as some toys, novelties (pillows, "bunk junk" and other hot items) and books. The shoe salespeople are true pros at fitting kids. The lower level houses a full junior department.

Lilliput   **$$ to $$$**
240 Lafayatte Street between Prince and Spring Streets, 965-9201
265 Lafayette Street between Prince and Spring Streets, 965-9567
www.lilliputsoho.com
These boutiques feature cool, chic, contemporary, mostly European clothes, shoes, layette and specialty toys. The 265 Lafayette Street store fits children up to eight years old, and the 240 Lafayette Street store fits from babies to teens. These shops offer a mix of high-fashion labels such as Diesel, Replay and Juicy and fine European brands such as I Golfini della Nonna.

Lincoln Center Performing Arts Gift Shop
136 West 65th Street, Lincoln Center, concourse level, 917 441-1195
www.lincolncenter.org
The Lincoln Center gift shop offers merchandise related to the performing arts for all ages.

Little Eric   **$$ to $$$**
1331 Third Avenue between 76th and 77th Streets, 288-8987
1118 Madison Avenue between 83rd and 84th Streets, 717-1513
This boutique offers a huge selection of high-fashion and adorable shoes for the younger set.

Little Extras   **$$ to $$$**
676 Amsterdam Avenue at 93rd Street, 721-6161
Come here for an assortment of unique decorative accessories, stuffed animals, backpacks, art supplies and furniture and toys, much of which can be personalized.

Little Folk Art   **$$ to $$$**
159 Duane Street between Hudson Street and West Broadway, 267-1500
www.littlefolkart.cc
This California-based company offers original designs and hand-crafted furniture and decorative accessories for the nursery, older child's room and playroom. Design services are available.

Little Folks $ to $$
123 East 23rd Street between Park and Lexington Avenues, 982-9669
This discount children's department store has two floors of everything you need for your baby and young child, including clothing in sizes 0 to 6x (basics from major brands and some imported), furniture (featuring CNT cribs from Italy), equipment and layette. For older kids, look for underwear, pajamas and outerwear up to size 14. Look for a large selection of infant toys and some toys for older kids.

Liz Lange $$$
958 Madison Avenue between 75th and 76th Streets, 879-2191
www.lizlange.com
Who said expectant mothers cannot have stylish, fabulous clothes? Not Liz Lange who serves up her very fashionable signature "must haves": slim pants, cashmere twin sets, skirts, bathing suits and evening clothes for chic moms-to-be.

Logos
1575 York Avenue between 83rd and 84th Streets, 517-7292
This neighborhood bookstore, which carries books for all ages and specializes in Christian literature, has a large children's section that stocks all kinds of books, including some Christian and Hebrew themed works.

Lord & Taylor $$
424 Fifth Avenue between 38th and 39th Streets, 391-3344
www.maycompany.com

The large children's department of this full-service department store carries clothing, layette, and some toys. This store, while not known for a super high-fashion look, has a very good selection of basics and designer labels.

Loro Piana $$$
821 Madison Avenue between 68th and 69th Streets, 980-7961
The New York outpost of this Italian luxury brand, known for its sumptuous cashmeres and casual clothing for adults, carries miniature versions of its signature quilted jackets and cashmere robes, sweaters, blankets and slippers for children up to sizes 4–6.

Lucky Brand Dungarees $$
38 Green Street at Grand Street, 625-0707
172 Fifth Avenue at 22nd Street, 917 606-1418 (no kids' department)
1151 Third Avenue at 67th Street 646 422-1192 (no kids' department)
216 Columbus Avenue at 70th Street, 579-1760
www.luckybrandjeans.com
This L.A.-based retailer specializes in casual clothes with a hip spin. In addition to great-fitting jeans and tops for adults, they have cute jeans, tops and more for children sizes 2–6. There are also some very stylish casual looks for tweens.

M & J Trimmings
1008 Sixth Avenue between 37th and 38th Streets, 391-9072
www.mjtrim.com
If your kids are into crafts, they will love perusing the trimmings (buttons, ribbons, tassels and more) and sewing supplies for all types of craft projects.

MacKenzie-Childs, Ltd. $$$
824 Madison Avenue at 69th Street, 570-6050, www.mackenzie-childs.com
This high-end home accessories emporium carries a selection of unique and whimsical multi-colored and multi-patterned goods (mostly hand-made, handpainted or handfinished), some of which are appropriate for children's rooms, baby gifts or children.

Macy's Herald Square $$
151 West 34th Street at Herald Square, 695-4400
www.macys.com
The very large children's department of this landmark full-service department store carries a broad variety of both designer and more moderate clothing, shoes, layette and toys. You can also find a full-service maternity department and a large selection of fashions and accessories for teen and tweens.

Magic Windows $$$
1186 Madison Avenue at 87th Street, 289-0028
M. W. Teen, 1188 Madison Avenue at 88th Street, 289-0181 (girls only)
Classically styled imported layette and clothing and accessories for boys and girls. You can also find bassinettes, infant baskets and changing tables. M.W. Teen has a large selection of special-occasion dresses and casual wear for preteen and junior-size girls.

Malo $$$
125 Wooster Street between Prince and Spring Streets, 941-7444
814 Madison Avenue at 68th Street, 396-4721
www.malo.it
Wrap your newborn in luxurious Italian cashmere sweaters, hats, booties and blankets. A real treat is the cashmere-covered hot-water bottle.

Mandee $$
2550 Broadway between 95th and 96th Street, 666-1652
www.mandee.com
This shop, which offers junior-size clothing, is popular among teens because of its mission to "deliver fashion at a fabulous price." Look here for well-priced, popular brands of clothing and shoes.

Manhattan Comics and Cards
228 West 23rd Street between Seventh and Eighth Avenues, 243-9349
Come here for new and vintage comics, sports cards, trading cards and action figures.

Manhattan Dollhouse

236 Third Avenue between 19th and 20th Streets, 253-9549
www.manhattandollhouseshop.com
A great source for new and vintage dollhouses and dollhouse accessories. Repair service is available.

Manny's Music

156 West 48th Street between Sixth and Seventh Avenues, 819-0576
www.mannysmusic.com
For your budding rock and roller, you will find a selection of guitars, drums, amplifiers, keyboards and recording equipment.

Marsha D. D. $$ to $$$

1574 Third Avenue between 88th and 89th Streets, 831-2422
A must-visit for cool kids, this is the place for the hottest clothing, small toys, "bunk junk" for camp, novelties and costume jewelry for ages 7 through preteen, teen and some adult sizes for girls and sizes 8–20 for boys.

Mary Arnold Toys

1010 Lexington Avenue between 72nd and 73rd Streets, 744-8510
More than just a neighborhood toy store, this shop has an extensive selection of high-quality toys, dolls (Madame Alexander and Carroll), Steiff animals and books.

Mason's Tennis Mart $$$

56 East 53rd Street between Madison and Park Avenues, 755-5805
This tennis shop stocks a decent selection of racquets and gear for kids ages 5 and up.

Maternity Works $

16 West 57th Street between Fifth and Sixth Avenues, 3rd floor, 399-9840
www.maternitymall.com, www.babystuff.com
Find discounted Mimi, Motherhood and A Pea in the Pod maternity basics at this outlet-style maternity store.

Maxilla and Mandible

451 Columbus Avenue between 81st and 82nd Streets, 724-6173
www.maxillaandmandible.com
Your young scientist will love "the world's first and only osteological store" stocked with bones and fossils and "world renowned natural history and science emporium museum quality specimens and reproductions."

Metropolitan Museum of Art Shop

113 Prince Street between Wooster and Greene Streets, 614-3000
151 West 34th Street at Herald Square (in Macy's), 268-7266
15 West 49th Street, Rockefeller Center, 332-1360
1000 Fifth Avenue between 80th and 84th Streets, 535-7710

The Cloisters at Ft. Tryon Park, 923-3700
LaGuardia Airport, Central Terminal WR1, 718 396-8594
www.metmuseum.org/store
This world-famous museum features a world-class gift shop with a terrific and bountiful selection of educational toys and books. The main store (located within the museum) stocks the most kids' stuff.

Mets Clubhouse Shop
143 East 54th Street between Lexington and Third Avenues, 888-7508
11 West 42nd Street between Fifth and Sixth Avenues, 768-9534
www.sportsavenue.com
What about those Mets? Get all your team paraphernalia and novelties in their official stores.

Michele Saint-Laurent $$$
1028 Lexington Avenue between 73rd and 74th Streets, 452-4200
www.michelesaintlaurent.com
The elegant French maternity clothes in this shop will make you look and feel downright Parisienne. If you need something for a special occasion, custom designs are available.

Mimi Maternity $$
1021 Third Avenue between 60th and 61st Streets, 832-2667
1125 Madison Avenue at 84th Street, 737-3784
2005 Broadway between 68th and 69th Streets, 721-1999
www.maternitymall.com
This national chain offers great well-priced, fashionable basics for work and play as well as some high fashion labels.

Miss Pym $$$
By appointment only, 879-9530, www.misspym.com
Miss Pym is where to turn for custom-made, lovely special-occasion dresses for girls 0–12. Made of the finest materials, these dresses are elegant, sophisticated and lovely. Accessories, including crinolines, slips, purses, jackets, capes and hair ornaments, are also available.

Modell's $$
1293 Broadway between 33rd and 34th Streets, 244-4544
51 East 42nd Street at Vanderbilt Avenue, 661-4242
1535 Third Avenue between 86th and 87th Streets, 996-3800
300 West 125th Street between St. Nicholas and Eighth Avenues,
    280-9100
www.modells.com
A great source for kid-sized (and grownup) sporting goods, gear and skates.

Mommy Chic $$ to $$$
235 Mulberry Street between Prince and Spring Streets, 646 613-1825
www.mommychic.com
Owner Angela Chew designs a line of chic maternity clothes, using mostly silk, cashmere and stretch fabrics with hand-done details (crochet and beading) from terrific basics to fabulous party clothes for the mother-to-be.

Mom's Night Out $$ to $$$
147 East 72nd Street between Lexington and Third Avenues, 744-6667
www.momsnightout.com
The expectant mom who needs an outfit for a special night out can rent one from this shop's own label maternity evening-wear and special-occasion clothing. If you prefer, you can have an outfit made for you to keep.

Morgane Le Fay $$$
67 Wooster Street between Broome and Spring Streets, 219-7672
746 Madison Avenue between 64th and 65th Streets, 879-9700
This boutique, known for its women's designs that combine romantic with interesting angles and shapes, also carries beautiful and unique party dresses for girls up to size 12.

Morris Bros. $ to $$
2322 Broadway at 84th Street, 724-9000
This New York institution has a very large selection of casual clothes for children and teens (which includes some adult sizes) and some layette. You can count on this store for a big selection of poplar brands (such as Quicksilver and And One for boys and Petit Bateau for girls) for your fashion-conscious kids. Morris Brothers also makes name labels (sew-in or iron-on) and is an official camp outfitter.

Moschino $$$
803 Madison Avenue between 67th and 68th Streets, 639-9600
Tucked within the Moschino store for adults are unique, very fashionable designer clothing and shoes for children ages 2 to 8.

Motherhood Maternity $
641 Sixth Avenue at 20th Street, 741-3488
901 Sixth Avenue at 33rd Street, Manhattan Mall, 868-9478
36 West 34th Street between Fifth and Sixth Avenues, 695-9106
16-18 West 57th Street between Fifth and Sixth Avenues, 399-9840
2384 Broadway at 86th Street, 917 441-4009
1449 Third Avenue at 82nd Street, 734-5984
www.motherhood.com
This is the place for excellent value in stylish maternity basics.

Museum of the City of New York Store
1220 Fifth Avenue at 103rd Street, 534-1672, www.mcny.org
This museum shop stocks a good selection of books and toys.

Museum of Modern Art Design Store
44 West 53rd Street between Fifth and Sixth Avenues, 767-1050 ext 72
81 Spring Street between Crosby and Broadway, 646 613-1367
www.momastore.org
The Design Store offers a treasure trove of modern design for the home, art books and a good selection of educational books and toys for kids. While the Museum (located at 11 West 53rd Street) undergoes a major renovation, visit MOMA QNS in Long Island City, Queens.

N.B.A. Store
666 Fifth Avenue at 52nd Street, 515-NBA1 (515-6221)
www.nba.com, www.wnba.com
If your kids love basketball, they will be in heaven in this megastore filled with NBA team paraphernalia and novelties. The store also hosts on-site special events.

NBC Experience Store
49th Street between Fifth and Sixth Avenues, in Rockefeller Plaza, 664-3700
www.nbcsuperstore.com
Visit this store for memorabilia, novelties, collectibles and T-shirts relating to your favorite NBC personalities and shows. Check the website for scheduled in-store celebrity events.

Neutral Ground
122 West 26th Street between Sixth and Seventh Avenues, 4th floor,
  633-1288, www.neutralground.com
Games enthusiasts will love this shop filled with trading cards, role-playing games, sci-fi books and magazines, miniatures (and painting supplies), computer games and some board games. There is even a play area where the shop holds daily tournaments.

New York City Kids $$
495 Seventh Avenue between 36th and 37th Streets, 868-6925, www.nyck.net
This fashion-district store is a great source of contemporary, popular-label clothing and shoes with brands such as Guess, Calvin Klein, Nicole Miller, Kenneth Cole, Candies and Timberland. Dresses are available up to size 18, and boys suits are stocked for sizes 4–20. The store also carries christening gowns, Communion dresses and tuxedos for boys.

New York Doll Hospital
787 Lexington Avenue between 61st and 62nd Streets, 2nd floor, 838-7527
This shop is your source for antique dolls, stuffed animals and related collectibles. Repair services are available.

New York Exchange for Woman's Work $ to $$$
149 East 60th Street between Lexington and Third Avenues, 753-2330
www.nywomans-exchange.com
This not-for-profit store sells wonderful handmade items, including children's clothing, toys, blankets, quilts and dolls.

New York Firefighter's Friend $$
263 Lafayette Street between Prince and Spring Streets, 226-3142
www.nyfirestore.com
Your little firefighter will love this store filled with firefighter-motif clothing, toys and official-looking boots. For children and adults.

New York Public Library Shop
455 Fifth Avenue at 40th Street, 340-0849
476 Fifth Avenue at 42nd Street, 930-0641
www.thelibraryshop.com
A visit to the main branch of the New York Public Library, and photo op with the lions, warrants a visit to this well-stocked shop. The children's section contains books as well as some toys, decorative accessories and novelties. The 40th Street shop has a larger selection of children's books.

New York Transit Museum Gift Shop
Boerum Place and Schermerhorn Street, Brooklyn, 718 243-3060 (closed
     while under renovation)
Grand Central Terminal, 42nd Street, Main Concourse, 878-0106
Times Square Visitors Center, Broadway between 46th and 47th Streets
www.mta.info

Remember your commuter experiences with a treasure trove of New York transit system souvenirs, toys, novelties and other goodies.

Niketown $$
6 East 57th Street between Fifth and Madison Avenues, 891-6453
www.nike.com
Shopping here is a real experience. Totally devoted to athletes and those who just want the look, this store sells all types of Nike activewear, accessories and athletic shoes for children and adults.

Nine West $$
577 Broadway between Houston and Prince Streets, 941-1597
115 Fifth Avenue at 19th Street, 777-1752
341 Madison Avenue at 44th Street, 370-9107
757 Third Avenue between 47th and 48th Streets, 371-4597
675 Fifth Avenue at 53rd Street, 319-6893
750 Lexington Avenue between 59th and 60th Streets, 486-8094
901 Sixth Avenue at 33rd Street, Manhattan Mall, 564-0063
1230 Sixth Avenue at Rockefeller Center, 397-0710
1195 Third Avenue between 69th and 70th Streets, 472-8750
184 East 86th Street between Lexington and Third Avenues, 987-9004

2305 Broadway between 83rd and 84th Streets, 799-7610
425 Lexington Avenue between 43rd and 44th Streets, 949-0037
179 Broadway between John Street and Maiden Lane, 346-0903
2 Broadway at Bowling Green, 968-1521
www.ninewest.com
Your teen (and your wallet) will love the well-priced trendy shoes and accessories inspired by designer looks from this chain.

Nursery Lines $$$
1034 Lexington Avenue at 74th Street, 396-4445
This exclusive boutique carries fine imported classic clothing (up to size 4), linens and unique handpainted furniture. Custom linens and design services available.

Oilily $$$
870 Madison Avenue between 70th and 71st Streets, 628-0100
www.oililyusa.com
This Dutch label is known for its whimsical collection of signature multi-color and multi-patterned clothing for children up to age 12 as well as distinctive accessories and crib bedding. Moms who like the look can visit the women's store on Madison Avenue between 68th and 69th Streets.

Old Navy Clothing $
610 Sixth Avenue at 18th Street, 645-0663
150 West 34th Street at Broadway, 594-0049
300 West 125th Street at Eighth Avenue, 531-1544
511 Broadway at Spring Street, 226-0865
www.oldnavy.com
This relative of the Gap offers the same casual look at meaningfully lower prices. At these prices, it is easy to indulge your child's fashion whims for cool, trendy clothes and accessories.

Olive & Bette's $$$
1070 Madison Avenue between 80th and 81st Streets, 717-9655
252 Columbus Avenue between 71st and 72nd Streets, 579-2178
www.oliveandbettes.com
Teens, and petite moms, frequent this shop for trendy casual clothes and great jeans from such labels as Michael Stars, Bulldog, Theory and Diesel.

Original Levi's Store $$
3 East 57th Street between Fifth and Madison Avenues, 838-2188
750 Lexington Avenue at 59th Street, 826-5957
www.levi.com
This is the spot for all types of Levis jeans and other clothing. The mezzanine floor of the flagship 57th Street store is devoted to kids up to size 16. The Lexington Avenue store does not stock kids' sizes, but has plenty for teens. Both stores feature "create your own" departments (custom-fit jeans) for adults.

Origins $$
402 West Broadway at Spring Street, 219-9764
175 Fifth Avenue at 22nd Street, 677-9100
75 Grand Central Terminal, Lexington Avenue, 808-4141
44 West 50th Street, Rockefeller Center, 698-2323
2327 Broadway between 84th and 85th Streets, 769-0970
www.origins.com
Origins features natural products for skin, hair and body as well as bath accessories. There is an entire line just for babies, and your teens and tweens will love the delicious-smelling bath products and aromatherapy gum balls.

OshKosh B'Gosh $$
586 Fifth Avenue between 47th and 48th Streets, 827-0098
www.oshkoshbgosh.com
Famous for its overalls, this label offers an entire line of children's basics and casual clothes (up to size 16) and several styles of shoes (up to age 5).

Paper House $
1020 Third Avenue between 60th and 61st Streets, 223-3774
180 East 86th Street between Lexington and Third Avenues, 410-7950
269 Amsterdam Avenue between 72nd and 73rd Streets, 724-8085
This shop is stocked with party supplies, seasonal decorations, wrapping papers and party paraphernalia.

Papoose $$$

311 East 81st Street between First and Second Avenues, 639-9577
This lovely shop carries fine European, classically-inspired-yet-modern clothing and accessories for children 0–8.

Paragon Athletic Goods $$
867 Broadway at 18th Street, 255-8036, www.paragonsports.com
Since 1908, this huge emporium has been selling sporting goods and out-door/camping supplies for all ages, including a large selection of sporting goods and activewear for children.

Party City $
38 West 14th Street between Fifth and Sixth Avenues, 271-7310
www.partycity.com
You can find everything you need for a great party at Party City, including paper goods featuring your child's favorite characters.

Patagonia $$ to $$$
101 Wooster Street between Prince and Spring Streets, 343-1776
426 Columbus Avenue between 80th and 81st Streets, 917 441-0011
www.patagonia.com
This high-end outdoor specialist for adults also carries a great line of high-performance and good-looking outerwear for children.

Paul and Shark $$$
772 Madison Avenue between 66th and 67th Streets, 452-9868
www.paulshark.it
This is Italian preppy at its most high tech. With a nautical spin (think yachting), this venerable Italian label offers high performance outerwear (in advanced high-tech fabrics) and very stylish casual clothing for men, women and boys (sizes 4–8).

Paul Mole
1031 Lexington Avenue at 74th Street, 2nd floor, 535-8461
For 80 years, barbers at this barbershop have cut and styled the hair of Upper East Side adults and children.

Payless Shoe Source $
34 East 14th Street at Union Square, 924-1492
1 Herald Square at 34th Street and Sixth Avenue, 947-0306
484 Eighth Avenue at 34th Street, 594-5715
590 Fifth Avenue between 47th and 48th Streets, 398-3823
250 West 57th Street at Broadway, 586-8625
www.paylessshoesource.com
As the name suggests, this is your source for very inexpensive contemporary shoes for the entire family.

A Pea in the Pod $$ to $$$
151 West 34th Street (in Macy's)
860 Madison Avenue at 70th Street, 988-8039
www.apeainthepod.com, www.maternitymall.com
This national chain carries a broad selection of well-priced, modern, chic maternity clothes and accessories.

Peanut Butter & Jane $$ to $$$
617 Hudson Street between Jane and West 12th Streets, 620-7952
This Village shop offers a terrific selection of mostly imported fun, upbeat and cool clothing (up to size 14/16 for girls and up to size 10 for boys), shoes and toys.

Pearl Paint $
308 Canal Street between Church Street and Broadway, 431-7932
www.pearlpaint.com
If you love arts and crafts, you will be in heaven in five floors of discounted art and craft supplies (for the serious artist as well as for the dabbler). Pearl also has a home-decorating center.

Pearl River Mart $
277 Canal Street at Broadway, 431-4770
200 Grand Street at Mulberry Street, 966-1010
www.pearlriver.com
Both Chinatown residents and fashionistas patronize this Chinese department store, which features a wonderful assortment of Chinese products, including silk pajamas, hats, purses, slippers, birdcages, novelties, housewares and games. The prices are great, too.

Peck & Goodie $$
917 Eighth Avenue between 54th and 55th Streets, 246-6123
In business for more than 50 years, this shop specializes in skates (roller, blades and ice), skateboards and accessories

Penny Whistle Toys
1283 Madison Avenue between 91st and 92nd Streets, 369-3868
448 Columbus Avenue between 81st and 82nd Streets, 873-9090
These cozy shops offer a selection of unique toys, art supplies and some books for younger children.

Peter Elliot $$$
1071 Madison Avenue at 81st Street, 570-1551
This women's boutique specializing in luxurious, casual clothing offers its signature cashmere sweaters and quilted and toggle jackets for children sizes 2 and up.

Peter Elliot, Jr. $$$
1067 Madison Avenue between 81st and 82nd Streets, 570-5747
This shop, complete with an on-site personal shopper and tailor and a play area for children, offers high-end (including special label cashmeres), mostly imported clothing and accessories for children sizes 2–12 as well as layette and infant clothing, gifts and novelties.

Petit Bateau $$ to $$$
1100 Madison Avenue at 82nd Street, 988-8884, www.petitbateau.com
This popular French brand has been making fine cotton garments since 1893 and now has a flagship store with a huge selection of adorable clothes for preemies and newborns and children up to size 18 (the larger sizes fit most moms). The T-shirts, which are available in a variety of styles and colors, are extremely popular with tweens, teens and adult women.

Pierre Deux $$$
625 Madison Avenue at 59th Street, 521-8012
www.pierredeux.com
You will feel transported to Provence in this home accessories and furniture shop featuring items made with traditional Provençal fabrics, pottery and pewter accessories and an especially popular quilted fabric diaper bag.

Plain Jane $$ to $$$
525 Amsterdam Avenue between 85th and 86th Streets, 595-6916
www.plainjanekids.com
This Upper West Side boutique offers unique vintage and retro-styled decorative accessories, furniture, bedding and layette for your child's room.

Planet Kids $$
247 East 86th Street between Second and Third Avenues, 426-2040
2688 Broadway between 102nd and 103rd Streets, 864-8705
www.planetkidsny.com
Planet Kids stocks everything you need for the new baby and young child, including equipment, furniture, layette, toys and books. The 86th Street store offers some clothing (up to size 4T); the Broadway store offers clothing up to teen sizes.

Pokemon Center
10 Rockefeller Plaza at 48th Street, 307-0900, www.pokemoncenter.com
Your Pokemon-loving child will adore this multimedia store dedicated to everything Pokemon, including the latest toys, cards and video games, with plenty of hands-on Pokemon.

Polo/Ralph Lauren $$$
867 Madison Avenue at 72nd Street, 606-2100
www.polo.com
Ralph Lauren creates his classically styled clothing for girls up to age 4, boys up to age 14, including cashmere sweaters, casual and dressy clothes and lots of logoed "polo" shirts. You will also find a good selection of suits and blazers for boys. Teens may want to shop in the adult department for expensive preppy looks or the Polo Sport store directly across the street for pricey activewear.

Pop Shop $$
292 Lafayette Street between Houston and Prince Streets, 219-2784
www.haring.com/popshop
This not-for-profit store for adults and children carries all things Keith Haring, including clothing and toys.

Porthault Linens $$$
18 East 69th Street between Fifth and Madison Avenues, 688-1660
www.dporthault.fr
Perhaps best known for its luxury floral-printed and scalloped-edged linens, Porthault also sells imported luxury children's linens, custom infant bedding, children's robes, hooded towels and pajamas for children ages 1 to 6.

Prada $$$
45 East 57th Street between Madison and Park Avenues, 308-2332
724 Fifth Avenue at 56th Street, 664-0010
841 Madison Avenue at 70th Street, 327-4200 (no kids' shoes)
www.prada.com
This high fashion and trendsetting Italian label (clothing, shoes and accessories for men and women) is known for its modern, distinctive sensibility and look. Your well-heeled children can stride in their own Prada shoes available in European sizes 23–33 (roughly equivalent to American children's sizes 6–13 and youth sizes 1–3). Chic moms love the logoed totes and backpacks for carting baby stuff. Moms, teens and tweens love the sport line of shoes.

Pratesi $$$
829 Madison Avenue between 69th and 70th Streets, 288-2315
www.pratesi.com
For a truly luxurious experience, you can wrap your baby or child in these sumptuous Italian linens. Pratesi offers crib and bassinet linens as well as robes for children ages 1 to 10.

Prince & Princess $$$
33 East 68th Street between Madison and Park Avenues, 879-8989
Your child will look and feel like royalty in the fine classic imported clothing and layette from this Upper East Side boutique. Come here for that special-occasion outfit.

Princeton Ski Shop $$
21 East 22nd Street between Broadway and Park Avenue, 228-4400
www.allskis.com
For over 80 years, Princeton Ski Shop has outfitted the family for winter adventures.

Promises Fulfilled $$ to $$$
1592 Second Avenue between 82nd and 83rd Streets, 472-1600
This children's gift shop specializes in a unique selection of personalized decorative accessories, furniture and toys. With artists on the premises, turnaround time is pretty quick. They do party favors, too.

P.S. I Love You $$
1242 Madison Avenue between 89th and 90th Streets, 722-6272
Tweens love this little shop packed with stickers, candles, trendy novelty items, "bunk junk" for camp and accessories.

Pumpkin Maternity $$ to $$$
407 Broome Street between Lafayette and Center Streets, 334-1809
www.pumpkinmaternity.com
Hip moms-to-be love the chic and trendy maternity clothes designed by the former leader of a rock band, Pumpkin Wentzel.

Radio Shack $$

114 Fulton Street, South Street Seaport, 732-1904
9 Broadway at Exchange Place, 482-8138
75 Maiden Lane between William and Gold Streets, 785-5893
626 Broadway at Houston and Bleecker Streets, 677-7069
360 Sixth Avenue at Washington Place, 473-2113
781 Broadway between 8th and 9th Streets, 228-6810
49 Seventh Avenue at 13th Street, 727-7641
7 East 14th Street between Fifth Avenue and University Place, 463-0143
866 Broadway at 17th Street, 982-9707
336 First Avenue between 19th and 20th Streets, 254-1558
641 Sixth Avenue at 20th Street, 604-0695
270 Park Avenue South at 21st Street, 533-1906
369 Third Avenue between 26th and 27th Streets, 685-8525
444 Park Avenue South between 30th and 31st Streets, 447-9819
534 Third Avenue between 35th and 36th Streets, 481-9139
205 West 23rd Street at Seventh Avenue, 924-3054
356 Seventh Avenue between 29th and 30th Streets, 244-0567
1359 Broadway between 36th and 37th Streets, 564-6139
Eighth Avenue and 41st Street, Port Authority Bus Terminal, 564-9427
1100 Sixth Avenue at 42nd Street, 944-2540
1134 Sixth Avenue at 44th Street, 575-2361
209 West 57th Street between Broadway and Seventh Avenue, 246-3940
333 West 57th Street between Eighth and Ninth Avenues, 586-1909
925 Lexington Avenue between 68th and 69th Streets, 249-3028
1477 Third Avenue between 83rd and 84th Streets, 327-0979
1267 Lexington Avenue between 85th and 86th Streets, 831-2765
240 West 72nd Street between Broadway and West End Avenue,
    787-1413
2372 Broadway between 86th and 87th Streets, 873-8919
36 East 23rd Street between Park and Madison Avenues, 673-3670
901 Sixth Avenue, Manhattan Mall, 279-1560
139 East 42nd Street at Lexington Avenue, 953-6050
1721 Broadway between 54th and 55th Streets, 307-9376
940 Third Avenue between 56th and 57th Streets, 750-8409
1668 First Avenue between 87th and 88th Streets, 426-2160
2505 Broadway between 93rd and 94th Streets, 665-8307
www.radioshack.com

This chain store offers its own brand of electronic gadgets, accessories and goodies. A good source for remote-controlled toys.

Rain or Shine General Store $$ to $$$

202 East 29th Street between Second and Third Avenues, 3rd floor,
    685-8556

Within the Rain or Shine play center, this charming shop offers colorful and unique items for children of all ages. In particular, they have cribs and furniture for older kids (and even adults) from such companies as Maine Cottage and Vermont Tubs, bedding and linens (including custom linens), decorative accessories, unique toys, select items of clothing (onesies, hand-knits, raincoats) and plenty of items for kids who like to play "dress up."

Rand-McNally Map Store
150 East 52nd Street between Lexington and Third Avenues, 758-7488
www.randmcnally.com
For the budding cartographer, here is the source for maps and travel books for all ages.

Red Caboose
23 West 45th Street between Fifth and Sixth Avenues, basement,
   575-0155
For the real train enthusiast, this store specializes in new electric train sets and accessories.

Reminiscence $
50 West 23rd Street between Fifth and Sixth Avenues, 243-2292
www.reminiscence.com
Formerly in the Village, Reminiscence has moved a bit further north but has not lost the downtown feel. This store, which features funky, basic and casual clothes (much with a retro feel), accessories, retro toys (such as inexpensive wind-ups), some vintage clothing and some housewares, has major appeal to teens looking for well-priced cool stuff.

Replay $$$
109 Prince Street at Greene Street, 800 250-6972, 673-6300
www.replay.it

This Italian label does an impressive job of creating a casual western-style look for adults and kids. The imported basic clothing (including great jeans) and shoes are available for kids from 6 months to 10 years.

Ricky's $ to $$
590 Broadway between Houston and Prince Streets, 226-5552
718 Broadway at Astor Place, 979-5232
44 East 8th Street between Mercer and Greene Streets, 254-5247
509 Fifth Avenue between 42nd and 43rd Streets, 352-8545
466 Sixth Avenue between 11th and 12th Streets, 924-3401
988 Eighth Avenue at 58th Street, 957-8343
1189 First Avenue at 64th Street, 879-8361
112 West 72nd Street between Broadway and Columbus Avenue, 769-3678
www.rickys-nyc.com
Ricky's is a hot spot, perhaps too hot for young wannabe tweens, but the store is loaded with makeup, jewelry, hair accessories and bags that true teens love.

Rizzoli Bookstores
31 West 57th Street between Fifth and Sixth Avenues, 759-2424
Best known for "coffee-table books" Rizzoli also offers books for all ages.

Robin's Nest $$ to $$$
1168 Lexington Avenue between 80th and 81st Streets, 737-2004
This tiny shop has a surprisingly large selection of unique, contemporary, casual clothing and accessories and layette featuring a number of chic European labels.

Ruby's Book Sale
119 Chambers Street at West Broadway, 732-8676
A neighborhood bookstore offering discounted books for all ages.

St. Mark's Bookshop
31 Third Avenue at 9th Street, 260-7853
www.stmarksbookshop.com
This East Village bookstore has a respectable selection of children's books and a knowledgeable staff.

St. Mark's Comics
11 St. Mark's Place between Second and Third Avenues, 598-9439
Your kids can spend hours choosing from a large selection of comics (new and vintage), action figures and related toys and trading cards

Saks Fifth Avenue $$ to $$$
611 Fifth Avenue at 49th Street, 753-4000
www.saksfifthavenue.com
The extensive children's department in this up-scale, full-service department store has a large selection of clothing (from classic to cool), layette and stuffed animals from a variety of top labels and a meaningful selection of special-occasion clothing for boys and girls. Teens can also do very well on the fifth floor for trendy clothes.

Sam Flax $$$
12 West 20th Street between Fifth and Sixth Avenues, 620-3038
425 Park Avenue at 55th Street, 935-5353
www.samflax.com
This very upscale and serious stationery and office and art-supply store offers a number of items for your budding artist as well as lots of great notebooks, presentation books, folders and photo albums. Some of the more avant-garde office furniture and furnishings would work well in an older child's room.

San Francisco $$
975 Lexington Avenue between 70th and 71st Streets, 472-8740
This shop, which sells adult clothing, also offers nostalgic classic clothing and some toys for girls and boys to size 6x.

Sanrio

233 West 42nd Street between Seventh and Eighth Avenues, 840-6011
www.sanrio.com

This store is dedicated entirely to Hello Kitty and all her friends—Chococat, Pocchaco, Badtz-Maru and others. You can get everything from school supplies to room accessories to hats, bags and T-shirts. Fun for the boys, too.

Schneider's Juvenile Furniture $$

20 Avenue A at East 2nd Street, 228-3540

This is your source for everything for the new baby and young child, including equipment, layette, furniture and toys as well as furniture for your older child's room.

The Scholastic Store

557 Broadway between Prince and Spring Streets, 343-6166
www.scholastic.com/sohostore

Your family can spend hours exploring 5,500 square feet of Scholastic products with displays featuring characters (Clifford, Harry Potter, Magic School Bus and others) and hands-on activities.

Schweitzer Linen $$$

1053 Lexington Avenue between 74th and 75th Streets, 570-0236
1132 Madison Avenue at 84th Street, 249-8361
457 Columbus Avenue between 80th and 81st Streets, 799-9629
www.schweitzer-linen.com

For more than 35 years, this family-owned and -run company has provided New Yorkers with high quality, luxury linens, including classic items for the nursery and children's rooms.

Scoop $$$

532 Broadway between Prince and Spring Streets, 925-2886
1273-1277 Third Avenue between 73rd and 74th Streets, 535-5577
873 Washington Street at 14th Street, 929-1244
www.scoopnyc.com

This hip women's store features very expensive high-fashion clothing and accessories. Because the shop carries a lot of very tiny sizes, it is very popular among older teen girls. In addition to items by cutting-edge designers, the shop features T-shirts from popular labels such as Juicy. Scoop also carries a line of Petit Bateau items for infants.

Screaming Mimi's $$

382 Lafayette Street between Great Jones and 4th Streets, 677-6464

Teens adore the huge selection of vintage clothing, shoes (vintage, but never worn) and accessories (some vintage, some new) at this popular downtown boutique.

Sephora $$

555 Broadway between Prince and Spring Streets, 625-1309

119 Fifth Avenue at 19th Street, 674-3570
130 West 34th Street between Broadway and Seventh Avenue, 629-9135
1500 Broadway between 43rd and 44th Streets, 944-6789
Columbus Circle location opening in 2003
1129 Third Avenue at 67th Street, 452-3336
2103 Broadway at 73rd Street, 362-1500
www.sephora.com

This high concept cosmetics emporium, stocked with top brands of makeup, fragrances and bath products as well as an extensive collection of excellent private-label products, is the perfect destination for teenage girls (and their moms) who love to play with makeup. Preteens can have fun searching for the perfect lip gloss.

Shakespeare & Co. Booksellers
1 Whitehall Street between Bridge and Stone Streets, 742-7025
716 Broadway between Astor Place and 4th Street, 529-1330
939 Lexington Avenue between 68th and 69th Streets, 570-0201
137 East 23rd Street at Lexington Avenue, 505-2021
www.shakeandco.com

This New York institution, known for its knowledgeable staff, stocks a comprehensive selection of books for all ages.

Shanghai Tang $$$
714 Madison Avenue between 63rd and 64th Streets, 888-0111
www.shanghaitang.com

This department store imported from Hong Kong carries a unique selection of upscale clothing, accessories and housewares, as well as lovely and original children's clothing for boys and girls in sizes 2–12. The sweaters and Chinese jackets and pajamas are especially cool.

The Sharper Image $$ to $$$
89 South Street Seaport, Pier 17, 693-0477
4 West 57th Street between Fifth and Sixth Avenues, 265-2550
900 Madison Avenue between 72nd and 73rd Streets, 794-4974
50 Rockefeller Plaza, 51st Street between Fifth and Sixth Avenues,
    646 557-0861
98 Greene Street between Prince and Spring Streets, 917 237-0221
www.sharperimage.com

If your family loves gadgets and electronics, then you will have fun visiting the NYC outposts of this national chain. Weary adults can rest on the massage chairs while the children shop.

Shoofly $$
42 Hudson Street between Duane and Thomas Streets, 406-3270
465 Amsterdam Avenue between 82nd and 83rd Streets, 580-4390
www.shooflynyc.com

This shop is filled with a unique selection of irresistible and fashionable shoes, hats and accessories.

Shu Uemura $$

121 Greene Street between Houston and Prince Streets, 979-5500

This Japanese cosmetics company, which offers an extensive line of products displayed and packaged in a particularly user-friendly way, is extremely popular among teen girls.

Sisley $$

469 West Broadway between Houston and Prince Streets, 375-0538
2308 Broadway between 83rd and 84th Streets, 769-0121
www.sisley.com

This brand, a part of the well-known Benetton company, offers a terrific adult-sized selection of reasonably priced, sophisticated and stylish basics and casual clothing for women and men, which is appropriate for teens as well.

Skechers $$

530 Broadway between Prince and Spring Streets, 431-8803
55 West 8th Street at Sixth Avenue, 253-5810
150 Fifth Avenue between 19th and 20th Streets, 627-9420
140 West 34th Street between Sixth and Seventh Avenues, 646 473-0490
2169 Broadway at 76th Street, 712-0539
www.skechers.com

This popular line of well-priced footwear with an athletic look is a favorite of kids, preteens and teens.

Small Change $$$

964 Lexington Avenue between 70th and 71st Streets, 772-6455

This charming shop features fine clothing, much of it imported, from contemporary to classic.

SoHo Baby

247 Elizabeth Street between Prince and Houston Streets, 625-8538

This shop offers a unique selection of (mostly) imported clothing and accessories for children up to size 8 as well as toys for younger children.

Space Kiddets $$

46 East 21st Street between Broadway and Park Avenue South, 420-9878

This hip shop is packed with funky, stylish clothing and accessories for girls up to size 6x and boys up to size 8–10, shoes for all ages, layette and some toys and vintage furniture. Upstairs, you will find fun, trendy and teen chic clothes and accessories for girls sizes 7–16, featuring such brands as Juicy, Paul Frank, and Tiki.

Speedo Authentic Fitness $$

90 Park Avenue at 39th Street, 682-3830
150 Columbus Avenue between 66th and 67th Streets, 501-8140
500 Fifth Avenue at 42nd Street, 768-7737
www.speedo.com

For the swimmers in your family, this is the place for a large selection of swimwear, swimming gear and activewear for adults and children ages 4+.

Sports Authority $$
636 Sixth Avenue at 19th Street, 929-8971
845 Third Avenue at 51st Street, 355-9725
57 West 57th Street at Sixth Avenue, 355-6430
www.sportsauthority.com
These all-purpose sporting-goods stores carry a wide selection of merchandise and gear for all sports. The stores do not carry clothing in children's sizes.

Spring Flowers $$$
1050 Third Avenue at 62nd Street, 758-2669
905 Madison Avenue between 72nd and 73rd Streets, 717-8182
This is the place for classic European clothing, layette and shoes for girls up to size 10 and boys up to size 8. The special-occasion and party clothes are particularly nice.

Staples $ to $$
200 Water Street at Fulton Street, 785-9521
488-492 Broadway between Spring and Broome Streets, 219-1299
769 Broadway between 8th and 9th Streets, 646 654-6660
5-9 Union Square at 14th Street, 929-6323
16 East 34th Street between Fifth and Madison Avenues, 683-8009
205 East 42nd Street between Second and Third Avenues, 697-1591
535 Fifth Avenue at 44th Street, 646 227-0585
730 Third Avenue at 45th Street, 867-9486
609 Fifth Avenue at 49th Street, 593-0623
575 Lexington Avenue at 51st Street, 644-2118
425 Park Avenue at 56th Street, 753-9640
250 West 34th Street between Seventh and Eighth Avenues, 629-3713
1065 Sixth Avenue at 40th Street, 997-4446
57 West 57th Street at Sixth Avenue, 308-0335
1280 Lexington Avenue between 86th and 87th Streets, 426-6190
2248 Broadway at West 81st Street, 712-9617
217 Broadway at Vesey Street, 346-9624
699 Sixth Avenue at 23rd Street, 675-5698
345 Park Avenue South at 26th Street, 683-3267
Penn Station, Amtrak Main Concourse, 646-674-1652
www.staples.com
Kids can literally spend hours in this discounted office- and school-supplies super store, which also stocks some children's art supplies, electronics and software.

Star Magic
745 Broadway between Astor Place and 8th Street, 228-7770
1256 Lexington Avenue between 84th and 85th Streets, 988-0300
www.starmagic.com
This unique store dedicated to science and stars, selling toys, books, and other unique objects, is a must for young astronomers or those interested in New Age pursuits.

Stationery & Toy World
125 West 72nd Street between Columbus and Amsterdam Avenues,
    580-3922
This tiny neighborhood store, a block from Central Park, is packed to the rafters with school supplies, toys, party goods and art supplies.

Steve Madden $$
540 Broadway between Prince and Spring Streets, 343-1800
41 West 34th Street between Fifth and Sixth Avenues, 736-3283
150 East 86th Street between Lexington and Third Avenues, 426-0538
    (women only)
2315 Broadway between 83rd and 84th Streets, 799-4221
www.stevemadden.com
Preteens, teens and even adults cannot get enough of this stylish, trendy and well-priced footwear for women and men.

The Stork Club $$$
142 Sullivan Street between Houston and Prince Streets, 505-1927
Do not miss this charming downtown shop stocked with unique, original and stylish, mostly imported clothes and accessories, including a large selection of hand-knit sweaters and some layette, for boys and girls from size 0 to 8/10. In the spring, look for a selection of imported shoes here, too.

Strand Book Store
95 Fulton Street between Gold and William Streets, 732-6070
828 Broadway at 12th Street, 473-1452
www.strandbooks.com
Since 1927, this family-owned, independent book store has supplied books to readers of all ages. Featuring "eight miles of books," this is also the place to find rare books, previously owned books and hard-to-find art and photography books.

Strawberry $
901 Sixth Avenue at 33rd Street, Manhattan Mall, 268-7855
14 West 34th Street between Fifth and Sixth Avenues, 279-8696
129 East 42nd Street at Lexington Avenue, 986-7030
120 West 49th Street between Sixth and Seventh Avenues, 391-8718
49 West 49th Street between Fifth and Sixth Avenues, 688-0348
501 Madison Avenue at 52nd Street, 753-5008
80 Broad Street at Beaver Street, 425-6627

258 Broadway between Murray and Warren Streets, 406-2330
111 John Street between Cliff and Pearl Streets, 964-8683
900 Third Avenue between 54th and 55th Streets, 223-2333
711 Lexington Avenue between 57th and 58th Streets, 355-9414
38 East 14th Street between Broadway and University Place, 353-2700
345 Park Avenue South at 25th Street, 725-5970
320 First Avenue between 19th and 20th Streets, 505-1291
www.strawberrystores.com
These stores are a good source of trendy, value-priced clothing for teen girls and women.

Stussy $$
140 Wooster Street between Houston and Prince Streets, 274-8855
Teen boys love the West Coast, California-surf–styled, relaxed streetwear and accessories.

Stuyvesant Trains & Hobbies
345 West 14th Street between Eighth and Ninth Avenues, 2nd floor, 675-2160, www.dept-56.com
This store carries train sets, accessories and specialty models.

SuperCuts
Call 800 SUPERCUT (787-3728) to locate the nearest salon.
Well-priced haircuts for all ages.

Swatch $$
640 Broadway at Bleecker Street, 777-1002
438 West Broadway at Prince Street, 646 613-0160
100 West 72nd Street at Columbus Avenue, 595-9640
Swatch Timeship, 5 East 57th Street between Fifth and Madison Avenues, 317-1100
www.swatch.com
Swatch was the original innovator for inexpensive fashion watches. These stylish timepieces are just the right price for kids. The flagship store at 57th Street provides a unique high-concept shopping environment with hands-on displays.

Syms $
42 Trinity Place at Rector Street, 797-1199
400 Park Avenue at 54th Street, 317-8200
www.syms.com
The children's department of this discount department store stocks discounted major brand and designer-label clothing, shoes, layette and some toys and books.

Tah Poozie $ to $$
50 Greenwich Avenue between West 6th and West 7th Streets,
   646 638-0750
78A Seventh Avenue at 15th Street, 647-0668
This self-styled "silly trinket shop" is packed with all kinds of little toys such as mini-slinkies, key chains and cards. A great source for party favors.

Takashimaya $$$
693 Fifth Avenue between 54th and 55th Streets, 350-0100
This high-end department store carries luxury layettes, clothing (0–24 months, pajamas to size 4), unique toys, silver gift items and vintage items such as silver cups and infant jewelry.

Talbots Kids & Babies $$
1523 Second Avenue at 79th Street, 570-1630, www.talbots.com
This is a great place to load up on well-made, well-priced contemporary basic clothing and accessories for boys and girls.

Tannen's Magic Company
24 West 25th Street between Broadway and Sixth Avenue, 2nd floor,
   929-4500, www.tannenmagic.com
Since 1933, this renowned magic shop has provided quality magic tricks, books, videos, accessories, props and paraphernalia to professional and amateur magicians. On site magicians are there to assist, advise and demonstrate. Tannen's runs a magic camp for children ages 12 to 18 and has its own woodworking and machine shop.

Tartine et Chocolat $$$
475 Park Avenue between 57th and 58th Streets, 508-0090
1047 Madison Avenue between 79th and 80th Streets, 717-2112
www.tartine-et-chocolat.com
Step into Paris at this charming boutique featuring elegant, beautiful Tartine et Chocolat clothing for boys and girls as well as lovely children's furniture and strollers. This is just the place for that perfect party dress.

Teacher's College Bookstore
1224 Amsterdam Avenue at 120th Street, 678-3920, www.BKSTORE.com
Serving Columbia University, this bookstore offers a good selection of children's books as well as many books on education and learning.

Tender Buttons
143 East 62nd Street between Lexington and Third Avenues, 758-7004
If you love to sew, decorate or just to create, you will love this store filled with buttons of every type, including some vintage buttons.

Terra Verde $$$
120 Wooster Street between Prince and Spring Streets, 925-4533
This environmentally sensitive shop offers all-natural clothing (0–24 months), layette and furniture, as well as other products for adults and the home. Some custom furniture available.

The Terrence Conran Shop $$ to $$$
407 East 59th Street at First Avenue/59th Street Bridge, 755-9079
This British import, best known for its clean, modern, very stylish furniture and housewares, also has a great selection of furnishings and other cool stuff (toys, decorative accessories) for kids.

Tiffany & Co. $$$
727 Fifth Avenue at 57th Street, 755-8000, www.tiffany.com
Renowned for jewelry, china, crystal, desk accessories and gifts, Tiffany's is a wonderful source for traditional silver baby gifts, children's dishes and picture frames. There is also a good selection of silver and gold jewelry appropriate for children and teens.

Tigers, Tutu's & Toes $$ to $$$
128 Second Avenue at St. Mark's Place, 228-7990
This East Village shop is related to the Ibiza shop on University Place and carries a less extensive, but similarly stylish, fun and funky collection of mostly European clothing, accessories and very adorable shoes for kids up to age 6 or 7.

Timberland $$ to $$$
709 Madison Avenue at 63rd Street, 754-0436, www.timberland.com
This outdoor specialist for adults also carries shoes for children.

Tiny Doll House
1179 Lexington Avenue between 80th and 81st Streets, 744-3719
This shop is a great source for dollhouses and dollhouse accessories and supplies.

Tip Top Kids Shoes $$
149 West 72nd Street between Columbus Avenue and Broadway, 874-1004
www.tiptopshoes.com
This Upper West Side source for comfort shoes (such as Birkenstock, Mephisto, Ecco) has finally opened an outpost for kids. The store features Stride Rite, New Balance, Keds, Timberland and more.

T. J. Maxx $
620 Sixth Avenue between 18th and 19th Streets, 229-0875
www.tjmaxx.com

As one of the largest off-price retailers in the country, T. J. Maxx is a great place to shop for brand-name and designer fashions for the entire family (from newborns through adults) and home accessories, as well as some toys and books.

Tod's $$$
650 Madison Avenue between 59th and 60th Streets, 644-5945
www.tods.com

Adults have become addicted to these high-quality, high-style casual driving moccasins, loafers and other shoes. Your well-heeled child can be shod just like mom and dad. The children's line is available in European sizes 23–35.

Tower Records
692 Broadway at 4th Street, 505-1500
383 Lafayette Street at 4th Street, 505-1166
721-725 Fifth Avenue at 56th Street (Trump Tower lower level), 838-8110
1961 Broadway at 66th Street, 799-2500
www.towerrecords.com

This chain, which pioneered the music superstore, offers up a terrific selection of music and other entertainment media for all ages and tastes.

Toys R Us $$
24-32 Union Square East at 15th Street, 674-8697
44th Street at Times Square, 800-869-7787
www.toysrus.com

It is hard to drag your children out of this store, which stocks an enormous selection of name-brand toys in every category you can imagine as well as strollers, car seats, bicycles and equipment of every type. The flagship store in Times Square, complete with Ferris wheel, is a total shopping experience.

Toys Tokyo
121 Second Avenue between Second Avenue and St. Mark's Place,
    2nd floor, 673-5424

This East Village shop specializes in vintage and collectible Japanese toys from the 1940s through the 1990s but also stocks Star Wars stuff, wind-ups and current favorites.

Train World
751 McDonald Avenue between Cortelyou Road and Ditmus, Brooklyn,
    718 436-7072, www.trainworld.com

Your little engineer will have a field day in this large store full of electric trains and train stuff.

Trash and Vaudeville
4 St. Marks Place between Second and Third Avenues, 982-3590
Strictly for teens, this store has a treasure trove of funky, trendy clothing, shoes and accessories that live up to the promise of the shop's name.

Triple Five Soul
290 Lafayette Street between Houston and Prince Streets, 431-2404
www.triplefivesoul.com
Teen boys (but not necessarily their parents) love the hip hop streetwear and accessories from this SoHo shop.

Trouvaille Française
By appointment only, 737-6015
If you are looking for that special christening gown, visit Muriel Clark for a unique, finely preserved, mostly English vintage Victorian-style selection, ranging in price from $125 to $500. You can also find antique table and bed linens here.

Tutti Bambini
1490 First Avenue between 77th and 78th Streets, 472-4238
This boutique is stocked with a great selection of contemporary and stylish clothing (a mix of European and American labels) and accessories for girls up to size 12, boys up to size 8/10.

United Colors of Benetton, see Benetton

United Nations Gift Center
United Nations, 46th Street at First Avenue, 963-7700
Complete a visit to the U.N. with a stop at the gift shop for such souvenirs as international dolls and flags and books.

Urban Outfitters
374 Sixth Avenue between Waverly and Washington Places, 677-9350
628 Broadway between Bleecker and Houston Streets, 475-0009
162 Second Avenue at 11th Street, 375-1277
2081 Broadway at 72nd Street, 579-3912
526 Sixth Avenue at 14th Street, 646 638-1646
www.urbanoutfitters.com
Teens love the hip, trendy, casual clothes for men and women and decorative accessories for their rooms.

Utrecht
111 Fourth Avenue between 11th and 12th Streets, 777-5353
www.utrechtart.com
Since 1966, Utrecht has been supplying quality, well-priced canvas, paints, papers, graphic arts and framing materials and other art supplies to New Yorkers. It's the perfect place to stock up for art-and-crafts projects.

Veronique
1321 Madison Avenue at 93rd Street, 831-7800
www.veroniquematernity.com
This Carnegie Hill boutique offers an exclusive line of chic maternity clothing and accessories imported from Paris and Milan.

Versace
647 Fifth Avenue between 51st and 52nd Streets, 317-0224, www.versace.com
The fourth floor of the Versace store is home to the Italian label's stylish collection for children ages 2 to 12. The kids' clothes are mostly casual, and there are usually some shoes as well.

Vilebrequin
436 West Broadway at Prince Street, 431-0673
1070 Madison Avenue at 81st Street, 650-0353
www.vilebrequin.com
Men and boys (sizes 2–12) hit the beach via San Tropez with these festive, bright-colored and printed bathing suits from France.

Village Chess Shop
230 Thompson Street at West 3rd Street, 475-9580, www.chess-shop.com
Since 1972, this shop, located in the heart of Greenwich Village, not only specializes in chess sets from around the world, but also offers a friendly environment in which to play chess. Chess instruction is available by appointment.

Village Comics
214 Sullivan Street between Bleecker and West 3rd Streets, 777-2770
www.villagecomics.com
This large store has a huge selection of comics (new and vintage), collectibles, model kits, figures and trading cards for kids of all ages.

Village Kidz
3 Charles Street between Seventh and Greenwich Avenues, 807-8542
This Greenwich Village boutique offers a great selection of contemporary, casual and stylish clothing, shoes, layette and specialty toys.

Violet
203 East 75th Street between Second and Third Avenues, 879-3605
Violets are "Blue" at this uptown outpost of the East Village's custom-designed Blue label party dresses. This location offers chic, stylish ready-to-wear party dresses for pre-teens, teens and women.

Virgin Megastore
52 East 14th Street at Union Square, 598-4666
1540 Broadway between 45th and 46th Streets, 921-1020
www.virginmega.com
This British import offers a huge selection of music, DVD, videos and other entertainment media for all ages and all tastes.

Warehouse of London
581 Broadway between Prince and Houston Streets, 941-0910
150 Fifth Avenue between 19th and 20th Streets, 243-7333
Teens will love the stylish, trendy, well-priced clothing from these downtown stores.

Wee Bee Kids
285 Broadway at Chambers Streets, 766-2147
93 Nassau Street at Fulton Street, 766-1494
A downtown source for everything for the new baby and young child, including equipment, layette, furniture and clothing for girls up to size 16 and boys up to size 20.

West Side Kids
498 Amsterdam Avenue at 84th Street, 496-7282
Not just a neighborhood toy store, this shop carries an excellent selection of unique and educational toys and books.

Wet Seal
670 Broadway at Bond Street, 253-2470
65 East 8th Street at Broadway, 228-6188
901 Sixth Avenue at 33rd Street, Manhattan Mall, 216-0622
www.wetseal.com
This national chain offers fashionable, trendy and hip brand-name and private-label well-priced clothes and accessories for fashion-conscious teen girls.

Whitney Museum of American Art Store
Madison Avenue at 75th Street, 570-3614, www.whitney.org
This museum shop has a children's section with a good selection of unique toy and books and some decorative accessories.

The Wicker Garden $$$
1327 Madison Avenue between 93rd and 94th Streets, 410-7001
This Upper East Side institution is the place to go for classic nursery furniture, decorative accessories and fine, imported, lovely layette and infant clothing up to size 18 months. You can also choose from a selection of beautiful party dresses for girls up to size 2.

The Wiz
726 Broadway between Astor and Waverly Places, 677-4111
17 Union Square West at 15th Street, 741-9500

555 Fifth Avenue at 46th Street, 557-7770
212 East 57th Street between Second and Third Avenues, 754-1600
871-873 Sixth Avenue at 31st Street, 594-2300
1534-1536 Third Avenue between 86th and 87th Streets, 876-4400
2577 Broadway at 97th Street, 663-8000
www.thewiz.com
New Yorkers know that "nobody beats the Wiz." The sales staff can be
somewhat aggressive, but The Wiz is still a good source for electronics for
the family.

Yankees Clubhouse
393 Fifth Avenue between 36th and 37th Streets, 685-4693
110 East 59th Street between Park and Lexington Avenues, 758-7844
245 West 42nd Street between Seventh and Eighth Avenues, 768-9555
8 Fulton Street, South Street Seaport, 514-7182
www.sportsavenue.com
Do not worry if you cannot get to a game, because you can get team paraphernalia, souvenirs and novelties at the official Yankees store.

York Barber Shop
981 Lexington Avenue between 70th and 71st Streets, 988-6136
This local barbershop, in business for over 75 years, is a great place to take
your child for a haircut.

Zany Brainy
112 East 86th Street between Park and Lexington Avenues, 427-6611
2407 Broadway between 88th and 89th Streets, 917 441-2066
www.zanybrainy.com
Offering "extraordinary toys for extraordinary kids," this chain stocks an
extensive selection of high-quality, safe, non-violent, gender-neutral educational toys, craft kits and art supplies at value pricing.

Z'Baby Company $$ to $$$
996 Lexington Avenue at 72nd Street, 472-2229
100 West 72nd Street between Columbus Avenue and Broadway, 579-2229
www.zbabycompany.com
This lovely boutique carries a fantastic selection of charming, chic, mostly
European clothing (including labels such as Sonia Rykiel and Kenzo), accessories and some shoes for boys and girls up to age 10.

Z Girl $$$
976 Lexington Avenue between 71st and 72nd Streets, 879-4990
This cool boutique carries hip, trendy clothes and some accessories for preteens and teens (cool moms can shop here too) in sizes 10 (girls) through
adult sizes.

Zitomer and Zittles $$ to $$$
969 Madison Avenue between 75th and 76th Streets, 737-4480
www.zitomer.com

The emphasis is on service at this unique pharmacy and department store. The first floor has a large selection of high-end (including Kiehl's) skincare, bath products (including products especially for children and babies) and cosmetics. The second floor has a large selection of layette and fabulous children's and pre-teen clothing, from basics to imported to designer and from classic to trendy as well as some decorative accessories. The Zittles toy store on the third floor is an Upper East Side favorite and carries both commercial and unique and educational toys and books.

GENERAL RESOURCES

www.allny.com
www.citidex.com
www.cityguideny.com
www.citysearch.com
www.digitalcity.com
www.go-newyorkcity.com
www.lasvegasroomfinders.com/
newyork/kids.htm

www.metronewyork.com
www.nyc.com
www.nyctourism.com
www.nycvisit.com
www.nytoday.com
www.urbanbaby.com

SHOPPING INDEX

Neighborhood Locator

bkln	Brooklyn
es	East Side, East 23rd Street through and including East 60th Street
jfk	John F. Kennedy Airport
lga	LaGuardia Airport
lm	Lower Manhattan, below 23rd Street
qns	Queens
ues	Upper East Side, East 61st Street up to 110th Street
um	Upper Manhattan, 110th Street and above
uws	Upper West Side, West 61st Street up to 110th Street
ws	West Side, West 23rd Street through and including West 60th Street

Accessories and Novelties
Alphabets **lm, uws**
Alphaville **lm**
Chimera **lm**
Claire's Accessories **es, lm, ws**
Details **lm, uws**

Dylan's Candy Bar **es**
E.A.T. Gifts **ues**
Fossil lm, **ws**
G.C. William **ues**
Girlprops.com **lm**
Halloween Adventure **lm**

Ibiza Boutique **lm**
Infinity **ues**
It's a Mod, Mod World **lm**
Kar'ikter **lm**
Kate Spade Store **lm**
Kids Cuts **es**
Le Sportsac **lm, ues**
Lester's **ues**
Little Extras **uws**
Marsha D.D. **ues**
Pearl River Mart **lm**
Peter Elliot, Jr. **ues**
Pop Shop **lm**
P.S. I Love You **ues**
Reminiscence **ws**
Sanrio **ws**
Screaming Mimi's **lm**
Shoofly **lm, uws**
Tah Poozie **lm**
Tender Buttons **ues**

Activewear, Dancewear, Outerwear,
  Sporting Goods and Swimwear
Blades Board & Skate **lm, ues, uws, ws**
Capezio **es, ues, ws**
Danskin **uws**
Diesel **lm**
Eastern Mountain Sports **lm, uws**
Freed of London **qns**
Jodi's Gymwear **ues**
Kids Foot Locker **ues, ws**
Mason's Tennis Mart **es**
Modell's **lm, es, ues, um, ws**
Niketown **es**
Paragon Athletic Goods **lm**
Patagonia **lm, uws**
Peck & Goodie **ws**
Princeton Ski Shop **lm**
Speedo Authentic Fitness **es, uws, ws**
Sports Authority **es, lm, ws**
Vilebrequin **lm, ues**

Art Supplies and Crafts
American Craft Museum Shop **ws**
Ben's For Kids **ues**
Brooklyn Museum of Art Shop **bkln**
Economy Handicrafts **qns**
Exploration Station **ues**
F.A.O. Schwarz **es**
Homboms **ues**
Kate's Paperie **lm, ues**
KB Toys **ws, uws, um**

Lee's Art Shop **ws**
Little Extras **uws**
M & J Trimmings **ws**
Pearl Paint **lm**
Penny Whistle Toys **ues, uws**
Sam Flax **es, lm**
Staples **es, lm, ues, uws, ws**
Stationery & Toy World **uws**
Tender Buttons **ues**
Utrecht **lm**
Zany Brainy **ues, uws**

Baby Gifts
ABC Carpet and Home **lm**
Cartier **es**
Christofle Pavillion **ues**
Gucci **es**
Henri Bendel **ws**
Hermes **ues**
Hoofbeats **ues**
Kirna Zabete **lm**
La Layette et Plus **ues**
MacKenzie-Childs, Ltd. **ues**
Peter Elliot, Jr. **ues**
Takashimaya **es**
Tiffany & Co. **es**
Trouvaille Française

Bookstores
Bank Street Bookstore **um**
Barnes & Noble Superstores **es, lm, ues,**
  uws, ws
Bookberries **ues**
Books of Wonder **lm**
Borders Books and Music **es**
City Store **lm, ws**
Corner Bookstore **ues**
Crawford Doyle Booksellers **ues**
Gryphon Bookshop **uws**
Integral Yoga Bookstore **lm**
Lenox Hill Bookstore **ues**
Logos **ues**
New York Public Library Shop **es, ws**
Rand-McNally Map Store **es**
Rizzoli Bookstores **ws**
Ruby's Book Sale **lm**
St. Marks Bookshop **lm**
Shakespeare & Co. Booksellers **lm, ues**
Strand Book Store **lm**
Teacher's College Bookstore **um**
The Scholastic Store **lm**

Clothing and Accessories

Abercrombie & Fitch **lm**
Albee's **uws**
Alskling **uws**
April Cornell **uws**
Au Chat Botte **ues**
Baby Depot at Burlington Coat
    Factory **ws**
Bambi's Baby Center **um**
Bambini **ues**
Barney's New York **lm, ues**
Bebe Thompson **ues**
Ben's For Kids **ues**
Bergdorf Goodman **was**
Berkley Girl **uws**
Betwixt **lm**
Bloomers **ues**
Bloomingdales **es**
Bombalulu's **lm, uws**
Bonne Nuit **uws**
Bonpoint **ues**
Brooks Brothers **es, lga, ws**
Bu and the Duck **lm**
Bunnies Children's Department
    Store **lm**
Burberry **es, lm**
C.J. Laing **ues**
Calypso Enfants & Bébé **lm**
Calypso **lm, ues**
Canal Jean Co. **lm**
Cashmere Cashmere **ues**
Catimini **ues**
Century 21 **bkln, lm**
Children's Place **lm, ues, um, uws, ws**
Chimera **lm**
Chocks **lm**
Conway Stores **es, lm, ws**
Cradle & All **ues**
Crembebe **lm**
Daffy's **es, lm, ws**
Dave's Army & Navy Store **lm**
Diesel **es**
Dinosaur Hill **lm**
Farmers Daughter and Son **es**
First & Second Cousin **lm**
G.C. William **ues**
Gap **es, lm, ues, uws, ws**
Geiger **es**
Granny Made **uws**
The Green Onion **bkln**
Greenstone's **uws**
Greenstone's, too **ues**

Gymboree Store **ues, uws**
H & M **lm ws**
Henri Bendel **ws**
Hermes **ues**
Hoyt & Bond **bkln**
Ibiza Boutique **lm**
Infinity **ues**
Jacadi **ues**
Jay Kos **ues**
Judy's Fancies
Julian & Sara **lm**
Jumpin' Julias **bkln**
Just for Tykes **lm**
Kidding Around **lm**
Kidstown **lm**
Kirna Zabete **lm**
Kmart Stores **lm, ws**
La Layette et Plus **ues**
La Petite Etoile **ues**
Lacoste **es**
Laura Ashley **uws**
Leeper Kids **es**
Lester's **ues**
Lilliput **lm**
Little Folks **lm**
Lord & Taylor **ws**
Loro Piana **ues**
Lucky Brand Dungarees **lm, uws**
Macy's Herald Square **ws**
Magic Windows **ues**
Malo **lm, ues**
Marsha D.D. **ues**
Miss Pym
Morgane Le Fay **lm, ues**
Morris Bros. **uws**
Moschino **ues**
New York City Kids **ws**
New York Exchange for Woman's
    Work **es**
Nursery Lines **ues**
Oilily **ues**
Old Navy Clothing **lm, um, ws**
Original Levi's Store **es**
Osh Kosh B'Gosh **ws**
Papoose **ues**
Paul and Shark **ues**
Peanut Butter & Jane **lm**
Pearl River Mart **lm**
Peter Elliot **ues**
Peter Elliot, Jr. **ues**
Petit Bateau **ues**
Planet Kids **ues, uws**

Polo/Ralph Lauren **ues**
Pop Shop **lm**
Prince & Princess **ues**
Rain or Shine General Store **es**
Reminiscence **ws**
Replay **lm**
Robin's Nest **ues**
Saks Fifth Avenue **es**
San Francisco **ues**
Scoop **lm, ues**
Shanghai Tang **ues**
Small Change **ues**
Sotto Baby **lm**
Space Kiddets **lm**
Spring Flowers **ues**
The Stork Club **lm**
Syms **es, lm**
T.J. Maxx **lm**
Takashimaya **es**
Talbots Kids & Babies **ues**
Tartine et Chocolat **es, ues**
Terra Verde **lm**
Tigers, Tutu's & Toes **lm**
Trouvaille Française
Tutti Bambini **ues**
Versace **es**
Village Kidz **lm**
Wee Bee Kids **lm**
The Wicker Garden **ues**
Z Girl **ues**
Z'Baby Company **ues, uws**
Zitomer and Zittles **ues**

Comics/trading cards
Alex's MVP Cards **ues**
Chameleon Comics **lm**
Collector's Universe **ws**
Cosmic Comics **es**
Forbidden Planet **lm**
Funny Business Comics **uws**
Gotham City Comics **ues**
It's "A" Nother Hit **ws**
Jim Hanley's Universe **ws**
Manhattan Comics and Cards **lm**
Neutral Ground **ws**
Pokemon Center **ws**
St. Mark's Comics **lm**
Village Comics **lm**

Cosmetics/bath accessories
Avon Salon & Spa **es**
Bath & Bodyworks **es, lm, ues, ws**
Bath Island **uws**

Bed Bath & Beyond **lm, ues**
The Body Shop **es, lm, um, ues, uws, ws**
Clyde's **ues**
Details **lm, uws**
Fresh **lm, ues**
H2O **es, lm**
Kiehl's **lm**
Origins **es, lm, uws, ws**
Sephora **lm, ues, uws, ws**
Shu Uemura **lm**
Zitomer **ues**

Dollhouses and Dollhouse Accessories
F.A.O. Schwarz **es**
Iris Brown's Victorian Doll Shop **es**
Manhattan Dollhouse **lm**
New York Doll Hospital **ues**
Tiny Doll House **ues**

Equipment
Albee's **uws**
Au Chat Botte **ues**
Baby Depot at Burlington Coat
    Factory **ws**
Bambi's Baby Center **um**
Ben's For Kids **ues**
Bunnies Children's Department Store **lm**
Granny's Rentals
Jacadi **ues**
Just for Tykes **lm**
Kidstown **lm**
Kmart Stores **lm, ws**
La Petite Etoile **ues**
Little Folks **lm**
Planet Kids **ues, uws**
Schneider's Juvenile Furniture **lm**
Tartine et Chocolat **es, ue**s
Toys R Us **lm, ws**
Wee Bee Kids **lm**

Furniture and/or Decorative Accessories
ABC Carpet and Home **lm**
Albee's **uws**
Art & Tapisserie **ues**
Au Chat Botte **ues**
Baby Depot at Burlington Coat
    Factory **ws**
Bambi's Baby Center **um**
Barney's New York **ues**
A Bear's Place Inc. **ues**
Bed Bath & Beyond **lm, ues**
Bellini Juvenile Designer Furniture **ues**
Ben's For Kids **ues**

Bergdorf Goodman **ws**
Bombalulu's lm, **uws**
Bu and the Duck **lm**
Bunnies Children's Department Store **lm**
Chelsea Kids Quarters **lm**
Cradle & All **ues**
Crate & Barrel **es, lm**
Details lm, **uws**
E.A.T. Gift **ues**
Ethan Allen **es, ues, uws**
The Gazebo **ues**
Girlprops.com **lm**
Gracious Home **ues, uws**
Granny Made **uws**
Granny's Rentals
The Green Onion **bkln**
Guggenheim (Solomon R.) Museum **ues**
Jacadi **ues**
Just for Tykes **lm**
Kar'ikter **lm**
Kids Supply Co. **ues**
Kidstown **lm**
La Layette et Plus **ues**
Laura Beth's Baby Collection
Little Extras **uws**
Little Folk Art **lm**
Little Folks **lm**
MacKenzie-Childs, Ltd. **ues**
Magic Windows **ues**
Nursery Lines **ues**
Pierre Deux **es**
Plain Jane **uws**
Planet Kids **ues, uws**
Promises Fulfilled **ues**
Rain or Shine General Store **es**
Schneider's Juvenile Furniture **lm**
Space Kiddets **lm**
T.J. Maxx **lm**
Tartine et Chocolat **es, ues**
Terra Verde **lm**
The Terrence Conran Shop **es**
Wee Bee Kids **lm**
The Wicker Garden **ues**

Gadgets and Electronics
Brookstone **jfk, lga, ws**
Hammacher Schlemmer **es**
J & R Music World **lm**
Radio Shack **es, lm, ues, uws, ws**
The Sharper Image **lm, ues, ws**
Staples **es, lm, ues, uws, ws**
The Wiz **es, lm ues, uws, ws**

Games and Hobbies
America's Hobby Center **lm**
Chess Forum **lm**
Chess Shop **lm**
Compleat Strategist **es**
Exploration Station **ues**
F.A.O. Schwarz **es**
Game Show **lm, ues**
Games Workshop **lm**
Jan's Hobby Shop **ues**
Maxilla and Mandible **uws**
Neutral Ground **ws**
Red Caboose **ws**
Star Magic **lm, ues**
Stuyvesant Trains & Hobbies **lm**
Train World **bkln**
Village Chess Shop **lm**

Haircuts
Astor Place Hair Designers **lm**
Cozy's Cuts for Kids **ues, uws**
Kids Cuts **es**
Paul Mole **ues**
SuperCuts
York Barber Shop **ues**

Layette
Albee's **uws**
Au Chat Botte **ues**
Baby Depot at Burlington Coat
 Factory **ws**
Bambi's Baby Center **um**
Bambini **ues**
Bebe Thompson **ues**
Ben's For Kids **ues**
Bergdorf Goodman **ws**
Bloomingdales **es**
Bonne Nuit **uws**
Bonpoint **ues**
Bunnies Children's Department Store **lm**
Calypso Enfants & Bébé **lm**
Catimini **ues**
Century 21 **bkln, lm**
Chocks **lm**
Conway Stores **es, lm, ws**
Cradle & All **ues**
Daffy's es, lm, **ws**
Dinosaur Hill **lm**
Gracious Home **ues, uws**
Granny Made **uws**
The Green Onion **bkln**

Hoofbeats **ues**
Jacadi **ues**
Julian & Sara **lm**
Kidstown **lm**
La Layette et Plus **ues**
La Petite Etoile **ues**
Lester's **ues**
Lilliput **lm**
Little Folks **lm**
Lord & Taylor **ws**
Macy's Herald Square **ws**
Magic Windows **ues**
Morris Bros. **uws**
Peter Elliot, Jr. **ues**
Petit Bateau **ues**
Plain Jane **uws**
Planet Kids **ues, uws**
Prince & Princess **ues**
Robin's Nest **ues**
Saks Fifth Avenue **es**
Schneider's Juvenile Furniture **lm**
Space Kiddets **lm**
Spring Flowers **ues**
The Stork Club **lm**
Syms **es, lm**
Takashimaya **es**
Terra Verde **lm**
Toys R Us **lm, ws**
Village Kidz **lm**
Wee Bee Kids **lm**
The Wicker Garden **ues**
Zitomer and Zittles **ues**

Linens
ABC Carpet and Home **lm**
Barney's New York **ues**
Bed Bath & Beyond **lm, ues**
Bellini Juvenile Designer Furniture **ues**
Bergdorf Goodman **ws**
Chelsea Kids Quarters **lm**
E. Braun & Co., Inc. **ues**
Frette **ues**
Gracious Home **ues, uws**
Jacadi **ues**
Just for Tykes **lm**
Kids Supply Co. **ues**
La Layette et Plus **ues**
Laura Beth's Baby Collection
Leron **ues**
Nursery Lines **ues**
Plain Jane **uws**
Porthault Linens **ues**
Pratesi **ues**

Rain or Shine General Store **es**
Schweitzer Linen **ues, uws**
Trouvaille Française

Magic
Abracadabra **lm**
Halloween Adventure **lm**
Tannen's Magic Company **ws**

Maternity
Bloomingdales **es**
Cadeau **lm**
Just for Tykes **lm**
Liz Lange **ues**
Macy's Herald Square **ws**
Maternity Works **ws**
Michele Saint-Laurent **ues**
Mimi Maternity **es, ues, uws**
Mommy Chic **lm**
Mom's Night Out **ues**
Motherhood Maternity **lm, ues, uws, ws**
A Pea in the Pod **ues, ws**
Pumpkin Maternity **lm**
Veronique **ues**

Museum Stores
American Craft Museum Shop **ws**
American Museum of Natural History Store **uws**
Brooklyn Museum of Art Shop **bkln**
Children's Museum of Manhattan Store **uws**
Cooper-Hewitt National Design Museum Shop **ues**
Guggenheim (Solomon R.) Museum **ues**
Jewish Museum Store **ues**
Lincoln Center Performing Arts Gift Shop **uws**
Metropolitan Museum of Art Shop **lm, lga, ues, um, ws**
Museum of Modern Art Design Store **lm, ws**
Museum of the City of New York Store **ues**
New York Public Library Shop **es, ws**
New York Transit Museum Gift Shop **bkln, es**
United Nations Gift Center **es**
Whitney Museum of American Art Store **ues**

Music
Borders Books and Music **es**
HMV **es, um, ws**
J & R Music World **lm**
Lincoln Center Performing Arts Gift
    Shop **uws**
Manny's Music **ws**
Tower Records **es, lm, uws**
Virgin Megastore **lm, ws**

Party Goods
The Balloon Man **uws**
Dylan's Candy Bar **es**
E.A.T. Gifts **ues**
F.A.O. Schwarz **es**
Paper House **es, ues, uws**
Party City **lm**
Stationery & Toy World **uws**

Resale
Children's Resale **ues**
Good Byes Children's Resale Shop **ues**
Jane's Exchange **lm**

Shoes
Bambini **ues**
Bombalulu's **lm, uws**
Bonpoint **ues**
Bu and the Duck **lm**
Calypso **lm, ues**
Century 21 **bkln, lm**
Daffy's **es, lm, ws**
David Z **lm, ws**
East Side Kids **ues**
G.C. William **ues**
Galo Shoes **ues**
Great Feet **ues**
The Green Onion **bkln**
Gucci **es**
Harry's Shoes **uws**
Hoyt & Bond **bkln**
Jacadi **ues**
Jumpin' Julias **bkln**
Juno **lm**
Kids Foot Locker **ues, ws**
Kmart Stores **lm, ws**
Lester's **ues**
Lilliput **lm**
Little Eric **ues**
Macy's Herald Square **ws**
Moschino **ues**
New York City Kids **ws**
Niketown **es**

Nine West **es, lm, ues, uws, ws**
Osh Kosh B'Gosh **ws**
Payless Shoe Source **lm, ws**
Peanut Butter & Jane **lm**
Prada **es, ues, ws**
Replay **lm**
Shoofly **lm, uws**
Skechers **lm, uws, ws**
Space Kiddets **lm**
Spring Flowers **ues**
Steve Madden **lm, ues, uws, ws**
Syms **es, lm**
Tigers, Tutu's & Toes **lm**
Timberland **ues**
Tip Top Kids Shoes **uws**
Tod's **es**
Versace **es**
Village Kidz **lm**
Z'Baby Company **ues, uws**

Stationery
Hyde Park Stationers **ues**
Kate's Paperie **lm, ues**
Sam Flax **es, lm**
Staples **es, lm, ues, uws, ws**

Teens
Abercrombie & Fitch **lm**
Adidas Originals **lm**
A/X Armani Exchange **es, lm**
Banana Republic **es, lm, ues, uws, ws**
Barney's New York **lm, ues**
Bath & Bodyworks **es, lm ues, ws**
Bath Island **uws**
Bebe **es, lm, ues**
Benetton **es, lm, ues**
Betsey Johnson **lm, ues, uws**
Bloomingdales **es**
The Body Shop **es, lm, um, ues, uws, was**
Burberry **es, lm**
Calypso **lm, ues**
Canal Jean Co. **lm**
Century 21 **bkln, lm**
Club Monaco **es, lm, ues, uws**
Clyde's **ues**
Contempo Casuals **lm**
Crush—Hip Stuff You'll Want **ues**
Diesel **es, lm**
DKNY **es, lm**
Dollhouse **lm**
Earl Jeans **lm**
Eclipse **lm**
Express **es, lm, uws, ws**

Filene's Basement **lm, uws**
Fossil **lm, ws**
French Connection **lm, uws, ws**
Fresh **lm, ues**
G.C. William **ues**
Gap **es, lm, ues, uws, ws**
Guess? **lm**
H & M **lm, ws**
H2O **es, lm**
Infinity **ues**
J. Crew **lm, ws**
Joyce Leslie **lm**
Kate Spade Store **lm**
Kenneth Cole **es, lm, uws, ws**
Kiehl's **lm**
Lacoste **es**
Le Chateau **lm, ws**
Lester's **ues**
Lilliput **lm**
Lucky Brand Dungarees **lm, ues, uws**
Macy's Herald Square **ws**
Magic Windows (M.W. Teen) **ues**
Mandee **uws**
Marsha D.D. **ues**
Morris Bros. **uws**
Nine West **es, lm, ues, uws, ws**
Olive & Bette's **ues, uws**
Original Levi's Store **es**
Origins **es, lm, uws, ws**
Petit Bateau **ues**
Planet Kids **uws**
Polo/Ralph Lauren **ues**
Reminiscence **ws**
Ricky's **es, lm, ues, uws, ws**
Saks Fifth Avenue **es**
Scoop **lm, ues**
Screaming Mimi's **lm**
Sephora **lm, ues, uws, ws**
Shu Uemura **lm**
Sisley **lm, uws**
Skechers **lm, uws, ws**
Space Kiddets **lm**
Steve Madden **lm, ues, uws, ws**
Strawberry **es, lm, ws**
Stussy **lm**
T.J. Maxx **lm**
Trash and Vaudeville **lm**
Triple Five Soul **lm**
Urban Outfitters **lm, uws**
Violet **ues**
Warehouse of London **lm**
Wet Seal **lm, ws**
Z Girl **ues**

Theme Stores
CBS Store **ws**
City Store **lm, ws**
Disney Store **es, uws, ws**
Fire Zone **ws**
MetsClubhouse Shop **es, ws**
N.B.A. Store **ws**
NBC Experience Store **ws**
New York Firefighter's Friend **lm**
Sanrio **ws**
Yankees Clubhouse Shop **es, lm, ws**

Toys and/or Books
Albee's **uws**
Alex's MVP Cards **ues**
Alphabets **lm, uws**
Alphaville **lm**
American Craft Museum Shop **ws**
American Museum of Natural History
   Store **uws**
Art & Tapisserie **ues**
Bambi's Baby Center **um**
Bank Street Bookstore **um**
A Bear's Place Inc. **ues**
Bebe Thompson **ues**
Bed Bath & Beyond **lm, ues**
Ben's For Kids **ues**
Big City Kite Company **ues**
Big Fun Toys **lm**
Bombalulu's **lm, uws**
Bonne Nuit **uws**
Books of Wonder **lm**
Brooklyn Museum of Art Shop **bkln**
Calypso Enfants & Bébé **lm**
Children's General Store **es, uws**
Children's Museum of Manhattan
   Store **uws**
Chimera **lm**
Classic Toys **lm**
Clyde's **ues**
Cooper-Hewitt National Design
   Museum Shop **ues**
Cozy's Cuts for Kids **ues, uws**
Crembebe **lm**
Daffy's **es, lm, ws**
Dinosaur Hill **lm**
E.A.T. Gifts **ues**
Enchanted Forest **lm**
F.A.O. Schwarz **es**
First & Second Cousin **lm**
Forbidden Planet **lm**
Geppetto's Toybox **lm**
The Green Onion **bkln**

Guggenheim (Solomon R.)
   Museum **ues**
Homboms **ues**
Hoyt & Bond **bkln**
Hyde Park Stationers **ues**
Ibiza Boutique **lm**
It's a Mod, Mod World **lm**
Jewish Museum Store **ues**
Julian & Sara **lm**
Just for Tykes **lm**
KB Toys **ws, uws, um**
Kidding Around **lm**
Kids Cuts **es**
Kidstown **lm**
Kmart Stores **lm, ws**
Lilliput **lm**
Little Extras **uws**
Little Folks **lm**
Lord & Taylor **ws**
Macy's Herald Square **ws**
Mary Arnold Toys **ues**
Metropolitan Museum of Art Shop **lm,**
   lga, ues, um, ws
Museum of Modern Art Design Store
   lm, ws
Museum of the City of New York
   Store **ues**
New York Exchange for Woman's
   Work **es**
New York Public Library Shop **es, ws**
New York Transit Museum Gift Shop
   bkln, es
Peanut Butter & Jane **lm**
Penny Whistle Toys **ues, uws**
Planet Kids **ues, uws**

Pokemon Center **ws**
Pop Shop **lm**
Promises Fulfilled **ues**
Rain or Shine General Store **es**
Reminiscence **ws**
San Francisco **ues**
Schneider's Juvenile Furniture **lm**
Sotto Baby **lm**
Space Kiddets **lm**
Star Magic **lm, ues**
Stationery & Toy World **uws**
Syms **es, lm**
T.J. Maxx **lm**
Terra Verde **lm**
The Terrence Conran Shop **es**
Toys R Us **lm, ws**
Toys Tokyo **lm**
Village Kidz **lm**
West Side Kids **uws**
Whitney Museum of American Art
   Store **ues**
Zany Brainy **ues, uws**
Zitomer and Zittles **ues**

Vintage
Crush—Hip Stuff You'll Want **ues**
Reminiscence **ws**
Screaming Mimi's **lm**
Space Kiddets **lm**
Trouvaille Française

Watches
Fossil **lm, ws**
G-Factory **lm**
Swatch **es, lm, uws**

HOT DOGS, BAGELS AND CAVIAR

With more than 18,000 eating establishments, New York's varied and flavorful gastronomic landscape provides an opportunity for the adventurous to embark on an international culinary tour. The younger members of your group may not yet have the palate to appreciate the diversity, but for the curious—or simply willing— epicure, new taste buds may be born. And for the recalcitrant, there are always chicken nuggets!

Since your time in New York is limited, you will likely want to selectively, rather than randomly, sample Big Apple fare. Dining out with kids might automatically eliminate some of the finer (translation, pricey) or more exotic destinations for which New York is famous, but the city is filled with plenty of delicious, family-friendly dining. And, it is fair to say that in most restaurants, children are accepted (or at least tolerated!) if not necessarily welcomed.

So, even if you are not intending to drag the kids to a string of the city's most renowned restaurants, you can still make dining a satisfying part of your visit. This chapter will provide you with some good food for thought and things to consider when planning your city meals to increase the odds that your dining experience gets four stars.

► **Where and when to go.** There is no magic answer to creating a great family dining experience. However, you can maximize the potential for a good time with some thought not only to your choice of restaurant but to the timing of the meal. Consider:

◩ **Where to go.** Until your youngster has moved beyond a staple of hamburgers, chicken nuggets and pasta, avoid more sophisticated restaurants unless they either specifically cater to kids or offer something your children will eat (even if it is just plain rice). Your best bet may be a restaurant with a children's menu. Try to select a restaurant where the noise level will camouflage the potentially loud noise coming from your own table rather than choosing a very formal adult restaurant.

Theme restaurants are always a popular family dining destination. While they do provide a certain level of entertainment for the kids, be aware that they often offer somewhat mediocre, but very expensive, food. Also, you can pretty much count on a long wait to be seated. Be prepared for an onslaught of pricey souvenirs your children will beg to bring home. If theme restaurants are on your list, be sure to review your visiting-the-gift-shop policy in advance.

Many restaurants bend over backward to attract families. These restaurants tend to be decorated in a playful way, providing an atmosphere that interests most kids. They usually have a children's menu, provide crayons or other table activities and are very busy and noisy. These types of restaurants lend themselves to family dining. Be forewarned that even though a restaurant may have entertainment of some kind, it may not offer the diversion needed to get through a whole meal. Some kids have a hard time keeping themselves in control either because of the noise or the level of activity.

◩ **When to go.** In Manhattan, prime time for lunch is between 12:30 and 1:30 p.m. and prime time for dinner begins between 7:00 and 7:30 p.m. To maximize the chance to be seated quickly and receive prompt service, choose an early dinner time (between 6:00 and 7:00 p.m.), especially on Friday and Saturday nights, and avoid the prime lunch hour by eating before it begins or when the rush is over. Additionally, try to streamline your meal. Most children are not prepared to sit through a two-hour dinner starting at 8:30 p.m. A night out with young children is not the night to have a four-course meal.

Do keep in mind that restaurants located in the theater district or near Lincoln Center often offer a pre-theater seating intended to get patrons out for an 8:00 p.m. curtain call, and so arriving without a reservation is likely to be a problem.

In general, it is best to avoid peak times, so that the staff will be less harried and the restaurant less crowded, noisy and busy. It is amazing what a difference 30 minutes can make for your dining experience.

☑ **About reservations.** If you are going to be dining at a restaurant that requires reservations and that would typically not be host to New York's youngest diners, let the maitre d' know (in advance if possible) that your party includes a child or children. Generally, a table can be selected that will present the fewest distractions to others. With advance notice, the restaurant may be able to provide you with a child seat or make arrangements for a child-friendly meal. Whenever possible, make a reservation, particularly if you are dining with a large party.

▶ **The Grownup's Guide's Hierarchy of Dining.** There are many categories of restaurants in New York. Your choices range from haute cuisine to fast food, from $100+ per person to $10 for the family and include every cuisine imaginable. Fast food and the corner coffee shop are easy choices when dining with children, but if you want an authentic taste of New York, you should venture beyond the "tried and true."

There are basically two ways to approach dining: feeding the troops or destination dining. In the case of the former, the goal is simply to get food into the group in the most expedient manner. In the latter case, dining is an end in itself. The restaurant is chosen for the cuisine, the atmosphere or the entertainment value. Most visitors will engage in a bit of each. In order to help you navigate the dining landscape, we have identified five very general categories of city dining:

◪ Fast food. This includes your basics such as McDonalds, Burger King, Sbarro's and others. As much as many diners love to hate fast food, when traveling with kids, this option can provide a quick, easy and cheap meal. Ironically, sometimes it becomes necessary to escape the very service you generally seek in a restaurant. Since most kids love fast food, it can become a useful bargaining tool for parents to keep the kids going for a while longer.

◪ Diners and Pizza Joints. Not quite as fast as fast food, diners and pizza joints are a staple for most New York families. Pizza parlors tend toward the inexpensive, with the exception of those featuring brick-oven pizza and a full menu of other selections. Diners however are not all created equal and can dramatically range in price and quality. For example, while a diner on Madison Avenue can set you back more than $50 for breakfast for four, breakfast at a more local neighborhood diner can cost half as much. Most diners have a children's menu.

◪ Family Restaurants. While there may not be cloths on the table (and there may be crayons for the kids), dining is taken a bit more seriously at this level, which includes establishments offering a huge range of cuisines at a variety of prices. In this category, you will find everything from burgers to ethnic fare. What makes this type of restaurant a good choice for the family is that there are food choices for both kids and adults and the environment is not too formal.

◪ Grownup Restaurants. Here you will find not only crystal and table linens (or the hip equivalent thereof), but sophisticated menus and very few children, especially at night. Patrons expect a high level of service commensurate with the prices. While such restaurants may not be formal per se, the intended clientele is definitely over 21. This type of dining is most suitable for older children, those with developed palates and those who are at ease in adult environments. If you want to take younger children for a grownup meal, it is recommended you dine early.

▰ **A True Gastronomic Experience.** Few children travel well in the world of haute cuisine. Even if you have a young "foodie" in your party, these exclusive, usually very pricey, restaurants are not really the place for younger kids although your teen may do just fine.

Trying different types of restaurants with your children can expand both their palates and their view of the world.

As you make your restaurant choices, do not feel compelled to linger in the fast food or diner categories, though they certainly have their place in the eating lexicon. Trying different types of restaurants with your children can expand both their palates and their view of the world. As long as you are realistic about what the group can handle and are mindful about your destination, you can have a delicious adventure.

▶ **Prix fixe?** Everything you heard about the high cost of eating out in New York is true. From coast to coast, we have all become accustomed to the $4.00 cup of gourmet Joe. In New York, however, that is just the beginning. While you can dine al fresco on a street vendor hot dog for $2.00, you can also spend $65 for an entrée in a pricey restaurant.

If you will be spending an entire day or more eating in restaurants, you can easily pass the $100-a-day mark feeding a family of four. If you add to your basic food costs the snacks you end up buying after meals are rejected because the food does not "look right," your food budget will scrape the sky. Suddenly, the price of meals (and gratuities) can become a consuming source of anxiety. So how do you fix the price and be left with more than pocket change?

Some ideas for keeping the check in check:

- ⟳ You do not always have to pay top dollar to get a great meal, but eating in a diner does not necessarily result in significant savings. Before you sit down and order, peruse the menu (usually posted in the window or, if not, ask to see one) and make sure that the restaurant is in your price range. Do not be intimidated into staying someplace that is not in your budget or does not serve something your children will eat.

- ⟳ In New York you pay for atmosphere as much as food. Eating establishments that market to tourists generally are a bit pricier than local favorites.

◑ A restaurant does not have to be glamorous or expensive to be good, but if an establishment looks run down, not clean and is very cheap, steer clear unless you have a reliable recommendation to eat there.

◑ If the restaurant has a children's menu, try to take advantage of it. In most cases, the portions will be child-sized (although sometimes the portion is large and only the price is child-sized) and significantly less expensive than the adult menu. If your child is insulted by the idea of ordering from the children's menu, you can use the moment as an opportunity to discuss the difference between pride and cash flow. Some restaurants that do not have a children's menu may offer "half orders" of certain dishes such as pastas or have appetizers that work as a main course for a child.

◑ If you are in town for a number of meals, consider mixing informal meals such as a slice of pizza and a salad and other less expensive options with meals at more expensive restaurants.

◑ If you are staying in a hotel (all of which are notorious for expensive room service meals), you can still eat in and keep costs down. Some hotels offer a breakfast meal plan, have kitchenettes in the room so you can prepare your own or may rent you a small in-room refrigerator or have space in the mini-bar for some essentials. Take-out breakfast (for example, bagels and beverages) or sandwiches for lunch or a snack in the room purchased from a local supermarket can bring down the overall food cost of your stay. We always travel with a small jar of peanut butter, crackers, breakfast bars, individual-sized cereal boxes, milk which does not need to be refrigerated and fruit, so that we do not have to eat every meal in a restaurant.

▶ **You are the ringmaster.** Wherever you dine *en famille*, it may seem as if you're running a three-ring circus. In many respects you are. That being said, you still can exercise authority over a disintegrating situation and keep things not only in perspective, but under control. The key is to remain calm and be flexible.

To more fully enjoy your restaurant experiences with children, it is important to acknowledge your children's physical and emotional limitations and to place appropriate limits on your children's behavior. Just as children need to be taught to use "indoor voices" in a museum, so too, must they learn about "restaurant manners" and the level of kid's conduct that passes muster at different types of restaurants.

While we have all had the opportunity to witness, in horror, someone else's dining disaster, we have also been in the parental hot seat and had to manage one of our own. When faced with a table of unruly kids, keep your cool and try not to salvage your meal at the expense of the other patrons. If you respect that others may not have children of their own and therefore may not be very accommodating or patient with your children, or that others may actually be escaping their own responsibilities of parenthood for a few hours, you can take children almost anywhere in New York. Dining with children may not be a relaxing experience, but it is a family one, and that is reason enough for undertaking such an effort. Some basics:

- Keep your child at the table. To allow children to wander among tables unattended is dangerous for both children and waiters carrying hot food and inconsiderate to other diners.

- Outlaw food fights and other disruptive behavior and stick to your position.

- Be prepared to leave or take your child outside for a little walk in case of meltdown during the meal. If all else fails, order dessert early, buy everyone a round of drinks and tip well.

► **Let's hear it for distractions and other strategies.** A key strategy against long waits, slow service or lack of interest in the table conversation is distraction. Distractions come in many forms. Some are edible (crackers, candy) and some consist of activities for the kids to do with you or on their own. Stickers, drawing materials, cards, trading cards, electronic hand-held games, books, Mad Libs and magazines help direct your child's energy and usually provide just the distraction necessary to buy the time you need to get in and out of the restaurant.

Some other ideas:

- Younger kids sometimes benefit from an adult-supervised walk either in an open area or outdoors between the time you order and the time the meal is served. This tactic can help to postpone a child's limited table-time attention span to the time when you need it the most—while you're eating.

↪ Particularly if your group is running out of steam, distractions alone may not salvage the meal. In such a case, keep it short. Skip the appetizer, order the kids' food immediately and let the children eat dessert while you have your entrée.

Letting a child have a coveted soft drink or dessert can be much more pleasant than spending the entire meal trying to get the greens down.

↪ Don't try to enforce a balanced meal in a restaurant. Eating in a restaurant marks a departure from regular meals and can be a good time to relax your rules. Letting a child have a coveted soft drink or dessert can be much more pleasant than spending the entire meal trying to get the greens down. A wise pediatrician once told us that a child's nutritional needs should be balanced over time, not necessarily at each meal or over a particular day. You are on vacation or having a special day, so go with the flow. Your children will be excited and will fondly remember the time they had candy for lunch (which may have bought you the cooperation to get through an exhibit at the Met!).

↪ If your child is an especially picky eater, or mealtime is running late and it is likely your child will hit the wall before food can be ordered and served, consider giving him or her a healthy snack before you get to the restaurant or bringing something with you to supplement the meal.

▶ **Have it your way.** Children are notoriously choosy when it comes to their food. We have all seen tears shed because the vegetables touched the pasta and tantrums thrown because the food was served with a garnish of icky "green stuff" that has to be removed piece by verdant piece. As a result, if the food ordered does not meet expectations, a child is likely to reject it (and if you are lucky, without much fanfare).

The best way to make sure that what is ordered actually has a chance of being eaten is to ask questions before you order and to be clear about any specific requests you may have regarding how it is prepared. For example, in a funky retro dinner, a grilled cheese may come on fluffy fresh-baked bread rather than "regular" bread. A hamburger may be oversized or served on an English muffin. Gourmet pizza may be garnished with herbs and not cut in triangles. Having that information will help your child decide what to order or how to modify the order to make it edible.

One last tip if you have young children who cannot manage well on an empty tummy. It is always a good idea to have the server bring the children's food as soon as it is prepared rather than waiting until everyone's meal is ready to be served.

► **Practice makes perfect.** The table manners emphasized at home are more likely to show up when you're out on the town than those that are not. Napkins on laps, elbows off the table, staying in one's seat, no horseplay and passing instead of reaching for items across the table are just a few of those basic rules of etiquette that make children seem less primitive.

However, even if your kids are usually civilized at the table at home, the excitement of being at a restaurant, on vacation or on a special outing or the cumulative effects of a day on the move may challenge even the most polite child. What to do? Be realistic. Do not expect your kids to be perfect and hold it together at every meal (especially if you are eating all of your meals in restaurants while here). After all, they are still children—drinks will spill, napkins will be on the floor, noise will be made. What you can prevent is silverware flying, standing on chairs and food fights.

You can help your children with restaurant readiness by role-playing at home. You can practice ordering, rehearse what to do if the food that arrives is different from what was expected and learn how to excuse yourself to go to the bathroom. You can review the basic place setting and your own restaurant rules. Most important, do not expect your kids to be suddenly transformed into grownups. With realistic expectations, clearly spelled out before you sit down to eat, you will enjoy many meals out with your children while they practice their way to dinner at Lutèce.

► **A change in your plans.** Nothing is more disappointing than having to cancel plans to which you are looking forward. However, we all know how uncomfortable it is for everyone when you push a child too far—you end up with a miserable child and a day ruined for all. As a parent, only you can gauge if your child is low on fuel or completely out of gas. A comment such as "this restaurant smells bad, it's going to make me throw up" from an otherwise cooperative and agreeable child needs to be evaluated seriously. Sometimes, that means calling off the plans and going home early or returning to an evening of room service and early bedtime. As parents, we will not always make the right choices, but we can improve the odds by reading the signals and clues the children may be giving us. Being realistic and ready to alter our own plans can substantially improve the odds of things working out for everyone involved.

► **Using this chapter.** Listed below are some restaurants we think are generally kid-friendly. We have not endeavored to include every eating establishment in every neighborhood. Rather, we have provided a modest sampler of restaurants around town that will satisfy a variety of tastes and budgets, including restaurants that do not necessarily have kids' menus or cool themes. We do not rate particular places; however we do provide simple descriptions about what you can expect to find at the listed restaurants. Hopefully, this information will provide some options no matter where you might find yourself thirsty and hungry. At the end of the restaurant listings are some general resources concerning dining in New York.

Bon appétit!

Restaurants

► **Price.** Our price indicator is based on dinner for a hypothetical family of four with two children under the age of 12. We assume both adults have one glass of wine or beer. Lunch and brunch menus tend to be less expensive.

$—inexpensive, under $40

$$—moderate, between $41 and $100

$$$—expensive, over $100

► **Reservations.** Reservations for dinner are always a good idea, and if you are traveling with a large party, reservations are also recommended for lunch. Note that some less formal restaurants do not take reservations, although they may take reservations for large parties (6 or 8+) or an early seating. Because reservations at popular restaurants may be hard to get, your hotel concierge can be quite helpful. Also, many credit cards offer reservation services for certain level cardholders.

► **Strollers.** Most restaurants are able to accommodate strollers, although "accommodate" has many meanings. In some cases, you can wheel your stroller up to the table. In others, it means there is a place where you can stash your folded stroller. Whatever the policy, expect that at peak times, if the restaurant is crowded, you will probably not be able to keep your stroller at the table.

► **Highchairs and booster seats.** Most restaurants will offer some type of seating for children, either in the form of a highchair, booster seat or sassy seat. The quality, cleanliness and availability of such seating is highly variable. High-end restaurants catering to an adult dinner crowd will be less likely to offer such seating than diners and informal eateries. If you require a child seat, it is best to call ahead and confirm.

► **Wheelchair accessibility.** This designation is actually more complicated than one would expect. For instance, restaurants that are wheelchair accessible may not have wheelchair accessible restrooms. Call ahead to clarify if the facility is suitable for your particular situation.

► **Brunch.** Brunch seems to be a meal that goes in and out of style with various restaurants. Some have it during certain seasons but not others. Some restaurants experiment with introducing it from time to time. Therefore, do not assume that a restaurant that serves lunch will have a weekend brunch menu. In addition, some restaurants that actually do have kids' menus do not have them for brunch and some that do not otherwise have kids' menus do have them for brunch. Call ahead to confirm.

▶ **Call ahead because things change**. All information listed is as of the date of this publication. Restaurants are notorious for frequently changing hours, menus and special features (brunch, live music, kids' menus). In all cases, if you need specific information, call ahead.

Unless otherwise specifically indicated, restaurants listed accept major credit cards (American Express, MasterCard, Visa) and reservations.

❖ = cash only

❀ = kid's menu

✗ = no reservations

America $$
9 East 18th Street between Broadway and Fifth Avenue, 505-2110
There's no need for a kid's menu at this America-themed eatery when the regular menu offers items like macaroni & cheese, Fluffernutters, shakes, hamburgers, grilled cheese, pasta and more, most of which are named after American cities. It's big, it's loud and there are often specially scheduled family-friendly events or promotions over weekends.

Annie's $
1381 Third Avenue between 78th and 79th Streets, 327-4853
The kids will love this popular neighborhood breakfast and lunch spot, especially the chocolate-chip pancakes, and both kids and mom and dad can choose from a variety of egg dishes, waffles, pancakes and salads. Annie's also serves dinner.

Arqua $$$
281 Church Street at White Street, 334-1888
This elegant, quintessential Tribeca restaurant featuring northern Italian dishes is an excellent choice when you want a delicious grownup Italian dinner. Perfect for celebrating a special occasion.

Artie's Delicatessen   ❀ ✗ $
2290 Broadway between 82nd and 83rd Streets, 579-5959
This family-friendly, traditional-style deli offers all the deli staples—potato pancakes, burgers, grilled cheese, Reubens, hot dogs, Dr. Brown's and grandma's chicken soup.

Barking Dog Luncheonette   ❖ ✗ $$
1453 York Avenue at 77th Street, 861-3600 (Dog fountain)
1678 Third Avenue at 94th Street, 831-1800
American comfort fare, such as burgers, fried chicken, mashed potatoes, meat loaf, gourmet mac and cheese, ice cream sodas and soda fountain choices are served up in a homey, dog-motif setting. Dog watching at the

canine drinking fountain at the 77th Street location is always a hoot, and the people food is delicious too.

Barney Greengrass—the Sturgeon King ❖ ✗ $$
541 Amsterdam Avenue between 86th and 87th Streets, 724-4707
This legendary Upper West Side deli, famous for its array of smoked fish— sturgeon, lox, "Nova," kippers, sable, pickled herring and whitefish—is a great spot for breakfast or lunch. If fish is not your thing, go for the egg dishes, chopped liver, borscht or bagels.

Bendix Diner ✗ $$
167 First Avenue between 10th and 11th Streets, 260-4220
This East Village diner has a mixed personality. Blending American diner favorites (burgers, tuna melts, pancakes) with Thai cuisine (noodles, coconut soup), the overall atmosphere is hip and friendly. The kitschy décor includes a godzilla and a full-sized plastic bathing beauty.

Benihana of Tokyo ❀ $$$
120 East 56th Street between Park and Lexington Avenues, 593-1627
47 West 56th Street between Fifth and Sixth Avenues, 581-0930
It may be touristy, and it may be part of a chain, but it is still a very enter- taining place to eat, especially for children under 12. Kids love watching the extravagant knife work of the table-side chef as he prepares Japanese- style chicken, beef or seafood entrées on the table-top grill. Be prepared: you may be seated with another family at a large table.

Benny's Burritos $
93 Avenue A at 6th Street, 254-2054
113 Greenwich Ave between Jane and West 12th Streets, 727-0584

This East Village eatery offers up huge burritos as well as other innovative Mexican fare. The meat-free crowd can find barbequed tofu, and Benny's is committed to lard-, MSG- and preservative-free food. If you cannot get a table, check out the takeout shop at 112 Greenwich Avenue.

The Boathouse in Central Park $$$
Central Park Lake at Park Drive North at 72nd Street, 517-2233
The Boathouse is better than a picnic in the park. This seasonal restaurant offering American cuisine overlooks the bucolic Central Park Lake. Pasta is a safe fallback if other items don't appeal. In season, rowboat rentals are available. Visit the adjoining Café for a less formal environment.

Brooklyn Diner $$
212 West 57th Street between 7th Avenue and Broadway, 581-8900
This retro diner serves up gigantic portions of reliable comfort food, includ- ing foot-long hot dogs, burgers, barbecue chicken sandwiches, onion rings, salads, shakes and other fountain drinks. Huge desserts include mile-high lemon meringue pie and chocolate blackout cake.

Brother Jimmy's BBQ ❀ $$

1485 Second Avenue between 77th and 78th Streets, 288-0999
428 Amsterdam Avenue between 80th and 81st Streets, 501-7211
1644 Third Avenue at 92nd Street, 426-2020

These southern barbeque joints offer stick-to-your-ribs, old fashioned fare including fried chicken, ribs, pulled pork, meat loaf, corn dogs, Cajun shrimp and more. Loud music, authentic roadhouse décor and Mississippi mud pie complete the scene. To keep the kids coming back, Jimmy's offers two free kids' meals with every adult entrée.

Bryant Park Café $$$

25 West 40th Street between Fifth and Sixth Avenues, behind the New
   York Public Library, 840-6500

The outdoor café serves up creative American cuisine in a wonderful outdoor setting that is open from April through October. The more upscale (and pricier) indoor Grill features a wall-of-windows view of the park.

Bubby's ❀ $$

120 Hudson Street between Franklin and North Moore Streets, 219-0666

This local downtown place is cluttered and informal and serves breakfast most of the day. Very popular with Tribeca families and frequented by local celebrities, Bubby's offers old-fashioned comfort food such as eggs, burgers, sandwiches, salads, lemonade, apple pie and chocolate cake plus some more gourmet offerings. Kids under 8 eat free on weekends (dinner only).

Burritoville $

36 Water Street at Broad Street, 747-1100
20 John Street between Broadway and Nassau Streets, 766-2020
144 Chambers Street at Hudson Street, 571-1144
298 Bleecker Street between Seventh Avenue South and Grove Street,
   633-9249
141 Second Avenue between 8th and 9th Streets, 260-3300
264 West 23rd Street between Seventh and Eighth Avenues, 367-9844
352 West 39th Street between Eighth and Ninth Avenues, 563-9088
625 Ninth Avenue at 44th Street, 333-5352
855 Third Avenue at 52nd Street, 980-4111
166 West 72nd Street between Columbus and Amsterdam Avenues,
   580-7700
1487 Second Avenue between 77th and 78th Streets, 472-8800
451 Amsterdam Avenue between 81st and 82nd Streets, 787-8181

Burritoville offers an alternative to fast food by stuffing enormous burritos with healthy ingredients. Choose from an array of tortillas, including toasted sesame, chipotle and whole wheat. Enchiladas and quesadillas are also available.

Café Edison   ❖ ✗ $$
228 West 47th Street between Broadway and Eighth Avenue, 354-0368
If you need an inexpensive and quick bite pre- or post-theater, this diner
(complete with pink vinyl booths) offers standard diner/deli fare and caters
not only to showgoers but Broadway biggies as well.

Café Luxembourg $$$
299 West 70th Street between Amsterdam and West End Avenues,
    873-7411
This Art Deco Upper West Side French bistro (cousin of downtown's
Odeon) offers up delicious steak frites, roast chicken and other classic
dishes. Though definitely an adult destination, this is a good choice to take
older children for a great meal in sophisticated surroundings (near Lincoln
Center).

California Pizza Kitchen   ❀ $$
201 East 60th Street between Second and Third Avenues, 755-7773
The Manhattan outpost of this popular pizza chain restaurant offers a wide
selection of specialty pizzas, pasta dishes and salads on two floors.

Candle Café $$
1307 Third Avenue between 74th and 75th Streets, 472-0970
This neighborhood café offers very fresh and tasty vegetarian and macro-
biotic fare, pasta, fresh juices and a good selection of desserts.

Carmine's $$
200 West 44th Street between Broadway and Eighth Avenue, 221-3800
2450 Broadway between 90th and 91st Streets, 362-2200
Reservations during prime dinner hours for parties of six or more.
Everything is big at Carmine's—especially the portions. Classic southern
Italian food is served on large family-sized platters for the table. Perfect for
large groups. Carmines is always busy and somewhat noisy. Be prepared to
wait if you do not have a reservation.

Carnegie Deli   ❖ ✗ $$
854 Seventh Avenue at 55th Street, 757-2245
This is the quintessential New York deli, with long wooden tables set with
the necessities of authentic deli dining—pickles, coleslaw and Dr. Brown's
soda. Enjoy huge portions, sandwiches with celebrity names and deli
favorites, including blintzes, hot dogs and knishes. Expect a big tourist
crowd in this popular restaurant.

Chat 'N Chew   ❀ ✗ $$
10 East 16th Street between Fifth Avenue and Union Square West,
    243-1616
Southern-style home cooking features po' boys, fried chicken, meat loaf,
mac and cheese, the renowned Holy Cow Burger and yummy desserts. This

casual friendly neighborhood spot, loaded with plenty of roadside decorations, is a popular family dining choice.

China Fun $$
1653 Broadway between 51st and 52nd Streets, 333-2622
1239 Second Avenue at 64th Street, 752-0810
246 Columbus Avenue between 71st and 72nd Streets, 580-1516
This chain of inexpensive, quick and friendly restaurants offers up a reliable variety of Chinese favorites, including dim sum, barbeque and dumplings in a modern, sleek environment. As an added bonus, the exposed kitchens let the kids take a peek at how dumplings are made.

Churrascaria Plataforma $$
316 West 49th Street between Eighth and Ninth Avenues, in the
    Belvedere Hotel, 245-0505
This Brazilian all-you-can-eat rodizio serves grilled meats right off the skewer at tableside, paired with a huge salad bar. Kids will enjoy using a coaster to signal the waiter when it's time to bring more food. Children under 10 eat for half price, children under 5 eat for free.

City Hall   ❀ $$
131 Duane Street between Church Street and West Broadway, 227-7777
This steakhouse offers up a variety of cuts and side dishes in a spacious, family-friendly restaurant filled with photos of old New York.

Coffee Shop   ❀ $$
29 Union Square West at 16th Street, 243-7969
This funky diner with a Brazilian twist attracts a young, hip crowd and many Village artists. On Saturdays and Sundays, an all-day brunch is served, accompanied by live samba music.

Comfort Diner   ❀ ✗ $
214 East 45th Street between Second and Third Avenues, 867-4555
142 East 86th Street at Lexington Avenue, 369-8628
As the name suggests, you will be transported to the golden age of the diner with a menu loaded with your favorite comfort foods in a kid-friendly environment.

Cookies & Couscous   ❖ ✗ except for large parties $
230 Thompson Street between Bleecker and West 3rd Streets, 477-6562
This small Moroccan eatery serves up plenty of couscous and lots more. The gregarious owner–chef goes out of his way to make his guests comfortable and happy.

Cowgirl Hall of Fame ❀ **$$**
519 Hudson Street at West 10th Street, 633-1133
Cowgirl memorabilia adorns the walls and Tex-Mex cuisine (including barbeque, chili, frito pie) is the specialty of the house. Don't miss the ice-cream desserts.

Cupping Room Café ✗ for weekend breakfast, brunch or lunch **$$$**
359 West Broadway between Broome and Grand Streets, 925-2898
496 Hudson Street between Christopher and Grove Streets, 226-2723
This SoHo staple since the late 1970s is a popular spot for a casual breakfast or brunch, but it has a regular lunch and dinner menu, too. The Hudson Street location is more of a casual bakery that also offers salads, sandwiches and desserts.

Dallas BBQ ❀ ✗ except for large parties **$**
132 Second Avenue at 8th Street, 777-5574
21 University Place at 8th Street, 674-4450
132 West 43rd Street between Broadway and Sixth Avenue, 221-9000
27 West 72nd Street between Columbus Avenue and Central Park West, 873-2004
1265 Third Avenue at 73rd Street, 772-9393
3956 Broadway at 166th Street, 568-3700
This chain offer huge portions of popular barbeque selections. Kids love the oversized non-alcoholic frozen drinks. Be prepared for a wait during prime-time dining hours.

Duke's ❀ ✗ except for parties of 6+ **$**
99 East 19th Street between Park Avenue South and Irving Place, 260-2922
The whole family can enjoy large portions of Southern barbeque plus family friendly service in this down-home spot. Family-size platters are available for some house specialties.

E.A.T. **$$$**
1064 Madison Avenue between 80th and 81st Streets, 772-0022
This tony, pricey Upper East Side café is frequented for breakfast and lunch by well-heeled mommies and kids and by the whole family for weekend brunch and lunch.

EJ's Luncheonette ❖ ❀ ✗ **$**
432 Sixth Avenue between 9th and 10th Streets, 473-5555
1271 Third Avenue at 73rd Street, 472-0600
477 Amsterdam Avenue between 81st and 82nd Streets, 873-3444
Quintessential retro American diner with some gourmet modifications of the conventional formula. Portions are large, and yummy breakfast fare is served all day. Steel yourself for a huge line on weekends.

Elephant and Castle ✗ $$
68 Greenwich Avenue between Seventh Avenue South and 11th Street, 243-1400

With a bohemian pub-like feeling, this Village institution offers reliable burgers, omelettes, crepes, salads and pastas. Don't miss the famed Boston Indian pudding (a sweet cornmeal-and-molasses confection).

Ellen's Stardust Diner ❀ ✗ except for parties of 8+ $
1650 Broadway at 51st Street, 956-5151

This 1950s retro diner boasts singing waiters, nostalgic memorabilia and a video screen on which '50's movies and black-and-white televisions show classic reruns.

Empire Diner ✗ $
210 Tenth Avenue at 22nd Street, 243-2736

This Art Deco 24-hour diner is popular with the late-night crowd but attracts Chelsea families at mealtime. It features lots of diner favorites, such as scrambled eggs, grilled cheese and burgers. In nicer weather, the large outdoor eating area gives kids a chance to spread their wings a bit.

Ernie's ❀ $$$
2150 Broadway between 75th and 76th Streets, 496-1588

Big portions and a family-friendly atmosphere make this huge, cavernous and noisy Italian Upper West Side eatery a hit with parents. Check out the garden room in the back.

ESPN Zone ❀✗ $$$
1472 Broadway at 42nd Street, 921-3776

Sports, sports and more sports is what's cooking at this Times Square themed restaurant. Expect a standard bar-and-grill menu with a healthy portion of sports entertainment, including scoreboards, giant TV monitors and an amazing assortment of sports-oriented interactive games on the top floor. Get your pager and play games upstairs while waiting for your table.

Fanelli's ✗ $
94 Prince Street at Mercer Street, 226-9412

It is said that in 1847 a grocery store opened on this site, and that grocery store quickly became the watering hole purchased in 1922 by Michael Fanelli that today claims to be the second-oldest drinking spot in the city. Filled with 19th-century atmosphere and serving simple pub cuisine, it is certainly a change of pace in otherwise trendy SoHo.

Florent ❖ ❀ $$
69 Gansevoort Street between Greenwich and Washington Streets, 989-5779

This very cool French bistro in the Meatpacking District is popular with the late-night club crowd, but during the day and for early dinners, it is surprisingly kid-friendly.

Fraunces Tavern   **$$$**
54 Pearl Street at Broad Street, 968-1776
This recently renovated and reopened landmark (which is part of the
Fraunces Tavern Museum) is where George Washington said farewell to his
officers in 1793. It offers a combination of traditional American fare and
more modern dishes.

Friend of a Farmer   ✗ **$$**
77 Irving Place between 18th and 19th Streets, 477-2188
Off Gramercy Park, this rustic eatery serves up fresh-baked muffins for
breakfast and hefty portions of traditional American standards for lunch
and dinner.

Gabriela's   ❀ **$$**
311 Amsterdam Avenue at 75th Street, 875-8532
685 Amsterdam Avenue at 93rd Street, 961-0574
Both branches of this popular Upper West Side restaurant offer a variety of
delicious Mexican appetizers, entrées and salads in a festive, cantina-style
setting.

Golden Unicorn   ✗ on weekends **$$**
18 East Broadway at Catherine Street, 941-0911
Dim Sum, Hong Kong style, is served here. Typically crowded and located
up three flights of stairs, this spot is better suited for older kids. The metal
carts ferrying tiny portions of a variety of foods will fascinate kids.

Good Enough To Eat   ❀ **$$**
483 Amsterdam Avenue between 83rd and 84th Streets, 496-0163
This country-style eatery, featuring omelettes, salads, soups, breakfast fare
and homemade biscuits, is popular among West Side mommies for break-
fast and lunch with the kids. Be prepared for long lines on weekends.

Googie's Italian Diner   ❀ ✗ **$$**
1491 Second Avenue at 78th Street, 717-1122
This popular Upper East Side spot offers up standard diner fare (don't miss
the shoestring fries), fountain favorites and hearty Italian staples.

Hard Rock Café   ❀ ✗ **$$**
Reservations for large groups only (but visit www.hardrock.com to secure a
    place in line)
221 West 57th Street between Broadway and Seventh Avenue, 489-6565
A 40-foot guitar-shaped bar, rock 'n' roll memorabilia and a gift shop make
this a hot spot for tourists. As with most of the themed restaurants, there
can be long waits. Best known for burgers.

Haru   **$$$**
205 West 43rd Street between Broadway and Eighth Avenue, 398-9810
280 Park Avenue on 48th Street between Park and Madison Avenues,
   490-9680
1327 Third Avenue at 76th Street, 452-1028
1329 Third Avenue at 76th Street, 452-2230
433 Amsterdam Avenue between 80th and 81st Streets, 579-5655
You can rely on these stylish sushi restaurants to provide high quality and tasty Japanese fare. If your kids will sample the raw stuff, there is much from which to choose, and if not, there are standbys like tempura and teriyaki to keep them busy while you have a great meal.

Il Cortile   **$$$**
125 Mulberry Street between Canal and Hester Streets, 226-6060
This Little Italy spot is known for its fine Italian food. Dining in the Garden Room feels like an al fresco experience.

Il Vagabondo   ✗ except for parties of 10+   **$$$**
351 East 62nd Street between First and Second Avenues, 832-9221
Traditional Italian cuisine is served up with a little bocce at this casual neighborhood spot. An indoor bocce court (players must be 18+) provides the entertainment.

Island Burgers and Shakes   ❖ ✗   **$**
766 Ninth Avenue between 51st and 52nd Streets, 307-7934
As the name suggests, this neighborhood spot serves delicious milk shakes and a huge variety (40+) of burgers, chicken sandwiches and sides (but no fries!!).

Jackson Hole   ❀ ✗ except for large parties   **$**
521 Third Avenue at 35th Street, 679-3264
232 East 64th Street between Second and Third Avenues, 371-7187
1611 Second Avenue between 83rd and 84th Streets, 737-8788
517 Columbus Avenue at 85th Street, 362-5177
1270 Madison Avenue at 91st Street, 427-2820
This popular chain serves gigantic burgers with all the fixin's.

Jekyll & Hyde Club   ❀ ✗ except for parties of 10+   **$$**
91 Seventh Avenue South between Barrow and West 4th Streets,
   989-7701 (Pub)
1409 Sixth Avenue between 57th and 58th Streets, 541-9517
"Eccentric explorers and mad scientists" and children are mesmerized by the spooky surroundings (body parts and weapons) and special effects at this themed restaurant offering American fare. Be prepared for long waits. Not appropriate for preschoolers.

Jerry's **$$**
101 Prince Street between Greene and Mercer Streets, 966-9464
A hangout for local artists, this upscale diner features high-end comfort food in a happening atmosphere with a menu that will not break the bank.

Johnny Rockets **❀ ✗ $**
42 East 8th Street between Greene Street and University Place, 253-8175
The Manhattan outpost of this chain of retro '50s soda shops offers burgers, shakes, fries and other diner staples.

John's of 12th Street **❖ $$**
302 East 12th Street between First and Second Avenues, 475-9531
This is the place for an old-fashioned Italian meal in a casual setting, featuring huge plates of pasta and unforgettable garlic bread. Although there is not a kids' menu, they are happy to offer kid-sized portions.

John's Pizzeria ❖ at Bleecker Street location; ✗ except for parties of 15+ **$**
278 Bleecker Street at Great Jones Street, 243-1680
260 West 44th Street between Broadway and Eighth Avenue, 391-7560
408 East 64th Street between First and York Avenues, 935-2895
You may have to order a whole pie, but you'll eat every last piece of the delicious thin-crust brick-oven pizza.

Katz's Delicatessen **$**
205 East Hudson Street at Ludlow Street, 254-2246
Some favorites on the regular menu include knishes, hot dogs and sandwiches. This Lower East Side institution (in business since 1888) is famed for its gigantic sandwiches, all beef hot dogs and other deli favorites. Fans of the movie *When Harry Met Sally* will recognize Katz's as the site of the memorable deli scene. The place is packed and service is cafeteria style, so it is best to avoid peak hours.

Kelly and Ping **✗ $$**
127 Greene Street between Houston and Prince Streets, 228-1212
This pan-Asian noodle shop also features dumplings, stir fry, spring rolls and other appetizers that will interest young diners. This cafeteria-style, very popular SoHo spot can get quite busy. Kids might enjoy perusing the Asian groceries for sale in the shop.

Kitchenette ✗ except for large parties (uptown only) **$$**
80 West Broadway at Warren Street, 267-6740
1272 Amsterdam Avenue between 122nd and 123rd Streets, 531-7600
Both the Tribeca and uptown locations offer old-fashioned home cooking and yummy desserts in a country-style environment. The downtown location is not open for dinner

La Caridad Luncheonette ❖ ✗ $
2199 Broadway at 78th Street, 874-2780
The Cuban–Chinese cuisine at this very casual Upper West Side spot is popular with families looking for a quick, inexpensive, but filling, meal.

La Cocina $$
430 Third Avenue at 30th Street, 532-1887
762 Eighth Avenue between 46th and 47th Streets, 730-1860
217 West 85th Street between Amsterdam Avenue and Broadway, 874-0770
2608 Broadway between 98th and 99th Streets, 865-7333
Here you'll find no thrills, just plain good food. This Mexican restaurant chain is popular with local families.

Lombardi's ❖ ✗ $$
32 Spring Street between Mott and Mulberry Streets, 941-7994
This popular, crowded, downtown spot is famed for its super-thin crust, brick-oven pizza.

Mangia e Bevi $$$
800 Ninth Avenue at 53rd Street, 956-3976
Spontaneous celebrating (singing waiters and tambourines all around) is part of the deal at this Southern Italian restaurant featuring home-made pasta and brick-oven pizza, located in the heart of Hell's Kitchen. That's amore!

Manhattan Chili Company ❀ $$
1500 Broadway at 43rd Street, 730-8666
1697 Broadway between 53rd and 54th Streets, 246-6555
These restaurants feature 11 types of chili as well as other hearty southwestern fare. Three-dimensional cartoon art adorns the walls, and a TV at the bar features the Cartoon Network.

Mars 2112 ❀ ✗ except for parties of 20+ $$$
1633 Broadway at 51st Street, 582-2112, www.mars2112.com
Enter this "interactive dining experience based on a virtual journey to, and exploration of, the planet Mars" via a Journey to Mars (a simulated space ride for all patrons age 3 years and up). American standards are served by Martians, and diners are surrounded by spacey special effects. The kids will love the interactive game room and Martian gift shop.

Mary Ann's   ❀ **$$**
107 West Broadway at Reade Street, 766-0911
80 Second Avenue at 5th Street, 475-5939
116 Eighth Avenue at 16th Street, 633-0877
1503 Second Avenue between 78th and 79th Streets, 249-6165
2454 Broadway at 91st Street, 877-0132
1803 Second Avenue at 93rd Street, 426-8350
This popular Mexican chain offers large portions of reliable, tasty fare.
Some of the locations have outdoor dining.

Mezzaluna   Amex or cash only **$$**
1295 Third Avenue between 74th and 75th Streets, 535-9600
This sophisticated Italian caffe featuring brick-oven pizza and homemade
pasta is a good spot for a casual, Upper East Side meal.

Mickey Mantle's   ❀ **$$**
42 Central Park South between Fifth and Sixth Avenues, 688-7777
Baseball fans will have a ball at this themed restaurant that serves Ameri-
can standards while featuring Mickey Mantle memorabilia, big TVs and
lots of baseball.

Miss Elle's Homesick Bar & Grill   **$$**
226 West 79th Street between Broadway and Amsterdam Avenue,
   595-4350
This American grill offering old-fashioned comfort food (kids will go for
the mac and cheese) has a special closet with toys to keep tots busy while
the adults in the party enjoy their meals.

Miss Rita's   Amex or cash only **$$**
Pier 60, Chelsea Piers, 604-0441
Located in the heart of Chelsea Piers, this good old-fashioned American
diner has a fun country-western–themed spin.

Monsoon   **$$$**
435 Amsterdam Avenue at 81st Street, 580-8686
This popular Upper West Side upscale Vietnamese restaurant offers an
extensive selection of authentic cuisine. Picky kids will enjoy the grilled
skewered meats and spring rolls.

New York Noodle Town   **$$**
28 1/2 Bowery at Bayard Street, 349-0923
This Chinatown noodle shop offers noodles your way—wet (in broth) or
dry (pan-fried or stir fried). Kids will enjoy seeing the display of meats and
poultry hanging in the window.

NoHo Star   X **$$**
330 Lafayette Street at Bleecker Street , 925-0070

The postmodern decor and friendly service make this an easy spot for downtown dining, featuring a mix of American (including a great burger and fries) and Chinese cuisines. Weekend brunch is a popular meal here. Though there is no kid's menu, small portions and grilled cheese sandwiches are available for children.

Odeon ❀ $$$
145 West Broadway between Duane and Thomas Streets, 233-0507
This French bistro with a wonderful Art Deco setting has been a downtown fixture for two decades. A very New York scene that, despite its cool clientele, makes room for the ever-increasing number of hipsters that travel in the family circle. Kids will enjoy the steak frites, burgers and roast free-range chicken.

Ollie's Noodle Shop & Grill ✗ $
200B West 44th Street between Broadway and Eighth Avenue, 921-5988
1991 Broadway between 67th and 68th Streets, 595-8181
2315 Broadway at 84th Street, 362-3712
2957 Broadway at 116th Street, 932-3300
Ollie's is a chain of Chinese eateries noted less for service than for its extensive offering of Cantonese, Mandarin and Szechwan dishes.

Patsy's Pizza ❖ ✗ $
67 University Place between 10th and 11th Streets, 533-3500
509 Third Avenue between 34th and 35th Streets, 689-7500
206 East 60th Street between Second and Third Avenues, 688-9707
1312 Second Avenue at 69th Street, 639-1000
61 West 74th Street between Central Park West and Columbus Avenue, 579-3000
2287-91 First Avenue between 117th and 118th Streets, 534-9783
Known for its delicious thin-crust pizza, Patsy's also serves up soups, salads, pasta and other dishes. The original location on First Avenue has been in business since the 1930s.

Peanut Butter & Co. $
240 Sullivan Street between Bleecker and West 3rd Streets, 677-3995
The whole menu at this tiny café is kid friendly, providing that the kid loves peanut butter. Freshly ground peanut butter provides the nuts and bolts of this sandwich emporium, which also does offer a few non–peanut-butter choices.

Petaluma $$$
1356 First Avenue at 73rd Street, 772-8800
Locals bring kids to dine on classic upscale Italian cuisine (including thin-crust pizza) in a relaxed environment with a bit of Upper East Side formality. Service is accommodating to families.

Pig Heaven $$
1540 Second Avenue between 80th and 81st Streets, 744-4333
This very hospitable Upper East Side Chinese institution features pork spe-
cialties, but there are plenty of other good non-pork dishes from which to
choose.

Pink Teacup   ❖ ✗ $$
42 Grove Street just west of Bleecker Street, 807-6755
Located in Greenwich Village, this tiny eatery serves up huge portions of
southern soul food. Be prepared for a crowd at weekend brunch.

Pintaille's Pizza   ✗ $$
1237 Second Avenue between 64th and 65th Streets, 752-6222
1443 York Avenue between 76th and 77th Streets, 717-4990
1577 York Avenue between 83rd and 84th Streets, 396-3479
26 East 91st Street between Fifth and Madison Avenues, 722-1967
This is a popular Upper East Side spot for thin-crust pizza with a variety of
gourmet toppings.

Pizzeria Uno   ❀ ✗ $$
89 South Street, South Street Seaport, 791-7999
391 Sixth Avenue between 8th Street and Waverly Place, 242-5230
55 Third Avenue between 10th and 11th Streets, 995-9668
432 Columbus Avenue at 81st Street, 595-4700
220 East 86th Street between Second and Third Avenues, 472-5656
Not an exclusive New York spot, but nonetheless this pizzeria chain, which
features both deep-dish and thin-crust pizza as well as pasta dishes and
main courses, bends over backwards for families.

Planet Hollywood   ❀ ✗ $$
1540 Broadway at 45th Street, 840-8326
The New York outpost of this international chain offering American stan-
dards is loaded with Hollywood memorabilia and a gift shop.

Popover Café   ❀ ✗ $$
551 Amsterdam Avenue between 86th and 87th Streets, 595-8555
This popular Upper West Side spot offers lots of comfort food, salads, burgers and many varieties of egg dishes in a cozy atmosphere (populated by a
serious assortment of teddy bears). Make sure to order a popover with
strawberry butter.

Rain $$
100 West 82nd Street at Columbus Avenue, 501-0776
1059 Third Avenue between 62nd and 63rd Streets, 223-3669
Tasty Pan-Asian cuisine is served in an exotic environment. Kids will enjoy
the chicken on skewers, steak and noodle dishes.

The Rock Center Café   ❀ **$$$**
20 West 50th Street between Fifth and Sixth Avenues, Rockefeller Center,
   332-7620
Enjoy fine creative cuisine as you watch the skaters glide past in winter,
and enjoy outdoor dining in summer in the heart of Rockefeller Center.

Rosa Mexicano   **$$$**
1063 First Avenue at 58th Street, 753-7407
61 Columbus Avenue at 62nd Street, 977-7700
Not your standard cantina, this very upscale Mexican restaurant is for the
more sophisticated palette (that is, older children). The guacamole (made
tableside) is renowned and the food is high quality. The Upper West Side
location is a postmodern fantasy complete with a wall of falling water. This
hip spot gets very busy. Better to go early and make reservations when dining as a family.

Ruby Foo's   ❀ **$$$**
1626 Broadway at 49th Street, 489-5600
2182 Broadway at 77th Street, 724-6700
These huge pan-Asian restaurants are decorated in tongue-in-cheek kitsch,
but the food is good, featuring everything from sushi to dumplings to Thai
specialties to dramatically presented desserts.

Saigon Grill   ✗ **$$**
1700 Second Avenue at 88th Street, 996-4600
620 Amsterdam at 90th Street, 875-9072
These restaurants are popular neighborhood destinations for reasonably
priced Vietnamese cuisine.

Sarabeth's   ✗ except for dinner **$$$**
Chelsea Market, 75 Ninth Avenue between 15th and 16th Streets,
   989-2424 (bakery)
Whitney Museum, 945 Madison Avenue at 75th Street, 570-3670
   (no dinner)
423 Amsterdam Avenue between 80th and 81st Streets, 496-6280
Hotel Wales, 1295 Madison Avenue at 92nd Street, 410-7335
Upscale home-style cooking is what you'll find at these charming eateries.
The Upper West Side and Hotel Wales locations are popular breakfast and
lunch spots for mommies and kids. Pancakes, eggs, sandwiches, salads,
fresh baked goods and homemade jams are among the wholesome goodies
to be sampled during the day. There can be a long wait for Sarabeth's deli-
cious fare at peak times.

Second Avenue Kosher Deli   ✗ **$$**
156 Second Avenue at 10th Street, 677-0606
This classic kosher (meat) deli offering such favorites as matzoh-ball soup,
chopped liver and overstuffed sandwiches along with lots of attitude is a
total Lower East Side experience.

Serafina ✗ except for large parties $$$
393 Lafayette Street at 4th Street, 995-9595
29 East 61st Street between Madison and Park Avenues, 702-9898
1022 Madison Avenue at 79th Street, 734-2676
While the menu features light Italian fare, the kids will love the thin-crust brick-oven gourmet pizzas and the pasta dishes at these very sophisticated, upscale, trendy, popular, bright, cheerfully decorated restaurants.

Serendipity 3 $$
225 East 60th Street between Second and Third Avenues, 838-3531
This New York institution has a large menu of American standards (kids particularly like the foot-long hot dogs), but the real attractions are the huge desserts, including the famed Frozen Hot Chocolate. Lines are long and kids tend to get waylaid at the toy and gift shop in the front of the restaurant.

79th Street Boat Basin Café ❀ ✗ $
West 79th Street at the Hudson River in Riverside Park, 496-5542
Open May through October (in October, weekends only, weather permitting), this open-air structure makes for a lovely outdoor café overlooking the Hudson. Casual setting and a view of the houseboat marina can make for relaxed family dining. The menu includes grilled seafood, burgers, seasonal salads and sandwiches. Sandwiches on white bread (including PB & J) and hot dogs are available for the kids.

Shun Lee $$$
155 East 55th Street between Lexington and Third Avenues, 371-8844
43 West 65th Street between Central Park West and Columbus Avenue,
    595-8895
These glamorous high-end restaurants offer gourmet Chinese cuisine in an elegant environment. The West Side location is great for a pre-theater dinner before a Lincoln Center performance.

Stage Deli ❀ ✗ except for parties of 10+ $
834 Seventh Avenue between 53rd and 54th Streets, 245-7850
1481 Second Avenue at 77th Street, 439-9989
This restaurant offers the quintessential New York deli experience, complete with menu items named after celebs. It is known for its overstuffed sandwiches and career wait-staff.

Tavern on the Green ❀ $$$
Central Park West at 67th Street (inside Central Park), 873-3200
www.tavernonthegreen.com (see menus and make reservations)
A popular tourist destination offering American fare, this spot looks festive year round with decorative lights illuminating the grounds. Although geared more for celebrating adults, Tavern on the Green frequently offers festive events and special offers for families with children, particularly on holidays.

T.G.I. Friday's   ✿ ✗ $$
47 Broadway at Exchange Place, 483-8322
47 East 42nd Street between Madison and Vanderbilt Avenues, 681-8458
1552 Broadway at 46th Street, 944-7352
604 Fifth Avenue between 48th and 49th Streets, 767-8335
761 Seventh Avenue at 50th Street, 767-8350
1680 Broadway at 53rd Street, 767-8326
This franchise restaurant, popular among tourists, is a reliable destination
for a kid-friendly atmosphere.

Tennessee Mountain   ✿ $$
143 Spring Street at Wooster Street, 431-3993
This SoHo barbeque restaurant, done in a farmhouse motif, is popular with
families. For little ones there are hats to color and crayons.

Time Café   ✗ $$
380 Lafayette Street at East 4th Street, 533-7000
2330 Broadway at 85th Street, 579-5100
This popular spot offers contemporary American fare as well as pasta, pizzas and "coffee shop" standards such as burgers and salads. Both locations
offer outdoor seating (weather permitting), which makes for fun people
watching.

Tony di Napoli $$
147 West 43rd Street between Sixth Avenue and Broadway, 221-0100
1606 Second Avenue between 83rd and 84th Streets, 861-8686
This Southern Italian eatery, offering huge portions of pasta and other
dishes served family style, is frequented by families. The Upper East Side
location is a popular neighborhood spot for celebrating birthdays with its
signature chocolate decadence dessert.

Tortilla Flats   ✿ $$
767 Washington Street at 12th Street, 243-1053
Though best known as a watering hole for a young, single crowd, this Tex-
Mex cantina caters to families before the singles arrive.

Totonno's Pizzeria Napolitano $$
1544 Second Avenue between 80th and 81st Street, 327-2800
1524 Neptune Avenue between West 15th Street and West 16th Streets,
    Coney Island, Brooklyn, 718 372-8606
Totonno's has been offering its legendary thin-crust pizza at Coney Island
since the 1920s. The Upper East Side location has a full menu.

Tribeca Grill $$$
375 Greenwich Street at Franklin Street, 941-3900
Creative American cuisine is the fare at this cool, casual, downtown and
surprisingly kid-friendly destination co-owned by Robert DeNiro. The food
is good, as is the celebrity-spotting.

Two Boots ❀ ✗ except 37 Avenue A location **$$**
74 Bleecker Street between Broadway and Lafayette Street, 777-1033
37 Avenue A between 2nd and 3rd Streets, 505-2276
42 Avenue A at 3rd Street, 254-1919
201 West 11th Street at Seventh Avenue, 633-9096
Grand Central Terminal, Lower Concourse, 557-7992
30 Rockefeller Center, Lower Concourse, 332-8800
This eatery features pizza with a Cajun twist. Dough is fashioned from cornmeal, and toppings include crawfish and andouille sausage. The name "Two Boots" was inspired by the shapes of Italy and Louisiana. All locations offer various salads and po' boy sandwiches and will make a kid's Face Pizza (small pizza with the toppings used to make a face). The 37 Avenue A location offers a full menu.

V & T Pizzeria-Restaurant ❀ ✗ except for parties of 12+ **$**
1024 Amsterdam Avenue between 110th and 111th Streets, 663-1708
This old-fashioned Italian eatery located near Columbia University is reasonably priced and offers pizza, baked ziti, lasagna and other classic favorites.

Virgil's Real BBQ ❀ **$$**
152 West 44th Street between Sixth Avenue and Broadway, 921-9494
Enjoy down-home authentic barbeque right in Times Square.

Won Jo **$$**
23 West 32nd Street between Broadway and Fifth Avenue, 695-5815
The first floor of this Korean restaurant features a sushi bar. It's the second floor, however, that will entice families. Each table has a built-in grill, allowing patrons to select beef, pork, chicken and other items to be grilled tableside. Other Korean specialties are offered as well.

The World ❀ ✗ **$$$**
1501 Broadway at 43rd Street, 398-2563, www.wwe.com
Wrestling fans won't want to miss this official World Wrestling Entertainment restaurant located within the 'one acre multi-platform entertainment complex' housed within a landmark theater in Times Square. There's plenty of official stuff to buy in the gift shop.

Bagels

Bagelry
1324 Lexington Avenue between 88th and 89th Streets, 996-0567
1380 Madison Avenue at 96th Street, 423-9590

David's Bagels
228 First Avenue between 13th and 14th Streets, 533-8766
331 First Avenue at 19th Street, 780-2308
1651 Second Avenue between 85th and 86th Streets, 439-7887

Ess-a-Bagel
359 First Avenue at 21st Street, 260-2252
831 Third Avenue between 50th and 51st Streets, 980-1010

H & H
639 West 46th at Twelfth Avenue, 765-7200 (24 hours)
2239 Broadway at 80th Street, 595-8003

H & H Midtown East
1551 Second Avenue between 80th and 81st Streets, 717-7312

Murray's Bagels
500 Sixth Avenue at 13th Street, 462-2830
242 Eighth Avenue between 22nd and 23rd Streets, 646 638-1335

Pick-a-Bagel
102 North End Avenue, Battery Park, 786-9200
601 Sixth Avenue between 17th and 18th Streets, 924-4999
297 Third Avenue between 22nd and 23rd Streets, 686-1414
200 West 57th Street at Seventh Avenue, 957-5151
1473 Second Avenue between 76th and 77th Streets, 717-4662
1101 Lexington Avenue at 77th Street, 517-6590

Tal Bagels
977 First Avenue between 53rd and 54th Streets, 753-9080
333 East 86th Street between First and Second Avenues, 427-6811
2446 Broadway between 90th and 91st Streets, 712-0171

Bakeries, Cafés, Ice Cream, Snack Attacks and Take-Out

Alice's Tea Cup $
102 West 73rd Street at Columbus Avenue, 799-3006
This charming, cozy Upper West Side tea salon features an Alice in Wonderland theme.

Amy's Bread $
Chelsea Market, 75 Ninth Avenue between 15th and 16th Streets,
    462-4338
672 Ninth Avenue between 46th and 47th Streets, 977-2670
972 Lexington Avenue between 70th and 71st Streets, 537-0270
This café and takeout shop offers an excellent assortment of delicious sandwiches, soups, breads (including organic breads) and baked goods (including yummy cupcakes). The hot chocolate is a favorite with the kids.

A Salt & Battery $
112 Greenwich Avenue between 12th and 13th Streets, 691-2713
Enjoy fish and chips served wrapped in a London newspaper.

Benfarmeo—The Lemon Ice King of Corona $

52-02 108th Street at 52nd Avenue, Queens, 718 699-5133

If you find yourself in Corona (perhaps visiting the Hall of Science), stop here for authentic homemade Italian ices (a.k.a. water ice).

Buttercup Bakeshop $$

973 Second Avenue between 51st and 52nd Streets, 350-4144

A simple old-fashioned bakeshop known for its delicious buttercream icing, delectable cupcakes, cakes and other goodies.

Café Lalo $$

201 West 83rd Street between Amsterdam Avenue and Broadway, 496-6031

This popular neighborhood café (located just opposite the Children's Museum of Manhattan) offers a variety of pastries and sweets as well as sandwiches and egg dishes.

Caffe Roma $$

385 Broome Street at Mulberry Street, 226-8413

Want a cannoli and hot cocoa? This old-fashioned Little Italy pastry shop with little tables will hit the spot.

Chinatown Ice Cream Factory $

65 Bayard Street between Elizabeth and Mott Streets, 608-4170

Try a scoop of green tea, red-bean, litchi, coconut or mango ice cream.

Ciao Bella $$

285 Mott Street between Houston and Prince Streets, 431-3591
35 Carmine Street between Bedford and Bleecker Streets, 646 230-0558
227 Sullivan Street between Bleecker and West 3rd Streets, 505-7100
27 East 92nd Street at Madison Avenue, 831-5555

Directly from its own factory, Ciao Bella offers rich, delicious authentic gelato in numerous flavors.

Columbus Bakery $$

957 First Avenue between 52nd and 53rd Streets, 421-0334
474 Columbus Avenue between 82nd and 83rd Streets, 724-6880

These café/bakeries are popular breakfast destinations (fresh baked goods, cappuccino and cocoa) for mommies and their kids. Service is cafeteria style, but the food is entirely upscale.

Cosi $$

841 Broadway at 13th Street, 614-8544
3 East 17th Street between Broadway and Fifth Avenue, 414-8468
202 West 36th Street between Seventh and Eighth Avenues, 967-9444
11 West 42nd Street between Fifth and Sixth Avenues, 398-6662
685 Third Avenue between 43rd and 44th Streets, 697-8449

38 East 45th Street between Madison and Vanderbilt Avenues, 949-7400
61 West 48th Street between Fifth and Sixth Avenues, 397-2674
1633 Broadway at 51st Street, 397-9838
165 East 52nd Street between Lexington and Third Avenues, 758-7800
60 East 56th Street between Madison and Park Avenues, 588-1225
This popular gourmet takeout and café creates great sandwiches served on fabulous freshly baked breads as well as other breakfast and lunch fare, in a sleek, cool environment.

Cupcake Café $
522 Ninth Avenue at 39th Street, 465-1530
This spot features cupcakes, muffins, doughnuts, coffeecake and sugar-dusted crullers, soups and quiches. Known for buttercream icing and birthday cake.

DTUT $$
1626 Second Avenue between 84th and 85th Streets, 327-1327
This cool coffee bar decorated with unmatched comfy sofas, chairs and tiny tables offers a variety of sweets as well as some sandwiches. Upper East Side families mix with young singles for the fruit fondue and s'mores.

Dylan's Candy Bar $$
1011 Third Avenue at 60th Street, 646 735-0078
This two-level candy store opened by Dylan Lauren is a candy-lover's dream. You can satisfy your sweet tooth with everything from Pez to M&Ms and pick your own personal favorites from walls of candy choices. Custom orders available.

Emack & Bolio's Ice Cream $
56 Seventh Avenue between 13th and 14th Streets, 727-1198
151 West 34th Street (Macy's Herald Square, 4th Floor), 494-5853
389 Amsterdam Avenue between 78th and 79th Streets, 362-2747
Ice cream and frozen yogurt in more flavors than you can imagine are available at the New York outposts of this Boston-based chain.

F & B $
269 West 23rd Street between Seventh and Eighth Avenues,
    646 486-4441
This is the place for tasty hot dogs with an interesting variety of toppings, twice-fried frites, sweet potato fries and beignets.

Fauchon $$$
442 Park Avenue at 56th Street, 308-5919
1000 Madison Avenue between 77th and 78th Streets, 570-2211
Have a taste of Paris in New York. Fauchon is the perfect spot for a fancy high tea or delicious French pastries.

Ferrara Pasticceria $$
195 Grand Street between Mott and Mulberry Streets, 226-6150
363 Madison Avenue between 45th and 46th Streets, 599-7800
This venerable Italian pastry shop (in business since the 1890s) is dessert heaven, offering everything from the basics to gelato and tiramisu.

Gray's Papaya $
402 Sixth Avenue at 8th Street, 260-3532
539 Eighth Avenue at 37th Street, 904-1588
2090 Broadway at 72nd Street, 799-0243
Try Gray's notable hot dogs and secret formula papaya and other fruit juices.

Krispy Kreme Doughnuts $
265 West 23rd Street between Seventh and Eighth Avenues, 620-0111
2 Penn Plaza, 33rd Street on the Amtrak level, 947-7175
625 Eighth Avenue between 40th and 41st Streets, Port Authority
   (no phone)
141 West 72nd Street between Columbus and Amsterdam Avenues,
   724-1100
1497 Third Avenue between 84th and 85th Streets, 879-9111
These famous doughnuts deserve their reputation as the tastiest ones around.

Mangia $$
40 Wall Street between Broad and William Streets, 425-4040
16 East 48th Street between Madison and Fifth Avenues, 754-0637
50 West 57th Street between Fifth and Sixth Avenues, 582-5882
This gourmet takeout and café offers terrific soups, sandwiches, salads and other Mediterranean-inspired fare with a good assortment of freshly baked cookies and other goodies.

Nathan's Famous $
1310 Surf Avenue at Stillwell Avenue, Coney Island, Brooklyn, 718 946-2202
This well-known establishment serves its famed hot dogs plus. Enough said!

Papaya King $
179 East 86th Street at Third Avenue, 369-0648
121 West 125th Street between Lenox and Seventh Avenues, 665-5732
Try the notable hot dogs and secret formula papaya and other fruit juices.

Payard Patisserie and Bistro $$$
1032 Lexington Avenue between 73rd and 74th Streets, 717-5252
While the main dining area offers French bistro cuisine and is not especially geared to kids, the junior members of your group will love to feast on the French pastries in the patisserie.

T Salon and T Emporium $$
11 East 20th Street between Fifth Avenue and Broadway, 358-0506

Not your typical high tea, but it's a wonderful location for an afternoon cup of tea with lots of atmosphere. Ideal for teen girls.

Two Little Red Hens $$
1652 Second Avenue between 85th and 86th Streets, 452-0476
The Manhattan outpost of this Park Slope shop offers an excellent selection of cakes, pies, tarts, cookies and cupcakes (including the Brooklyn Blackout, loaded with pudding).

Veniero's Pasticceria and Caffe $$
342 East 11th Street between First and Second Avenues, 674-7070
A long line will surely be between you and the dessert goodies at this café, which has been specializing in Italian pastry since the 1890s.

White Castle $
325 Fifth Avenue between 32nd and 33rd Streets, 718 899-8404
525 Eighth Avenue at 36th Street, 718 899-8404
You've heard about those square burgers (Slyders). If the kids have never tried them, they will get a kick out of this fast-food institution.

Yonah Schimmel's Knishery $$
137 East Hudson Street between First and Second Avenues, 477-2858
What began a century ago as a pushcart stand is now a Lower East Side institution offering renowned knishes and potato pancakes.

Kosher restaurants

Abigael's on Broadway $$$
1407 Broadway between 38th and 39th Streets, 575-1407
Kosher haute cuisine (meat).

Darna $$
600 Columbus Avenue at 89th Street, 721-9123
A family restaurant serving Moroccan specialties (meat).

Haikara Grill $$$
1016 Second Avenue between 53rd and 54th Streets, 355-7000
Kosher sushi and more.

Il Patrizio $$
206 East 63rd Street between Second and Third Avenues, 980-4007
Roman style Italian fare (dairy).

Kosher Delight $
1365 Broadway between 36th and 37th Streets, 563-3366
10 West 46th Street between Fifth and Sixth Avenues, 869-6699
Basics including burgers and grilled chicken sandwiches plus Middle Eastern and Chinese dishes.

Le Marais $$$
150 West 46th Street between Sixth and Seventh Avenues, 869-0900
French cuisine in the theater district (meat).

Levana $$$
141 West 69th Street between Columbus Avenue and Broadway,
    877-8457
Stylish meat restaurant.

Pastrami Queen $$
1269 Lexington Avenue between 85th and 86th Streets, 828-0007
Old-fashioned deli fare (meat).

The Prime Grill $$$
60 East 49th Street between Madison and Park Avenues, 692-9292
Old-fashioned steakhouse known for large portions.

Second Avenue Deli, see above

Va Bene $$$
1589 Second Avenue between 82nd and 83rd Streets, 517-4448
High-end Italian food (dairy).

Markets

Agata & Valentina
1505 First Avenue at 79th Street, 452-0690
This Upper East Side market offers an incredible selection of fresh meat,
prepared foods, breads, cheeses and gourmet items.

Balducci's
424 Sixth Avenue at 9th Street, 673-2600
155A West 66th Street between Amsterdam Avenue and Broadway,
    653-8320
Though no longer a family business, this market still offers premium pro-
duce, prepared foods, breads, desserts and delectable gourmet items.

Citarella
2135 Broadway at 75th Street, 874-0383
1313 Third Avenue at 75th Street, 874-0383

With an incredible selection of fresh meat, fish, prepared food, produce, breads, desserts and gourmet items, this is a perfect stop for creating your own meal.

Dean & Deluca
560 Broadway at Prince Street, 431-1691
This famed gourmet market offers an amazing array of high-end gourmet items, prepared foods, breads, desserts and premium produce. Be prepared for sticker shock.

Eli's
1411 Third Avenue at 80th Street, 717-8100
431 East 91st Street between First and York Avenues, 987-0885 (Vinegar Factory)
These huge emporia are filled with fresh meat, fish, premium produce (much of it organic), prepared food, breads, desserts and other high-end grocery and gourmet items. The Vinegar Factory's upstairs restaurant has a popular weekend brunch. The 80th Street store also has a restaurant.

Fairway
2127 Broadway at 74th Street, 595-1888
2328 Twelfth Avenue between 132nd and 133rd Streets, 234-3883
These huge markets offer an enormous range of produce, prepared foods, gourmet items, organic products, breads, desserts and groceries at surprisingly value prices. The Upper West Side location has a juice bar. The upper Manhattan location, which offers a fun shopping experience, has free parking.

Gourmet Garage
453 Broome Street at Mercer Street, 941-5850
301 East 64th Street between First and Second Avenues, 535-6271
2567 Broadway between 96th and 97th Streets, 663-0656
These markets offers fantastic produce (especially hard-to-find items), prepared food, breads, desserts, grocery and gourmet items at refreshingly decent prices.

Grace's Marketplace
1237 Third Avenue at 71st Street, 737-0600
Serving the Upper East Side, this shop offers high-end (i.e., expensive) produce, fresh meat and fish, prepared food, breads, desserts, grocery and gourmet items.

Jefferson Market
450 Sixth Avenue between 10th and 11th Streets, 533-3377
This family-owned store has been offering premium fresh meats, produce, prepared foods, grocery and gourmet items for more than 75 years.

Union Square Greenmarket

This open-air market, at which local and regional farmers sell their wares (organic produce, cheeses, jams, breads), operates in Union Square on Mondays, Wednesdays, Fridays and Saturdays from 8 a.m. to 6 p.m. Cash only. See www.cenyc.org for other greenmarket locations.

Whole Foods
250 Seventh Avenue at 24th Street, 924-5969

This huge mega supermarket outpost of the Texas-based chain offers all-natural, healthy products in all categories.

Zabars
2245 Broadway at 80th Street, 787-2000

This Upper West Side institution is the place to go for smoked fish, prepared foods, cheeses, breads, desserts, gourmet items and specialty products. Visit the upper level for an incredible selection of cooking supplies and household wares.

RESOURCES

References Books

Manners

Barnes, Bob, and Emilie Barnes. *A Little Book of Manners for Boys* (Harvest House Publishers, 2000). Most appropriate for ages 9–12.

Barnes, Emilie. *A Little Book of Manners: Etiquette for Young Ladies* (Harvest House, 1998). Most appropriate for ages 4–8.

Hoving, Walter. *Tiffany's Table Manners for Teenagers* (Random House, 1989). Most appropriate for young adults.

Samuel, Catherine, and Maggie Swanson. *Elmo's Good Manners Game* (Sesame Street) (CTW Books, 1999). Most appropriate for preschool children.

Restaurant guides

The New York Times Guide to New York City Restaurants (New York Times, 2002)

Time Out New York Eating and Drinking Guide (Time Out New York, 2003), updated annually

Zagat Survey – New York City Restaurants. An annual compilation of surveys completed by local restaurant "consumers," this guide to one of the world's most dynamic and varied restaurant scenes provides valuable information on dining options. Available in bookstores and specialty shops or by calling 800 333-3421.

Web Sites

www.allny.com

www.citidex.com

www.cityguideny.com

www.citysearch.com

www.cuisinenet.com

www.dailycandy.com

www.digitalcity.com

www.go-newyorkcity.com

www.kerrymenu.com

www.metronewyork.com

www.nyc.com

www.nyctourism.com

www.nycvisit.com

www.nytimes.com

www.nytoday.com

www.timeoutny.com

www.zagat.com

RESTAURANT INDEX

Neighborhood Locator

es	East Side, East 23rd Street through and including East 60th Street
lm	Lower Manhattan, below 23rd Street
ues	Upper East Side, East 61st Street up to 110th Street
um	Upper Manhattan, 110th Street and above
uws	Upper West Side, West 61st Street up to 110th Street, including Central Park
ws	West Side, West 23rd Street through and including West 60th Street
bklyn	Brooklyn
qns	Queens

American

America **lm**

Barking Dog Luncheonette **ues**

The Boathouse in Central Park **uws**

Bryant Park Café **ws**

Bubby's **lm**

Chat 'N Chew **lm**

City Hall **lm**

Elephant and Castle **lm**

Fanelli's **lm**

Fraunces Tavern **lm**

Friend of a Farmer **lm**

Island Burgers and Shakes **ws**

Jackson Hole **es, ues, uws**

Kitchenette **lm, um**

Miss Elle's Homesick Bar & Grill **uws**

NoHo Star **lm**

Popover Café **uws**

The Prime Grill **es**

The Rock Center Café **ws**

Serendipity 3 **es**

79th Street Boat Basin Café **uws**

Tavern on the Green **uws**

T.G.I. Friday's **es, lm, ws**

Time Café **lm, uws**

Tribeca Grill **lm**

Asian

Benihana of Tokyo **es, ws**

China Fun **ues, uws, ws**

Golden Unicorn **lm**

Haikara Grill **es**

Haru **es, ues, uws, ws**
Kelly and Ping **lm**
Kosher Delight **ws**
La Caridad Luncheonette **uws**
Monsoon **uws**
New York Noodle Town **lm**
NoHo Star **lm**
Ollie's Noodle Shop & Grill **um, uws, ws**
Pig Heaven **ues**
Rain **ues, uws**
Ruby Foo's **uws, ws**
Saigon Grill **ues, uws**
Shun Lee **es, uws**
Won Jo **ws**

Bagels
Bagelry **ues**
David's Bagels **lm, ues**
Ess-a-Bagel **es, lm**
H & H **ws, uws**
H & H Midtown East **ues**
Murray's Bagels **lm**
Pick-a-Bagel **lm, ues, ws**
Tal Bagels **es, ues, uws**

*Bakeries, Cafés, Ice Cream, Snack Attacks
   and Take-Out*
Alice's Tea Cup **uws**
Amy's Bread **lm, ues, ws**
A Salt & Battery **lm**
Benfarmeo—The Lemon Ice King of
   Corona **qns**
Buttercup Bakeshop **es**
Café Lalo **uws**
Caffe Roma **lm**
Chinatown Ice Cream Factory **lm**
Ciao Bella **lm, ues**
Columbus Bakery **es, uws**
Cosi **es, lm, ws**
Cupcake Café **ws**
DTUT **ues**
Dylan's Candy Bar **es**
Emack & Bolio's Ice Cream **lm, uws, ws**
F & B **ws**
Fauchon **es, ues**
Ferrara Pasticceria **es, lm**
Gray's Papaya **lm, uws, ws**
Krispy Kreme Doughnuts **ues, uws, ws**
Mangia **es, lm, ws**
Nathan's Famous **bklyn**
Papaya King **ues, um**
Payard Patisserie and Bistro **ues**

T Salon and T Emporium **lm**
Two Little Red Hens **ues**
Veniero's Pasticceria and Caffe **lm**
White Castle **es, ws**
Yonah Schimmel's Knishery **lm**

Barbeque
Brother Jimmy's BBQ **ues, uws**
Cowgirl Hall of Fame **lm**
Dallas BBQ **lm, ues, um, uws, ws**
Duke's **lm**
Tennessee Mountain **lm**
Virgil's Real BBQ **ws**

Brazilian
Churrascaria Plataforma **ws**
Coffee Shop **lm**

Breakfast
Annie's **ues**
Barney Greengrass—the Sturgeon King
   uws
Bubby's **lm**
Cupping Room Café **lm**
E.A.T. **ues**
Friend of a Farmer **lm**
Good Enough To Eat **uws**
Sarabeth's **lm, ues, uws**

Delis
Artie's Delicatessen **uws**
Carnegie Deli **ws**
Katz's Delicatessen **lm**
Pastrami Queen **ues**
Second Avenue Kosher Deli **lm**
Stage Deli **ues, ws**

Diners
Bendix Diner **lm**
Brooklyn Diner **ws**
Café Edison **ws**
Coffee Shop **lm**
Comfort Diner **es, ues**
EJ's Luncheonette **lm, ues, uws**
Ellen's Stardust Diner **ws**
Empire Diner **lm**
Googie's Italian Diner **ues**
Jerry's **lm**
Johnny Rockets **lm**
Miss Rita's **lm**

French
Café Luxembourg **uws**
Florent **lm**
Le Marais **ws**
Odeon **lm**

Italian
Arqua **lm**
California Pizza Kitchen **es**
Carmine's **uws, ws**
Ernie's **uws**
Googie's Italian Diner **ues**
Il Cortile **lm**
Il Patrizio **ues**
Il Vagabondo **ues**
John's of 12th Street **lm**
John's Pizzeria **lm, ues, ws**
Lombardi's **lm**
Mangia e Bevi **ws**
Mezzaluna **ues**
Patsy's Pizza **es, lm, ues, um, uws**
Petaluma **ues**
Pintaille's Pizza **ues**
Pizzeria Uno **lm, ues, uws**
Serafina **lm, ues**
Tony di Napoli **ues, ws**
Totonno's Pizzeria Napolitano **ues, bklyn**
Two Boots **es, lm, ws**
V & T Pizzeria-Restaurant **um**
Va Bene **ues**

Kosher
Abigael's on Broadway **ws**
Darna **uws**
Haikara Grill **es**
Il Patrizio **ues**
Kosher Delight **ws**
Le Marais **ws**
Levana **uws**
Pastrami Queen **ues**
The Prime Grill **es**
Second Avenue Kosher Deli **lm**
Va Bene **ues**

Markets
Agata & Valentina **ues**
Balducci's **lm, uws**
Citarella **ues, uws**
Dean & Deluca **lm**
Eli's **ues**
Fairway **um, uws**
Gourmet Garage **lm, ues, uws**

Grace's Marketplace **ues**
Jefferson Market **lm**
Union Square Greenmarket **lm**
Whole Foods **ws**
Zabars **uws**

Mexican
Benny's Burritos **lm**
Burritoville **es, lm, ues, uws, ws**
Cowgirl Hall of Fame **lm**
Gabriela's **uws**
La Cocina **es, uws, ws**
Mary Ann's **lm, ues, uws**
Rosa Mexicano **es, uws**
Tortilla Flats **lm**

Middle Eastern
Cookies & Couscous **lm**
Darna **uws**
Kosher Delight **ws**

Sandwiches & desserts
Amy's Bread **lm, ues, ws**
Cupping Room Café **lm**
E.A.T. **ues**
Peanut Butter & Co. **lm**
Sarabeth's **lm, ues, uws**

Southern and Southwestern
Chat 'N Chew **lm**
Manhattan Chili Company **ws**
Pink Teacup **lm**

Theme restaurants
America **lm**
ESPN Zone **ws**
Hard Rock Café **ws**
Jekyll & Hyde Club **lm, ws**
Mars 2112 **ws**
Mickey Mantle's **ws**
Miss Rita's **lm**
Peanut Butter & Co. **lm**
Planet Hollywood **ws**
The World **ws**

Vegetarian/Macrobiotic
Candle Café **ues**

Chapter 9

HOME SWEET HOME-AWAY-FROM-HOME

While it is said that New York is the city that never sleeps, after a long day exploring the sights, where you will rest your head and put up your feet takes on a whole new significance. With more than 66,000 hotel rooms citywide, there are accommodations to suit every family and every budget.

The allure of hotel living, exemplified by one of children's literature's most quirky heroines, Eloise, has fascinated imaginations for generations. Upon checking in to a hotel, the travails of travel are quickly forgotten as the beds are tested and claimed, the room and its contents are explored (with special attention to the contents of the minibar and the tiny bottles of bath products), the television is inspected (just how many stations are there?) and the room-service menu is perused. The magical combination of chocolates on the pillow at night, someone to make the beds in the morning and a break from the routines of home signals to the entire family that the vacation has truly commenced.

Most likely, if you are staying in a hotel for more than a few days, you will probably experience both the pleasures—whirlpools and bubble baths, room service—and the challenges—lights out at eight to get the kids to sleep, endless whining for more television time, cabin fever from too much togetherness—of hotel life. To that end, before booking that great hotel deal, it is worth spending some time considering what type of accommodations will best suit your group, where you want to be located in town, what amenities you really need and how much you are willing to spend.

► **Location, Location, Location.** Since there is a good selection of hotels in all price ranges throughout the city, it is not hard to locate one in the area you want to stay in that will fit in your budget. Deciding in which area you want to stay, however, can be a bit more complicated. Some factors to consider:

⬛ Proximity to attractions. Many tourists are attracted to the large midtown hotels because of their proximity to destinations such as Times Square, theaters, Fifth Avenue shopping, the Empire State Building, Rockefeller Center and other landmarks. Other tourists seek to avoid the typical tourist locations and prefer to stay in particular neighborhoods that they want to explore or near a particular destination such as Museum Mile or the South Street Seaport. Whatever your preference, it is useful to choose a hotel that will maximize your ability to easily get to as many of the attractions—landmarks, shopping, cultural attractions, activities and restaurants—you want to visit and minimize the inconvenience to easily accessible transportation, taking into consideration your preferred means of transportation (on foot, by mass transit, by taxi or car).

⬛ Residential, business or commercial areas. Each type of area offers its own unique experience. Staying in a residential area allows you to soak up the neighborhood atmosphere and avoid feeling like a tourist all of the time. Residential areas often have parks or playgrounds that can offer a diversion for the kids, but they may not have as many attractions or public transportation options. Business districts or commercial areas allow you to see New

York in action—the hustle and bustle of commerce, lots of busy people, a large selection of shops and restaurants—but some areas are deserted after business hours. On the other hand, midtown business and commercial areas are centrally located and provide a good base from which to visit attractions uptown and downtown with readily accessible public transportation.

▟ **Love thy neighbor.** Certain locations attract particular clientele. Cool downtown boutique hotels often have many celebrity guests and young, single hipsters, whereas city classics like the Plaza Hotel or Waldorf-Astoria typically attract tourists. Hotels near convention centers or those with large conference facilities tend to draw business travelers, while all-suite hotels may cater to families. Hotels located in tonier neighborhoods may be surrounded by higher priced shops and restaurants, while those located in less fancy neighborhoods may be far from the shopping and dining you desire.

▟ **Noise.** If your group contains some light sleepers or you are not used to urban sounds, the noise factor can negatively affect your ability to get a good night's sleep. In general, residential areas tend to be quiet in the evening, particularly on the Upper East Side. Commercial or business areas that empty out at night (such as the Wall Street area and parts of midtown Manhattan) will also be relatively quiet at night, but noisy and congested during business hours. Conversely, the Times Square area will be noisy and crowded 24/7. While many hotels have sound-resistant windows, expect the noise to be reduced rather than eliminated. If noise is your issue, be sure to request a quiet room, but note that quiet rooms are generally located in the back of the hotel and may not have much of a view.

▟ **Safety.** While specific safety issues regarding hotel stays are reviewed and discussed in Chapter 10, it is useful to consider how a hotel's location plays a part in safety. For example, if you are traveling with teenagers and know that they will want to explore on their own in the evening, selecting a hotel in an area that is well trafficked and populated might make sense. On the other hand, if you are traveling with more than one very small child, you may prefer to be in a residential neighborhood where it is less crowded and hectic and easier to navigate with a double stroller and to keep your eye on busy toddlers.

► **How suite it is.** A hotel room is certainly not your home, but choosing a hotel that has clean, pleasant accommodations, good service, appropriate amenities and is family friendly can make all the difference to the quality of your visit.

For starters, there is no longer such a thing as a "basic" hotel room. Hotel rooms come in many varieties: one room with either one bed (twin, full, queen, king) or more than one bed (combinations of twin, full, queen, king beds); connecting rooms which either connect through a door in the wall of each room or connect off a small hallway behind a single door; suites of all types—junior (usually one bedroom with another room that may or may not have a pull-out bed or accommodate a cot); larger suites with multiple bedrooms and some type of common room, with or without a kitchen; and suites that are actually apartments with one or more bedrooms, a dining area or common room and a kitchen.

Deciding what is best for your group has a lot to do with the number of people and the needs of your group. Can everyone reasonably fit in one room? How many bathrooms does your family need to get out in the morning and ready for bed at night? Will you need some space to take breaks from each other at the end of a long day? If chilling out with some television at the end of the day is important for some and torture for others, do you need more than one area to which the whole group can retire? Are you traveling with adolescents (and grownups!) who require extra privacy? Will everyone be going to sleep and waking up at the same time? Are the children old enough to sleep in a room without an adult?

In general, New York hotel rooms are not very large, real estate being the precious urban commodity that it is, and so if the group does not do well in tight quarters, finding a hotel with spacious rooms or taking more than one room will be a priority. On the other hand, if you intend to spend most of your time out of the hotel, the group may be able to tolerate less space and put up with some inconvenience so as not to allocate a major chunk of your vacation budget to the hotel room.

The ages of the children in your party also affect your hotel decision. For example, babies and small children who cannot be left on their own in a hotel room will generally comfortably share a room with parents, either in a single hotel room or some type of suite accommodation. On the other hand, older children who are too big to share with parents or to share beds with siblings may need their own room for sleeping, but not yet be old enough to sleep in a separate room behind their own door. Teenagers may want their own rooms, but parents may prefer to have the family more connected. Once you are beyond the single room stage, you have to decide among connecting rooms, individual rooms or some type of suite.

The ages of the children in your party also affect your hotel decision.

If you are in a situation where there are more children than beds in the room, options can include choosing a room with a pull-out bed or having the hotel send in a cot or rollaway bed to accommodate the overflow. Whatever option you choose, you should be prepared for disputes over who sleeps in the 'real' beds.

Traveling families who will be staying for more than a few days may also want to consider our favorite type of accommodation: a suite that is set up like an apartment with a kitchen, one or more sleeping rooms and some kind of common area for eating and relaxing. The all-suite hotels generally have full hotel services, and some suites even have their own laundry facilities (a huge convenience if your children like to change their clothes as often as ours do). This type of accommodation allows families to spread out, take some meals or snacks (perhaps take-out from a local gourmet market) at "home," providing a respite from a steady diet of restaurant food and manners and offering more physical spaces to get some time off (for naps, calling in to the office, watching television, reading or just relaxing).

▶ **All about amenities.** These days, even the most basic of hotels will offer cable television, some type of in-room movie service (for which you pay per movie viewed), alarm clocks, laundry facilities (either hotel laundry service or coin-operated machines), safes (in-room safes or safe-deposit boxes at the front desk), telephone service (often with multiple lines and voice mail) and cribs (either for a rental charge or for free). Recently built or renovated hotels, hotels catering to business travelers and hotels that are part of large chains will generally be fully handicapped accessible and are increasingly likely to offer in-room data ports for Internet access. What separates hotels, however, is the level and scope of other amenities offered.

In general, luxury hotels will offer high level concierge service; luxury linens and bath products; elegant, luxurious décor and bathrooms; larger rooms (though not always); some type of fitness center; 24-hour room service; well-stocked minibars; higher-end electronic equipment (televisions, music, fax machines and data ports); and a high level of service. Budget hotels typically will have more modest furnishings and fewer extras and services available for guests. In between these categories, you will find various levels of service and accommodations.

Since additional levels of services and amenities are usually accompanied by higher room rates, it is worth focusing on what level of amenities you want or need in order to enjoy your stay and evaluating the importance to you of the amenities offered. While some rooms come with all kinds of bells and whistles, you don't want to pay for amenities you are unlikely to use as a guest traveling with children. For example, a kitchenette, in-room video games and movies, children's room-service menu, a pool and an activity room for kids are practical amenities, whereas spa services, teleconferencing, business support capabilities and a fabulous cocktail lounge may be superfluous on your family vacation.

Some other things you may want to investigate as you select your hotel include the availability of smoke-free rooms or floors; the proximity of the room to the elevator or to restaurants or lounges which may be noisy or emit cooking smells; whether there is a bath or stall shower (relevant to bathing young children); how recently the hotel has been decorated or refurbished (relevant to the appointments being relatively new or well-worn and perhaps less fresh); and whether the hotel offers any club or private key-access floors with additional amenities (very useful for snacks and a break from being in the room).

◢ At your service. Larger hotels, including the less expensive chain hotels, tend to have a 'concierge' on site. What that title means, however, varies from hotel to hotel. At the high end, the concierge is available to assist with almost anything the guest may need or desire, such as organizing reservations, tickets and private guides; orchestrating amazing experiences; locating unusual merchandise or services and recommending and planning things to do and see. At a less expensive hotel where the concierge is effectively the front-desk manager, however, the services will be much more basic. Having a knowledgeable concierge available is enormously helpful, but if you are resourceful, it is not a total necessity.

◢ Electronics. The electronics in the room are generally of far more interest to the kids than the grownups. If you are not spending a lot of time in your room, it may not be very important that you get 100 channels on the satellite television or that you can rent video games. Alternatively, if you are traveling with a laptop or mixing business with pleasure, access to a data port, fax machine, multiple phone lines and voice mail could make all the difference.

◢ Fitness facilities. This is one for the adults. Having access to a gym can give parents a chance to burn off some steam without the kids. At some hotels, the fitness facilities include some spa features (steam room or sauna, whirlpool, massage). Fitness centers can range from serious all-purpose gyms either on the premises or near to the hotel to an old treadmill and a couple of hand weights. If working out away from home is important to you, make sure that the fitness facilities will meet your needs.

◢ Food. Since traveling requires eating many meals in restaurants, having food available at the hotel is very useful. High-end hotels may offer exclusive (that is, expensive) restaurants where breakfast can easily run upwards of $25 per person. Other hotels will have more modest coffee shops or complimentary continental breakfast (usually consisting of hot beverages and pastries). The availability of room service is especially helpful for avoiding long breakfasts or when everyone just needs a night in. If your hotel does not offer any food on the premises, you can use the minibar refrigerator (or if there is no minibar, you may want to arrange for an in-room small refrigerator) for basic snacks. If avoiding restaurant dining is a priority, consider an apartment-type suite where you can organize your own meals or, at least, have the option.

■ **Kid Stuff.** If you are traveling with little kids, it is very important to make certain that your hotel will be able to provide you with adequate equipment, such as a sturdy and safe crib or cot, a high-chair if you need one and a tub suitable for bathing baby. While many hotels provide cribs and other equipment free of charge, others will charge some type of rental fee. Many parents find it helpful to bring along their own crib sheets and blankets as sometimes the ones provided by the hotel are not appropriate.

Other amenities for children can include a kids' welcome packages, bedtime snacks (such as complimentary cookies and milk in the evening), a selection of children's videos, DVDs, toys, video-game units and board games that can be "borrowed" during your stay; children's bath products; and coloring books and crayons. Really kid-friendly hotels will have a stash of disposable diapers and extra strollers.

Most hotels, especially the larger or the higher-end ones, can arrange for babysitters, usually through an agency or sometimes from among hotel staff.

An amenity that parents often seek is access to a swimming pool. Having a pool creates an automatic activity if the kids need some cool-down time or an opportunity for contained physical activity. Unfortunately, very few city hotels have pools, but the few that do may deserve some extra consideration.

■ **Parking.** If you are coming into the city by car, parking becomes a meaningful concern. Parking services offered by hotels vary from valet service or on-site parking to a "special" rate at a garage some-where near the hotel. Be aware that most parking rates are based on the assumption that you will not be moving your car several times throughout the day, but rather that it will stay in the garage most of the time. If you plan to use the car to get around the city, be prepared to be charged each time the car is removed and brought back.

► **What you will find in this chapter.** With literally hundreds of hotels in Manhattan alone, it would be impossible to list every hotel that would be of interest to a family visiting New York. Rather, we have decided to identify a modest list of those Manhattan hotels in various price ranges that would appeal to families either because they are special or unique New York destinations in and of themselves, particularly wonderful finds, or particularly kid-friendly in a Big Apple kind of way. And, because staying in an apartment or suite can be especially helpful when traveling with kids, we have a separate section listing all-suite (or predominantly all-suite) and extended-stay hotels that can accommodate families. We have also compiled a list of a number of the chain hotels with properties in the city and hotels located near the three area airports.

► **A word about price.** For most families, cost is the determining factor in choosing a hotel room. When booking, be sure to inquire about special promotional packages; discounts (corporate, organization membership); upgrades (credit-card promotions); frequent-flyer tie-ins; meal plans (the inclusion of breakfast can create significant savings); and complimentary airport transfers.

For purposes of helping you evaluate hotels, we separate hotel room rates into four categories based on the hotels' stated "rack rates" (the full fare, without any discounts or promotions) for a double room (that is, a room with two full or queen beds) at peak times. Be aware that you will almost never pay the full rack rate, since all hotels feature a variety of substantially lower promotional, specialty (such as corporate), Internet booking and package rates throughout the year. Make sure to inquire whether there are any additional charges for more than two guests per room and whether children stay for free, a reduced rate or the full rate. Also, if you are booking on the Internet, be sure to compare prices over a variety of websites before you make your reservation, as the proliferation of Internet deals makes rate shopping relatively easy.

$ —less than $150
$$ —from $151 to $250
$$$ —from $251 to $450
$$$$ —over $450

Note that all hotels charge a 13.25% tax (8.25% of which is sales tax, 5% of which is a hotel tax) plus a $2 per night occupancy tax.

🎩	=	concierge
🏃	=	fitness facility
🍽	=	restaurant
☕	=	room service
△	=	parking
🐰	=	pet friendly
♿	=	handicapped accessible

Manhattan Hotels

The Algonquin   🎩 🏃 🍽 ☕ ♿ $$$
59 West 44th Street between Fifth and Sixth Avenues, 840-6800, 800 555-8000, www.algonquinhotel.com   174 rooms and suites
Located in midtown Manhattan on "Club Row," this landmark hotel, home to the famed literary Round Table of the 1920s, was completely renovated in 1998 but retains its architectural ambience as an "oasis of civility amid the hectic pace of New York." The Algonquin has had a resident cat since the 1930s, and children will enjoy meeting Matilda, the current hotel pet, whose birthday is celebrated with an annual fete. Parents will enjoy the New Yorker cartoon wallpaper. Afternoon tea in the lobby is an Algonquin tradition.

The Carlyle   🎩 🏃 🍽 ☕ △ 🐰 ♿ $$$$
35 East 76th Street at Madison Avenue, 744-1600, 800 227-5737, www.carlyle.com   180 rooms and suites
Since 1931, this elegant, high-service and genteel Upper East Side luxury hotel (with rooms decorated by Mark Hampton) has hosted diplomats, dignitaries and celebrities from around the world. Some suites offer kitchens, terraces and even grand pianos. Adults will enjoy the Café Carlyle, the famed cabaret venue featuring Bobby Short, Eartha Kitt and other renowned performers.

Central Park Inter-Continental   🎩 🏃 🍽 ☕ △ ♿ $$$$
112 Central Park South between Sixth and Seventh Avenues, 757-1900, 800 327-0200, www.intercontinental.com   207 rooms and suites
This recently renovated, elegant, old-world luxury hotel, fashioned after an 18th-century English manor, overlooks Central Park and is located on the West Side.

Essex House ⬚ 🧍 🍽 ☕ ♿ **$$$$**
160 Central Park South between Sixth and Seventh Avenues, 247-0300,
800 937-8461, www.westin.com
501 rooms and suites, spa, restaurants (including Alain Ducasse), kids' amenities
This famed luxury hotel overlooking Central Park is located in a landmark
Art Deco tower on Central Park South on the West Side. The recently renovated hotel has luxuriously appointed rooms featuring the Heavenly Bed
(and Heavenly Crib), Westin's deluxe mattresses. Amenities for children
include a welcome pack (logo item, coloring materials), baby bath products
and an over-the-phone "story line" for children up to age six.

Excelsior Hotel ⬚ 🧍 △ **$$$**
45 West 81st Street between Central Park West and Columbus Avenue,
362-9200, 800 368-4575, www.excelsiorhotelny.com
196 rooms and suites, entertainment room, breakfast room
Located on the Upper West Side just off Central Park West and overlooking
the American Museum of Natural History, this hotel is in a lovely residen-
tial neighborhood. Rooms are decorated in a French motif, and the hotel
features an entertainment room with a library, fireplace, books and board
games and a big-screen television.

Flatotel ⬚ 🧍 🍽 ☕ △♿ **$$$-$$$$**
135 West 52nd Street between Sixth and Seventh Avenues, 887-9400,
800 552-8683, www.flatotel-intl.com
288 rooms and suites, access to an off-site full health club with pool
This reasonably priced, chic hotel located on the West Side offers high-tech
amenities in spacious modern surroundings inspired by the designs of
Frank Lloyd Wright. The well-appointed, large one-bedroom suites are very
popular with families. Many rooms contain refrigerators and microwaves
and many of the suites contain full kitchens. Suites are available on an
extended-stay (30+ days) basis for a monthly charge.

Four Seasons New York ⬚ 🧍 🍽 ☕ △♿ **$$$$**
57 East 57th Street between Park and Madison Avenues, 758-5700, 800
819-5053, www.fourseasons.com   368 rooms and suites, spa, kids' amenities
This sleek, chic modern hotel designed by I. M. Pei is a favorite for Holly-
wood moguls in town to take a meeting. As glamorous as this hotel is, it is
still extremely welcoming to families and offers a kids' welcome pack
(including milk and cookies), video games, child-sized robes, children's
menus (in the restaurant and for room service) baby bath products and
toys and baby equipment. The towering lobby features a lounge with an
excellent afternoon tea.

Gramercy Park Hotel 🧍 🍽 ☕ ♿ **$$**
2 Lexington Avenue at 21st Street , 475-4320, 800 221-4083,
www.gramercyparkhotel.com   509 rooms and suites
Though somewhat faded, the Gramercy Park Hotel has been family-owned
since 1924 and has hosted many celebrities (including Babe Ruth and

Humphrey Bogart) over the years. Rooms and suites (many with kitchenettes) are old-fashioned with only the most basic amenities. What makes this hotel unique is that guests have access to famed Gramercy Park, a locked gated square to which only neighborhood residents have the key. The hotel also features a roof deck.

Grand Hyatt
Park Avenue at Grand Central Terminal, 883-1234, 800 233-1234,
www.hyatt.com   1336 rooms and suites, access to an off-site full service health club

This huge hotel located in the heart of midtown Manhattan at Grand Central Terminal offers upscale accommodations in a central location. The hotel offers key-access concierge Regency Club accommodations on two floors, which feature a club lounge, a private concierge and deluxe bath amenities.

Hotel Beacon
2130 Broadway at 75th Street, 787-1100, 800 572-4969,
www.beaconhotel.com   240 rooms and suites

Originally an apartment-hotel, the rooms and suites at this no-frills, modestly-priced hotel on the Upper West Side located right on Broadway (the neighborhood's main commercial and shopping street) have fully equipped kitchenettes. Coin-operated laundry facilities are available. In 2003, there will be access to a full-service health club located in the building.

Hôtel Plaza Athénée
37 East 64th Street at Madison Avenue, 734-9100, 800 447-8800,
www.plaza-athenee.com   117 rooms and suites

This boutique, European-style hotel located on a lovely residential street on the Upper East Side, is a member of the Leading Hotels of the World. The recently renovated luxury hotel is dedicated to providing a high level of service and amenities to its guests.

Hotel Wales
1295 Madison Avenue between 92nd and 93rd Streets, 876-6000,
877 847-4444, www.waleshotel.com

88 rooms and suites, access to a full health-club facility with pool, video and CD library

This very civilized, Victorian style hotel on the Upper East Side offers reasonably priced, charming accommodations in a lovely residential neighborhood. Rooms are not terribly large (although suites are more spacious) but are well appointed with luxury amenities. A breakfast buffet (featuring live harp music) and snacks are available in the cozy lobby, and meals are available at Sarabeth's, a popular restaurant frequented by uptown mommies and their kids for breakfast and lunch. Adults will enjoy the complimentary espresso and cappuccino, available all day.

Hudson
🎩 🕴 🍽 ☕ △ ♿ $$$

356 West 58th Street between Eighth and Ninth Avenues, 554-6000, 800 444-4786, www.ianschragerhotels.com

1000 rooms and suites, indoor/outdoor private park, library, refreshment lounge on every floor

The Hudson, designed by Philippe Starck, is a "stylish, democratic, affordable, young at heart and utterly cool" hotel. The dramatic public spaces, including an illuminated glass floor, ivy covered walls with flowering vines, eclectic furnishings and art exhibits, together with popular trendy restaurants, create an "urban adventure." The rooms, which are all very chic and modern, tend to be small. All the Ian Schrager hotels are implementing a program that offers child-friendly amenities, including a welcome gift and complimentary snack on the first night, board games, children's videos and video game units, baby bath amenities, jogging strollers and other baby equipment, toys and bedtime cookies with milk or juice.

Intercontinental The Barclay New York
🎩 🕴 🍽 ☕ △ ♿ $$$$

111 East 48th Street at Lexington Avenue, 755-5900, www.new-york-barclay.new-york.intercontinental.com

686 rooms and suites

This elegant luxury hotel located in midtown Manhattan features high-end amenities and services and has many connecting rooms.

Kitano
🎩 🍽 ☕ △ ♿ $$$$

66 Park Avenue at 38th Street, 885-7000, 800 548-2666, www.kitano.com

149 rooms and suites, access to health club

This Japanese-owned luxury hotel located in Murray Hill combines "modern Manhattan at its most elegant, old Japan at its most gracious and graceful." Recently renovated, the hotel features beautifully appointed rooms, deluxe bath amenities, complimentary Japanese tea, a serious art collection including the bronze "Dog" by Fernando Botero and a world-class kaiseki restaurant.

The Lowell
🎩 🕴 🍽 ☕ △ ♿ $$$$

28 East 63rd Street between Madison and Park Avenues, 838-1400, 800 221-4444, www.lhw.com   23 rooms and 47 suites

This charming hotel, located on the Upper East Side in a residential neighborhood, features a high level of service and luxury amenities. Many of the suites have wood-burning fireplaces, some have terraces and most have fully equipped kitchens. Member of the Leading Small Hotels of the World.

The Mark
🎩 🕴 🍽 ☕ △ ♿ $$$$

25 East 77th Street at Madison Avenue, 744-4300, 800 843-6275, www.themarkhotel.com   180 rooms and suites

Decorated in the "refined English-Italian style inspired by [18th century English architect Sir John] Sloane," this elegant Upper East Side hotel features a high level of service and luxury amenities. Many of the suites have fully-equipped kitchenettes.

Mayflower Hotel on the Park   🧍 ☕ △ ♿ $$-$$$
15 Central Park West at 61st Street, 265-0060, 800 223-4164,
www.mayflowerhotel.com   365 rooms and suites
Overlooking Central Park, this affordable (but somewhat faded) no-frills
Upper West Side hotel offers rooms with serving pantries outfitted with a
sink and refrigerator. Some suites have terraces.

The Melrose (formerly the Barbizon Hotel)   🎩 🧍 🍽 △ ♿ $$$
140 East 63rd Street at Lexington Avenue, 838-5700, 800 635-7673,
www.thebarbizon.com
306 rooms and suites, access to the Equinox (a full-service health club and spa
located in the building)
Opened in 1927 as a residence for genteel young ladies, this recently renovated hotel located in a landmark building in midtown on the Upper East
Side just steps from Bloomingdale's and other shopping, features classic
style and amenities. Of particular note are the grand Tower Suites, each of
which offers unique architectural elements such as stained-glass windows
or terraces.

The Mercer   🎩 🍽 ☕ △ ♿ $$$$
147 Mercer Street at Prince Street, 212 966-6060, 800 918-6060,
www.mercerhotel.com
75 rooms and suites, access to health club, CD/video/book libraries
Operated by hotelier Andre Balazs and designed by Christian Liagre, this
downtown hotel is very cool and oh-so-chic. Amenities are luxurious and
service is taken very seriously. The restaurant, operated by celebrity chef
Jean Georges Vongerichten, is a downtown hot spot and is best for older
children.

Morgans   🎩 🧍 🍽 ☕ △ ♿ $$$
237 Madison Avenue between 37th and 38th Streets, 686-0300,
800 334-3408, www.ianschragerhotels.com   154 rooms and suites
This "quietly sophisticated" hotel located in Murray Hill with interiors by
Andree Putnam creates a "chic, residential feel" for its guests. Amenities are
luxurious. Guests appreciate the complimentary continental breakfast and
coffee-and-tea service throughout the day. All the Ian Schrager hotels are
implementing a program that offers child-friendly amenities, including a
welcome gift and complimentary snack on the first night, board games,
children's videos and video game units, baby bath amenities, jogging
strollers and other baby equipment, toys and bedtime cookies with milk or
juice.

New York Palace and The Towers   🎩 🧍 🍽 ☕ △ $$$$
455 Madison Avenue at 51st Street, 888-7000, 800 697-2522,
www.newyorkpalace.com   896 rooms and suites
This luxury hotel located in midtown on the East Side, combines the opu-
lent neo-Italian Renaissance style Villard Houses (the mansion of financier
Henry Villard, completed in 1882) with a modern 55-story tower. The

hotel, which offers spacious rooms, consists of a main hotel through the 29th floor, executive rooms on floors 30 through 39 (featuring a private common room with complimentary food and beverages throughout the day) and The Towers on floors 41 to the top of the building. The Towers functions as a "hotel within a hotel," featuring 175 rooms, suites and triplexes, dedicated elevators, separate lobby, maître d'étage service on each floor, exclusive luxury amenities, classical style décor on even-numbered floors and Art Deco décor on odd-numbered floors. The renowned Le Cirque 2000 is located in the Villard Houses.

The Paramount   🎩 🏃 🍽 ☕ △ **$$$**
235 West 46th Street between Broadway and Eighth Avenue, 764-5500, 800 225-7474, www.ianschragerhotels.com   610 rooms and suites
With interiors designed by Philippe Starck, this midtown hotel features "witty, whimsical" décor and a dramatic lobby. Though rooms are smallish, the amenities are luxurious. All the Ian Schrager hotels are implementing a program that offers child-friendly amenities, including a welcome gift and complimentary snack on the first night, board games, children's videos and video game units, baby bath amenities, jogging strollers and other baby equipment, toys and bedtime cookies with milk or juice.

Le Parker Meridien   🎩 🏃 🍽 ☕ △ ♿ **$$$$**
119 West 56th Street between Sixth and Seventh Avenues, 245-5000, 800 543-4300, www.parkermeridien.com   730 rooms and suites, pool
Located in the heart of midtown and steps from Fifth Avenue shopping and Carnegie Hall, Le Parker Meridien boasts ergonomically inspired rooms and suites and upscale amenities. Most suites have full kitchens. Restaurants include Norma's, which serves breakfast all day, and the New Burger Joint.

The Peninsula   🎩 🏃 🍽 ☕ △ ♿ **$$$$**
700 Fifth Avenue at 55th Street, 956-2888, 800 262-9467, www.peninsula.com   239 rooms and suites, spa, pool
Located in the heart of midtown on Fifth Avenue and fully renovated in 1998, this luxury hotel, decorated in a classic contemporary style with Art Nouveau accents, features deluxe amenities, serious service and state-of-the-art electronics. The spa provides an idyllic respite for weary moms and dads.

The Pierre   🎩 🏃 🍽 ☕ △ ♿ **$$$$**
2 East 61st Street at Fifth Avenue, 838-8000, 800 332-3442, www.fourseasons.com/pierre   201 rooms and suites, kids' amenities
Long a destination for New York visitors, this landmark luxury hotel located on Fifth Avenue on the Upper East Side features deluxe amenities, a high level of service (the hotel will even arrange for in-room exercise equipment) and a taste of classic, grand New York. Amenities for children include a welcome gift, bedtime cookies and milk, child-sized robes, children's bath products, children's room service menu (including pureed food for baby), books, toys and baby products (diapers, strollers, bathing equip-

ment, bottle warmers and Frette linens for the crib). Rooms can be child-proofed on request. Grand suites have dining rooms.

The Plaza   🎩 🧍 🍽 ☕ △ 🐰 ♿ **$$-$$$**
768 Fifth Avenue at 59th Street, 759-3000, 800 441-1414,
www.fairmont.com   805 rooms and suites, spa, kids' amenities
Located on Fifth Avenue, this legendary hotel (it became a designated National Historic Landmark in 1969) has welcomed dignitaries, celebrities and travelers from around the world since 1907. Amenities and services are deluxe. The Plaza features the Young Plaza Ambassadors membership program (see www.plazaypa.com) for kids (free with a two-night stay, otherwise a fee applies), which includes a YPA wallet and photo i.d., discounts with local merchants and etiquette and cooking classes. Older kids will enjoy formal high-tea service in the lobby's famed Palm Court.

The Regency   🎩 🧍 🍽 ☕ △ 🐰 ♿ **$$$$**
540 Park Avenue between 61st and 62nd Streets, 759-4100, 800 235-6397,
www.loewshotels.com   351 rooms and suites, kids' amenities
This recently renovated luxury hotel located on Park Avenue offers top-drawer amenities in a contemporary setting. The Loews Loves Kids program offers a variety of special features for families and children, including a welcome gift for kids, children's menus, lending library, milk and cookies, childproofing kits, kids' videos, toys and games, baby equipment (including strollers). Grandparents traveling with their grandchildren can take advantage of Generation G packages that feature specially priced rooms, many giveaways (photo album, cookbook, luggage, snacks) and discounted city tours. Some rooms have kitchenettes and some suites have full kitchens. Grownups will enjoy Feinstein's, a nightclub and cabaret.

Regent Wall Street   🎩 🧍 🍽 ☕ △ ♿ **$$$$**
55 Wall Street at William Street, 845-8600, 800 545-4000,
www.regenthotels.com   144 rooms and suites, spa
Located downtown in the financial district in a 1842 combination Greek Revival and Italian Renaissance landmark building that has housed the Merchants Exchange, Customs House and National City Bank before becoming a luxury hotel, this property features spacious accommodations (the décor is a "modern interpretation of traditional Italian design"), first-class amenities and plenty of service.

Renaissance New York Hotel Times Square 🎩 🧍 🍽 ☕ △ 🐰 ♿ **$$$$**
714 Seventh Avenue between 47th and 48th Streets, 765-7676,
800 468-3571, www.renaissancehotels.com   305 rooms and suites
Located in the heart of Times Square, this hotel offers an alternative to the other gigantic area hotels and features deluxe amenities.

Ritz-Carlton New York Battery Park 🎩 🧍 🍽 ☕ △ ♿ $$$$

2 West Street, Battery Park City, 344-0800, 800 241-3333,
www.ritzcarlton.com   298 rooms and suites, spa, kids' amenities

Located in lower Manhattan overlooking the Hudson River, this luxury hotel features spacious rooms, deluxe amenities and serious service. The Ritz Kids program welcomes families with such features as a "toy menu" with games from FAO Schwarz, a selection of G-rated movies and teddy bears tucked into kid's beds at turndown. Harborfront rooms come equipped with telescopes.

Ritz-Carlton New York Central Park 🎩 🧍 🍽 ☕ △ ♿ $$$$

50 Central Park South between Fifth and Sixth Avenues, 308-9100,
800 241-3333, www.ritzcarlton.com 298 rooms and suites, spa, kids' amenities

Overlooking Central Park from Central Park South, this luxury hotel features spacious rooms, first-class amenities and serious service. Children receive a welcome gift, and the hotel can provide baby bath products, cookies and milk, strollers and toys and games. Club-level accommodations, which offer a dedicated concierge and lounge, are available.

The Royalton 🎩 🧍 🍽 ☕ △ $$$-$$$$

44 West 44th Street between Fifth and Sixth Avenues, 869-4400,
800 635-9013, www.ianschragerhotels.com   205 rooms and suites

Located in midtown, this Philippe Starck–designed hotel features post-modern décor and "stage set elegance." Amenities are deluxe, facilities are high-tech and service is a priority. Some rooms have working fireplaces. All the Ian Schrager hotels are implementing a program that offers child-friendly amenities, including a welcome gift and complimentary snack on the first night, board games, children's videos and video game units, baby bath amenities, jogging strollers and other baby equipment, toys and bedtime cookies with milk or juice.

St. Regis Hotel 🎩 🧍 🍽 ☕ △ ♿ $$$$

2 East 55th Street at Fifth Avenue, 753-4500, 800 325-3589,
www.stregis.com   315 rooms and suites

Housed in a 1904 Beaux Art landmark in prime shopping territory on Fifth Avenue, this hotel features "the atmosphere and attentive service found in the most gracious residences of that era" combined with modern amenities. The décor is traditional Louis XVI–style and the rooms are spacious. Some suites have kitchenettes.

The Sherry-Netherland Hotel 🎩 🧍 ☕ △ ♿ $$$$

781 Fifth Avenue between 59th and 60th Streets, 355-2800, 800 297-4377,
www.sherrynetherland.com   70 rooms and suites

Long a Fifth Avenue landmark, this grand, white-glove luxury hotel, decorated with antiques, marble mosaic floors and crystal chandeliers, is elegance personified and prides itself on "unyielding personal service and meticulous attention to your every need." Rooms are large and have "dramatically" high ceilings and amazing Central Park views. Some suites have working fireplaces. Complimentary continental breakfast is available in the Harry Cipriani Restaurant. The property also has many permanent residents.

SoHo Grand Hotel

310 West Broadway between Grand and Canal Streets, 965-3000, 800 965-3000, www.sohogrand.com   369 rooms and suites

This "ultra-chic, downtown boutique hotel" located in the heart of Soho features both luxurious amenities and high-level service. Kids will enjoy having a vacation pet—goldfish are provided on request.

The Stanhope Park Hyatt

995 Fifth Avenue at 81st Street, 774-1234, 800 233-1234, www.parkhyatt.com   242 rooms and suites

Located on Museum Mile overlooking the Metropolitan Museum of Art, this luxury hotel features deluxe amenities and service. A renovation of the hotel is scheduled to commence in 2003.

Swissotel New York – The Drake

440 Park Avenue at 56th Street, 421-0900, 888 737-9477, www.swissotel.com   495 rooms and suites, spa

This recently renovated midtown hotel features high-ceilinged rooms, contemporary décor and high level service. The hotel offers more than 100 suites with wet bars and refrigerators.

Tribeca Grand Hotel

2 Sixth Avenue at White Street, 519-6600, 877 519-6600, www.tribecagrand.com   203 rooms and suites

The sister hotel of the SoHo Grand is located in the heart of Tribeca and offers cutting-edge facilities in a "calm, clutter-free environment." This technologically sophisticated hotel prides itself on "exceptionally personable, whatever you need, whenever you need it service." The rooms feature floor-to-ceiling windows and high-tech appointments.

Trump International Hotel and Tower

1 Central Park West at Columbus Circle, 299-1000, 888 448-7867, www.trumpintl.com   167 rooms and suites, spa, pool

Located on Columbus Circle overlooking Central Park, this luxury hotel does things in a big Trump way. Rooms have floor-to-ceiling windows and come equipped with telescopes, deluxe bath amenities, fresh flowers. Many rooms and suites offer European-style kitchens, and personal in-room chefs are available. Personal service for all guests is provided by Trump Attachés. The restaurant, Jean Georges, is operated by celebrity chef Jean-Georges Vongerichten.

Waldorf-Astoria and Waldorf Towers   🔲 🏃 🍽 ♨ △ ♿ **$$$$**

301 Park Avenue between 49th and 50th Streets, 355-3000, 800 925-3673, www.waldorfastoria.com   1400 rooms and suites, spa

A landmark grand hotel that has been welcoming guests for over a century, the Waldorf has been housed in its Park Avenue Art Deco tower since 1931. This gigantic hotel (currently operated by the Hilton hotel chain) features spacious, high-ceilinged rooms, luxury amenities and comfortable accommodations. The Waldorf Towers, located on floors 28 through 42 with a separate entrance, features super-luxury accommodations (available for long-term residency), all with either kitchenettes or wet bars and refrigerators, with a high level of personal service

Washington Square Hotel   🏃 🍽 △ **$$**

103 Waverly Place between MacDougal and Waverly, 777-9515, 800 222-0418, www.wshotel.com   170 rooms

This hotel located on historic Washington Square in Greenwich Village features reasonably priced, comfortable rooms with basic amenities. The lobby was recently renovated; rooms are scheduled for renovation commencing in 2003. Complimentary continental breakfast is available in the North Square Restaurant.

▟▙

All-Suite Hotels and Extended Stay Residences

The facilities listed in this section function as either hotel accommodations or extended-stay properties or, in some cases, both. The hotels can accommodate guests for short or long stays. The extended-stay properties are designed to accommodate long-term visitors (usually requiring a minimum stay of 30 days) such as guests on extended vacations or who otherwise need to be in Manhattan for a month or more, recent arrivals to town who have not yet found a permanent home, people who are awaiting completion of an apartment renovation or are otherwise in need of an interim residence, frequent visitors who require a city pied-à-terre and company apartments. Certain extended-stay properties may accommodate stays of under 30 days if the property is not otherwise booked.

The Bridge Suite Apartments   **$**

351 East 60th Street at First Avenue, 221-8300, www.bridgesuites.com

Seventy-five recently renovated studio apartments are available at this extended-stay residence. There is a doorman, but no housekeeping services or hotel amenities are provided.

Bristol Plaza   ·   🛄 🕴 △ ♿ $$
210 East 65th Street at Third Avenue, 753-7900, www.bristolplaza.com
This Upper East Side luxury extended-stay residence offers suites with full kitchens, daily housekeeping service, 24-hour doorman, valet service and a pool.

Doubletree Guest Suites   🛄 🕴 🍽 ☕ △ ♿ $$$
1568 Broadway between 47th and 48th Streets, 800 222-8733,
www.doubletree.com   460 suites, full or self-service laundry
All of the suites in this all-suite hotel located in the heart of Times Square come equipped with a Sony Playstation and kitchenette. Especially for families, the Doubletree features a floor of childproofed suites, a children's room-service menu, a children's playroom, a kids' club and a welcome pack and the Hilton Vacation Station, a program of services and amenities for families, including free welcome information, a lending desk with toys and games and a souvenir for children ages 1–12, summer only.

Embassy Suites Hotel   🛄 🕴 🍽 ☕ ♿ $$$
102 North End Avenue, near Murray Street, 945-0100, 800 362-2779,
www.embassysuites.com   463 suites, full- or self-service laundry
Located on the waterfront in lower Manhattan, this upscale all-suite hotel offers complimentary beverage and breakfast areas and scheduled children's activities on summer weekends.

The Envoy Club   🕴 △ ♿ $$$$
377 East 33rd Street at First Avenue, 481-4600, www.envoyclub.com
This Murray Hill luxury extended-stay hotel (located on the first seven floors of an apartment building) offers 57 studios and one- and two-bedroom suites, all with kitchens. Services include daily housekeeping service, valet service, a children's play area and a small movie screening room.

Kimberly Hotel   🛄 🍽 ☕ △ ♿ $$$
145 East 50th Street between Lexington and Third Avenues, 755-0400,
800 683-0400, www.kimberlyhotel.com
186 rooms and suites, access to full service health club
This East Side hotel offers both regular hotel rooms and one- or two-bedroom suites with fully equipped kitchens, living rooms and dining areas.

The Lowell, see above.

Manhattan East Suite Hotels
800 637-8483, www.mesuite.com
This family-owned business operates nine all-suite hotels containing 2,100 suites on the Upper East Side and midtown Manhattan. All properties are in the luxury category and offer hotel amenities (such as daily housekeeping service), fitness facilities, grocery shopping, valet service as well as self-service laundry facilities, concierge services and data ports. Most have been recently renovated and offer on-premises dining and room service and parking. Price classification is based on the cost of a one-bedroom suite.

Beekman Tower Hotel   🎩 🧍 🍽 ☕ △ ♿ $$$$
3 Mitchell Place at 49th Street and First Avenue, 355-7300
174 suites. Located in an Art Deco–designated landmark near the United Nations.

The Benjamin Hotel   🎩 🧍 🍽 ☕ △ ♿ $$$$
125 East 50th Street, 715-2500, www.thebenjamin.com
209 suites. Located in midtown on the East Side in a restored 1927 building, this luxury property is a certified Five-Globe ECOTEL and offers a spa.

Dumont Plaza   🎩 🧍 △ ♿ $$$$
150 East 34th Street between Third and Lexington Avenues, 481-7600
248 suites. This Murray Hill property offers a spa.

Eastgate Tower   🎩 🧍 🍽 ☕ △ ♿ $$$$
222 East 39th Street between Second and Third Avenues, 687-8000
187 suites. Located in Murray Hill.

Lyden Gardens   🎩 🧍 △ ♿ $$$$
215 East 64th Street between Second and Third Avenues, 355-1230
131 suites. Several suites at this Upper East Side property have private patios.

Plaza Fifty   🎩 🧍 ☕ ♿ $$$$
155 East 50th Street between Third and Lexington Avenues, 751-5710
211 suites. Located in midtown Manhattan, this property offers room service from a neighborhood restaurant.

Shelburne Murray Hill   🎩 🧍 🍽 ☕ △ ♿ $$$$
303 Lexington Avenue at 37th Street, 689-5200
253 suites. Located in Murray Hill.

Southgate Tower   🎩 🧍 🍽 ☕ △ ♿ $$$$
371 Seventh Avenue at 31st Street, 563-1800
527 suites. Located in the fashion district on Seventh Avenue.

Surrey Hotel   🎩 🧍 🍽 ☕ △ ♿ $$$$
20 East 76th Street between Fifth and Madison Avenues, 288-3700
131 suites. This Upper East Side Property is extremely popular with families and features the renowned Café Boulud restaurant.

The Marmara-Manhattan   🎩 ♿ $$$
301 East 94th Street at Second Avenue, 427-3100, 800 621-9029, www.marmara-manhattan.com
This chic, stylish, luxury extended-stay property located on the Upper East Side offers 102 studio and one-, two- and three-bedroom suites with fully equipped kitchens, daily housekeeping service, a 24-hour doorman, valet service, roof terrace and a selection of toys and children's videos.

The Phillips Club 🎩 ♿ $$$$
155 West 66th Street at Broadway, 835-8800, 877 854-8880,
www.phillipsclub.com
Located on the Upper West Side, this chic, stylish, luxury extended-stay property also accommodates short stays and offers junior and one-, two- and three-bedroom suites, all with full kitchens, access to the Reebok Sports Club/NY, delivery from area restaurants and daily housekeeping service.

RIHGA Royal 🎩 🏃 🍽 ☕ △ ♿ $$$$
151 West 54th between Sixth and Seventh Avenues, 307-5000,
800 937-5454, www.rihga.com
Most of the 506 suites in this midtown luxury all-suite hotel are one-bedroom with a living room. Sofa beds or rollaways can be arranged. The suites do not have kitchens. Executive floor accommodation available.

The Sutton 🏃 🍽 ☕ ♿ $$$$
330 East 56th Street between First and Second Avenues, 752-8888,
www.thesutton.com
This East Side extended-stay property offers luxury suites with kitchens, a pool and daily housekeeping service.

Apartment rentals/extended-stay websites

Abode Apartment Rentals, 472-2000, 800 835-8880, www.abodenyc.com

Homestay New York, 718 434-2071, www.homestaynyc.com

Manhattan Getaways, 956-2010, www.manhattangetaways.com

Manhattan Lodgings, 677-7616, www.manhattanlodgings.com

West Village Reservations, 614-3034, www.citysonnet.com

Chains

This is a sampling of the many hotels chains that operate hotels in New York City. See also Airport Hotels.

Best Western www.bestwestern.com

Best Western Ambassador 🎩 △ $
132 West 45th Street between Sixth Avenue and Broadway, 921-7600,
800 242-8935 70 rooms, children 12 and under stay free

Best Western Convention Center Hotel △ ♿ $
522 West 38th Street between Tenth and Eleventh Avenues, 405-1700
83 rooms, located near Jacob Javits Convention Center, children 17 and under stay free

Best Western Hospitality House △ $$-$$$
149 East 49th Street between Lexington and Third Avenues, 753-8781
35 suites, all-suite hotel, suites have kitchens, children 13 and under stay free

Best Western Majestic △ $-$$
210 West 55th Street between Broadway and Seventh Avenue, 247-2000, 800 336-4110   175 rooms, off-site health club

Best Western Manhattan 🏃 🍴 △ ♿ $
17 West 32nd Street between Fifth Avenue and Broadway, 736-1600, 800 567-7720   182 rooms, children 12 and under stay free

Best Western President Hotel 🍴 ♿ $
234 West 48th Street between Broadway and Eighth Avenue, 246-8800, 800 826-4667
334 rooms, off-site health club, children 12 and under stay free

Best Western Seaport Inn 🏃 ♿ $$
33 Peck Slip, South Street Seaport, 766-6600, 800 468-3569
72 rooms, children 17 and under stay free

Comfort Inn/Clarion/Quality   www.comfortinn.com

Comfort Inn ♿ $
442 West 36th Street between Ninth and Tenth Avenues, 714-6699
56 rooms, off-site fitness facility

Comfort Inn Central Park West 🏃 △ ♿ $
31 West 71st Street between Central Park West and Columbus Avenue, 721-4770, 877 727-5236   96 rooms

Comfort Inn Manhattan $
42 West 35th Street between Fifth and Sixth Avenues, 947-0200, 800 228-5150   131 rooms

Comfort Inn Midtown 🏃 △ $
129 West 46th Street between Sixth Avenue and Broadway, 221-2600, 800 567-7720   80 rooms

Clarion Hotel Fifth Avenue 🍴 ♿ $$-$$$
3 East 40th Street between Fifth and Madison Avenues, 447-1500
189 rooms, children under 18 stay free

Clarion Hotel Park Avenue   △ $$
429 Park Avenue South between 29th and 30th Streets, 532-4860
60 rooms

Quality Hotel on Broadway   △ �& $
215 West 94th Street at Broadway, 866-6400   359 rooms

Crowne Plaza   www.crowneplaza.com

Crowne Plaza Hotel at the United Nations   ▣ ◉ △ �& $$-$$$
304 East 42nd Street at Second Avenue, 986-8800, 800 227-6963
300 rooms and suites

Crowne Plaza Manhattan at Times Square   ▣ ◉ △ �& $$$
1605 Broadway between 48th and 49th Streets, 977-4000, 800 243-6969
770 rooms and suites

Hilton   www.hilton.com

Hilton Times Square   ▣ 夵 ◉ �& $$$
234 West 42nd Street between Broadway and Eighth Avenue, 840-8222,
800 445-8667, www.timessquarehilton.com   444 rooms
Offers Hilton Vacation Station, a program of services and amenities for
families, including free welcome information, a lending desk with toys
and games and a souvenir for children ages 1–12, summer only.

Millenium Hilton $$$
55 Church Street between Fulton and Dey Streets, 693-2001,
800 445-8667
This hotel, which was damaged in the September 11, 2001, attack on
New York, is undergoing a total renovation and is scheduled to reopen
in early 2003.

New York Hilton & Towers   ▣ ◉ △ ᅀ $$$
1335 Sixth Avenue between 53rd and 54th Streets, 840-8222,
800 445-8667, www.newyorktowers.hilton.com
2000+ rooms and suites, executive floors
Offers Hilton Vacation Station, a program of services and amenities for
families, including free welcome information, a lending desk with toys
and games and a souvenir for children ages 1–12, summer only.

Holiday Inn   www.holiday-inn.com

Holiday Inn Downtown/Soho   ▣ ◉ △ ᅀ $$$
138 Lafayette Street between Canal and Howard Streets, 966-8898,
800 465-4329   239 rooms and suites

Holiday Inn Martinique on Broadway   🎩 🍽 △ 🎄 ♿ $$
49 West 32nd Street between Broadway and Fifth Avenue, 736-3800,
888 694-6543   538 rooms and suites

Holiday Inn Midtown   🍽 △ ♿ $$
440 West 57th Street between Ninth and Tenth Avenues, 581-8100,
800 231-0405   602 rooms and suites, outdoor rooftop pool

Holiday Inn Wall Street   🎩 🍽 △ ♿ $$$
15 Gold Street at Platt Street, 232-7800, 800 465-4329
138 rooms and one suite

Marriott/Courtyard   www.marriott.com

New York Marriott Brooklyn   🎩 🏃 🍽 △ ♿ $$
333 Adams Street between Tillary and Willingby Streets, 718 246-7000,
800 436-3579   376 rooms, indoor pool

New York Marriott East Side   🎩 🏃 🍽 △ ♿ $$-$$$
525 Lexington Avenue at 49th Street, 755-4000, 800 242-8684
643 rooms and suites

New York Marriott Financial Center   🎩 🏃 🍽 △ ♿ $$$
85 West Street at Carlisle Street, 385-4900, 800 242-8685
500 rooms, indoor pool, executive floor

New York Marriott Marquis   🎩 🏃 🍽 △ 🎄 ♿ $$-$$$
1535 Broadway between 45th and 46th Streets, 398-1900, 800 843-4898
2002 rooms and suites, executive floor

Courtyard NYC Manhattan Midtown East   🎩 🏃 🍽 ♿ $$-$$$
866 Third Avenue between 52nd and 53rd Streets, 644-1300,
800 321-2211   314 rooms and suites

Courtyard NYC Manhattan Times Square South 🎩 🏃 🍽 ♿ $$-$$$
114 West 40th Street between Broadway and Sixth Avenue, 391-0088,
800 321-2211   248 rooms and suites

Sheraton   www.sheraton.com

Sheraton Manhattan   🎩 🏃 🍽 △ ♿ $$$-$$$$
790 Seventh Avenue at 52nd Street, 581-3300, 800 325-3535
660 rooms, club-level rooms, indoor pool

Sheraton New York Hotel & Towers   🎩 🏃 🍽 △ ♿ $$$
811 Seventh Avenue between 52nd and 53rd Streets, 581-1000,
800 325-3535   1750 rooms and suites, club-level rooms

Sheraton Russell Hotel   🎩 🕴 △ ♿ **$$$**
45 Park Avenue at 37th Street, 685-7676, 800 325-3535
146 rooms, club-level rooms

W   www.whotels.com

W New York   🎩 🕴 🍽 △ ♿ **$$$$**
541 Lexington Avenue at 49th Street, 755-1200, 877 946-8357
713 rooms and suites, modern luxury hotel, concierge (whatever/whenever
department), trendy gourmet restaurant

W New York, The Court   🎩 🍽 △ 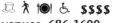 ♿ **$$$$**
130 East 39th Street between Lexington and Park Avenues, 685-1100,
877 946-8357
198 rooms and suites, modern luxury hotel, concierge (whatever/whenever
department), off-site fitness center, trendy gourmet restaurant

W New York, Times Square   🎩 🕴 🍽 ♿ **$$$$**
1567 Broadway at 47th Street, 930-7400, 877 946-8357
509 rooms and suites, modern luxury hotel, concierge (whatever/whenever
department), trendy gourmet restaurant

W New York, The Tuscany   🎩 🕴 🍽 ♿ **$$$$**
120 East 39th Street between Lexington and Park Avenues, 686-1600,
877 946-8357
122 rooms and suites, modern luxury hotel, concierge (whatever/whenever
department), trendy restaurant

W Union Square   🎩 🕴 🍽 ♿ **$$$$**
201 Park Avenue South at 17th Street, 253-9119, 877 946-8357
286 rooms and suites, modern luxury hotel, concierge (whatever/whenever
department), trendy gourmet restaurant

Westin   www.westin.com

The Westin New York at Times Square   🎩 🕴 △ ♿ **$$$**
43rd Street and Eighth Avenue, 201-2700, 800 WESTIN1
863 rooms and suites, concierge-level rooms

Airport Hotels

La Guardia Airport

Crowne Plaza Hotel La Guardia   iOi △ & $$
104-04 Ditmars Boulevard at 23rd Avenue, East Elmhurst, Queens,
718 457-6300, 800 692-5429, www.crowneplaza.com
358 rooms plus suites, swimming pool

Courtyard LaGuardia   ⵇ iOi △ & $$
90-10 Grand Central Parkway, East Elmhurst, Queens, 446-4800,
800 321-2211, www.marriott.com   295 rooms and suites, outdoor pool

La Guardia Marriott   ⛢ ⵇ iOi △ & $$$
102-05 Ditmars Boulevard at 23rd Avenue, East Elmhurst, Queens,
718 565-8900, 800 228-9290, www.marriott.com
439 rooms and suites, indoor pool

Sheraton LaGuardia East Hotel   ⛢ ⵇ iOi △ & $$-$$$
135-20 39th Avenue, Flushing, Queens, 718 460-6666, 800 325-3535,
www.sheraton.com   173 rooms

JFK Airport

Courtyard JFK Airport   ⛢ ⵇ iOi △ & $$
145-11 North Conduit Avenue, Jamaica, Queens, 718 848-2121,
800 880-1934, www.marriott.com   166 rooms

Hampton Inn JFK Airport   △ & $
144-10 135th Avenue, Jamaica, Queens, 718 322-7500, 800 426-7866,
www.hilton.com   216 rooms, off-site fitness center

Holiday Inn JFK Airport   ⛢ iOi △ & $$
144-02 135th Avenue, Jamaica, Queens, 718 659-0200, 800 692-5350,
www.holidayinnjfk.com   360 rooms plus suites, indoor–outdoor pool

Radisson Hotel JFK Airport   ⛢ ⵇ iOi △ & $$
135-30 140th Street, Jamaica, Queens, 718 322-2300, 800 333-3333,
www.radisson.com   386 rooms

Ramada Plaza JFK Airport   ⵇ iOi △ & $$
JFK Airport, Van Wyck Expressway, Jamaica, Queens, 718 995-9000,
888 535-7262, www.ramadajfk.com   478 rooms

Sheraton JFK Airport   ⟨icons⟩ $$
151-20 Baisley Boulevard, Jamaica, Queens, 718 489-1000, 800 325-3535,
www.sheraton.com   184 rooms

Newark International Airport

Courtyard Newark Airport   ⟨icons⟩ $$
600 Route 1 & 9 South, Newark, NJ, 973-643-8500, 800 321-2211,
www.marriott.com   158 rooms and suites, indoor pool

Hilton Newark Airport   ⟨icons⟩ $$
1170 Spring Street, Elizabeth, NJ, 908 351-3900, 800 774-1500,
www.hilton.com   378 rooms, indoor pool

Newark Airport Holiday Inn   ⟨icons⟩ $
160 Frontage Road, Newark, NJ, 973-589-1000, 800 465-4329,
www.holiday-inn.com   412 rooms

Newark Airport Marriott   ⟨icons⟩ $$
Newark International Airport, Newark, NJ, 973 623-0006, 800 882-1037,
www.marriott.com   597 rooms and suites, executive floor, indoor–outdoor pool

Sheraton Newark Airport Hotel   ⟨icons⟩ $$
128 Frontage Road, Newark, NJ, 973 690-5500, 800 325-3535,
www.sheraton.com   504 rooms

HOTEL INDEX

$ - less than $150

$$ - from $151 to $250

Lower Manhattan
Best Western Seaport Inn
Gramercy Park Hotel
Washington Square Hotel

West Side
Best Western Majestic
Courtyard NYC Manhattan Times
   Square South
Holiday Inn Martinique on Broadway
Holiday Inn Midtown
New York Marriott Marquis
The Plaza

Upper West Side
Hotel Beacon
Mayflower Hotel on the Park

East Side
Best Western Hospitality House
Clarion Hotel Fifth Avenue
Clarion Hotel Park Avenue
Courtyard NYC Manhattan Midtown East
Crowne Plaza Hotel at the United
   Nations
New York Marriott East Side

Upper East Side
Bristol Plaza

Airports
Courtyard JFK Airport
Holiday Inn JFK Airport
Radisson Hotel JFK Airport
Ramada Plaza JFK Airport
Sheraton JFK Airport

Courtyard LaGuardia
Crowne Plaza Hotel La Guardia
Sheraton LaGuardia East Hotel

Courtyard Newark Airport
Hilton Newark Airport
Newark Airport Marriott
Sheraton Newark Airport Hotel

Brooklyn
New York Marriott Brooklyn

$$$ - from $251 to $450

Lower Manhattan
Embassy Suites Hotel
Holiday Inn Downtown/Soho
Holiday Inn Wall Street
Millenium Hilton
New York Marriott Financial Center

West Side
The Algonquin
Courtyard NYC Manhattan Times
   Square South
Crowne Plaza Manhattan at Times
   Square
Doubletree Guest Suites
Flatotel
Hilton Times Square
The Hudson
New York Hilton & Towers
New York Marriott Marquis
The Paramount
The Plaza

The Royalton
Sheraton Manhattan
Sheraton New York Hotel & Towers
The Westin New York at Times Square

Upper West Side
Excelsior Hotel
Mayflower Hotel on the Park

East Side
Best Western Hospitality House
Clarion Hotel Fifth Avenue
Courtyard NYC Manhattan Midtown East
Crowne Plaza Hotel at the United
   Nations
Grand Hyatt
Kimberly Hotel
Morgans
New York Marriott East Side
Sheraton Russell Hotel

$$$ - from $251 to $450 continued

Upper East Side
Hotel Wales
The Marmara-Manhattan
The Melrose

Airports
La Guardia Marriott
Sheraton LaGuardia East Hotel

$$$$ - over $450

Lower Manhattan
The Mercer
Regent Wall Street
Ritz-Carlton New York Battery Park
SoHo Grand Hotel
Tribeca Grand Hotel
W Union Square

West Side
Central Park Inter-Continental
Essex House
Flatotel
Le Parker-Meridien
The Peninsula
Renaissance New York Hotel Times
    Square
RIHGA Royal
Ritz-Carlton New York Central Park
The Royalton
Sheraton Manhattan
Southgate Tower
Trump International Hotel and Tower
W New York, Times Square

Upper West Side
The Phillips Club

East Side
Beekman Tower Hotel
The Benjamin Hotel
Dumont Plaza
Eastgate Tower
The Envoy Club
Four Seasons New York
Intercontinental The Barclay New York
Kitano
New York Palace and The Towers
Plaza Fifty
St. Regis Hotel
Shelburne Murray Hill
The Sherry-Netherland
The Sutton
Swissotel New York – The Drake
W New York
W New York, The Court
W New York, The Tuscany
Waldorf-Astoria and Waldorf Towers

Upper East Side
The Carlyle
Hôtel Plaza Athénée
The Lowell
Lyden Gardens
The Mark
The Pierre
The Regency
The Stanhope Park Hyatt
Surrey Hotel

Chapter 10

SAFE AND HEALTHY ON THE STREETS OF NEW YORK

O ut-of-towners tend to see New York City as either a very danger-ous place, with peril and temptation lurking around every corner, or the venue for nonstop excitement and adventure. For those who have never been here before, or have never been here with chil-dren, the city can indeed be a very intimidating place. Whatever your perspective, when you visit New York with children, you want to have a positive experience. To do so, it is important to think about how to get around and use the city in a way that will be enjoyable and safe for everyone.

Preparing yourself for a visit to New York does not require a crash course in guerilla street tactics or self-defense. To the contrary, the last several years have brought a welcome improvement in the quality of life in the Big Apple. Since 1993, when then-Mayor Rudolph W. Giuliani embarked on a crusade to improve life in the city, it has become a safer, cleaner and more civil and vibrant metropolis. Not only have the notorious "squeegee men" been virtually eliminated, but overall crime has decreased by more than 49 percent and tremendous strides have been made in enforcing traffic laws, raising taxi safety standards, reducing reckless bicycle riding by those infamous bike messengers and decreasing noise pollution, litter and panhandling.

Indeed, according to FBI statistics, New York City, with more than 40,000 uniformed police officers, has become since 1993 one of the safest large cities in the country. That being said, however, residents and visitors alike must deal with the realities of urban life when in New York, and take care and exercise caution when out and about.

In this chapter, we will discuss keeping yourself and your children safe while moving around on the streets of New York, dealing with illness and emergencies and mastering the basics of hotel and fire safety. At the end of the chapter, you will find a list of resources that will help make your visit to the city as safe as possible for your family.

 🏙

The Sidewalks of New York

▶ **Out on the streets.** New York City is home to more than eight million people from all cultures and walks of life. In addition, many thousands commute into New York every day for work and entertainment. You can expect to be in close proximity to others the moment you step outside, and yet among all those people, you may find yourself surprisingly alone at certain times or in some locations.

Even for well-traveled kids, the hustle and bustle can be very disconcerting. If you are coming from a suburban or rural environment, the noise and activity of the city streets can be quite a shock. Although the safety rules most children already know apply to any location, the inherent differences between home and the city, not to mention the excitement and wonder that often accompany a city visit, can often initiate bouts of safety-rule amnesia.

There are very few absolutes when it comes to safety rules. While we want to protect our children against all harm, we cannot anticipate everything that can potentially happen. The trick is to teach your children not only specific words and actions, but also, and perhaps more important, strategies to deal with events for which they are not expressly prepared. The key skills include how to observe situations, formulate strategies, feel confident about their decisions and take decisive action appropriate to the situation. Developing these skills is a lifelong process that begins in childhood.

Traveling to a new place, or even a somewhat familiar one that is still different from your home turf, is the perfect time to review safety rules and adjust them as need be.

► **Safety basics for kids.** City safety rules are really not very different from the ones you probably already have at home. You may, however, want to modify or add to your regular rules to deal with being in an unfamiliar place and to address the fact that New York City may be busier or more crowded than home.

Even the youngest children need to be taught such safety basics as how to use the telephone, how and when to use 911 and how to deal with strangers. When children are able, they should learn their full names, their parents' names, and their addresses and phone numbers.

As soon as you feel that the children are old enough, you can give them a list to carry with all relevant emergency numbers (cellular phones, beepers, office numbers or friends or relatives to call in an emergency). You can point out city landmarks to help them orient themselves (such as in relation to where the car is parked or where the hotel is located) and arrange for a contingency plan in case you become separated. If you are staying in a hotel, make sure the children have the name, phone number and address of the hotel on hand at all times. If you are in New York for the day, make sure your children know where the car is parked or, if you are traveling by train or bus, the name of the line on which you travel and the station from which you depart.

It is important to prepare your children for situations where an adult is not present, even if only for a moment, and work out strategies with them for getting help. They need to know how to conduct themselves if approached by a stranger in a store, on the street, in a crowd, at the park or anywhere else. They need strategies to get help if they become separated from you. They need to be empowered to protect themselves against potential physical harm. As much as we may not want to have to discuss these issues with our children, as responsible parents it is our duty to give them the tools to protect themselves.

Your safety rules should be clearly communicated to all care-givers who may be with the children during your visit to the city, including grandparents, relatives or friends who may be watching the children or taking them on an outing. Do not assume that an otherwise responsible adult who is not used to being with children in the city will have the same rules as you do. Often, adults who do not spend time with children, or have not done so in a long time, are not focused on how easily curious children can wander off or how much vigilance is necessary to keep them safe.

If you are traveling with a caregiver and staying at a hotel, your caregiver should have the name and address of the hotel, any other pertinent information, a contingency plan in case you become sep-arated, some cash for carfare or an emergency and instructions on how to handle an emergency. We know of one family who lost their nanny in Rome for an entire day because she did not know where the family was staying and did not know how to use the local tele-phone or have carfare to return to the museum where she started out the day. If you are in town for the day, your caregiver should know how to get back to where your car is parked or which train or bus you plan to take home.

When traveling anywhere with children, it is a good idea to have an identification kit on hand that includes recent photographs and fingerprints of your child. If you assemble an identification kit, you may also want to include a description of any identifying marks (for example, birthmarks, scars, chipped tooth) or characteristics (for example, handedness, pitch of voice or a tendency to giggle or lisp), a lock of hair, and frequently updated measurements, clothing and shoe sizes and a photo. Many local police departments will help parents assemble a child identification package that includes fin-gerprints and front and side view photos of your child. Call your local police station in your home town to see if they will assist you in putting together your kit.

► **All-purpose safety guidelines**. Your children probably already know these things, but it is always a good idea to review them before your trip:

▰ **Stay connected.** Children should always stay with an adult or their group. On crowded streets or in places where it is easy to get separated, including a busy playground, children should not run ahead or lag behind or be out of the supervising adult's line of sight. At busy intersections, it is important that your children not turn the corner before you get to the end of the block. A good reminder is to tell your children that you must always be able to see them.

▰ **No wandering.** Children should always let an adult know where they are going. Even if they are not allowed to go far, it is good practice to get them in the habit of letting you know where they are. For example, in a store your child should not wander off to the next display but should say "I am going to look at the books."

▰ **Pay attention.** Children should always pay attention to their surroundings, look alert and self-confident and walk with purpose. Help your children by pointing out, and teaching them to take note of, landmarks and the people around them.

▰ **Stranger danger.** Help your children understand that a stranger is any person they do not know. This can be a very confusing subject for your children to tackle. For example, an employee at a hotel may be very helpful and even get to know your child by name, but that person is still a stranger. A helpful approach is to teach children to be on the lookout for certain kinds of situations or actions (for example, an adult asking for a child to help find a lost puppy) rather than certain kinds of individuals.

▰ **Help!** If in trouble, a child should shout "help," "call the police" or "fire" to attract attention. Knowing how to get help—calling 911 or looking for a police officer or other uniformed guard—may sound like a simple task, but without preparation, many kids faced with danger will either dissolve into tears or be paralyzed with fear. If your child is separated from you in a place of business, he or she should go to an employee—salesperson, waiter, usher, doorman— before asking for or accepting help from a patron. Help your child be comfortable asking for help from a police officer (who might be intimidating to a child) as well as saying "no" to an adult stranger.

◤ **Lost in the crowd.** It is surprisingly common for children to become separated from you, a caregiver, a group leader or other adult with whom they are supposed to be, particularly at parades, street fairs, ball parks, theaters or other crowded public events. A strategy suggested to us by a police officer for making it easier to find a child lost in a crowd is to have him or her wear distinctive brightly colored clothing when you are expecting to go to a crowded event such as a parade. Distinguishing clothing is much easier to spot and you can yell out "My son/daughter is missing. He/she is wearing a yellow shirt" which will get people in the vicinity focused on locating your child.

◤ **Getting around.** Children should be reminded of the basics about crossing the street, following traffic signs and rules and being alert to vehicles that cannot see them or are backing up. If your child uses a bicycle, skateboard, scooter or in-line skates, make sure he or she uses appropriate safety gear, rides safely and understands how to conduct him or herself in traffic (pedestrian and vehicular). Note that if you will be bicycle riding in Central Park, you are required to ride with, not against, the traffic flow.

◤ **Elevator and bathroom safety.** Children, and younger children in particular, should not go into an elevator ahead of you. Electronic doors can close very quickly and your child could end up in the elevator without you. Children not familiar with riding elevators need to know never to try to stop the doors from closing by putting their arm or leg in the door, as they can easily be crushed. City parents are typically very conservative about sending children off to public restrooms on their own. A typical rule of thumb when sending your child to a bathroom that is a single room rather than a multi-stall bathroom is not to let the child go to the bathroom alone unless you can see the door (for example, from your table in the restaurant) or stand at the door. It is always a good idea to accompany your child to a bathroom with multiple stalls. If your older child of the opposite sex needs to use a public restroom, stand by the door and make sure that your child is not in the bathroom for an unusually long time.

◪ **Show off.** City streets are not an appropriate place to count money, show others your new purchases or other valuables or loudly discuss your plans. Money and wallets should be kept out of view.

◪ **Hello operator.** Children should know how to use a public telephone and make collect or credit-card calls.

◪ **Out alone.** If you have not let your children go out without an adult in your own home town, letting them explore the streets of New York on their own is definitely not the place to start. In fact, even if your child is used to going out alone at home, it is wise to err on the side of caution and not do so, or have much stricter parameters for going out alone, in New York.

▶ **A word about teenagers.** Teenagers visiting New York City will no doubt expect to venture out without you, particularly if they have siblings or friends along. We do not recommend letting younger teenagers out without adult supervision, particularly if they do not go out alone at home or if they are not used to the city. If, however, you have decided that it is safe to let your older teenager go out without an adult, here are some things to consider:

◪ **Street safety.** Your teens should pay attention, look alert and self-confident and walk with a purpose. They should stick to well-lit, well-traveled areas, avoid construction sites, empty or closed stores and deserted buildings, and not take shortcuts through the park (stick to streets instead). Well-lit commercial streets are generally safer than quiet streets, and the park side of a street should be avoided. Lingering in a large, noisy crowd on the street can attract unwanted attention and should be avoided. Work out with them the best strategies for dealing with strangers and what to do if they are followed on foot or by a car.

◪ **The buddy system.** Going it alone is not necessarily a safe plan for a teenager. Traveling in small groups of two, three or four is a much better choice.

☑ **Transportation.** Bus, subway and taxi safety are extremely important. Teenagers riding the bus or subway should be instructed on specific procedures, such as avoiding isolated bus stops, having extra change or a MetroCard on hand, staying clear of the platform edge and riding in the car with the motorman (usually the center car). If using the subways at night, they should wait for the train in the area marked "Off-Peak Waiting Areas." Teens using taxis should take only yellow cabs or cars from a telephone car service (making sure not to get into unmarked cars or car-service cars that cannot identify by name the person they are supposed to pick up). At night it is advisable to take a taxi, even if only for a few blocks, rather than walk. The Parents League of New York (a not-for-profit organization of parents and independent schools) recommends that children riding in taxis always carry about $3.00 of "escape money" that can be quickly handed to a driver as the child exits the taxi at a traffic light if he or she is uncomfortable in the taxi. If a teen is driving a car, the doors and windows and trunk should be kept locked. Check the back seat for unwanted guests before getting into a parked car.

☑ **Dress for success.** Notwithstanding your teens' desire to look cool, they should not wear visible or flashy jewelry or trendy accessories. These types of sought-after items are targets for mugging or assault. If your teen is approached by a mugger, the NYPD advises giving up your property rather than engaging in a fight with an assailant who may be mentally unstable, substance impaired or armed.

☑ **Curfew.** It is important to set a curfew for your teens and to agree on the places they may go and the modes of transportation they may use.

☑ **Communication.** As cellular phones and even high-tech walkie-talkies become more available and accessible, you may want to consider using technology to remain in contact with your older child as he or she begins to be out and about without you. At the very least, it is important to institute a system of regular check-ins by telephone so that you always know where your teen is.

▶ **It's the law.** Despite the common belief in the lawlessness of New York City, there are in fact many laws on the books that address safety issues. A sampler:

◤ **Pedestrians.** Notwithstanding the fact that native New Yorkers seem to enjoy tempting drivers to hit them by stepping into the street and crossing between lights, pedestrians can and do get ticketed for jaywalking. If you are walking, you should always stop at the corner and wait on the curb for the Walk sign. Avoid crossing mid-block or from between parked cars. It is particularly dangerous to push your stroller into the street while you are waiting to cross because your stroller can be an easy target for a car making a speedy, tight turn. It is best to give yourself the most time to cross by waiting for a newly turned green light rather than running through a blinking Don't Walk sign. Unfortunately, city drivers often regard the yellow traffic light as a signal to step on the gas rather than to slow down. Therefore, avoid the temptation to wait in the street, and remain on the sidewalk until it is safe to go. By law, cars making a turn must yield to pedestrians at the crosswalk. Drivers are required to come to a complete stop before the crosswalk for a red light or a stop sign. The New York Police Department recommends that if the sidewalk is blocked and you must walk in the road, walk facing traffic so that drivers can see you.

◤ **Bicyclists.** All bicycle riders under the age of 14 are required by law to wear a helmet. Riders 13 years or older must drive in the street and not on the sidewalk. When riding in the street, riders must ride with the flow of traffic, stop at stop signs and obey all other traffic signals and rules, including yielding to pedestrians. Visitors should be aware that cycling rules apply even on streets that run through city parks.

◤ **Drivers.** All passengers in the front seat of cars are required to wear a seat belt. All children under the age of 16 must wear a seat belt whether they are sitting in the back or front seats. Children under the age of 4 must be in a federally approved car safety seat. Drivers can receive a fine of up to $100 if a passenger under the age of 16 is not properly buckled up. (See Chapter 3 for information about using seat belts in taxis). Within New York City limits, drivers *may not* turn right on red, unless otherwise specifically advised by posted signs.

Safety Ideas for the Whole Family

▶ **Steering clear of street crime.** There is no surer way for your trip to New York to be ruined than to become the victim of a street crime. The NYPD offers these tips to avoid becoming the target of a pickpocket or con artist:

- ⤴ Carry purses that close tightly (a zipper or locking flap) and carry them securely, with the flap close to your body. Do not hang purses, backpacks or shopping bags on the back of your chair or set them next to you on the floor.

- ⤴ Carry wallets inside your coat or in your side pants pockets rather than in your back pocket.

- ⤴ Beware of loud arguments or commotions, because they may be incidents staged to distract people while being pickpocketed. Do not be distracted by strangers asking you for directions. Another common distraction technique is for a stranger to direct your attention to something on your clothes (such as a mustard or ketchup stain).

- ⤴ If you are bumped, jostled or crowded, a pickpocket may be responsible.

- ⤴ Be on guard at an ATM machine. A pickpocket may tell you that you dropped money as a distraction.

- ⤴ Avoid three-card Monty or other street games. Do not buy watches or jewelry on the street from other than vendors with posted vendor licenses.

- ⤴ On a bus or on the stairs or an escalator, do not be distracted if someone appears to stumble or drop something in front of you or while getting on or off the bus or escalator. A person pushing or shoving you or moving quickly to the exit may be a pickpocket.

- ⤴ If you are in your car, it is best to drive with the windows up and the doors locked. Store your purse, shopping bags and other items out of sight on the floor rather than on the seat. If a driver bumps your car or indicates that you should stop your car and get out (a common ruse is to say you have a flat tire), do not get out but proceed to a populated, well-lit area to get help. If you have a cellular phone, call for assistance.

► **Hotel safety.** Hotel safety is important not only for older children who may be without an adult in the room but to the entire family. Some safety tips to keep in mind:

- When you are in your room, always lock the door and use the door security chain. When you leave the room, do not just let the door close behind you; make sure to close the door manually.

- Do not keep valuables exposed in your room. Use an in-room safe or one of the hotel safe-deposit boxes.

- Do not open your door to anyone you are not expecting or to other than appropriate hotel staff. If someone comes to your door claiming to be a repair or delivery person, call the front desk before opening the door to confirm that the person is supposed to be coming to your room.

- Do not discuss plans or activities in front of strangers. Keep your hotel room number confidential. Rather than carrying your room key, deposit it with the front desk when you leave the hotel.

- Do not leave luggage unattended in the hotel. Store it with the Bell Desk instead.

- If you need to leave your room, do not leave the door propped open. Instead, close and lock the door behind you.

► **Home away from home . . . alone.** Wherever you live, sooner or later, the day will come when you agree to let your children stay home for some period of time without an adult in the house. And if a child has had the experience of being home without an adult, he or she will probably expect the same privilege on your city vacation.

Leaving your child home alone is a very controversial issue. We are not expressing a view as to whether or not you should do this or the age at which it is appropriate to do so. Your decision as to when to leave your *older* child alone in the house is strictly a family matter *except that it is never appropriate to leave an infant, toddler, or very young child alone or in the care of another child. Do not leave your child alone if there is not adequate security or your accommodations are not safe for an unattended child.* Of course, if your child has never been alone at home, a hotel room would definitely not be the place to start.

The fact that your child can stay home alone in your own house does not mean that it is appropriate to stay alone in a hotel room or to explore the hotel unsupervised. At home, your child has a routine, is in familiar surroundings and has friends, neighbors and family to call upon if necessary. Vacation is another story entirely. Hotels have many employees, guests and visitors on the floor, in the elevators, in the restaurants, in public restrooms, in the lobby and in other public areas at any given time. Unfortunately, unwitting children are easy targets for individuals with less-than-good intentions.

Even if your children are allowed to be without an adult in your own home, we strongly recommend that you *not leave any children in a hotel without an adult or let them explore the hotel without adult supervision.* This would even apply to young (or less mature) teenagers. So, when your adolescent is complaining about being dragged to yet another art museum and would rather stay in the room and channel surf, hang tough and find a compromise that does not involve your child going solo in the hotel.

If you do determine that it is appropriate to leave your *teenager* in the hotel without an adult, here are some considerations:

◢ **Is your teen ready?** Even though your teenager may be comfortable being at home alone, he or she may be less comfortable about being alone in a hotel. Consider whether your teenager wants to be alone, is not afraid to be alone, has good problem-solving skills, is responsible and self-motivated, can recognize a problem and take action, follows instructions and the rules and would feel comfortable seeking help (from hotel staff, by phone, calling 911).

◢ **Make sure your teen is prepared.** Before you leave, review: emergency procedures; what to do if there is a fire; how to reach you, another adult, building personnel or police or firefighters; how to handle phone calls, visitors or deliveries during your absence; what to do if you are late coming home. Make sure he or she has one or more adults to call upon if there is a problem (concierge, doorman, friend, relative) and that he or she has a way to reach you (beeper, cellular phone, other phone numbers). As you develop contingency plans, make sure to review them with your teen and consider writing them down for easy reference.

☑ **Telephone.** How should the telephone be answered? What information may your teen give to callers (for example, who is there and when you will be back)? Would you prefer that calls go on hotel voice mail or to the operator rather than be answered?

☑ **Answering the door.** To whom may your teen open the door? What should he or she say before opening the door (who is it?) or if he or she is not going to open the door (we are not expecting anyone now)?

☑ **Hotel personnel and services.** Are any employees allowed in your room while you are out? What services may the kids call for when you are not there (housekeeping, room service, none) and are delivery people allowed into the room? What amenities can they use in your absence (video games, videos, pay-per-view movies, minibar)?

☑ **Leaving the room.** Where may the kids go in the hotel (game room, ice machine, vending machines, pool, gym, lobby, restaurant, no place)? If they are planning to leave the room, how will they let you know where to find them and what time they will return (leave a note, call you on the cell phone)?

☑ **Checking in.** If your teen will be coming back to your hotel room when you will be out, establish procedures for him or her to check in with you or another designated adult upon arrival at the hotel and spell out how to contact you if his or her schedule will change. Make certain your teen will be able to get back into the hotel room. Instruct him or her not to enter the hotel room if the door is open or not properly locked.

▶ **Safety programs in Manhattan.** The Parents League has been a leader in dealing with safety issues. The Safe Haven Program, begun in the 1970s by the Parents League in conjunction with the East Side Chamber of Commerce, registers merchants who agree to provide a sanctuary to a child or adult who is in danger or otherwise feels threatened. Safe Haven participants display a distinctive yellow and black sticker in their window or on the door and receive training to assist the person in need by providing shelter, allowing or making a telephone call (either to the police or someone else) and giving help. The Safe Haven Program has recently expanded to include apartment buildings on routes commonly traveled by schoolchildren. It is well worth educating your children to recognize and look for Safe Havens.

It is well worth educating your children to recognize and look for Safe Havens.

Every fire department in New York City is also a safe haven for children through the Firecap program. Under this program, every firehouse and fire truck is considered a safe haven for a child or adult. The Firecap decal consists of a white square, bordered in black, with a red helmet in the middle and two children holding hands, and says "If you're in trouble, or if someone's bothering you, say NO and get away. You can always go to a firefighter or firehouse for help." When someone comes to them for help, they will notify appropriate authorities and take the necessary steps to help the person in need.

Every fire department in New York City is also a safe haven for children through the Firecap program.

► **A final thought.** While the issues raised in this section may send you running for cover, we want to emphasize that the many safety programs and police officers keep the city safe for residents and visitors alike. Helping children develop the judgment and strategies to handle difficult situations and giving them the tools to feel secure and help themselves will serve them well anywhere and all of the time. We urge you to spend time thinking about these issues and educating and working with your children to reduce the likelihood that you or they will become victims of crime. By doing so, you will improve the odds that you will leave New York city with only good memories.

Mommy, I Don't Feel Well

Every parent has heard these unfortunate words at least once on a family outing or vacation, usually at the most inconvenient time possible. The fact is that traveling with kids creates the perfect conditions for falling prey to viruses, infections and other mishaps. A day trip into the city, including sampling new and different foods, can set an unsuspecting tummy into turmoil. When on vacation, we disrupt our family routines (and perhaps even time zones), eat more meals in restaurants, sample different foods (often at odd times), eat more treats, stay up late, miss naps, do more in a day than we do at home and just generally operate at a higher level of activity and excitement. If you add air travel into the equation, you are almost guaranteed to end up with at least one episode of physical meltdown.

While most travel illnesses will do little more than truncate a day trip or require an early night or day of hotel room cable TV and room service, there will be times when you need to consult with a doctor. If you are planning to stay in New York City, it is a good idea to ask your local doctor if he or she has a colleague to recommend in the city so that you have someone to call if necessary. If not, but you have friends or family in town, you can use their city doctor (or one referred by their doctor) should the need arise. If you are staying in a hotel, the concierge or manager can usually provide you with a referral. Of course, if your child is extremely ill, your best bet is to get to an emergency room either on your own or by ambulance (see below).

Most of the time, you can resolve a minor travel illness with a call home to your own doctor for advice and an interim fix. Many parents find it useful to carry the medicines their children use so that a midnight fever does not necessitate a panicked search for a 24-hour pharmacy. Common travel items include acetaminophen, ibuprofen, antihistamine, cold/cough syrup, a thermometer, topical antibiotic cream, topical cortisone cream, medicine for upset tummies, saline drops for stuffy noses and any prescription medication your child requires. For children suffering from asthma, many parents purchase a small travel-size nebulizer that can be easily packed.

Emergencies

The last thing you want to think about is coping with an emergency, particularly an emergency occurring outside your home turf. However, the best thing you can do in the event of an emergency is to be prepared. This does not mean that you have to live your life waiting for the moment when your lifesaving, self-defense or other survival skills are put to the test, but it does mean that you and the members of your household traveling with you, which includes your children, their caregivers and anyone else with whom you leave your children (grandparents, friends, and so on), have a current working knowledge of how to handle themselves and what to do if an emergency occurs.

▶ **Medical Emergencies.** It is extremely important for you and those who take care of your children to be prepared to handle a medical emergency. At the very least, you should travel with a basic first-aid kit and a handy list of important emergency phone numbers, such as your cellular numbers, the pediatrician (or any other doctor your family uses), the dentist, poison control, and a family member, neighbor or friend who should be called if you are not available. It is also wise for you and your child's other caregivers to be trained in CPR and other emergency techniques, such as how to treat a choking victim, being sure to update the training regularly.

In the event of a medical emergency (which includes dental emergencies), if you do not have a New York City doctor to call, you will probably need an emergency room. If the situation is not dire, you may have time to call your home pediatrician for advice, but if the child needs to be physically examined, you will need either a referral to a local doctor (which can generally be made by your hotel) or know how to find the ER.

In the case of a dire emergency, you should call 911 before anything else. If you have a local doctor and you have the choice, try to have the ambulance take your child to the hospital with which your doctor is affiliated (see below). If the situation is not dire, and you have a local doctor, you can call that doctor and ask to be met or called at the emergency room or for the doctor to call ahead to the emergency room on your behalf so that you can be met by an appropriate specialist (for example, an orthopedist if a broken bone is suspected). *If you are not sure how bad the situation is, do not waste time trying to decide. Call 911.*

When your children are in the care of another adult, such as a grandparent, relative, friend or other caregiver, another important element of preparation is to give that person an envelope that contains cab fare to get to a doctor's office or hospital and a signed consent form authorizing treatment of your child. Keep in mind that in some circumstances, the doctor or emergency room cannot administer treatment without parental consent. Your consent form should state that your child may receive treatment if deemed necessary by his or her physician or the hospital physician in the event that you cannot be reached. It should also include any pertinent information about allergies, chronic conditions, medications taken regularly by the child and medical insurance.

▶ **EMS.** The New York City Emergency Medical Service (EMS), which operates under the auspices of the City Health and Hospitals Corporation, is the primary emergency medical care provider in the city. EMS operates a fleet of more than 350 ambulances that are deployed throughout, and constantly patrol, the five boroughs.

If you need an emergency service, call 911. Your call will be routed by the police operator to the high-tech EMS communications center in Maspeth, Queens, for triage and dispatching of an ambulance. EMS will transmit information directly to a mobile data terminal located in the dispatched ambulance. Be sure to give the EMS operator all relevant information and the telephone number of the phone from which you are calling. Be certain not to hang up until the EMS operator tells you to, so that the automatic location indicator and automatic number indicator can be activated and all relevant information can be obtained. If possible, have someone meet the ambulance to lead the crew to where the patient is located. Remember to use 911 only for a true emergency.

Once you are in an ambulance, you have a limited ability to direct EMS to the hospital of your choice. EMS is required to take you to the closest 911 Receiving Emergency Facility (an emergency room certified by EMS and relevant state authorities). You can request that EMS take you to a specific hospital, which EMS will endeavor to do only under the following circumstances: the patient is not *in extremis* and the hospital you request is *not more than* either (1) ten minutes from the closest hospital to which you would have otherwise been taken or (2) 20 minutes from where the ambulance picks you up (that is, not more than 20 minutes of total travel time). The decision as to the medical condition of the patient and the estimated travel time is at the discretion of EMS, not you.

At the end of this chapter, you will find a list of New York City emergency rooms, trauma centers, burn centers, replantation units and other special services.

► **Reporting a crime.** There are two types of situations involving crimes: emergencies and nonemergencies. In an emergency situation, the crime is in progress, or if not actually still in progress, the person or persons who committed the crime may still be in the vicinity. In a nonemergency situation, the crime has been committed and some amount of time has elapsed.

You should report a crime in an emergency situation by calling 911. If your child is missing, treat it as an emergency and *report it immediately*. Patrol cars are dispatched by 911, so calling the local police precinct will delay police response. Your report should include as much information as you have about what happened, where it happened and descriptions of the perpetrator(s). The information you provide will be broadcast over the police radio. The responding officer will interview the victim and witnesses, if any, and file a complaint. A detective will be assigned if appropriate under applicable police procedures.

You may report a crime in a nonemergency situation by contacting the relevant local precinct (see the list at the end of this chapter). Assaults can generally be reported by telephone, although robbery complaints must be filed in person. The complainant will be interviewed and a detective will be assigned if appropriate under applicable police procedures.

► **In case of a fire.** The New York City Fire Department recommends the following procedures in the event of a fire:

☑ **Get Help.** Call 911 to report smoke, a fire or a suspected fire. If you are able, leave the area immediately and call from a safe location.

☑ **Smoke.** If you smell smoke, call 911 to reach the fire department and, if applicable, activate the building fire-alarm system. Since smoke rises, stay low. If you cannot escape, use wet towels or tape to seal the door and room vents and turn off air conditioners and fans. Open a window, but do not break it as you may need to close the window to prevent smoke from a lower floor entering through your window.

☑ **Escape.** Identify fire exits in any unfamiliar building. If you are staying in a hotel, point out the exits to your children and work out a family escape plan and meeting place outside the hotel. In a hotel, count the number of doors between your room and the exits in case the lights go out. Fire officials recommend that you plan two ways out of the building and plan what you will do if you cannot escape. Before leaving the room, check the door with the back of your hand. If it is cool, stay low to the ground and open slowly (be prepared to close quickly if there is smoke or fire in the hallway). Use the stairs. Do not use the elevator to escape a fire. Close the door behind you but do not lock it (or take your key) in case you need to turn back. As you move to the exit, keep low to the ground where the air is cooler. The safest escape may be to stay where you are and await help. Stay calm.

☑ **Or Stay Put.** If you cannot escape, fill the bathtub with water with which to cool down the door if it gets hot. Wave a sheet out the window to signal the fire department that you are in your room.

☑ **Alarm.** Do not depend on someone else to call the fire department. Always call the fire department even if you think the fire is out. Do not depend on the building alarm system, as it may not be directly connected to the fire department or it may not be functioning.

☑ **Prevention.** Complain to the hotel management if you notice blocked fire exits, locked fire doors, fire doors wedged open or trash stored in fire exits.

◪ **Stop, Drop and Roll,** if your clothes catch fire.

For additional information on fire safety and prevention, you can contact the New York City Department Office of Public Safety and Education at 718 999-2343 or visit
www.nyc.gov/html/fdny/html/safety/firesafety.html
or
the U.S. Fire Administration at www.usfa.fema.gov.

► **Don't panic.** While there is surely a great deal of potential for accidents to occur or for our children to land in dangerous or unsafe situations, in many ways being in New York City makes you no more or less vulnerable than being anywhere else in the country. We cannot and should not scare ourselves or our children away from partaking in the fun and pleasure of being in this city. What we can do is take reasonable precautions and give our children the tools and security to handle the situations we and they may encounter.

RESOURCES

Animal Bites

New York City Department of Health, Bureau of Veterinary Public Health Services, Animal Bite Unit 676-2483

Dental Emergencies

Emergency Dental Service, New York County Dental Society, 573-9502

Emergency Rooms (ER), Manhattan

Bellevue Hospital (911 receiving facility), 462 First Avenue, 562-4141. ER entrance on the corner of First Avenue and 27th Street. Bellevue maintains specific pediatric emergency facilities staffed with a member of the Child Life Program. Pediatric Trauma Unit, Trauma Unit, Replantation Unit, Spinal Cord Injury Center

Beth Israel Medical Center (911 receiving facility) (downtown), First Avenue and 16th Street, 420-2840. ER entrance on 16th Street between First and Second Avenues. Beth Israel maintains specific pediatric emergency facilities.

Beth Israel Medical Center (911 receiving facility) (uptown), 170 East End Avenue, 870-9000. ER entrance on East 88th Street off East End Avenue.

Cabrini Medical Center, 227 East 19th Street, 995-6620. ER entrance on 20th Street between Second and Third Avenues.

Harlem Hospital Center (911 receiving facility), 506 Lenox Avenue, 939-1000. ER entrance on Lenox Avenue between 135th and 136th Streets. Harlem Hospital maintains specific pediatric emergency facilities. Trauma Unit

Hospital for Joint Diseases Orthopaedic Institute, 301 East 17th Street at corner of Second Avenue, 598-6000. Specialized hospital. ER for private ambulance only, not serviced by EMS. Entrance through main lobby. Immediate care center for broken bones, sprains, and so on.

Jacobi Medical Center (911 receiving facility), 1400 Pelham Parkway South, Eastchester Road, Bronx, NY 10461, 718 918-5000. Hyperbaric center and snakebite center

Lenox Hill Hospital (911 receiving facility), 100 East 77th Street, 434-3030. ER entrance at 120 East 77th Street between Park and Lexington Avenues. Lenox Hill maintains specific pediatric emergency facilities.

Manhattan Eye, Ear and Throat Hospital, 210 East 64th Street, 838-9200. Specialized services for eye, ear, nose or throat emergencies. ER entrance through main hospital entrance on 64th Street between Second and Third Avenues.

Metropolitan Hospital (911 receiving facility), 1901 First Avenue, 423-6262. ER entrance on 97th Street between First and Second Avenues. Metropolitan maintains specific pediatric emergency facilities.

Mt. Sinai Medical Center (911 receiving facility), One Gustave L. Levy Place, 241-6500. ER entrance on Madison Avenue between 100th and 101st Streets. Mt. Sinai maintains specific pediatric emergency facilities staffed with a member of the Child Life Program.

New York Eye and Ear Infirmary, 310 East 14th Street, 979-4000. Specialized services for eye, ear, nose or throat emergencies. ER entrance on Second Avenue between 13th and 14th Streets.

New York Presbyterian Hospital (911 receiving facility)

    Columbia-Presbyterian Campus (formerly Columbia Presbyterian Medical Center), 622 West 168th Street, 305-2500. ER entrance on 168th Street between Broadway and Ft. Washington Avenue. Columbia-Presbyterian Campus maintains specific pediatric emergency facilities. Pediatric Trauma Unit

    New York-Cornell Campus (formerly New York Hospital Cornell Medical Center), 525 East 68th Street, 746-5454. ER entrance on 68th Street between York Avenue and the FDR Drive. New York-Cornell Campus maintains specific pediatric emergency facilities. Burn Center, Trauma Unit

New York University Medical Center (911 receiving facility), 550 First Avenue, 263-5550. ER entrance on First Avenue at 33rd Street.

NYU DOWNTOWN HOSPITAL, 170 William Street, 312-5063. ER entrance at Spruce and Beekman.

ST. LUKE'S-ROOSEVELT HOSPITAL CENTER (911 receiving facility), 523-4000 (general number for St. Lukes and Roosevelt divisions)

> **ST. LUKES DIVISION,** 1111 Amsterdam Avenue. ER entrance on the corner of 113th and Amsterdam Avenue. St. Luke's maintains a pediatric emergency room. Trauma Unit

> **ROOSEVELT DIVISION** (911 receiving facility), 1000 Tenth Avenue. ER entrance on West 59th Street between Ninth and Tenth Avenues. St. Luke's maintains a specific pediatric emergency department

ST. VINCENT'S HOSPITAL AND MEDICAL CENTER OF NEW YORK (911 receiving facility), 153 West 11th Street, 604-7000. ER entrance on Seventh Avenue between 11th and 12th Streets. St.Vincent's maintains special pediatric emergency facilities. Trauma Unit

Fire Safety

New York City Fire Department, 9 Metrotech Center, Brooklyn, NY 11201, www.nyc.gov

> 718 999-2000 (headquarters)
> 718 999-2343 (fire safety education department)
> 718 999-2056 (public information—Fire Department and EMS)

National Fire Protection Association, 11 Tracy Drive, Avon, MA 02322, 800 344-3555, www.nfpa.org (includes a list of publications)

U.S. Fire Administration, www.usfa.fema.gov

Hotel Safety

American Hotel & Lodging Association, webprod.ahma.com

Park Emergencies

New York City Parks Department, nycparks.completeinet.com
800 201-PARK (7275)

Poison Control

Poison Control Center, POISONS (764-7667) or VENENOS (836-3667)

Police Information

General information 646/718 610-5000
Child abuse hotline 800 342-3720
Crime victim services (Safe Horizons) 577-7777
Crimestoppers 577-TIPS (8477) or 800 577-TIPS (8477);
    Spanish 888 57 PISTA (74784)
Domestic violence 800 621-4673
Missing persons case status 646 610-6914
Sex crime report unit 267-RAPE

Terrorism Hotline 888 NYC SAFE (692-7233)
www.nyc.gov (official website of city government)

Manhattan

1st Precinct
16 Ericsson Place
334-0611

5th Precinct
19 Elizabeth Street
334-0711

6th Precinct
233 West 10th Street
741-4811

7th Precinct
19 1/2 Pitt Street
477-7311

9th Precinct
321 East 5th Street
477-7811

10th Precinct
230 West 20th Street
741-8211

13th Precinct
230 East 21st Street
477-7411

Midtown South Precinct
357 West 35th Street
239-9811

17th Precinct
167 East 51st Street
826-3211

Midtown North Precinct
306 West 54th Street
760-8300

19th Precinct
153 East 67th Street
452-0600

20th Precinct
120 West 82nd Street
580-6411

Central Park Precinct
86th Street Transverse
570-4820

23rd Precinct
164 East 102nd Street
860-6411

24th Precinct
151 West 100th Street
678-1811

25th Precinct
120 East 119th Street
860-6511

26th Precinct
520 West 126th Street
678-1311

28th Precinct
2271 Eighth Avenue
678-1611

30th Precinct
451 West 151st Street
690-8811

32nd Precinct
250 West 135th Street
690-6311

33rd Precinct
2120 Amsterdam Avenue
927-3200

34th Precinct
4295 Broadway
927-9711

West Side Crime Prevention Program
866-8603

Public Services

ConEdison (gas and electric). General Information, gas emergency, fallen power lines, damaged electrical equipment or hazardous conditions, 800 75 CON ED (800 752-6633), www.coned.com

New York City Department of Environmental Protection, 718 DEP-HELP (337-4357) (24-hour complaint number for water, sewer, air, noise), www.nyc.gov

New York City Department of Health and Mental Hygiene, Central information and referrals 877 692-3647, Communicable disease information 788-9830

New York State Department of Health Ozone alert 800 535-1345

Safety—General Information

National Center for Missing and Exploited Children, 699 Prince Street, Alexandria, VA 22314, 800 THE LOST (843-5678) www.missingkids.com www.safekids.org

24-Hour Pharmacies

Police precincts maintain lists of neighborhood pharmacies that are open 24 hours.

CVS. Call 800 SHOP CVS (746-7287) for the location of the closest 24-hour CVS pharmacy
    First Avenue and 23rd Street 473-5750
    Ninth Avenue and 59th Street 245-0611
    Second Avenue and 72nd Street 249-5062
    Third Avenue and 91st Street 876-7212

Duane Reade. (store is open, pharmacy may not be)
    Broadway and Houston 683-3042
    Waverly Place and 6th Avenue 674-5357
    Lexington Avenue and 47th Street 682-5338
    Broadway and 57th Street 541-9708
    Second Avenue and 63rd Street 355-5944
    Third Avenue and 74th Street 744-2668
    Madison Avenue and 89th Street 360-6586
    Broadway and 91st Street 799-3172

Rite Aid. Call 800 RITE AID (748-3243) for the location of the closest 24-hour Rite Aid pharmacy
    Grand Street and Hudson Street 529-7115
    Second Avenue and 30th Street 213-9887
    Eighth Avenue and 50th Street 247-8384
    Lexington Avenue and 86th Street 876-0600
    Amsterdam Avenue and 89th Street 787-2903
    Broadway and 110th Street 663-3135

Pharmacies containing alternative/natural remedies

Statscript Pharmacy
197 Eighth Avenue, 691-9050

Hickey Chemists, Ltd.
888 Second Avenue, 223-6333
1258 Third Avenue, 744-5944

Nutrapharm
45 East 45th Street, 983-8291

INDEX

INDEX

INDEX

INDEX

INDEX

INDEX

INDEX

INDEX

Diane Chernoff-Rosen, mother of two, is a graduate of Cornell University, Georgetown University Law Center and New York University Stern School of Business and has practiced law in New York City. In addition to raising her children, she is the principal of Grownup's Guide Publishing LLC and is actively involved in volunteer activities. She has lived in Manhattan for 23 years.

Lisa Levinson, mother of two, is a graduate of Boston University and has worked in advertising, marketing and promotion.